Taste *of* Home®

one pot

favorites

one pot
favorites

TASTE OF HOME BOOKS • RDA ENTHUSIAST BRANDS, LLC • MILWAUKEE, WI

Visit us at tasteofhome.com for other
Taste of Home books and products.

International Standard Book Number:
978-1-61765-893-8 (Wire Bound)
978-1-61765-927-0 (Paperback)

**Library of Congress
Control Number:** 2019947871

Executive Editor: Mark Hagen
Senior Art Director: Raeann Thompson
Editor: Hazel Wheaton
Assistant Art Director: Courtney Lovetere
Designer: Jazmin Delgado
Copy Editor: Amy Rabideau Silvers
Editorial Intern: Daniella Peters

Cover Photography:
Photographer: Dan Roberts
Set Stylist: Melissa Franco
Food Stylist: Josh Rink

Pictured on front cover:
Chickpea Tortilla Soup, p. 305

Pictured on title page:
Garlicky Chicken Dinner, p. 225

Pictured on back cover:
Bacon & Spinach Pizza, p. 254
Slow-Cooked Pork Stew, p. 64
Five-Cheese Ziti al Forno, p. 433
Skillet Zucchini & Sausage, p. 181
Favorite Hamburger Stew, p. 319
Southern Hash Browns &
Ham Sheet-Pan Bake, p. 239

Printed in China.
1 3 5 7 9 10 8 6 4 2

**Make your one-pot meals shine with
the Taste of Home enameled cast-iron
Dutch oven seen on the cover. Learn more
about this amazing ovenproof nonstick
pot and all the Taste of Home cookware
at www.tasteofhome.com/cookwithtoh.**

Contents

More ways to connect with us:

SHOPTASTEOFHOME.COM

Dip into These One-Dish Wonders!

Simplicity is key when getting dinner on the table—and what could be simpler than a meal-in-one dish? From stir-fries and skillet suppers that come together quickly on the stovetop to casseroles and Dutch oven creations that slow-simmer for hours, these recipes offer the ultimate in efficiency. Whether you're looking for an entree that cooks in one pot, or a full meal that's served up all in one dish, you'll always find what you need with *Taste of Home One Pot Favorites*.

Look for these highlights:

- A chapter of sheet-pan meals brings these convenient recipes together in one spot.

- An Instant Pot & Slow-Cooker chapter—cook it fast or slow, this chapter has what you're looking for.

- ❄ Freeze It icons throughout the book identify recipes that freeze well, making it a snap to have dishes ready and waiting just when you need them.

- 🍎 Eat Smart icons are your guide to choosing healthier recipes that your whole family will love.

- Nutritional information with every recipe help you make sure your family is eating right.

- Hundreds of full-color photos show you the way, so it's even easier to make sure your meal comes out just right, every time.

The recipes in *One Pot Favorites* help you work your magic in the kitchen any night of the week—from busy work nights to special weekend get-togethers. Every recipe is approved by the **Taste of Home Test Kitchen,** so you're guaranteed success. Best of all, the only thing easier than making a one-dish meal is cleaning up after dinner. So choose a dish, choose a recipe, and start serving hearty favorites today!

Slow Cooker & Instant Pot®

favorites

Beef

STOUT & HONEY BEEF ROAST

Here's a heartwarming meal that's ideal for chilly days and hectic nights. Honey, beer and seasonings make the sauce different and oh-so-good.
—*Taste of Home* Test Kitchen

Prep: 15 min. • **Cook:** 8 hours
Makes: 12 servings

- 12 small red potatoes
  (about 1½ lbs.), scrubbed
- 6 to 7 medium carrots (about 1 lb.),
  peeled and cut into ½-in. pieces
- 2 medium onions, quartered
- 1 boneless beef chuck roast
  (4 lbs.), trimmed
- 1 can (14½ oz.) beef broth
- 1 cup beer or additional beef broth
- ½ cup honey
- 3 garlic cloves, minced
- 1 tsp. dried marjoram
- 1 tsp. dried thyme
- ½ tsp. salt
- ½ tsp. pepper
- ¼ tsp. ground cinnamon
- 2 Tbsp. cornstarch
- ¼ cup cold water
  Minced fresh thyme, optional

1. Place potatoes, carrots and onion in a 5-qt. slow cooker. Cut roast in half; transfer to slow cooker. In a small bowl, combine the next 9 ingredients; pour over top. Cook, covered, on low until the meat and vegetables are tender, 8-10 hours.
2. Slice the beef and keep warm. Strain the cooking juices, reserving vegetables and 1 cup liquid. Skim fat from the reserved liquid; transfer liquid to a small saucepan. Bring to a boil. Combine cornstarch and water until smooth; gradually stir into the juices. Bring to a boil; cook and stir until thickened, about 2 minutes. Serve with beef and vegetables. If desired, top with fresh thyme.

1 serving: 361 cal., 15g fat (6g sat. fat), 98mg chol., 340mg sod., 25g carb. (14g sugars, 2g fiber), 31g pro.

EASY CORNED BEEF & CABBAGE

I first tried this fuss-free way to cook traditional corned beef and cabbage for St. Patrick's Day a few years ago. Now it's a regular in my menu planning. This is terrific with Dijon mustard and crusty bread.
—Karen Waters, Laurel, MD

Prep: 15 min. • **Cook:** 8 hours
Makes: 8 servings

- 1 medium onion, cut into wedges
- 4 large red potatoes, quartered
- 1 lb. baby carrots
- 3 cups water
- 3 garlic cloves, minced
- 1 bay leaf
- 2 Tbsp. sugar
- 2 Tbsp. cider vinegar
- ½ tsp. pepper
- 1 corned beef brisket with spice packet (2½ to 3 lbs.), cut in half
- 1 small head cabbage,
  cut into wedges

1. Place the onion, potatoes and carrots in a 6- to 7-qt. slow cooker. Combine the water, garlic, bay leaf, sugar, vinegar, pepper and the contents of the spice packet; pour over the vegetables. Top with brisket and cabbage wedges.
2. Cover and cook on low for 8-9 hours or until the meat and vegetables are tender. Discard bay leaf before serving.

1 serving: 414 cal., 19g fat (6g sat. fat), 97mg chol., 1191mg sod., 38g carb. (11g sugars, 6g fiber), 23g pro.

PRESSURE-COOKER POT ROAST HASH

I love to cook a Sunday-style pot roast for weeknights. Whether cooked fresh or as leftovers, it's easy to make it into pot roast hash for any day of the week.
—Gina Jackson, Ogdensburg, NY

Prep: 20 min. • **Cook:** 45 min. + releasing
Makes: 10 servings

- 1 cup warm water (110° to 115°)
- 1 Tbsp. beef base
- ½ lb. sliced fresh mushrooms
- 1 large onion, coarsely chopped
- 3 garlic cloves, minced
- 1 boneless beef chuck roast (3 lbs.)
- ½ tsp. pepper
- 1 Tbsp. Worcestershire sauce
- 1 pkg. (28 oz.) frozen O'Brien potatoes

EGGS
- 2 Tbsp. butter, divided
- 10 large eggs, divided
- ½ tsp. salt, divided
- ½ tsp. pepper, divided
  Minced chives

1. In a 6-qt. electric pressure cooker, whisk water and beef base; add mushrooms, onion and garlic. Sprinkle roast with pepper; transfer to pressure cooker. Drizzle with Worcestershire sauce. Lock lid; close pressure-release vent. Adjust to pressure-cook on high for 45 minutes. Allow pressure to naturally release for 10 minutes, then quick-release any remaining pressure.
2. Remove roast; when cool enough to handle, shred meat with 2 forks. In a large skillet, cook potatoes according to package directions; stir in shredded beef. Using a slotted spoon, transfer vegetables from pressure cooker to skillet; heat through. Discard the cooking juices.
3. For the eggs, heat 1 Tbsp. butter over medium-high heat in another large skillet. Break 5 eggs, 1 at a time, into pan. Sprinkle with half the salt and pepper. Reduce heat to low. Cook until the eggs reach desired doneness, turning after whites are set if desired. Repeat with the remaining butter, eggs, salt and pepper. Serve eggs over hash; sprinkle with chives.

1 serving: 429 cal., 24g fat (8g sat. fat), 281mg chol., 15mg sod., 15g carb. (2g sugars, 2g fiber), 35g pro.

You can serve this with scrambled eggs if you prefer. Top with fresh salsa, ketchup or Sriracha.

ZESTY ORANGE BEEF

I put this recipe together in the morning before I leave for work. In the evening, the aroma hits me as soon as I open the door. All I have to do is cook some rice, and dinner is served.
—Deborah Puette, Lilburn, GA

- -

Prep: 15 min. • **Cook:** 5 hours
Makes: 5 servings

1	beef top sirloin steak (1½ lbs.), cut into ¼-in. strips
2½	cups sliced fresh shiitake mushrooms
1	medium onion, cut into wedges
3	dried hot chiles
¼	cup packed brown sugar
¼	cup orange juice
¼	cup reduced-sodium soy sauce
3	Tbsp. cider vinegar
1	Tbsp. cornstarch
1	Tbsp. minced fresh gingerroot
1	Tbsp. sesame oil
2	garlic cloves, minced
1¾	cups fresh snow peas
1	Tbsp. grated orange zest
	Hot cooked rice

1. Place beef in a 4-qt. slow cooker. Add the mushrooms, onion and chiles. In a small bowl, combine the brown sugar, orange juice, soy sauce, vinegar, cornstarch, ginger, oil and garlic. Pour over the meat.
2. Cover and cook on high for 5-6 hours or until the meat is tender, adding snow peas during the last 30 minutes of cooking. Stir in orange zest. Serve with rice.
1 cup: 310 cal., 8g fat (3g sat. fat), 55mg chol., 554mg sod., 24g carb. (16g sugars, 3g fiber), 33g pro. **Diabetic exchanges:** 4 lean meat, 1½ starch, ½ fat.

CHILI MAC

This recipe has regularly appeared on my family menus for decades, and it's never failed to please at potlucks and gatherings. Sometimes I turn it into soup by adding a can of beef broth.
—Marie Posavec, Berwyn, IL

Prep: 15 min. • **Cook:** 6 hours
Makes: 6 servings

- 1 lb. lean ground beef (90% lean), cooked and drained
- 2 cans (16 oz. each) hot chili beans, undrained
- 2 large green peppers, chopped
- 1 large onion, chopped
- 4 celery ribs, chopped
- 1 can (8 oz.) no-salt-added tomato sauce
- 2 Tbsp. chili seasoning mix
- 2 garlic cloves, minced
- 1 pkg. (7 oz.) elbow macaroni, cooked and drained
   Salt and pepper to taste

In a 5-qt. slow cooker, combine the first 8 ingredients. Cover and cook on low for 6 hours or until heated through. Stir in macaroni. Season with salt and pepper.
1 serving: 348 cal., 8g fat (3g sat. fat), 47mg chol., 713mg sod., 49g carb. (8g sugars, 12g fiber), 27g pro. **Diabetic exchanges:** 3 starch, 3 lean meat.

PRESSURE-COOKER GROUND BEEF STROGANOFF

My mother gave me this recipe 40 years ago. It's a wonderfully tasty dish to share around the dinner table.
—Sue Mims, Macclenny, FL

Prep: 25 min. • **Cook:** 10 min.
Makes: 8 servings

- 2 lbs. ground beef
- 1½ tsp. salt
- 1 tsp. pepper

- 1 Tbsp. butter
- ½ lb. sliced fresh mushrooms
- 2 medium onions, chopped
- 2 garlic cloves, minced
- 2 Tbsp. tomato paste
- 1 can (10½ oz.) condensed beef consomme, undiluted
- ⅓ cup all-purpose flour
- ⅓ cup water
- 1½ cups sour cream
   Hot cooked noodles, optional
   Minced fresh parsley

1. Select saute setting on a 6-qt. electric pressure cooker and adjust for medium heat. Add half each of the ground beef, salt and pepper. Cook and stir, crumbling the beef, until no longer pink, 6-8 minutes. Remove meat; drain any liquid from the pressure cooker. Repeat with the remaining ground beef, salt and pepper.

2. Add butter, mushrooms and onions to pressure cooker; saute until the onions are tender and the mushrooms have released their liquid and are beginning to brown, 6-8 minutes. Add garlic; cook 1 minute longer. Return the meat to the cooker; add tomato paste and consomme. Press cancel.

3. Lock lid; close the pressure-release valve. Adjust to pressure-cook on high for 5 minutes. Quick-release pressure.

4. Select saute setting and adjust for low heat. In a small bowl, whisk together flour and water. Pour over the meat mixture; stir to combine. Cook and stir until thickened. Stir in sour cream; cook until heated through. Serve with noodles, if desired, and minced parsley.

1 serving: 357 cal., 22g fat (11g sat. fat), 104mg chol., 802mg sod., 10g carb. (4g sugars, 1g fiber), 25g pro.

1. Select saute setting on a 6-qt. electric pressure cooker and adjust for medium heat. Add 2 tsp. oil. Sprinkle beef with salt and pepper. Brown meat in batches, adding oil as needed. Transfer meat to a bowl.
2. Add wine to cooker, stirring to loosen browned bits. Press cancel. Return beef to cooker; add the mushrooms, onion, broth and Worcestershire sauce. Lock lid; close the pressure-release valve. Adjust to pressure-cook on high for 15 minutes. Quick-release cooker pressure.
3. Select saute setting and adjust for low heat; bring the liquid to a boil. In a small bowl, mix cornstarch and water until smooth; gradually stir into beef mixture. Cook and stir until the sauce is thickened, 1-2 minutes. Serve with mashed potatoes.

1 cup: 212 cal., 7g fat (2g sat. fat), 46mg chol., 836mg sod., 8g carb. (2g sugars, 1g fiber), 27g pro. **Diabetic exchanges:** 3 lean meat, ½ starch, ½ fat.

TEST KITCHEN TIP

To make good use of leftovers— if there are any—stir a little heavy cream or sour cream into leftover sauce and serve over pasta.

PRESSURE-COOKER BEEF TIPS
These beef tips remind me of a favorite childhood meal. I like to cook them with mushrooms and serve them over brown rice, noodles or mashed potatoes.
—Amy Lents, Grand Forks, ND

- -

Prep: 20 min. • **Cook:** 15 min.
Makes: 4 servings

- 3 tsp. olive oil
- 1 beef top sirloin steak (1 lb.), cubed
- ½ tsp. salt
- ¼ tsp. pepper
- ⅓ cup dry red wine or beef broth
- ½ lb. sliced baby portobello mushrooms
- 1 small onion, halved and sliced
- 2 cups beef broth
- 1 Tbsp. Worcestershire sauce
- 3 to 4 Tbsp. cornstarch
- ¼ cup cold water
   Hot cooked mashed potatoes

ZIPPY SPAGHETTI SAUCE

This thick and hearty sauce goes a long way to fill my hungry family. They enjoy any leftovers ladled over thick slices of grilled garlic bread. To make sure I have the ingredients on hand, I always keep a bag of chopped green pepper in my freezer and minced garlic in my fridge.
—Elaine Priest, Dover, PA

Prep: 20 min. • **Cook:** 6 hours
Makes: 12 servings (3 qt.)

- 2   lbs. ground beef
- 1   cup chopped onion
- ½   cup chopped green pepper
- 2   cans (15 oz. each) tomato sauce
- 1   can (28 oz.) diced tomatoes, undrained
- 1   can (12 oz.) tomato paste
- ½   lb. sliced fresh mushrooms
- 1   cup grated Parmesan cheese
- ½ to ¾ cup dry red wine or beef broth
- ½   cup sliced pimiento-stuffed olives
- ¼   cup dried parsley flakes
- 1 to 2 Tbsp. dried oregano
- 2   tsp. Italian seasoning
- 2   tsp. minced garlic
- 1   tsp. salt
- 1   tsp. pepper
  Hot cooked spaghetti

1. In a large skillet, cook the beef, onion and green pepper over medium heat until the meat is no longer pink; drain.
2. Transfer to a 5-qt. slow cooker. Stir in the tomato sauce, tomatoes, tomato paste, mushrooms, cheese, wine, olives, parsley, oregano, Italian seasoning, garlic, salt and pepper. Cover and cook on low for 6-8 hours. Serve with spaghetti.
1 cup: 255 cal., 13g fat (4g sat. fat), 52mg chol., 930mg sod., 16g carb. (7g sugars, 4g fiber), 20g pro.

SPICY GOULASH

Ground cumin, chili powder and a can of Mexican diced tomatoes jazz up my goulash recipe. Even the elbow macaroni is prepared in the slow cooker.
—Melissa Polk, West Lafayette, IN

Prep: 25 min. • **Cook:** 5½ hours
Makes: 12 servings

- 1   lb. lean ground beef (90% lean)
- 4   cans (14½ oz. each) Mexican diced tomatoes, undrained
- 2   cans (16 oz. each) kidney beans, rinsed and drained
- 2   cups water
- 1   medium onion, chopped
- 1   medium green pepper, chopped
- ¼   cup red wine vinegar
- 2   Tbsp. chili powder
- 1   Tbsp. Worcestershire sauce
- 2   tsp. beef bouillon granules
- 1   tsp. dried basil
- 1   tsp. dried parsley flakes
- 1   tsp. ground cumin
- ¼   tsp. pepper
- 2   cups uncooked elbow macaroni

1. In a large skillet, cook beef over medium heat until no longer pink; drain.
2. Transfer beef to a 5-qt. slow cooker. Stir in tomatoes, beans, water, onion, green pepper, vinegar, chili powder, Worcestershire sauce, bouillon and seasonings. Cover and cook on low for 5-6 hours or until heated through.
3. Stir in macaroni; cover and cook 30 minutes longer or until the macaroni is tender.
1 cup: 222 cal., 5g fat (2g sat. fat), 23mg chol., 585mg sod., 30g carb. (7g sugars, 6g fiber), 15g pro. **Diabetic exchanges:** 2 lean meat, 1½ starch, 1 vegetable.

PRESSURE-COOKER SAUERBRATEN

One of my all-time favorite German dishes is sauerbraten, but I don't love that the traditional version takes five to 10 days to make. Using an electric pressure cooker, I think I've captured that same distinctive flavor in less than two hours.
—James Schend, Pleasant Prairie, WI

- -

Prep: 20 min. + standing • **Cook:** 20 min.
Makes: 4 servings

- 4 whole cloves
- 4 whole peppercorns
- 1 bay leaf
- ½ cup water
- ½ cup white vinegar
- 2 tsp. sugar
- ½ tsp. salt
  Dash ground ginger
- 1 lb. boneless beef top round steak, cut into 1-in. cubes
- 3 medium carrots, cut into ½-in. slices
- 2 celery ribs, cut into ½-in. slices
- 1 small onion, chopped
- ⅓ cup crushed gingersnaps
  Hot cooked egg noodles
  Optional: Chopped fresh parsley and coarsely ground pepper,

1. Place the cloves, peppercorns and bay leaf on a double thickness of cheesecloth; bring up the corners of the cloth and tie with kitchen string to form a bag. In a large bowl, combine water, vinegar, sugar, salt, ginger. Add beef and spice bag; let stand at room temperature for 30 minutes.

2. Transfer all to a 6-qt. electric pressure cooker. Add the carrots, celery and onion. Lock the lid and close pressure-release valve. Adjust to pressure-cook on high for 10 minutes. Quick-release pressure. Select saute setting and adjust for medium heat; bring liquid to a boil. Discard spice bag. Stir in gingersnaps; cook and stir until thickened, about 3 minutes. Serve with egg noodles. If desired, top with parsley and pepper.

Freeze option: Freeze cooled sauerbraten in freezer containers. To use, partially thaw in refrigerator overnight. Heat through in a saucepan, stirring occasionally and adding a little broth or water if necessary.

1 cup: 228 cal., 5g fat (2g sat. fat), 63mg chol., 436mg sod., 18g carb. (8g sugars, 2g fiber), 27g pro. **Diabetic exchanges:** 3 lean meat, 1 starch, 1 vegetable.

FIESTA BEEF BOWLS

This easy entree will knock your socks off. Zesty ingredients turn round steak, beans and rice into a phenomenal meal.
—Deborah Linn, Valdez, AK

Prep: 25 min. • **Cook:** 8½ hours
Makes: 6 servings

- 1½ lbs. boneless beef top round steak
- 1 can (10 oz.) diced tomatoes and green chiles
- 1 medium onion, chopped
- 2 garlic cloves, minced
- 1 tsp. dried oregano
- 1 tsp. chili powder
- 1 tsp. ground cumin
- ¼ tsp. salt
- ¼ tsp. pepper
- 2 cans (15 oz. each) pinto beans, rinsed and drained
- 3 cups hot cooked rice
- ½ cup shredded cheddar cheese
- 6 Tbsp. sliced ripe olives
- 6 Tbsp. thinly sliced green onions
- 6 Tbsp. guacamole

1. Place round steak in a 3-qt. slow cooker. In a small bowl, combine the tomatoes, onion, garlic and seasonings; pour over steak. Cover and cook on low for 8-9 hours or until the meat is tender.

2. Remove meat from slow cooker. Add beans to the tomato mixture. Cover and cook on high for 30 minutes or until the beans are heated through. When the meat is cool enough to handle, slice. In individual bowls, layer the rice, meat and bean mixture. Top with cheese, olives, green onions and guacamole.

1 serving: 460 cal., 11g fat (4g sat. fat), 74mg chol., 720mg sod., 52g carb. (4g sugars, 9g fiber), 38g pro.

MOROCCAN BRAISED BEEF

Curry powder is a blend of up to 20 spices, herbs and seeds. Add a pinch of curry to your favorite soups, stews, salads and even rice for an exotic flavor. In this Moroccan stew, begin with 2 tsp. curry, then add more to your taste.
—*Taste of Home* Test Kitchen

Prep: 20 min. • **Cook:** 7 hours
Makes: 6 servings

- ⅓ cup all-purpose flour
- 2 lbs. boneless beef chuck roast, cut into 1-in. cubes
- 3 Tbsp. olive oil
- 2 cans (14½ oz. each) beef broth
- 2 cups chopped onions
- 1 can (14½ oz.) diced tomatoes, undrained
- 1 cup dry red wine
- 1 Tbsp. curry powder
- 1 Tbsp. paprika
- 1 tsp. salt
- 1 tsp. ground cumin
- 1 tsp. ground coriander
- ½ tsp. cayenne pepper
- 1½ cups golden raisins
  Hot cooked couscous, optional

1. Place flour in a large shallow dish; add beef and toss to coat. In a large skillet, brown beef in oil. Transfer to a 5-qt. slow cooker. Stir in the broth, onions, tomatoes, wine and seasonings. Cover and cook on low for 7-8 hours or until the meat is tender.
2. During the last 30 minutes of cooking, stir in the raisins. Serve with couscous if desired.
Freeze option: Freeze cooled beef mixture in freezer containers. To use, partially thaw in refrigerator overnight. Heat through in a saucepan, stirring occasionally; add a little broth if necessary. Serve as directed.
1⅓ cups beef mixture: 533 cal., 22g fat (7g sat. fat), 98mg chol., 620mg sod., 45g carb. (30g sugars, 5g fiber), 34g pro.

MEXICAN BUBBLE PIZZA

This tasty pizza offers a new way to experience Mexican cuisine. Serve it at your next party and watch it disappear before your eyes.
—Jackie Hannahs, Cedar Springs, MI

Prep: 15 min. • **Cook:** 3 hours
Makes: 6 servings

- 1½ lbs. ground beef
- 1 can (10¾ oz.) condensed tomato soup, undiluted
- ¾ cup water
- 1 envelope taco seasoning
- 1 tube (16.3 oz.) large refrigerated buttermilk biscuits
- 2 cups shredded cheddar cheese
  Optional toppings: Shredded lettuce, chopped tomatoes, salsa, sliced ripe olives, sour cream and thinly sliced green onions

1. Line a 6-qt. slow cooker with a double thickness of heavy-duty foil. Coat with cooking spray.
2. In a large skillet, cook beef over medium heat until no longer pink, 6-8 minutes, breaking into crumbles; drain. Stir in soup, water and taco seasoning. Bring to a boil. Reduce heat; simmer, uncovered, until slightly thickened, 3-5 minutes.
3. Cut each biscuit into 4 pieces; gently stir into the beef mixture. Transfer all to slow cooker. Cook, covered, on low until the dough is cooked through, 3-4 hours. Sprinkle with cheddar cheese. Cook, covered, until the cheese is melted, about 5 minutes longer. Serve with toppings of your choice.
1 serving: 643 cal., 35g fat (15g sat. fat), 109mg chol., 1870mg sod., 46g carb. (8g sugars, 2g fiber), 35g pro.

SLOW-COOKED PIZZA CASSEROLE

A friend from church gave me the recipe for this satisfying slow-cooked casserole. It's always one of the first dishes emptied at potlucks, and it can easily be adapted to personal tastes.
—Julie Sterchi, Campbellsville, KY

Prep: 25 min. • **Cook:** 4 hours
Makes: 12 servings

- 3 lbs. ground beef
- ½ cup chopped onion
- 1 jar (24 oz.) pasta sauce
- 2 jars (4½ oz. each) sliced mushrooms, drained
- 1 tsp. salt
- ½ tsp. garlic powder
- ½ tsp. dried oregano
  Dash pepper
- 1 pkg. (16 oz.) wide egg noodles, cooked and drained
- 2 pkg. (3½ oz. each) sliced pepperoni
- 2 cups shredded cheddar cheese
- 2 cups shredded part-skim mozzarella cheese

1. In a Dutch oven, brown the beef and onion over medium heat until the meat is no longer pink; drain. Add spaghetti sauce, mushrooms, salt, garlic powder, oregano and pepper; heat through.
2. Spoon half the mixture into a 5-qt. slow cooker. Top with half the noodles, pepperoni and cheeses. Repeat layers. Cover and cook on low for 4-5 hours or until the cheese is melted.
1 serving: 534 cal., 26g fat (13g sat. fat), 131mg chol., 1009mg sod., 36g carb. (6g sugars, 3g fiber), 37g pro.

SLOW-COOKED BEEF & VEGGIES

My husband and I came up with this soothing slow-cooker recipe. It's simple and filling, with lots of flavor.
—LaDonna Reed, Ponca City, OK

Prep: 15 min. + marinating • **Cook:** 8 hours
Makes: 2 servings

- 1 boneless beef top round steak (½ lb.), cut into 2 pieces
  Dash seasoned salt, optional
  Dash pepper
  Dash garlic powder
- 1 cup Italian salad dressing
- ½ cup water
- 1 Tbsp. browning sauce, optional
- 2 medium carrots, cut into 2-in. pieces
- 2 medium red potatoes, cubed
- 1 small onion, sliced
- ½ small green pepper, cut into small chunks

1. Sprinkle 1 side of steak with seasoned salt (if desired) and pepper; sprinkle the other side with garlic powder. Cover and refrigerate for 2-3 hours or overnight.
2. In a 3-qt. slow cooker, combine the salad dressing, water and browning sauce. Add carrots and potatoes; toss to coat. Add the steak and coat with sauce. Top with onion and green pepper.
3. Cover and cook on low until the meat is tender, 8-9 hours.
1 serving: 505 cal., 22g fat (3g sat. fat), 63mg chol., 1283mg sod., 36g carb. (14g sugars, 5g fiber), 29g pro.

BARBECUED BEEF RIBS

These tender ribs with a tangy sauce taste slow-cooked but come together in a flash in the pressure cooker. They're great for picnics and parties.
—Erin Glass, White Hall, MD

Prep: 15 min. • **Cook:** 45 min. + releasing
Makes: 8 servings

- 2 Tbsp. canola oil
- 4 lbs. bone-in beef short ribs, trimmed
- 1 large sweet onion, halved and sliced
- ½ cup water
- 1 bottle (12 oz.) chili sauce
- ¾ cup plum preserves or preserves of your choice
- 2 Tbsp. packed brown sugar
- 2 Tbsp. red wine vinegar
- 2 Tbsp. Worcestershire sauce
- 2 Tbsp. Dijon mustard
- ¼ tsp. ground cloves

1. Select saute setting on a 6-qt. electric pressure cooker and adjust for medium heat; add oil. Brown ribs in batches, adding additional oil as needed. Remove the ribs. Brown onions. Add the ribs back to the pressure cooker. Add water. Lock lid; close pressure-release valve. Adjust to pressure-cook on high for 40 minutes. Let pressure release naturally for 10 minutes and then quick-release any remaining pressure.

2. In a small saucepan, combine the remaining ingredients; cook and stir over medium heat until heated through. Remove ribs from the pressure cooker; discard the cooking juices. Return ribs to the pressure cooker. Pour sauce over top. Lock lid; close pressure-release valve. Adjust to pressure-cook on low for 5 minutes. Allow pressure to naturally release for 5 minutes and then quick-release any remaining pressure. Serve ribs with sauce.

1 serving: 359 cal., 14g fat (5g sat. fat), 55mg chol., 860mg sod., 40g carb. (33g sugars, 0 fiber), 18g pro.

DID YOU KNOW?

Both light and dark brown sugar are a mix of sugar and molasses, and either can be used depending on your personal preference. Dark brown has a more intense molasses flavor, while light brown sugar has a more delicate flavor.

BEEF & BEANS

This deliciously spicy steak and beans over rice will have family and friends asking for more. It's a favorite in my recipe collection.
—Marie Leamon, Bethesda, MD

- -

Prep: 10 min. • **Cook:** 6½ hours
Makes: 8 servings

- 1½ lbs. boneless round steak
- 1 Tbsp. prepared mustard
- 1 Tbsp. chili powder
- ½ tsp. salt
- ¼ tsp. pepper
- 1 garlic clove, minced
- 2 cans (14½ oz. each) diced tomatoes, undrained
- 1 medium onion, chopped
- 1 tsp. beef bouillon granules
- 1 can (16 oz.) kidney beans, rinsed and drained
    Hot cooked rice

Cut steak into thin strips. Combine the mustard, chili powder, salt, pepper and garlic in a bowl; add the steak and toss to coat. Transfer steak to a 3-qt. slow cooker; add tomatoes, onion and bouillon. Cover and cook on low for 6-8 hours. Stir in beans; cook 30 minutes longer. Serve over rice.
1 cup: 185 cal., 3g fat (1g sat. fat), 47mg chol., 584mg sod., 16g carb. (5g sugars, 5g fiber), 24g pro. **Diabetic exchanges:** 2 lean meat, 1 starch, 1 vegetable.

FRENCH DIP SANDWICHES

Beef chuck roast gives this classic sandwich and its rich broth a hearty flavor. Add a crusty roll and you have a filling meal. This make-ahead recipe also can be prepared several days before serving.
—*Taste of Home* Test Kitchen

- -

Prep: 20 min. • **Cook:** 1¼ hour + releasing
Makes: 8 servings

- 1 boneless beef chuck roast (about 3 lbs.)
- 1 tsp. dried oregano
- 1 tsp. dried rosemary, crushed
- ½ tsp. seasoned salt
- ¼ tsp. pepper
- 3 cups beef broth
- 1 bay leaf
- 1 garlic clove, peeled
  French bread, sliced

1. Place roast on a trivet in a 6 qt. pressure cooker; sprinkle with oregano, rosemary, seasoned salt and pepper. Add broth, bay leaf and garlic. Lock lid; close pressure-release valve. Adjust to pressure-cook on high for 75 minutes.

2. Let the pressure release naturally for 10 minutes and then quick-release any remaining pressure. A thermometer inserted in beef should read at least 145°.

3. Remove the beef; shred with 2 forks. Discard bay leaf and garlic from broth. Serve shredded beef on French bread with broth for dipping.

1 serving: 237 cal., 13g fat (5g sat. fat), 88mg chol., 378mg sod., 1g carb. (0 sugars, 0 fiber), 27g pro.

FRESH SPINACH TAMALE PIE

I got this recipe from my mother, who loved making quick and easy meals. I added spinach, bell peppers and fresh corn. The changes were well worth it—my family and friends love this dish!
—Nancy Heishman, Las Vegas, NV

- -

Prep: 20 min. • **Cook:** 3 hours
Makes: 10 servings

- 8 frozen beef tamales, thawed
- 2 cans (15 oz. each) pinto beans, rinsed and drained
- 2 cups fresh or frozen corn
- 4 green onions, chopped
- 1 can (2¼ oz.) sliced ripe olives, drained
- ½ tsp. garlic powder
- ¾ cup chopped sweet red pepper
- ¾ cup sour cream
- 1 can (4 oz.) whole green chiles, drained and chopped
- 3 cups chopped fresh spinach
- 12 bacon strips, cooked and crumbled
- 2 cups shredded cheddar cheese
  Additional green onions, chopped

Place tamales in a single layer in a greased 6-qt. slow cooker. In a bowl, combine beans, corn, onions, olives and garlic powder; spoon over the tamales. In the same bowl, combine pepper, sour cream and chiles; spoon over the bean mixture. Top with spinach. Cook, covered, on low until heated through, 3-4 hours. Sprinkle with bacon, cheese and additional green onions.

1 serving: 459 cal., 24g fat (9g sat. fat), 49mg chol., 1013mg sod., 40g carb. (4g sugars, 7g fiber), 23g pro.

2. Add beer and bouillon granules to the skillet, stirring to loosen any browned bits from pan; pour over meat. In a large bowl, combine the remaining ingredients; add to the slow cooker.

3. Cover and cook on low for 8-10 hours or until the meat and vegetables are tender. Discard bay leaf. To serve, thinly slice across the grain.

Note: This recipe uses a fresh beef brisket, not corned beef.

1 serving: 352 cal., 9g fat (3g sat. fat), 72mg chol., 722mg sod., 25g carb. (13g sugars, 2g fiber), 38g pro. **Diabetic exchanges:** 5 lean meat, 1 starch, 1 vegetable, ½ fat.

SLOW-COOKED ENCHILADA CASSEROLE

Tortilla chips and a side salad turn this casserole into a fun and festive meal with very little effort.
—Denise Waller, Omaha, NE

- -

Prep: 20 min. • **Cook:** 6 hours
Makes: 6 servings

- 1 lb. ground beef
- 2 cans (10 oz. each) enchilada sauce
- 1 can (10¾ oz.) condensed cream of onion soup, undiluted
- ¼ tsp. salt
- 1 pkg. (8½ oz.) flour tortillas, torn
- 3 cups shredded cheddar cheese

1. In a skillet, cook the beef over medium heat until no longer pink; drain. Stir in the enchilada sauce, soup and salt.

2. In a 3-qt. slow cooker, layer a third of the beef mixture, tortillas and cheese. Repeat the layers twice. Cover and cook on low until heated through, 6-8 hours.

1 serving: 568 cal., 35g fat (16g sat. fat), 105mg chol., 1610mg sod., 30g carb. (4g sugars, 3g fiber), 31g pro.

ALL-DAY BRISKET WITH POTATOES

I think the slow cooker was invented with brisket in mind! This sweet and savory version is perfection. It's important to buy first-cut or flat-cut brisket, which has far less fat than other cuts.
—Lana Gryga, Glen Flora, WI

- -

Prep: 30 min. • **Cook:** 8 hours
Makes: 8 servings

- 2 medium potatoes, peeled and cut into ¼-in. slices
- 2 celery ribs, sliced
- 1 fresh beef brisket (3 lbs.)
- 1 Tbsp. canola oil
- 1 large onion, sliced
- 2 garlic cloves, minced
- 1 can (12 oz.) beer
- ½ tsp. beef bouillon granules
- ¾ cup stewed tomatoes
- ⅓ cup tomato paste
- ¼ cup red wine vinegar
- 3 Tbsp. brown sugar
- 3 Tbsp. Dijon mustard
- 3 Tbsp. soy sauce
- 2 Tbsp. molasses
- ½ tsp. paprika
- ¼ tsp. salt
- ⅛ tsp. pepper
- 1 bay leaf

1. Place potatoes and celery in a 5-qt. slow cooker. Cut brisket in half. In a large skillet, brown beef in oil on all sides; transfer to the slow cooker. In the same pan, saute onion until tender. Add garlic; cook for 1 minute longer. Add to the slow cooker.

CARIBBEAN POT ROAST

This dish is definitely a year-round recipe. Sweet potatoes, orange zest and baking cocoa are my surprise ingredients.
—Jenn Tidwell, Fair Oaks, CA

Prep: 30 min. • **Cook:** 6 hours
Makes: 10 servings

- 2   medium sweet potatoes, cubed
- 2   large carrots, sliced
- ¼   cup chopped celery
- 1   boneless beef chuck roast (2½ lbs.)
- 1   Tbsp. canola oil
- 1   large onion, chopped
- 2   garlic cloves, minced
- 1   Tbsp. all-purpose flour
- 1   Tbsp. sugar
- 1   Tbsp. brown sugar
- 1   tsp. ground cumin
- ¾   tsp. salt
- ¾   tsp. ground coriander
- ¾   tsp. chili powder
- ½   tsp. dried oregano
- ⅛   tsp. ground cinnamon
- ¾   tsp. grated orange zest
- ¾   tsp. baking cocoa
- 1   can (15 oz.) tomato sauce

1. Place potatoes, carrots and celery in a 5-qt. slow cooker. In a large skillet, brown roast in oil on all sides. Transfer meat to slow cooker.
2. In the same skillet, saute the onion in drippings until tender. Add garlic; cook for 1 minute longer. Combine the flour, sugar, brown sugar, seasonings, orange zest and cocoa. Stir in tomato sauce; add to skillet and heat through. Pour over the beef.
3. Cover and cook on low until the beef and vegetables are tender, 6-8 hours.
3 oz. cooked beef with ½ cup vegetable mixture: 278 cal., 12g fat (4g sat. fat), 74mg chol., 453mg sod., 16g carb. (8g sugars, 3g fiber), 25g pro. **Diabetic exchanges:** 3 lean meat, 1 starch, 1 vegetable, ½ fat.

SLOW-COOKER LASAGNA

Convenient no-cook lasagna noodles take the work out of this traditional favorite adapted for the slow cooker. It's so easy to assemble for workdays or weekends. We like it accompanied by Parmesan bread or garlic cheese toast.
—Lisa Micheletti, Collierville, TN

Prep: 25 min. • **Cook:** 4 hours
Makes: 8 servings

- 1   lb. ground beef
- 1   large onion, chopped
- 2   garlic cloves, minced
- 1   can (29 oz.) tomato sauce
- 1   cup water
- 1   can (6 oz.) tomato paste
- 1   tsp. salt
- 1   tsp. dried oregano
- 1   pkg. (8 oz.) no-cook lasagna noodles
- 4   cups shredded part-skim mozzarella cheese
- 1½ cups 4% cottage cheese
- ½   cup grated Parmesan cheese

1. In a skillet, cook beef and onion over medium heat until the meat is no longer pink. Add garlic; cook for 1 minute longer. Drain. Stir in the tomato sauce, water, tomato paste, salt and oregano.
2. Spread a fourth of the meat sauce in an ungreased 5-qt. slow cooker. Arrange a third of the noodles over the sauce (break the noodles to fit if necessary). Combine the cheeses; spoon a third of the cheese mixture over noodles. Repeat layers twice. Top with the remaining meat sauce.
3. Cover and cook on low for 4-5 hours or until the noodles are tender.
1 slice: 482 cal., 20g fat (11g sat. fat), 84mg chol., 1317mg sod., 36g carb. (10g sugars, 4g fiber), 38g pro.

SLOW-COOKED TAMALE CASSEROLE

I've been making this recipe for years because my family really likes it. I'll make it on busy Saturdays when we want a comforting and filling dinner. Stirring the cornmeal into the beef creates a thick, savory filling.
—Diana Briggs, Veneta, OR

- -

Prep: 15 min. • **Cook:** 4 hours
Makes: 6 servings

- 1 lb. ground beef
- 1 large egg, beaten
- 1½ cups whole milk
- ¾ cup cornmeal
- 1 can (15¼ oz.) whole kernel corn, drained
- 1 can (14½ oz.) diced tomatoes, undrained
- 1 can (2¼ oz.) sliced ripe olives, drained
- 1 envelope chili seasoning
- 1 tsp. seasoned salt
- 1 cup shredded cheddar cheese

1. In a skillet, cook beef over medium heat until it is no longer pink; drain. In a large bowl, combine the egg, milk and cornmeal until smooth. Add corn, tomatoes, olives, chili seasoning, seasoned salt and the browned beef.

2. Transfer to a greased 3-qt. slow cooker. Cover and cook on high for 3 hours and 45 minutes. Sprinkle with cheddar cheese; cover and cook for 15 minutes longer or until cheese is melted.

1 serving: 386 cal., 17g fat (9g sat. fat), 101mg chol., 1255mg sod., 31g carb. (9g sugars, 4g fiber), 24g pro.

SAUSAGE-STUFFED FLANK STEAK

This rich and hearty entree is perfect for entertaining but easy enough for weeknight meals with the family.
—Julie Merriman, Seattle, WA

- -

Prep: 40 min. + standing
Cook: 15 min. + releasing
Makes: 4 servings

- ¾ cup dry red wine or beef broth, divided
- ¼ cup dried cherries, coarsely chopped
- 1 beef flank steak (1½ lbs.)
- ½ tsp. salt
- ½ tsp. pepper, divided
- 3 Tbsp. olive oil, divided
- 1 medium onion, finely chopped
- 4 garlic cloves, minced
- ½ cup seasoned bread crumbs
- ¼ cup pitted Greek olives, coarsely chopped
- ¼ cup grated Parmesan cheese
- ¼ cup minced fresh basil
- ½ lb. bulk hot Italian sausage
- 1 jar (24 oz.) marinara sauce
  Hot cooked noodles

1. Combine ¼ cup wine with cherries; let stand 10 minutes. Meanwhile, cut steak into 4 serving-size pieces; pound with a meat mallet to ¼-in. thickness. Using ½ tsp. salt and ¼ tsp. pepper, season both sides.
2. Select saute setting on a 6-qt. electric pressure cooker and adjust for medium heat. Add 1 Tbsp. oil; cook onion until tender. Add garlic; cook 1 minute longer. Press cancel. Transfer to a large bowl; stir in the bread crumbs, olives, cheese, basil, cherry mixture and remaining pepper. Crumble sausage over the bread crumb mixture; mix well.
3. Divide sausage mixture into 4 portions; spread evenly over each steak piece. Roll up each steak jelly-roll style, starting with a long side; tie with kitchen string.
4. Select saute setting and adjust for medium heat. Add the remaining oil; brown meat on all sides. Top with marinara sauce and the remaining wine. Press cancel. Lock lid; close pressure-release valve. Adjust to pressure-cook on high for 15 minutes. Allow pressure to naturally release for 10 minutes, then quick-release any remaining pressure. Serve with pasta.

1 serving: 758 cal., 45g fat (13g sat. fat), 128mg chol., 2202mg sod., 39g carb. (19g sugars, 5g fiber), 48g pro.

Mild Italian or turkey Italian sausage can be used in place of hot Italian sausage if you like your food with less bite!

Chicken

V Good

CHICKEN VEGETABLE CURRY

This comfort dish gets fabulous flavor when I add chicken, sweet red peppers, coconut milk and the all-important curry powder for seasoning.
—Roxana Lambeth, Moreno Valley, CA

- -

Prep: 20 min. • **Cook:** 4 hours
Makes: 6 servings

1½ lbs. boneless skinless chicken thighs, cut into 1½-in. pieces
2 medium red potatoes, chopped (about 1½ cups)
1 small sweet red pepper, coarsely chopped
1 medium onion, coarsely chopped
1 medium carrot, chopped
3 garlic cloves, minced
1 can (13.66 oz.) coconut milk
½ cup chicken broth
3 tsp. curry powder —2
1½ tsp. salt
1 tsp. ground cumin
1 Tbsp. minced fresh cilantro
Hot cooked couscous

1. Place the first 6 ingredients in a 3- or 4-qt. slow cooker. In a small bowl, whisk together the coconut milk, broth and dry seasonings; stir into the chicken mixture.
2. Cook, covered, on low until the chicken and vegetables are tender, 4-5 hours. Stir in cilantro. Serve with couscous.

1 cup curry: 339 cal., 22g fat (14g sat. fat), 76mg chol., 755mg sod., 12g carb. (2g sugars, 2g fiber), 24g pro.

TEST KITCHEN TIP

Chicken thighs tend to do better in the slow cooker than chicken breasts. They aren't as lean as breasts, so the longer cook time won't dry them out.

SLOW-COOKER ORANGE CHICKEN

Kids cheer on the nights that this easy, family-friendly recipe is on the table— and the bright, distinctive flavors make it a fine choice for dinner guests, too.
—Sherry Kozlowski, Morgantown, WV

- -

Prep: 20 min. • **Cook:** 3½ hours
Makes: 6 servings

1 cup chicken broth
1 cup orange juice
½ cup honey
½ cup packed brown sugar
1 to 2 tsp. crushed red pepper flakes
2 Tbsp. rice vinegar
1 Tbsp. soy sauce
1 Tbsp. sesame oil
2 garlic cloves, minced
¼ tsp. ground ginger
6 boneless skinless chicken breast halves (about 6 oz. each)
3 Tbsp. cornstarch
¼ cup water
4 oz. uncooked rice noodles
Chopped green onions

1. Combine the first 10 ingredients until well mixed. Place chicken in a 4- or 5-qt. slow cooker; add broth mixture. Cook, covered, on low until tender, 3-4 hours. Remove chicken; when cool enough to handle, coarsely shred meat with 2 forks. Set aside.
2. In a small bowl, mix cornstarch and water until smooth; stir into cooking juices. Return chicken to slow cooker; add noodles. Cook, covered, on low for 15 minutes. Stir; cook until thickened and the noodles are tender, 15 minutes longer. Sprinkle individual servings with chopped green onions.

1 serving: 473 cal., 6g fat (1g sat. fat), 95mg chol., 520mg sod., 67g carb. (46g sugars, 1g fiber), 36g pro.

SLOW-ROASTED CHICKEN WITH VEGETABLES

This dish could not be easier—even a beginner cook can follow the recipe and get perfect results. Just a few minutes of prep in the morning and you'll come home to a delicious dinner.
—Anita Bell, Hermitage, TN

- -

Prep: 15 min. • **Cook:** 6 hours + standing
Makes: 6 servings

- 2   medium carrots, peeled, halved lengthwise and cut into 3-in. pieces
- 2   celery ribs, halved lengthwise and cut into 3-in. pieces
- 8   small red potatoes, quartered
- ¾   tsp. salt, divided
- ⅛   tsp. pepper
- 1   medium lemon, halved
- 2   garlic cloves, minced
- 1   broiler/fryer chicken (3 to 4 lbs.)
- 1   Tbsp. dried rosemary, crushed
- 1   Tbsp. lemon juice
- 1   Tbsp. olive oil
- 2½ tsp. paprika

1. Place carrots, celery and potatoes in a 6-qt. slow cooker; sprinkle with ¼ tsp. salt and pepper. Place lemon halves and garlic in chicken cavity. Tuck wings under chicken; tie drumsticks together. Place chicken over the vegetables, breast side up. Mix together the rosemary, lemon juice, oil, paprika and remaining salt; rub over chicken.
2. Cook, covered, on low until a meat thermometer inserted in thigh reads at least 170° and the vegetables are tender, 6-8 hours.
3. Remove chicken from slow cooker; tent with foil. Let stand for 15 minutes before carving. Serve with vegetables.

3 oz. cooked chicken with ⅔ cup vegetables: 329 cal., 17g fat (4g sat. fat), 88mg chol., 400mg sod., 14g carb. (2g sugars, 3g fiber), 29g pro.

SLOW-COOKER CHICKEN BOG

Chicken Bog is a South Carolina tradition with lots of variations (think herbs, spices and fresh veggies), but the standard bog ingredients remain: sausage, chicken and rice. This slow-cooked rendition is a simple take on the classic.
—Anna Hanson, Spanish Fork, UT

- -

Prep: 20 min. • **Cook:** 4 hours
Makes: 6 servings

- 1   Tbsp. canola oil
- 1   medium onion, chopped
- 8   oz. smoked sausage, halved and sliced ½-in. thick
- 3   garlic cloves, minced
- 5   cups chicken broth, divided
- 2   cups uncooked converted rice
- 1   tsp. salt
- 1   tsp. pepper
- 1   rotisserie chicken (about 3 lbs.), meat removed and shredded
      Thinly sliced green onions, optional
      Hot sauce

1. In a large skillet, heat oil over medium heat. Add onion and sausage; cook until the sausage is lightly browned. Add garlic and cook 1 minute longer; transfer to a 5-qt. slow cooker.
2. Stir in 4 cups broth, rice, salt and pepper. Cook, covered, on low until the rice is tender, 4-5 hours. Stir in chicken and the remaining broth. Cook, covered, on low until the chicken is heated through, about 30 minutes. If desired, sprinkle with green onions. Serve with hot sauce.

Freeze option: Omit green onions and hot sauce; freeze cooled meat mixture, juices and rice in freezer containers. To use, partially thaw in refrigerator overnight. Microwave, covered, on high until heated through, stirring gently; add a little broth or water if necessary.

1⅓ cups: 681 cal., 30g fat (9g sat. fat), 134mg chol., 1728mg sod., 54g carb. (3g sugars, 0 fiber), 45g pro.

CHICKEN CORNBREAD CASSEROLE

I love this super easy chicken slow-cooker recipe because it tastes like Thanksgiving, but without all the hassle. It's a hearty, satisfying meal for the fall or winter season.
—Nancy Barker, Peoria, AZ

- -

Prep: 40 min. • **Cook:** 3 hours
Makes: 6 servings

- 5 cups cubed cornbread
- ¼ cup butter, cubed
- 1 large onion, chopped (about 2 cups)
- 4 celery ribs, chopped (about 2 cups)
- 3 cups shredded cooked chicken
- 1 can (10¾ oz.) condensed cream of chicken soup, undiluted
- 1 can (10¾ oz.) condensed cream of mushroom soup, undiluted
- ½ cup reduced-sodium chicken broth
- 1 tsp. poultry seasoning
- ½ tsp. salt
- ½ tsp. rubbed sage
- ¼ tsp. pepper

1. Preheat oven to 350°. Place bread cubes on an ungreased 15x10x1-in. baking pan. Bake 20-25 minutes or until toasted. Let cool on the baking pan.
2. In a large skillet, heat the butter over medium-high heat. Add onion and celery; cook and stir for 6-8 minutes or until tender. Transfer to a greased 4-qt. slow cooker. Stir in cornbread cubes, chicken, soups, broth and seasonings.
3. Cook, covered, on low 3-4 hours or until heated through.

1⅓ cups: 500 cal., 21g fat (8g sat. fat), 89mg chol., 1657mg sod., 48g carb. (5g sugars, 5g fiber), 27g pro.

NORTH AFRICAN CHICKEN & RICE

I'm always looking to try recipes from different cultures and this one is a huge favorite. We love the spice combinations. This cooks equally well in a slow cooker or pressure cooker.
—Courtney Stultz, Weir, KS

- -

Prep: 10 min. • **Cook:** 4 hours
Makes: 8 servings

- 1 medium onion, diced
- 1 Tbsp. olive oil
- 8 boneless skinless chicken thighs (about 2 lbs.)
- 1 Tbsp. minced fresh cilantro
- 1 tsp. ground turmeric
- 1 tsp. paprika
- 1 tsp. sea salt
- ½ tsp. pepper
- ½ tsp. ground cinnamon
- ½ tsp. chili powder
- 1 cup golden raisins
- ½ to 1 cup chopped pitted green olives
- 1 medium lemon, sliced
- 2 garlic cloves, minced
- ½ cup chicken broth or water
- 4 cups hot cooked brown rice

In a 3- or 4-qt. slow cooker, combine onion and oil. Place chicken thighs on top of the onion; sprinkle with the next 7 ingredients. Top with raisins, olives, lemon and garlic. Add broth. Cook, covered, on low until the chicken is tender, 4-5 hours. Serve with hot cooked rice.

1 serving: 386 cal., 13g fat (3g sat. fat), 76mg chol., 556mg sod., 44g carb. (12g sugars, 3g fiber), 25g pro.

PRESSURE-COOKER COQ AU VIN

Don't be intimidated by the elegant name, this classic French dish is now made easier! It has all of the classic flavors of a rich red wine-and-mushroom sauce but is so simple to make. My family enjoys it with French bread or whole-grain bread, both perfect for dipping in the extra sauce.
—Julie Peterson, Crofton, MD

- -

Prep: 25 min. • **Cook:** 5 min.
Makes: 6 servings

- 3 thick-sliced bacon strips, chopped
- 1 medium onion, chopped
- 2 Tbsp. tomato paste
- 5 garlic cloves, minced
- 1½ cups dry red wine or reduced-sodium chicken broth
- 1½ lbs. boneless skinless chicken thighs
- 4 medium carrots, chopped
- 2 cups sliced baby portobello mushrooms
- 1 cup reduced-sodium chicken broth
- 4 fresh thyme sprigs
- 2 bay leaves
- ½ tsp. kosher salt
- ¼ tsp. pepper

1. Select saute setting on a 6-qt. electric pressure cooker. Adjust for medium heat; add bacon. Cook and stir until crisp. Remove with a slotted spoon; drain on paper towels. Discard drippings, reserving 1 Tbsp. in pressure cooker. Brown chicken on both sides in the remaining drippings; remove and set aside.
2. Add onion, tomato paste and garlic to pressure cooker; cook and stir 5 minutes. Add wine; cook 2 minutes. Press cancel.
3. Add chicken, carrots, mushrooms, broth, thyme, bay leaves, salt and pepper to pressure cooker. Lock lid; close pressure-release valve. Adjust to pressure-cook on high for 5 minutes. Quick-release pressure. A thermometer inserted in the chicken should read at least 170°. Press cancel.
4. Remove the chicken and vegetables to a serving platter; keep warm. Discard thyme and bay leaves. Select saute setting and adjust for low heat. Simmer cooking juices, stirring constantly, until reduced by half, 10-15 minutes. Stir in the reserved bacon. Serve with chicken and vegetables.

1 serving: 244 cal., 11g fat (3g sat. fat), 78mg chol., 356mg sod., 9g carb. (4g sugars, 2g fiber), 23g pro. **Diabetic exchanges:** 3 lean meat, 1 vegetable, ½ fat.

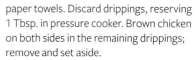

This dish is easy to make in a slow cooker, too. Follow the instructions for Step 1 and 2, substituting a large skillet over medium heat for the saute function of the pressure cooker. Increase the heat to medium-high before adding the wine.

Transfer to a 4- or 5-qt. slow cooker and add the remaining ingredients. Cook, covered, on low until chicken is tender, 6-7 hours. Follow the instructions for Step 4, using a large saucepan to reduce the cooking juices.

SIMPLE SOUTHWEST CHICKEN

Chicken breasts are cooked until tender and then combined with corn, black beans, cheese and salsa for this festive dish with southwestern flair. The garnishes are optional, but they really make the meal!
—Maddymoo,
Taste of Home online community

Prep: 15 min. • **Cook:** 4 hours
Makes: 6 servings

1   **can (15¼ oz.) whole kernel corn, drained**
1   **can (15 oz.) black beans, rinsed and drained**
1   **jar (16 oz.) mild salsa**
4   **boneless skinless chicken breast halves (5 oz. each)**
    Optional toppings: Sweet red and yellow pepper strips, sour cream, shredded cheddar cheese and sliced green onions

1. In a 3-qt. slow cooker, layer three-fourths each of the corn and beans and half the salsa. Arrange chicken over the salsa; top with the remaining corn, beans and salsa. Cover and cook on low for 4-5 hours or until chicken is tender.

2. Shred chicken with 2 forks and return meat to the slow cooker; heat through. Top with peppers, sour cream, cheddar cheese and onions as desired.

1 cup: 234 cal., 3g fat (1g sat. fat), 52mg chol., 678mg sod., 23g carb. (6g sugars, 4g fiber), 24g pro. **Diabetic exchanges:** 3 lean meat, 1 starch, 1 vegetable.

GREEN CHILE CHICKEN ENCHILADA PIE

My husband likes some heat in our meals, but our children—not so much. This is the best of both worlds. Serve with additional chopped cilantro and a dollop of sour cream if desired.
—Dana Beery, Ione, WA

Prep: 30 min. • **Cook:** 4 hours + standing
Makes: 6 servings

3 cups shredded cooked chicken
1 can (15 oz.) black beans, rinsed and drained
1 can (10½ oz.) condensed cream of chicken soup, undiluted
1 can (10 oz.) mild green enchilada sauce
1 can (4 to 4½ oz.) chopped green chiles
¼ cup minced fresh cilantro
1 Tbsp. lime juice
9 corn tortillas (6 in.)
3 cups shredded Colby-Monterey Jack cheese
  Optional toppings: Minced fresh cilantro, lime wedges, salsa and sour cream

1. In a large bowl, combine the first 7 ingredients. Cut three 30x6-in. strips of heavy-duty foil; crisscross the strips so they resemble the spokes of a wheel. Place strips on bottom and up the sides of a 4- or 5-qt. slow cooker. Coat the strips with cooking spray. Spread ¼ cup chicken mixture over the bottom of the slow cooker. Top with three tortillas, overlapping and tearing to fit, a third of the remaining chicken mixture and a third of the cheese. Repeat twice.

2. Cook, covered, on low until a meat thermometer reads 165°, about 4 hours. To avoid scorching, rotate the slow cooker insert one-half turn midway through cooking, lifting carefully with oven mitts. Turn off slow cooker; let stand, uncovered, 15 minutes before serving. Using foil strips as handles, remove pie to a platter. Cut into wedges. If desired, serve with additional cilantro, salsa, sour cream and lime wedges.

1 serving: 541 cal., 27g fat (15g sat. fat), 116mg chol., 1202mg sod., 36g carb. (2g sugars, 6g fiber), 39g pro.

This enchilada pie makes a complete meal, but you can also pair it with Spanish rice or a side salad.

COUNTRY CAPTAIN CHICKEN

Legend has it this dish was brought to the region by a British sailor—hence its name. Whether or not the story is accurate, Country Captain Chicken has been around Georgia since the 1800s. Traditionally served over rice, it's also delicious with noodles or mashed potatoes.
—Suzanne Banfield, Basking Ridge, NJ

- -

Prep: 25 min. • **Cook:** 10 min.
Makes: 8 servings

1	large onion, chopped
1	medium sweet red pepper, chopped
2	garlic cloves, minced
3	lbs. boneless skinless chicken thighs
½	cup chicken broth
1	Tbsp. brown sugar
1	Tbsp. curry powder
1	tsp. ground ginger
1	tsp. ground cinnamon
1	tsp. dried thyme
1	can (14½ oz.) diced tomatoes, undrained
½	cup golden raisins or raisins
	Hot cooked rice
	Chopped fresh parsley, optional

1. Place onion, red pepper and garlic in a 6-qt. electric pressure cooker; top with chicken. In a small bowl, whisk broth, brown sugar and seasonings; pour over chicken. Top with tomatoes and raisins. Lock lid; close pressure-release valve. Adjust to pressure-cook on high for 6 minutes.

2. Quick-release pressure. A thermometer inserted in chicken should read at least 170°. Thicken cooking juices if desired. Serve with rice and, if desired, parsley.

Freeze option: Place chicken and vegetables in freezer containers; top with the cooking juices. Cool and freeze. To use, partially thaw in refrigerator overnight. Heat through in a covered saucepan, stirring gently and adding a little broth if necessary.

1 serving: 298 cal., 13g fat (3g sat. fat), 114mg chol., 159mg sod., 13g carb. (9g sugars, 2g fiber), 32g pro. Diabetic exchanges: 4 lean meat, 1 vegetable, ½ starch.

TEST KITCHEN TIP

If it's tomato season, you can substitute 2 cups of diced fresh tomatoes per 14½ oz. can in your recipes. But if tomatoes aren't in season, canned are usually the better flavor option.

SAUCY INDIAN-STYLE CHICKEN & VEGETABLES

This Indian-style dish seems to develop a devoted following. Prepared sauce makes it easy to bring the rich flavors of Indian cuisine to your family. Feel free to use more or less tikka masala sauce according to your personal taste.
—Erica Polly, Sun Prairie, WI

Prep: 15 min. • **Cook:** 4 hours
Makes: 8 servings

- 2 medium sweet potatoes, peeled and cut into 1½-in. pieces
- 2 tablespoons water
- 2 medium sweet red peppers, cut into 1-in. pieces
- 3 cups fresh cauliflowerets
- 2 lbs. boneless skinlesss chicken thighs, cubed
- 2 jars (15 oz. each) tikka masala curry sauce
- ¾ tsp. salt
  Minced fresh cilantro, optional
  Naan flatbreads, warmed

1. Microwave sweet potatoes and water, covered, on high just until potatoes begin to soften, 3-4 minutes.
2. In a 5- or 6-qt. slow cooker, combine the vegetables and chicken; add sauce and salt. Cook, covered, on low until the meat is tender, 4-5 hours. If desired, top with minced cilantro; serve with warmed naan.

Freeze option: Omitting cilantro and naan, freeze cooled chicken and vegetable mixture in freezer containers. To use, partially thaw in refrigerator overnight. Microwave, covered, on high in a microwave-safe dish until heated through, stirring gently and adding a little water if necessary. If desired, sprinkle with cilantro. Serve with warmed naan.

1¼ cup: 334 cal., 15g fat (4g sat. fat), 80mg chol., 686mg sod., 25g carb. (12g sugars, 5g fiber), 25g pro. **Diabetic exchanges:** 3 lean meat, 2 fat, 1½ starch.

RISOTTO WITH CHICKEN & MUSHROOMS

Portobello mushrooms add earthy flavor to this creamy classic; the convenience of rotisserie chicken and the speed of the pressure cooker make it a snap to prepare.
—Charlene Chambers, Ormond Beach, FL

- -

Takes: 30 min. • **Makes:** 4 servings

- 4 Tbsp. unsalted butter, divided
- 2 Tbsp. olive oil
- ½ lb. sliced baby portobello mushrooms
- 1 small onion, finely chopped
- 1½ cups uncooked arborio rice
- ½ cup white wine or chicken broth
- 1 Tbsp. lemon juice
- 1 carton (32 oz.) chicken broth
- 2 cups shredded rotisserie chicken
- 3 Tbsp. grated Parmesan cheese
- 2 Tbsp. minced fresh parsley
- ½ tsp. salt
- ¼ tsp. pepper

1. On a 6-qt. electric pressure cooker, select saute setting; adjust for medium heat. Add 2 Tbsp. butter and oil. Add mushrooms and onion; cook and stir until tender, 6-8 minutes. Add rice; cook and stir until rice is coated, 2-3 minutes.
2. Stir in wine and lemon juice; cook and stir until wine mixture is absorbed. Press cancel. Pour in the broth. Lock lid; close pressure-release valve. Adjust to pressure-cook on low for 4 minutes. Quick-release pressure. Stir until combined and creamy.
3. Stir in the remaining ingredients and the remaining 2 Tbsp. butter. Select the saute setting and adjust for low heat; heat through. Serve immediately.
1½ cups: 636 cal., 26g fat (10g sat. fat), 101mg chol., 1411mg sod., 66g carb. (4g sugars, 2g fiber), 29g pro.

SAUCY CHICKEN & TORTELLINI

This heartwarming dish is something I first threw together years ago for my oldest daughter. When she's having a rough day, I turn on the slow cooker and prepare this special recipe.
—Mary Morgan, Dallas, TX

- -

Prep: 10 min. • **Cook:** 6¼ hours
Makes: 8 servings

- 1½ lbs. boneless skinless chicken breasts, cut into 1-in. cubes
- ½ lb. sliced fresh mushrooms
- 1 large onion, chopped
- 1 medium sweet red pepper, cut into ½-in. pieces
- 1 medium green pepper, cut into ½-in. pieces
- 1 can (2¼ oz.) sliced ripe olives, drained
- 1 jar (24 oz.) marinara sauce
- 1 jar (15 oz.) Alfredo sauce
- 2 pkg. (9 oz. each) refrigerated cheese tortellini
  Optional toppings: Grated Parmesan cheese and torn fresh basil

1. In a 5-qt. slow cooker, combine first 7 ingredients. Cook, covered, on low until the chicken is tender, 6-8 hours.
2. Stir in Alfredo sauce and cheese tortellini. Cook, covered, until the tortellini are tender, 15-20 minutes. Top with Parmesan cheese and basil if desired.
Freeze option: Freeze cooled, cooked mixture in freezer containers. To use, partially thaw in refrigerator overnight. Microwave, covered, on high, in a microwave-safe dish until heated through, stirring gently; add water if necessary.
1¼ cups: 437 cal., 15g fat (7g sat. fat), 91mg chol., 922mg sod., 44g carb. (8g sugars, 5g fiber), 31g pro.

AUTUMN APPLE CHICKEN

Chicken with apples and barbecue sauce fills the house with the most marvelous smell! This is a meal you won't want to wait to dig into.
—Caitlyn Hauser, Brookline, NH

- -

Prep: 25 min. • **Cook:** 20 min. + releasing
Makes: 4 servings

4	bone-in chicken thighs (about 1½ lbs.), skin removed
¼	tsp. salt
¼	tsp. pepper
1	Tbsp. canola oil
½	cup apple cider or juice
1	medium onion, chopped
⅓	cup barbecue sauce
1	Tbsp. honey
1	garlic clove, minced
2	medium Fuji or Gala apples, coarsely chopped

1. Sprinkle chicken with salt and pepper. Select saute or browning setting on a 6-qt. electric pressure cooker. Adjust for medium heat; add oil. When the oil is hot, brown chicken; remove and keep warm.

2. Add apple cider, stirring to loosen any browned bits from pot. Stir in chopped onion, barbecue sauce, honey, garlic and chicken. Press cancel. Lock the lid; close pressure-release valve. Adjust to pressure-cook on high for 10 minutes. Let pressure release naturally for 5 minutes and then quick-release any remaining pressure. Press cancel. A thermometer inserted in chicken should read at least 170°.

3. Remove chicken; keep warm. Select saute setting and adjust for low heat. Add apples; simmer, stirring constantly, until the apples are tender, about 10 minutes. Serve apple mixture over the chicken.

1 chicken thigh with ½ cup apple mixture: 340 cal., 13g fat (3g sat. fat), 87mg chol., 458mg sod., 31g carb. (24g sugars, 3g fiber), 25g pro. **Diabetic exchanges:** 4 lean meat, 1½ starch, ½ fruit.

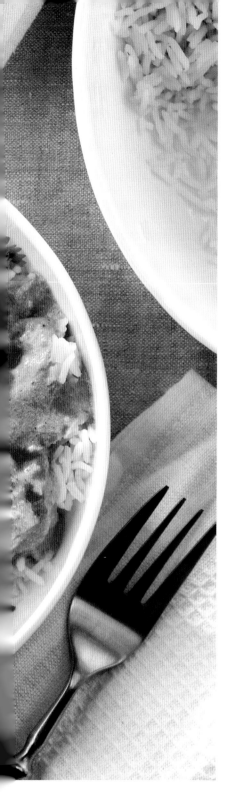

CHICKEN TIKKA MASALA

The flavors of this Indian-style entree keep me coming back for more. The dish isn't fancy, and it's simply spiced—but it's simply amazing.
—Jaclyn Bell, Logan, UT

- -

Prep: 20 min. • **Cook:** 20 min.
Makes: 8 servings

2 Tbsp. olive oil
½ large onion, finely chopped
4½ tsp. minced fresh gingerroot
4 garlic cloves, minced
1 Tbsp. garam masala
2½ tsp. salt
1½ tsp. ground cumin
1 tsp. paprika
¾ tsp. pepper
½ tsp. cayenne pepper
¼ tsp. ground cinnamon
2½ lbs. boneless skinless chicken breasts, cut into 1½-in. cubes
1 can (29 oz.) tomato puree
⅓ cup water
1 jalapeno pepper, halved and seeded
1 bay leaf
1 Tbsp. cornstarch
1½ cups plain yogurt
Hot cooked basmati rice
Chopped fresh cilantro, optional

1. Select saute setting on a 6-qt. electric pressure cooker and adjust for medium heat; add oil. Cook onion until tender. Add ginger and garlic; cook 1 minute. Stir in seasonings and cook 30 seconds. Press cancel. Add chicken, tomato puree, water, jalapeno and bay leaf.
2. Lock lid; close pressure-release valve. Adjust to pressure-cook on high for 10 minutes. Quick-release the pressure. discard bay leaf.
3. Select saute setting and adjust for medium heat; bring mixture to a boil. In a small bowl, mix cornstarch and yogurt until smooth; gradually stir into sauce. Cook and stir until sauce is thickened, about 3 minutes. Serve with hot basmati rice. If desired, sprinkle with cilantro.

1 cup chicken mixture: 279 cal., 8g fat (2g sat. fat), 84mg chol., 856mg sod., 13g carb. (5g sugars, 2g fiber), 32g pro. **Diabetic exchanges:** 4 lean meat, 1 starch, 1 fat.

DID YOU KNOW?

Tikka masala has no standard recipe. It varies from family to family in Indian culture. Traditionally, chicken is marinated in the yogurt and spice mixture and cooked in a tandoori oven.

SLOW-COOKER MUSHROOM CHICKEN & PEAS

Some amazingly fresh mushrooms I found at our local farmers market inspired this recipe. When you start with the best ingredients, you can't go wrong.
—Jenn Tidwell, Fair Oaks, CA

Prep: 10 min. • **Cook:** 3 hours 10 min.
Makes: 4 servings

- 4 boneless skinless chicken breast halves (6 oz. each)
- 1 envelope onion mushroom soup mix
- 1 cup water
- ½ lb. sliced baby portobello mushrooms
- 1 medium onion, chopped
- 4 garlic cloves, minced
- 2 cups frozen peas, thawed

1. Place chicken in a 3-qt. slow cooker. Sprinkle with soup mix, pressing to help the seasonings adhere. Add water, mushrooms, onion and garlic.
2. Cook, covered, on low 3-4 hours or until chicken is tender (a thermometer inserted in the chicken should read at least 165°). Stir in peas; cook, covered, 10 minutes longer or until heated through.

1 chicken breast half with ¾ cup vegetable mixture: 292 cal., 5g fat (1g sat. fat), 94mg chol., 566mg sod., 20g carb. (7g sugars, 5g fiber), 41g pro. **Diabetic exchanges:** 5 lean meat, 1 starch, 1 vegetable.

MEDITERRANEAN CHICKEN ORZO

Orzo pasta with chicken, olives and herbes de Provence has the bright flavors of Mediterranean cuisine. Here's a bonus: Leftovers reheat well.
—Thomas Faglon, Somerset, NJ

Prep: 15 min. • **Cook:** 5 min. + standing
Makes: 6 servings

- 6 boneless skinless chicken thighs (about 1½ lbs.), cut into 1-in. pieces
- 2 cups reduced-sodium chicken broth
- 2 medium tomatoes, chopped
- 1 cup sliced pitted green olives, drained
- 1 cup sliced pitted ripe olives, drained
- 1 large carrot, halved lengthwise and chopped
- 1 small red onion, finely chopped
- 1 Tbsp. grated lemon zest
- 3 Tbsp. lemon juice
- 2 Tbsp. butter
- 1 Tbsp. herbes de Provence
- 1 cup uncooked orzo pasta

1. In a 6-qt. electric pressure cooker, combine the first 11 ingredients; stir to combine. Lock lid; close pressure-release valve. Adjust to pressure-cook on high for 8 minutes. Quick-release pressure.
2. Add orzo. Lock lid; close pressure-release valve. Adjust to pressure-cook on low for 3 minutes. Allow pressure to naturally release for 4 minutes, then quick-release any remaining pressure. Let stand for 8-10 minutes before serving.

1 serving: 415 cal., 19g fat (5g sat. fat), 86mg chol., 941mg sod., 33g carb. (4g sugars, 3g fiber), 27g pro.

1. Sprinkle chicken with ¼ tsp. salt and ¼ tsp. pepper. Meanwhile, in a large skillet, heat oil over medium-high heat. Add the chicken; cook and stir until no longer pink, 6-8 minutes. Transfer to a 6-qt. slow cooker.

2. In same skillet, cook celery, carrots and onion until tender, 6-8 minutes. Add the garlic, tomato paste and remaining salt and pepper; cook 1 minute. Stir in flour; cook 1 minute longer. Whisk in 2 cups chicken broth, cooking and stirring until thickened. Transfer to slow cooker. Stir in bay leaves, thyme and remaining chicken broth.

3. For dumplings, whisk together flour, baking powder, salt and pepper in a large bowl. Stir in milk and butter to form a thick batter. Drop by ¼ cupfuls over chicken mixture. Cook, covered, on low until bubbly and dumplings are set, 6-8 hours. Discard bay leaves. Remove insert and let stand, uncovered, for 15 minutes.

1 dumpling with 1 cup sauce: 370 cal., 15g fat (6g sat. fat), 77mg chol., 1245mg sod., 35g carb. (4g sugars, 2g fiber), 22g pro.

DID YOU KNOW?

Unless otherwise specified, *Taste of Home* recipes are tested with lightly salted butter. Unsalted, or sweet, butter is sometimes used to achieve a buttery flavor, such as in shortbread cookies or buttercream frosting—in these recipes, added salt would detract from the buttery taste desired.

SLOW-COOKER CHICKEN & DUMPLINGS

Here's a homey dish that people just can't wait to dive into! Yes, you can have chicken and dumplings from the slow cooker. The homemade classic takes a bit of work but is certainly worth it.
—Daniel Anderson, Kenosha, WI

- -

Prep: 20 min. • **Cook:** 6 hours + standing
Makes: 8 servings

6	boneless skinless chicken thighs, chopped
½	tsp. salt, divided
½	tsp. pepper, divided
1	Tbsp. canola oil

3	celery ribs, chopped
2	medium carrots, peeled and chopped
1	large onion, chopped
3	garlic cloves, minced
2	Tbsp. tomato paste
⅓	cup all-purpose flour
4	cups chicken broth, divided
2	bay leaves
1	tsp. dried thyme

DUMPLINGS
2	cups all-purpose flour
3	tsp. baking powder
1	tsp. salt
¼	tsp. pepper
1	cup whole milk
4	Tbsp. melted butter

TARRAGON CHICKEN

I tried this dish one night when I had friends coming over for dinner and was pleased with how fresh-tasting it was. Serve it with crusty French bread to soak up all the delectable sauce.
—Shanelle Lee, Ephrata, PA

Prep: 30 min. • **Cook:** 6 hours
Makes: 6 servings

- 1 lb. fresh baby carrots
- ½ lb. medium fresh mushrooms, halved
- 1 small onion, chopped
- 6 bone-in chicken thighs (about 2¼ lbs.), skin removed
- 1 cup chicken broth
- 1 tsp. dried tarragon
- ½ tsp. salt
- ¼ tsp. pepper
- 2 Tbsp. cornstarch
- ½ cup heavy whipping cream

1. In a 5-qt. slow cooker, combine carrots, mushrooms and onion. Top with chicken. In a small bowl, combine broth, tarragon, salt and pepper; pour over the chicken. Cook, covered, on low until the chicken is tender, 6-8 hours. Remove chicken; when cool enough to handle, shred with 2 forks. Transfer shredded chicken and vegetables to a serving platter; keep warm.
2. Pour juices into a small saucepan. Skim fat. In a small bowl, mix cornstarch with ½ cup cooking juices until smooth. Whisk into the pan. Bring to a boil; cook and stir until thickened, 1-2 minutes. Add cream; heat through. Serve sauce with the chicken and vegetables.

1 chicken thigh with ⅓ cup sauce: 309 cal., 17g fat (7g sat. fat), 110mg chol., 497mg sod., 12g carb. (5g sugars, 2g fiber), 26g pro.

CAJUN CHICKEN ALFREDO

This recipe is a true comfort food! Cajun spice adds a nice heat to the creamy Alfredo sauce. And nothing beats only having to clean one pot. Add more or less seasoning depending on your preferred spice level. This recipe would also be tasty with shrimp or smoked sausage.
—Jennifer Stowell, Deep River, IA

Prep: 20 min. • **Cook:** 10 min.
Makes: 6 servings

- 2 Tbsp. olive oil, divided
- 2 medium green peppers, chopped
- 2 boneless skinless chicken breasts (6 oz. each), cubed
- 2 Tbsp. Cajun seasoning, divided
- 1 pkg. (16 oz.) bow tie pasta
- 3 cups chicken stock
- 2 cups water
- 2 cups heavy whipping cream
- 1 cup shredded Parmesan cheese

1. Select saute setting on a 6-qt. electric pressure cooker and adjust for medium heat; add 1 Tbsp. oil. When the oil is hot, add the peppers; cook and stir until peppers are crisp-tender, 3-4 minutes. Remove and keep warm. Heat the remaining 1 Tbsp. oil. Add chicken and 1 Tbsp. Cajun seasoning. Cook and stir until browned, 3-4 minutes. Press cancel.
2. Add pasta, stock and water (do not stir). Lock lid; close pressure-release valve. Adjust to pressure-cook on high for 6 minutes. Allow pressure to release naturally for 3 minutes; quick-release any remaining pressure. Press cancel.
3. Select saute setting, and adjust for low heat. Stir in cream, Parmesan cheese, the remaining 1 Tbsp. Cajun seasoning and the peppers. Cook until heated through (do not boil).

1⅔ cups: 717 cal., 40g fat (22g sat. fat), 131mg chol., 935mg sod., 60g carb. (6g sugars, 3g fiber), 31g pro.

TANGERINE CHICKEN TAGINE

My family and friends love foods from around the world, especially Moroccan entrees, so I created this flavorful dish. Cooking it in the slow cooker keeps each morsel moist and rich in flavor.
—Brenda Watts, Gaffney, SC

Prep: 20 min. • **Cook:** 6 hours
Makes: 8 servings

- 2 Tbsp. brown sugar
- 1 tsp. curry powder
- 1 tsp. ground cinnamon
- 1 tsp. cumin seeds
- ½ tsp. ground ginger
- 1 roasting chicken (5 to 6 lbs.), patted dry
- 1 lb. carrots, peeled and thinly sliced
- 1 lb. parsnips, peeled and thinly sliced
- 2 large tangerines, peeled and sliced
- 1 cup chopped dried apricots
- ½ cup slivered almonds
- ½ cup chicken broth

Combine the first 5 ingredients; rub the spice mixture over chicken until well coated. Arrange the carrots, parsnips, tangerines, apricots and almonds in the bottom of a 6-qt. slow cooker. Place chicken breast side up on the vegetables; pour in broth. Cook, covered, on low until a thermometer inserted in thigh reads 170° and the chicken is tender, 6-8 hours. Remove chicken, vegetables and fruits to a serving platter; let stand 5-10 minutes before carving chicken.
1 serving: 503 cal., 24g fat (6g sat. fat), 112mg chol., 232mg sod., 35g carb. (20g sugars, 6g fiber), 39g pro.

 FORGOTTEN JAMBALAYA

During chilly times of the year, I fix this jambalaya at least once a month. It's so easy...just chop the vegetables, dump everything in the slow cooker and forget about it! Even my sons, who are picky about spicy things, love this dish.
—Cindi Coss, Coppell, TX

- -

Prep: 35 min. • **Cook:** 4¼ hours
Makes: 11 servings

1 can (14½ oz.) diced tomatoes, undrained
1 can (14½ oz.) beef or chicken broth
1 can (6 oz.) tomato paste
3 celery ribs, chopped
2 medium green peppers, chopped
1 medium onion, chopped
5 garlic cloves, minced
3 tsp. dried parsley flakes
2 tsp. dried basil
1½ tsp. dried oregano
1¼ tsp. salt
½ tsp. cayenne pepper
½ tsp. hot pepper sauce
1 lb. boneless skinless chicken breasts, cut into 1-in. cubes
1 lb. smoked sausage, halved and cut into ¼-in. slices
½ lb. uncooked medium shrimp, peeled and deveined
   Hot cooked rice

1. In a 5-qt. slow cooker, combine the tomatoes, broth and tomato paste. Stir in the celery, green peppers, onion, garlic and seasonings. Stir in chicken and sausage.
2. Cover and cook on low for 4-6 hours or until the chicken is no longer pink. Stir in shrimp. Cover and cook 15-30 minutes longer or until the shrimp turn pink. Serve with rice.

Freeze option: Freeze individual portions of cooled stew in freezer containers. To use, partially thaw in refrigerator overnight. Heat through in a saucepan, stirring occasionally and adding a little water if necessary.

1 cup: 230 cal., 13g fat (5g sat. fat), 75mg chol., 1016mg sod., 9g carb. (5g sugars, 2g fiber), 20g pro.

It's much easier to cut raw chicken if it's slightly frozen. Place the chicken breasts in the freezer for 10-15 minutes before cutting them into cubes.

Pork

TUSCAN PORK STEW

Tender chunks of pork slowly cook in a nicely seasoned, wine-infused sauce. Add some crushed red pepper flakes for a little extra kick.
—Penny Hawkins, Mebane, NC

- -

Prep: 15 min. • **Cook:** 8½ hours
Makes: 8 servings (2 qt.)

- 1½ lbs. boneless pork loin roast, cut into 1-in. cubes
- 2 Tbsp. olive oil
- 2 cans (14½ oz. each) Italian diced tomatoes, undrained
- 2 cups reduced-sodium chicken broth
- 2 cups frozen pepper stir-fry vegetable blend, thawed
- ½ cup dry red wine or additional reduced-sodium chicken broth
- ¼ cup orange marmalade
- 2 garlic cloves, minced
- 1 tsp. dried oregano
- ½ tsp. fennel seed
- ½ tsp. pepper
- ⅛ tsp. crushed red pepper flakes, optional
- 2 Tbsp. cornstarch
- 2 Tbsp. cold water
  Hot cooked fettuccine, optional

1. In a large skillet, brown pork in oil; drain. Transfer to a 5-qt. slow cooker.
2. Stir in the tomatoes, broth, vegetable blend, wine, marmalade, garlic, oregano, fennel seed and pepper, and the pepper flakes if desired. Cover and cook on low until the meat is tender, 8-10 hours.
3. Combine cornstarch and water until smooth; gradually stir into the stew. Cover and cook on high until thickened, about 30 minutes. Serve stew over fettuccine if desired.

1 cup: 232 cal., 7g fat (2g sat. fat), 42mg chol., 614mg sod., 19g carb. (12g sugars, 1g fiber), 19g pro. **Diabetic exchanges:** 2 lean meat, 1 starch, 1 vegetable, ½ fat.

EASY CHILI VERDE

I love chili verde and I order it whenever I can at restaurants. A few years ago I figured out how to make an easy, tasty version at home. There are never leftovers when I make it for my family.
—Julie Rowland, Salt Lake City, UT

- -

Prep: 10 min. • **Cook:** 5 hours
Makes: 12 servings (3 qt.)

- 1 boneless pork shoulder roast (4 to 5 lbs.), cut into 1-in. pieces
- 3 cans (10 oz. each) green enchilada sauce
- 1 cup salsa verde
- 1 can (4 oz.) chopped green chiles
- ½ tsp. salt
  Hot cooked rice
  Sour cream, optional

In a 5-qt. slow cooker, combine pork, enchilada sauce, salsa verde, green chiles and salt. Cook, covered, on low until the pork is tender, 5-6 hours. Serve with rice. If desired, top with sour cream.

1 cup: 287 cal., 17g fat (5g sat. fat), 90mg chol., 729mg sod., 5g carb. (1g sugars, 0 fiber), 27g pro.

SLOW-COOKED PORK CHOPS WITH SCALLOPED POTATOES

Here's a meal that feels homey and Sunday-special. When my sister gave me this recipe, it was for a casserole baked in the oven, but I've adapted it to the slow cooker as well as the stovetop.
—Elizabeth Johnston, Glendale, AZ

Prep: 30 min. • **Cook:** 8 hours
Makes: 6 servings

- 4 medium potatoes, peeled and thinly sliced
- 6 bone-in pork loin chops (7 oz. each)
- 1 Tbsp. canola oil
- 2 large onions, sliced and separated into rings
- 2 tsp. butter
- 3 Tbsp. all-purpose flour
- ¼ tsp. salt
- ¼ tsp. pepper
- 1 can (14½ oz.) reduced-sodium chicken broth
- 1 cup fat-free milk

1. Place sliced potatoes in a 5- or 6-qt. slow cooker coated with cooking spray. In a large nonstick skillet, brown the pork chops in oil in batches.

2. Place chops over potatoes. Saute the onions in drippings until tender; place over the chops. Melt butter in skillet. In a bowl, combine flour, salt, pepper and broth until smooth. Stir into the skillet. Add milk. Bring to a boil; cook and stir for 2 minutes or until thickened.

3. Pour sauce over the onions. Cover and cook on low for 8-10 hours or until the pork is tender. Skim fat and thicken the cooking juices if desired.

1 serving: 372 cal., 12g fat (4g sat. fat), 90mg chol., 389mg sod., 29g carb. (6g sugars, 2g fiber), 35g pro. **Diabetic exchanges:** 4 lean meat, 2 starch, 1 fat.

OKTOBERFEST PORK ROAST

My mom used to make a version of this roast when I was growing up. It has all of our favorite fall flavors, such as apples, pork roast, sauerkraut and potatoes.
—Tonya Swain, Seville, OH

Prep: 35 min. • **Cook:** 8 hours
Makes: 8 servings

- 16 small red potatoes
- 1 can (14 oz.) sauerkraut, rinsed and well drained
- 2 large tart apples, peeled and cut into wedges
- 1 lb. smoked kielbasa or Polish sausage, cut into 16 slices
- 2 Tbsp. brown sugar
- 1 tsp. caraway seeds
- 1 tsp. salt, divided
- 1 tsp. pepper, divided
- 1 boneless pork loin roast (3 lbs.)
- 3 Tbsp. canola oil

1. Place red potatoes in a greased 6-qt. slow cooker. Top with sauerkraut, apples wedges and sliced kielbasa. Sprinkle with brown sugar, caraway seeds, ½ tsp. salt and ½ tsp. pepper.

2. Cut pork roast in half; sprinkle with the remaining salt and pepper. In a large skillet, brown the meat in oil on all sides. Transfer to the slow cooker.

3. Cover and cook on low until the meat and vegetables are tender, 8-10 hours. Skim the fat and thicken cooking liquid if desired.

1 serving: 562 cal., 29g fat (9g sat. fat), 123mg chol., 1290mg sod., 31g carb. (10g sugars, 4g fiber), 43g pro.

PRESSURE-COOKER RED BEANS & RICE

My family loves New Orleans-style cooking, so I make this dish often. I appreciate how simple it is—and the smoky ham flavor is simply scrumptious.
—Celinda Dahlgren, Napa, CA

- -

Prep: 20 min. • **Cook:** 45 min. + releasing
Makes: 6 servings

3	cups water
2	smoked ham hocks (about 1 lb.)
1	cup dried red beans
1	medium onion, chopped
1½	tsp. minced garlic
1	tsp. ground cumin
1	medium tomato, chopped
1	medium green pepper, chopped
1	tsp. salt
4	cups hot cooked rice

1. Place first 6 ingredients in a 6-qt. electric pressure cooker. Lock lid; close pressure-release valve. Adjust to pressure-cook on high for 35 minutes.
2. Let pressure naturally release. Remove ham hocks; cool slightly. Remove meat from bones. Finely chop the meat and return to pressure cooker; discard bones. Stir in the tomato, green pepper and salt. Select saute setting and adjust for low heat. Simmer, stirring constantly, until pepper is tender, 8-10 minutes. Serve with rice.

Freeze option: Freeze cooled bean mixture in freezer containers. To use, partially thaw in refrigerator overnight. Microwave, covered, on high in a microwave-safe dish until heated through, gently stirring and adding a little water if necessary.

⅔ cup bean mixture with ⅔ cup rice: 216 cal., 2g fat (0 sat. fat), 9mg chol., 671mg sod., 49g carb. (3g sugars, 12g fiber), 12g pro.

GERMAN POTATO SALAD WITH SAUSAGE

Hearty and saucy, this potato salad is an old family recipe that was updated using cream of potato soup to ease preparation. Despite the "salad" name, this is a hot and filling dish that brings comfort food to the supper. The sausage and sauerkraut give it a special zip.
—Teresa McGill, Trotwood, OH

- -

Prep: 30 min. • **Cook:** 6 hours
Makes: 5 servings

- 8 bacon strips, finely chopped
- 1 large onion, chopped
- 1 lb. smoked kielbasa or Polish sausage, halved and cut into ½-in. slices
- 2 lbs. medium red potatoes, cut into chunks
- 1 can (10¾ oz.) condensed cream of potato soup, undiluted
- 1 cup sauerkraut, rinsed and well drained
- ½ cup water
- ¼ cup cider vinegar
- 1 Tbsp. sugar
- ½ tsp. salt
- ½ tsp. coarsely ground pepper

1. In a large skillet, cook bacon over medium heat until crisp. Remove to paper towels with a slotted spoon to drain. Saute onion in drippings for 1 minute. Add sausage; cook until lightly browned. Add potatoes; cook 2 minutes longer. Drain.
2. Transfer the sausage mixture to a 3-qt. slow cooker. In a small bowl, combine the soup, sauerkraut, water, vinegar, sugar, salt and pepper. Pour over the sausage mixture. Sprinkle with bacon. Cover and cook on low until the potatoes are tender, 6-7 hours.
1⅔ cups: 674 cal., 44g fat (15g sat. fat), 92mg chol., 1643mg sod., 46g carb. (9g sugars, 5g fiber), 22g pro.

CANTONESE SWEET & SOUR PORK

Step away from the takeout menu—there's no reason to dial up delivery once you try this version of sweet and sour pork. The tender vegetables, juicy pork and flavorful sauce are delicious served over rice.
—Nancy Tews, Antigo, WI

- -

Prep: 20 min. • **Cook:** 7½ hours
Makes: 6 servings

- 1 can (15 oz.) tomato sauce
- 1 medium onion, halved and sliced
- 1 medium green pepper, cut into strips
- 1 can (4½ oz.) sliced mushrooms, drained
- 3 Tbsp. brown sugar
- 4½ tsp. white vinegar
- 2 tsp. steak sauce
- 1 tsp. salt
- 1½ lbs. pork tenderloin, cut into 1-in. cubes
- 1 Tbsp. olive oil
- 1 can (8 oz.) unsweetened pineapple chunks, drained
  Hot cooked rice

1. In a large bowl, combine the first 8 ingredients; set aside.
2. In a large skillet, brown pork in oil in batches. Transfer to a 3- or 4-qt. slow cooker. Pour the tomato sauce mixture over the pork. Cover and cook on low for 7-8 hours or until the meat is tender.
3. Add pineapple; cover and cook for 30 minutes longer or until heated through. Serve with rice.
1 cup: 231 cal., 6g fat (2g sat. fat), 63mg chol., 889mg sod., 19g carb. (14g sugars, 2g fiber), 25g pro.

1. Halve the roast. Mix flour, herbes de Provence, salt and pepper; rub over pork. Select saute or browning setting on a 6-qt. electric pressure cooker. Adjust for medium heat; add 1 Tbsp. oil. When oil is hot, brown a roast half on all sides. Remove; repeat with remaining pork and oil.

2. Add cider to pressure cooker. Cook for 1 minute, stirring to loosen browned bits from pot. Press cancel. Add onions, stock, bay leaves and roast.

3. Lock lid; close pressure-release valve. Adjust to pressure-cook on high for 25 minutes. Let pressure release naturally for 10 minutes; quick-release any remaining pressure. A thermometer inserted in pork should read at least 145°. Press cancel. Remove roast and onions to a serving platter, discarding bay leaves; tent with foil.

4. Select saute setting and adjust for low heat. Add apples and dried plums; simmer, uncovered, until the apples are tender, 6-8 minutes, stirring occasionally. Serve with roast.

4 oz. cooked pork with ¾ cup fruit mixture: 286 cal., 9g fat (3g sat. fat), 68mg chol., 449mg sod., 22g carb. (13g sugars, 2g fiber), 28g pro.

DID YOU KNOW?

Dried plums—or prunes—are known mostly as a snack in the United States. But in time-honored European cooking, their earthy, completely natural sweetness makes them perfect for both sweet and savory recipes. Some chefs even use pureed prunes as a substitute for butter in baking.

PORK WITH APPLES & DRIED PLUMS

The classic flavors of herbes de Provence, apples and dried plums make this easy cooked pork taste like a meal at a French country cafe. For a traditional pairing, serve the pork with braised lentils.
—Suzanne Banfield, Basking Ridge, NJ

- -

Prep: 20 min. + standing
Cook: 35 min. + releasing
Makes: 10 servings

1	boneless pork loin roast (3 to 4 lbs.)
2	Tbsp. all-purpose flour
1	Tbsp. herbes de Provence
1½	tsp. salt
¾	tsp. pepper
2	Tbsp. olive oil
1	cup apple cider or unsweetened apple juice
2	medium onions, halved and thinly sliced
1	cup beef stock
2	bay leaves
2	large tart apples, peeled and chopped
1	cup pitted dried plums

BRAZILIAN PORK & BLACK BEAN STEW

During high school, I spent a year in Brazil and fell in love with the culture and food. I introduced this Brazilian-style recipe to my family and it has become one of our favorite comfort foods.
—Andrea Romanczyk, Magna, UT

Prep: 15 min. + soaking • **Cook:** 7 hours
Makes: 8 servings

- 1½ cups dried black beans
- 1 lb. smoked kielbasa or Polish sausage, sliced
- 1 lb. boneless country-style pork ribs
- 1 pkg. (12 oz.) fully cooked Spanish chorizo links, sliced
- 1 smoked ham hock
- 1 large onion, chopped
- 3 garlic cloves, minced
- 2 bay leaves
- ¾ tsp. salt
- ½ tsp. pepper
- 5 cups water
  Hot cooked rice

1. Rinse and sort beans; soak according to package directions. Drain and rinse, discarding the soaking liquid.
2. In a 6-qt. slow cooker, combine beans with next nine ingredients. Add water; cook, covered, on low until meat and beans are tender, 7-9 hours.
3. Remove pork ribs and ham hock. When cool enough to handle, remove meat from bones; discard the bones and bay leaves. Shred meat with two forks; return to slow cooker. Serve with hot cooked rice.
Freeze option: Freeze cooled stew in freezer containers. To use, partially thaw in refrigerator overnight. Heat through in a saucepan, stirring occasionally and adding a little water if necessary.
1½ cups: 531 cal., 33g fat (11g sat. fat), 101mg chol., 1069mg sod., 27g carb. (3g sugars, 6g fiber), 33g pro.

PORK CHOPS & ACORN SQUASH

My husband and I are crazy for the squash we grow in our garden. For a sweet and tangy dish, we pressure-cook it with pork chops and orange juice.
—Mary Johnson, Coloma, WI

Prep: 15 min. • **Cook:** 5 min.
Makes: 6 servings

- 6 boneless pork loin chops (4 oz. each)
- 2 medium acorn squash, halved lengthwise, seeded and sliced
- ½ cup packed brown sugar
- ½ cup reduced-sodium chicken broth
- 2 Tbsp. butter, melted
- 1 Tbsp. orange juice
- ¾ tsp. salt
- ¾ tsp. browning sauce, optional
- ½ tsp. grated orange zest

Place pork chops in a 6-qt. electric pressure cooker; add squash. In a small bowl, mix the remaining ingredients; pour over the squash. Lock lid; close pressure-release valve. Adjust to pressure-cook on high for 4 minutes. Quick-release pressure. A thermometer inserted in pork should read at least 145°.
1 serving: 349 cal., 11g fat (5g sat. fat), 65mg chol., 416mg sod., 42g carb. (23g sugars, 3g fiber), 24g pro.

CAJUN PORK & RICE

I created this recipe after returning home from a trip and finding little food in the house. I used the ingredients I had available in the refrigerator and pantry. My husband loves this pork dish because it's tasty, and I love it because it's easy!
—Allison Gapinski, Cary, NC

- -

Prep: 20 min. • **Cook:** 20 min.
Makes: 4 servings

- 1 tsp. olive oil
- 1 medium green pepper, julienned
- 1½ tsp. ground cumin
- 1½ tsp. chili powder
- 1½ lbs. boneless pork loin chops
- 1 can (14½ oz.) petite diced tomatoes, undrained
- 1 small onion, finely chopped
- 1 celery rib, chopped
- 1 small carrot, julienned
- 1 garlic cloves, minced
- ½ tsp. Louisiana-style hot sauce
- ¼ tsp. salt
- ¾ cup reduced-sodium chicken broth
- 1½ cups uncooked instant rice

1. Select saute setting on a 6-qt. electric pressure cooker and adjust for medium heat; add oil. Add green pepper; cook and stir 4-5 minutes or until crisp-tender. Remove pepper and set aside. Press cancel.
2. Mix cumin and chili powder; sprinkle pork chops with 2 tsp. spice mixture. Place pork in pressure cooker. In a small bowl, mix the tomatoes, onion, celery, carrot, garlic, hot sauce, salt and the remaining spice mixture; pour over pork. Lock lid; close pressure-release valve. Adjust to pressure-cook on high for 6 minutes. Allow pressure to naturally release for 5 minutes, then quick-release any remaining pressure.
3. Stir in chicken broth, breaking up the pork into pieces. Select saute setting and adjust for low heat; bring to a boil. Add rice. Cook until rice is tender, 5 minutes longer. Serve with sauteed green pepper.

1 serving: 423 cal., 12g fat (4g sat. fat), 2mg chol., 573mg sod., 40g carb. (6g sugars, 4g fiber), 38g pro. **Diabetic exchanges:** 5 lean meat, 2 starch, 1 vegetable.

Instant rice and long grain rice cannot be substituted for each other in a recipe that calls for uncooked rice. However, you can use either kind of rice in a recipe that calls for cooked rice.

CREAMY MUSHROOM HAM & POTATOES

This comforting dish couldn't be easier—it uses only seven ingredients and is finished in the slow cooker. Best of all, folks always come back for seconds!
—Traci Meadows, Monett, MO

- -

Prep: 25 min. • **Cook:** 4 hours
Makes: 4 servings

- 1 can (10¾ oz.) condensed cream of mushroom soup, undiluted
- ½ cup 2% milk
- 1 Tbsp. dried parsley flakes
- 6 medium potatoes, peeled and thinly sliced
- 1 small onion, chopped
- 1½ cups cubed fully cooked ham
- 6 slices American cheese

In a small bowl, combine the soup, milk and parsley. In a greased 3-qt. slow cooker, layer half each of the potatoes, onion, ham, cheese and soup mixture. Repeat layers. Cover and cook on low for 4-5 hours or until the potatoes are tender.

1½ cups: 432 cal., 14g fat (7g sat. fat), 57mg chol., 1589mg sod., 55g carb. (8g sugars, 5g fiber), 23g pro.

PENNSYLVANIA POT ROAST

This heartwarming one-dish meal is adapted from a Pennsylvania Dutch recipe. I start the pot roast cooking before I leave for church, adding the vegetables when I get home. Then I just sit back and relax until it's done.
—Donna Wilkinson, Monrovia, MD

- -

Prep: 10 min. • **Cook:** 5 hours
Makes: 6 servings

- 1 boneless pork shoulder butt roast (2½ to 3 lbs.), halved
- 1½ cups beef broth
- ½ cup sliced green onions
- 1 tsp. dried basil
- 1 tsp. dried marjoram
- ½ tsp. salt
- ½ tsp. pepper
- 1 bay leaf
- 6 medium red potatoes, cut into 2-in. chunks
- 4 medium carrots, cut into 2-in. chunks
- ½ lb. medium fresh mushrooms, quartered
- ¼ cup all-purpose flour
- ½ cup cold water
   Browning sauce, optional

1. Place roast in a 5-qt. slow cooker; add the broth, onions and seasonings. Cook, covered, on high for 4 hours. Add the potatoes, carrots and mushrooms. Cook, covered, on high for 1 hour longer or until the vegetables are tender. Remove the meat and vegetables; keep warm. Discard bay leaf.
2. In a saucepan, combine flour and cold water until smooth; stir in 1½ cups cooking juices. Bring to a boil. Cook and stir until thickened, about 2 minutes. If desired, add browning sauce. Serve with the roast and vegetables.

1 serving: 331 cal., 12g fat (4g sat. fat), 78mg chol., 490mg sod., 28g carb. (5g sugars, 4g fiber), 26g pro.

GERMAN SCHNITZEL & POTATOES WITH GORGONZOLA CREAM

I lived in Germany for five years and ate a lot of schnitzel. I developed this recipe so it wasn't as time-consuming to make. I get asked for the recipe every time I make it.
—Beth Taylor, Pleasant Grove, UT

- -

Prep: 20 min. • **Cook:** 4 hours
Makes: 4 servings

- 1 pork tenderloin (1 lb.)
- 1 cup dry bread crumbs
- 2 lbs. medium Yukon Gold potatoes, peeled and cut into ¼-in. slices
- 2 cups heavy whipping cream
- ⅔ cup crumbled Gorgonzola cheese
- 1 tsp. salt
- ¼ cup minced fresh Italian parsley
   Lemon wedges

1. Cut the tenderloin into 12 slices. Pound with a meat mallet to ¼-in. thickness. Place 4 slices in a 3- or 4-qt. slow cooker. Layer with ¼ cup bread crumbs and a third of the potatoes. Repeat layers twice; top with the remaining bread crumbs.
2. In a small bowl, combine the cream, crumbled Gorgonzola and salt. Pour over the pork mixture; cook on low, covered, until the meat and potatoes are tender, 4-6 hours. Sprinkle with parsley; serve with lemon wedges.

3 slices pork with 1 cup potato mixture: 926 cal., 54g fat (33g sat. fat), 216mg chol., 1132mg sod., 73g carb. (9g sugars, 5g fiber), 38g pro.

2. Stir in beans and sausage. Cook, covered, on low until the meat and beans are tender, 5-6 hours. Discard bay leaf. Remove the short ribs. When cool enough to handle, remove meat from bones; discard bones. Shred the meat with 2 forks and return it to the slow cooker. Top individual servings with orange wedges. If desired, serve with hot cooked rice.

1 CUP: 481 cal., 27g fat (11g sat. fat), 123mg chol., 772mg sod., 17g carb. (2g sugars, 4g fiber), 41g pro.

BARBECUED PORK CHOP SUPPER

I start this recipe in the slow cooker in the morning and enjoy a tasty supper later without any last-minute work.
—Jacqueline Jones, Round Lake Beach, IL

Prep: 10 min. • **Cook:** 8 hours
Makes: 8 servings

- 6 small red potatoes, cut into quarters
- 6 medium carrots, cut into 1-in. pieces
- 8 bone-in pork loin or rib chops (½ in. thick and 8 oz. each)
- 1 tsp. salt
- ¼ tsp. pepper
- 1 bottle (28 oz.) barbecue sauce
- 1 cup ketchup
- 1 cup cola
- 2 Tbsp. Worcestershire sauce

1. Place potatoes and carrots in a 5-qt. slow cooker. Top with pork chops. Sprinkle with salt and pepper. In a small bowl, combine the barbecue sauce, ketchup, cola and Worcestershire sauce; pour over the pork chops.

2. Cover and cook on low for 8-9 hours or until the meat and vegetables are tender.

1 serving: 575 cal., 19g fat (7g sat. fat), 111mg chol., 1846mg sod., 61g carb. (46g sugars, 3g fiber), 38g pro.

MY BRAZILIAN FEIJOADA

A co-worker shared fond memories of his favorite meal—his mother's feijoada, a traditional Brazilian dish—so I made him my own version. You can use ham hocks instead of sausage, or substitute lean white meat for the red meat if you prefer.
—Christiane Counts, Webster, TX

Prep: 20 min. + soaking • **Cook:** 7 hours
Makes: 10 servings

- 8 oz. dried black beans (about 1 cup)
- 2 lbs. boneless pork shoulder butt roast, trimmed and cut into 1-in. cubes
- 3 bone-in beef short ribs (about 1½ lbs.)
- 4 bacon strips, cooked and crumbled
- 1¼ cups diced onion
- 3 garlic cloves, minced
- 1 bay leaf
- ¾ tsp. salt
- ¾ tsp. pepper
- 1½ cups chicken broth
- 1 cup water
- ½ cup beef broth
- 8 oz. smoked sausage, cut into ½-in. slices
  Orange wedges, including peel
  Hot cooked rice, optional

1. Rinse and sort beans; soak according to package directions. Meanwhile, place the pork roast, short ribs and bacon in a 6-qt. slow cooker. Add onion, garlic, bay leaf and seasonings; pour chicken broth, water and beef broth over meat. Cook, covered, on high for 2 hours.

CONGA LIME PORK

Dinner guests won't be too shy to get in line when this yummy pork in chipotle and molasses sauce moves to the buffet table!
—Janice Elder, Charlotte, NC

- -

Prep: 20 min. • **Cook:** 4 hours
Makes: 6 servings

1   tsp. salt, divided
½   tsp. pepper, divided
1   boneless pork shoulder butt roast (2 to 3 lbs.)
1   Tbsp. canola oil
1   large onion, chopped
3   garlic cloves, peeled and thinly sliced
½   cup water
2   chipotle peppers in adobo sauce, seeded and chopped
2   Tbsp. molasses
2   cups broccoli coleslaw mix
1   medium mango, peeled and chopped
2   Tbsp. lime juice
1½ tsp. grated lime zest
6   prepared corn muffins
    Lime wedges, optional

1. Sprinkle ¾ tsp. salt and ¼ tsp. pepper over roast. In a large skillet, brown pork in oil on all sides. Transfer to a 3- or 4-qt. slow cooker.

2. In the same skillet, saute onion until tender. Add garlic; cook 1 minute longer. Add water, chipotle peppers and molasses, stirring to loosen browned bits from pan. Pour over the pork. Cover and cook on high for 4-5 hours or until the meat is tender.

3. Remove roast; cool slightly. Skim fat from cooking juices. Shred pork with 2 forks and return to slow cooker; heat through. In a large bowl, combine coleslaw mix, mango, lime juice, lime zest and the remaining salt and pepper. Serve pork with muffins and, if desired, lime wedges; top with slaw.

Note: Wear disposable gloves when cutting hot peppers; the oils can burn skin. Avoid touching your face.

⅔ cup pork mixture with 1 muffin and ½ cup slaw: 514 cal., 23g fat (7g sat. fat), 135mg chol., 877mg sod., 46g carb. (21g sugars, 3g fiber), 31g pro.

TEST KITCHEN TIP

Molasses is notoriously slow and sticky, but there are tricks to make it easier to deal with. Wipe the inside of the measuring spoon or cup with a paper towel dipped in a bit of oil, and the molasses won't stick. You'll get a more accurate measurement and with less mess!

PRESSURE-COOKER PORK & CABBAGE DINNER

This classic slow-cooker recipe was adapted for the new pressure cookers by the Test Kitchen. Fast or slow, it makes an excellent option on busy weeknights. The meal is complete with vegetables but is also satisfying with a side of your family's favorite potatoes.
—Trina Hinkel, Minneapolis, MN

- -

Prep: 15 min. • **Cook:** 55 min. + releasing
Makes: 8 servings

1½ cups water
1 envelope onion soup mix
2 garlic cloves, minced
½ tsp. celery seed
1 boneless pork shoulder butt roast (4 to 5 lbs.)
½ tsp. salt
¼ tsp. pepper
1 small head cabbage (1½ lbs.), cut into 2-in. pieces
1 lb. medium carrots, halved lengthwise and cut into 2-in. pieces

1. Place water, soup mix, garlic and celery seed in a 6-qt. electric pressure cooker. Cut roast in half; place in cooker. Sprinkle with salt and pepper. Lock lid; close pressure-release valve. Adjust to pressure-cook on high for 50 minutes. Let pressure release naturally for 10 minutes; quick-release any remaining pressure. A thermometer inserted in pork should read at least 145°.
2. Add cabbage and carrots to pressure cooker. Lock lid; close pressure-release valve. Adjust pressure to pressure-cook on high for 5 minutes. Quick-release pressure.
3. Remove roast and vegetables to a serving plate; keep warm. If desired, skim fat and thicken cooking juices for gravy. Serve with the roast.
1 serving: 424 cal., 23g fat (8g sat. fat), 135mg chol., 647mg sod., 13g carb. (6g sugars, 4g fiber), 40g pro.

PORK CHILI VERDE

Pork slowly stews with jalapenos, onion, green enchilada sauce and spices in this flavor-packed Mexican dish. It's great on its own or stuffed in a warm tortilla with sour cream, grated cheese or olives on the side.
—Kimberly Burke, Chico, CA

Prep: 25 min. • **Cook:** 6½ hours
Makes: 8 servings

- 1 boneless pork sirloin roast (3 lbs.), cut into 1-in. cubes
- 4 medium carrots, sliced
- 1 medium onion, thinly sliced
- 4 garlic cloves, minced
- 3 Tbsp. canola oil
- 1 can (28 oz.) green enchilada sauce
- ¼ cup cold water
- 2 jalapeno peppers, seeded and chopped
- 1 cup minced fresh cilantro
    Hot cooked rice
    Flour tortillas, warmed

In a large skillet, saute the pork, carrots, onion and garlic in oil in batches until the pork is browned. Transfer to a 5-qt. slow cooker. Add the enchilada sauce, water, jalapenos and cilantro. Cover and cook on low for 6 hours or until the meat is tender. Serve with rice and tortillas.

Note: Wear disposable gloves when cutting hot peppers; the oils can burn skin. Avoid touching your face.

1 cup: 345 cal., 18g fat (4g sat. fat), 102mg chol., 545mg sod., 12g carb. (4g sugars, 1g fiber), 35g pro.

SLOW-COOKED PORK STEW

This rich and fragrant stew is easy to put together, but tastes like you've been working in the kitchen all day. It's even better served over polenta, egg noodles or mashed potatoes.
—Nancy Elliott, Houston, TX

Prep: 15 min. • **Cook:** 5 hours
Makes: 8 servings

- 2 pork tenderloins (1 lb. each), cut into 2-in. pieces
- 1 tsp. salt
- ½ tsp. pepper
- 2 large carrots, cut into ½-in. slices
- 2 celery ribs, coarsely chopped
- 1 medium onion, coarsely chopped
- 3 cups beef broth
- 2 Tbsp. tomato paste
- ⅓ cup pitted dried plums, chopped
- 4 garlic cloves, minced
- 2 bay leaves
- 1 fresh rosemary sprig
- 1 fresh thyme sprig
- ⅓ cup Greek olives, optional
    Chopped fresh parsley, optional
    Hot cooked mashed potatoes, optional

1. Sprinkle the pork with salt and pepper; transfer to a 4-qt. slow cooker. Add carrots, celery and onion. In a small bowl, whisk broth and tomato paste; pour over the vegetables. Add plums, garlic, bay leaves, rosemary, thyme and, if desired, olives. Cook, covered, on low for 5-6 hours or until the meat and vegetables are tender.
2. Discard bay leaves, rosemary and thyme. If desired, sprinkle stew with parsley and serve with potatoes.

1 cup: 177 cal., 4g fat (1g sat. fat), 64mg chol., 698mg sod., 9g carb. (4g sugars, 1g fiber), 24g pro. **Diabetic exchanges:** 3 lean meat, ½ starch.

COUNTRY RIBS DINNER

Ribs slow-cooked with carrots, celery, onions and red potatoes are pure comfort food for our family. To add a little zip, we sometimes sprinkle in some cayenne.
—Rose Ingall, Manistee, MI

- -

Prep: 10 min. • **Cook:** 6¼ hours
Makes: 4 servings

- 2 lbs. boneless country-style pork ribs
- ½ tsp. salt
- ¼ tsp. pepper
- 8 small red potatoes (about 1 lb.), halved
- 4 medium carrots, cut into 1-in. pieces
- 3 celery ribs, cut into ½-in. pieces
- 1 medium onion, coarsely chopped
- ¾ cup water
- 1 garlic clove, crushed
- 1 can (10¾ oz.) condensed cream of mushroom soup, undiluted

1. Sprinkle ribs with salt and pepper; transfer to a 4-qt. slow cooker. Add potatoes, carrots, celery, onion, water and garlic. Cook, covered, on low until the meat and vegetables are tender, 6-8 hours.
2. Remove meat and vegetables; skim fat from cooking juices. Whisk soup into the cooking juices; return meat and vegetables to slow cooker. Cook, covered, until heated through, 15-30 minutes longer.
5 oz. cooked meat with 1 cup vegetables and ¼ cup gravy: 528 cal., 25g fat (8g sat. fat), 134mg chol., 1016mg sod., 30g carb. (6g sugars, 6g fiber), 43g pro.

SPICY PORK & SQUASH RAGU

This recipe is a marvelously spicy combo perfect for cooler fall weather—so satisfying after a day spent outdoors.
—Monica Osterhaus, Paducah, KY

- -

Prep: 20 min. • **Cook:** 15 min. + releasing
Makes: 10 servings

- 2 cans (14½ oz. each) stewed tomatoes, undrained
- 1 pkg. (12 oz.) frozen cooked winter squash, thawed
- 1 large sweet onion, cut into ½-in. pieces
- 1 medium sweet red pepper, cut into ½-in. pieces
- ¾ cup reduced-sodium chicken broth
- 1½ tsp. crushed red pepper flakes
- 2 lbs. boneless country-style pork ribs
- 1 tsp. salt
- ¼ tsp. garlic powder
- ¼ tsp. pepper
  Hot cooked pasta
  Shaved Parmesan cheese, optional

1. Combine the first 6 ingredients in a 6-qt. electric pressure cooker. Sprinkle ribs with salt, garlic powder and pepper; place in pressure cooker. Lock lid; close pressure-release valve. Adjust to pressure-cook on high for 15 minutes. Let pressure release naturally for 10 minutes; quick-release any remaining pressure.
2. Remove cover; stir to break pork into smaller pieces. Serve with pasta. If desired, top with Parmesan cheese.
Freeze option: Freeze cooled ragu in freezer containers. To use, partially thaw in refrigerator overnight. Heat through in a saucepan, stirring occasionally.
1 cup ragu: 196 cal., 8g fat (3g sat. fat), 52mg chol., 469mg sod., 13g carb. (6g sugars, 2g fiber), 18g pro. **Diabetic exchanges:** 2 lean meat, 1 starch.

1. In a 6-qt. electric pressure cooker, combine the first 9 ingredients. Lock lid; close pressure-release valve. Adjust to pressure-cook on high for 3 minutes. Quick-release pressure. A thermometer inserted in pork should read at least 145°.
2. Add apple to pressure cooker. In a small bowl, combine cornstarch and water until smooth; stir into pressure cooker. Select saute setting and adjust for low heat. Simmer, stirring constantly, until thickened and the apple is tender, 3-5 minutes.
3. If desired, serve with rice. Sprinkle each serving with raisins and coconut.

⅔ cup: 174 cal., 6g fat (2g sat. fat), 57mg chol., 287mg sod., 8g carb. (4g sugars, 1g fiber), 22g pro. **Diabetic exchanges:** 3 lean meat, ½ starch.

BBQ PORK & PEPPERS

This was the first recipe I ever made in a slow cooker, and it was the first recipe my husband taught me! I usually pair this with white rice and a salad.
—Rachael Hughes, Southampton, PA

- -

Prep: 10 min. • **Cook:** 8 hours
Makes: 4 servings

- 4   bone-in pork loin chops (7 oz. each)
- 1   large onion, chopped
- 1   large sweet red pepper, chopped
- 1   large green pepper, chopped
- 1   cup barbecue sauce
   Chopped fresh parsley, optional

Place chops in a 4-qt. slow cooker coated with cooking spray. Top with onion, peppers and barbecue sauce. Cover and cook on low for 8-10 hours or until the pork is tender. If desired, top with chopped fresh parsley.

1 chop with ¾ cup sauce: 291 cal., 10g fat (3g sat. fat), 86mg chol., 638mg sod., 17g carb. (12g sugars, 3g fiber), 33g pro. **Diabetic exchanges:** 4 lean meat, 1 vegetable, ½ starch.

PORK & APPLE CURRY

Here's a gentle curry dish that won't overwhelm more delicate palates. For fun, try varying the garnish—add a few chopped peanuts or a little chutney.
—Nancy Reck, Mill Valley, CA

- -

Prep: 15 min. • **Cook:** 10 min.
Makes: 8 servings

- 2   lbs. boneless pork loin roast, cut into 1-in. cubes
- 1   small onion, chopped
- ½   cup orange juice
- 1   Tbsp. curry powder
- 1   tsp. chicken bouillon granules
- 1   garlic clove, minced
- ½   tsp. salt
- ½   tsp. ground ginger
- ¼   tsp. ground cinnamon
- 1   medium apple, peeled and chopped
- 2   Tbsp. cornstarch
- 2   Tbsp. cold water
   Hot cooked rice, optional
- ¼   cup raisins
- ¼   cup sweetened shredded coconut, toasted

Seafood & Meatless

PRESSURE-COOKER STUFFED PEPPERS

Here's a good-for-you dinner that's also a meal-in-one classic. Add a salad if you like and, in just moments, call everyone to the table.
—Michelle Gurnsey, Lincoln, NE

- -

Prep: 15 min. • **Cook:** 5 min. + releasing
Makes: 4 servings

- 4   medium sweet red peppers
- 1   can (15 oz.) black beans, rinsed and drained
- 1   cup shredded pepper jack cheese
- ¾   cup salsa
- 1   small onion, chopped
- ½   cup frozen corn
- ⅓   cup uncooked converted long grain rice
- 1¼ tsp. chili powder
- ½   tsp. ground cumin
      Reduced-fat sour cream, optional

1. Place trivet insert and 1 cup water in a 6-qt. electric pressure cooker.
2. Cut and discard tops from peppers; remove seeds. In a large bowl, mix beans, cheese, salsa, onion, corn, rice, chili powder and cumin; spoon into the peppers. Set the peppers on the trivet.
3. Lock lid; close pressure-release valve. Adjust to pressure-cook on high for 5 minutes. Let pressure release naturally. If desired, serve with sour cream.
1 stuffed pepper: 333 cal., 10g fat (5g sat. fat), 30mg chol., 582mg sod., 45g carb. (8g sugars, 8g fiber), 15g pro. **Diabetic exchanges:** 2 starch, 2 lean meat, 2 vegetable, 1 fat.

BAYOU GULF SHRIMP GUMBO

This recipe skips the hard-to-find spices found in traditional versions but still delivers the true seafood flavor beloved in the Louisiana bayou and beyond.
—Wolfgang Hanau, West Palm Beach, FL

- -

Prep: 35 min. • **Cook:** 5 hours
Makes: 6 servings

- ½   lb. bacon strips, chopped
- 3   celery ribs, chopped
- 1   medium onion, chopped
- 1   medium green pepper, chopped
- 2   garlic cloves, minced
- 2   bottles (8 oz. each) clam juice
- 1   can (14½ oz.) diced tomatoes, undrained
- 2   Tbsp. Worcestershire sauce
- 1   tsp. dried marjoram
- 2   lbs. uncooked large shrimp, peeled and deveined
- 2½ cups frozen sliced okra, thawed
      Hot cooked brown rice, optional

1. In a large skillet, cook the bacon over medium heat until crisp. Remove to paper towels with a slotted spoon. Drain and reserve 2 Tbsp. drippings. Saute celery, onion, green pepper and garlic in the drippings until tender.
2. Transfer vegetables to a 4-qt. slow cooker. Stir in the bacon, clam juice, tomatoes, Worcestershire sauce and marjoram. Cover and cook on low for 4 hours.
3. Stir in shrimp and okra. Cover and cook 1 hour longer or until the shrimp turn pink and the okra is heated through. Serve with rice if desired.
1½ cups: 287 cal., 12g fat (4g sat. fat), 204mg chol., 792mg sod., 13g carb. (5g sugars, 3g fiber), 31g pro. **Diabetic exchanges:** 4 lean meat, 2 vegetable, 2 fat.

PRESSURE-COOKER FISH STEW

I love fish and chowder, so this stew is a favorite of mine. It's made without cream or whole milk so I don't have to worry about keeping those on hand. Feel free to top servings with a little grated cheddar.
—Jane Whittaker, Pensacola, FL

Prep: 25 min. • **Cook:** 5 min. + releasing
Makes: 8 servings (3 qt.)

- 1 lb. potatoes (about 2 medium), peeled and finely chopped
- 1 can (14½ oz.) diced tomatoes, undrained
- 1 can (10½ oz.) condensed cream of celery soup, undiluted
- 1 pkg. (10 oz.) frozen corn, thawed
- 1½ cups frozen lima beans, thawed
- 1½ cups vegetable or chicken broth
- 1 large onion, finely chopped
- 1 celery rib, finely chopped
- 1 medium carrot, finely chopped
- ½ cup white wine or additional vegetable broth
- 4 garlic cloves, minced
- 1 bay leaf
- 1 tsp. lemon-pepper seasoning
- 1 tsp. dried parsley flakes
- 1 tsp. dried rosemary, crushed
- ½ tsp. salt
- 1 lb. cod fillets, cut into 1-in. pieces
- 1 can (12 oz.) fat-free evaporated milk

1. Combine the first 16 ingredients in a 6-qt. electric pressure cooker; top with cod. Lock lid; close pressure-release valve. Adjust to pressure-cook on high for 2 minutes.
2. Let pressure release naturally. Discard bay leaf. Stir in milk until heated through.
1½ cups: 233 cal., 3g fat (1g sat. fat), 25mg chol., 701mg sod., 36g carb. (11g sugars, 5g fiber), 18g pro. **Diabetic exchanges:** 2 starch, 2 lean meat.

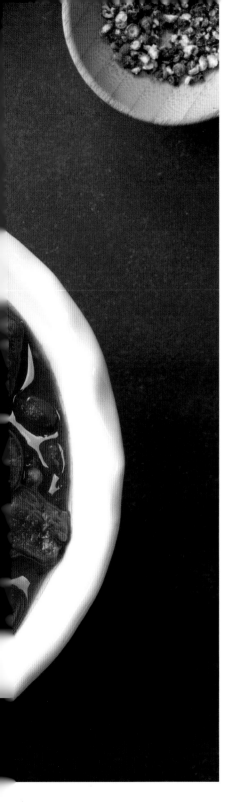

MANCHESTER STEW

While studying abroad, I was pleasantly surprised by how delicious and diverse vegetarian food in Britain could be. After returning to the States, I re-created my favorite meal from my favorite restaurant and named it after the University of Manchester. When the enticing aroma fills the kitchen, I'm back in England!
—Kimberly Hammond, Kingwood, TX

Prep: 25 min. • **Cook:** 5 min. + releasing
Makes: 6 servings

2 Tbsp. olive oil
2 medium onions, chopped
2 garlic cloves, minced
1 tsp. dried oregano
1 cup dry red wine
1 lb. small red potatoes, quartered
1 can (16 oz.) kidney beans, rinsed and drained
½ lb. sliced fresh mushrooms
2 medium leeks (white portion only), sliced
1 cup fresh baby carrots
2½ cups water
1 can (14½ oz.) no-salt-added diced tomatoes
1 tsp. dried thyme
½ tsp. salt
¼ tsp. pepper
Fresh basil leaves

1. Select saute setting on a 6-qt. electric pressure cooker. Adjust for medium heat; add oil. When oil is hot, cook and stir onions until crisp-tender, 2-3 minutes. Add the garlic and oregano; cook and stir 1 minute longer. Stir in wine. Bring to a boil; cook until liquid is reduced by half, 3-4 minutes. Press cancel.

2. Add potatoes, beans, mushrooms, leeks and carrots. Stir in water, tomatoes, thyme, salt and pepper. Lock lid; close pressure-release valve. Adjust to pressure-cook on high for 3 minutes. Let pressure release naturally for 10 minutes; quick-release any remaining pressure. Top with basil.

1⅔ cups: 221 cal., 5g fat (1g sat. fat), 0 chol., 354mg sod., 38g carb. (8g sugars, 8g fiber), 8g pro. **Diabetic exchanges:** 2 starch, 1 vegetable, 1 fat.

Buy leeks with crisp, bright leaves and an unblemished white stalk. Leeks that are larger than 1½ inches in diameter will be less tender. Before using, cut off the roots and trim the tough leaf ends. Slit the leek lengthwise and wash thoroughly under cold water to remove dirt trapped between the leaf layers.

CAROLINA SHRIMP & CHEDDAR GRITS

Shrimp and grits are a house favorite, if only we could agree on a recipe! I stirred things up with Cajun seasoning and some cheddar to find a winner that everyone in my family loves.
—Charlotte Price, Raleigh, NC

Prep: 15 min. • **Cook:** 2¾ hours
Makes: 6 servings

- 1 cup uncooked stone-ground grits
- 1 large garlic clove, minced
- ½ tsp. salt
- ¼ tsp. pepper
- 4 cups water
- 2 cups shredded cheddar cheese
- ¼ cup butter, cubed
- 1 lb. peeled and deveined cooked shrimp (31-40 per lb.)
- 2 medium tomatoes, seeded and finely chopped
- 4 green onions, finely chopped
- 2 Tbsp. chopped fresh parsley
- 4 tsp. lemon juice
- 2 to 3 tsp. Cajun seasoning

1. Place the first 5 ingredients in a 3-qt. slow cooker; stir to combine. Cook, covered, on high until the water is absorbed and the grits are tender, 2½-3 hours, stirring every 45 minutes.

2. Stir in cheese and butter until melted. Stir in remaining ingredients; cook, covered, on high until heated through, 15-30 minutes.
1⅓ cups: 417 cal., 22g fat (13g sat. fat), 175mg chol., 788mg sod., 27g carb. (2g sugars, 2g fiber), 27g pro.

SIMPLE POACHED SALMON

I love this recipe because it's healthy and almost effortless. The salmon always cooks to perfection and is ready in hardly any time. Preparation takes longer than cooking—and prep is only 10 minutes!
—Erin Chilcoat, Central Islip, NY

Prep: 10 min. • **Cook:** 5 min.
Makes: 4 servings

- 2 cups water
- 1 cup white wine
- 1 medium onion, sliced
- 1 celery rib, sliced
- 1 medium carrot, sliced
- 2 Tbsp. lemon juice
- 3 fresh thyme sprigs
- 1 fresh rosemary sprig
- 1 bay leaf
- ½ tsp. salt
- ¼ tsp. pepper
- 4 salmon fillets (1¼ in. thick and 6 oz. each) Lemon wedges

1. Combine the first 11 ingredients in a 6-qt. electric pressure cooker; top with salmon. Lock lid; close pressure-release valve. Adjust to pressure cook on high for 3 minutes. Quick-release the pressure. A thermometer inserted in fish should read at least 145°.

2. Remove fish from pressure cooker. Serve warm or cold with lemon wedges.
1 salmon fillet: 270 cal., 16g fat (3g sat. fat), 85mg chol., 115mg sod., 0 carb. (0 sugars, 0 fiber), 29g pro. **Diabetic exchanges:** 4 lean meat.

FRITTATA PROVENCAL

This meatless pressure-cooker meal makes a delectable dinner for busy weeknights as well as elegant brunch for lazy weekend mornings.
—Connie Eaton, Pittsburgh, PA

- -

Prep: 30 min. • **Cook:** 35 min. + releasing
Makes: 6 servings

1 Tbsp. olive oil
1 medium Yukon Gold potato, peeled and sliced
1 small onion, thinly sliced
½ tsp. smoked paprika
12 large eggs
1 tsp. minced fresh thyme or ¼ tsp. dried thyme
1 tsp. hot pepper sauce
½ tsp. salt
¼ tsp. pepper
1 log (4 oz.) crumbled fresh goat cheese, divided
½ cup chopped sun-dried tomatoes (not packed in oil)

1. Select saute setting on a 6-qt. electric pressure cooker; adjust for medium heat and heat oil. Add the potato and onion slices; cook and stir until potato is lightly browned, 5-7 minutes. Stir in paprika. Transfer the potato mixture to a greased 1½-qt. souffle or baking dish. Wipe pressure cooker clean.
2. In a large bowl, whisk next 5 ingredients; stir in 2 oz. cheese. Pour over the potato mixture. Top with tomatoes and remaining goat cheese. Cover baking dish with foil. Place trivet insert and 1 cup water in the pressure cooker. Fold an 18x12-in. piece of foil lengthwise into thirds, making a sling. Use the sling to lower the dish onto the trivet. Lock lid; close pressure-release valve.
3. Adjust to pressure-cook on high for 35 minutes. Allow pressure to naturally release for 10 minutes, then quick-release any remaining pressure. Using foil sling, carefully remove baking dish. Let stand 10 minutes.

1 serving: 245 cal., 14g fat (5g sat. fat), 385mg chol., 12mg sod., 12g carb. (4g sugars, 2g fiber), 15g pro.

DID YOU KNOW?

If you're watching your cholesterol, you can use egg whites or egg substitute instead of whole eggs in frittatas, omelets and quiches. One whole egg equals two egg whites or ¼ cup egg substitute.

ASPARAGUS TUNA NOODLE CASSEROLE

I updated a traditional tuna casserole using fresh asparagus and asparagus soup. This is so different and so delicious. When fresh asparagus isn't in season, use frozen.
—Nancy Heishman, Las Vegas, NV

Prep: 20 min. • **Cook:** 5 hours
Makes: 8 servings

- 2 cups uncooked elbow macaroni
- 2 cans (10½ oz. each) condensed cream of asparagus soup, undiluted
- 2 cups sliced fresh mushrooms
- 1 medium sweet red pepper, chopped
- 1 small onion, chopped
- ¼ cup lemon juice
- 1 Tbsp. dried parsley flakes, divided
- 1½ tsp. smoked paprika, divided
- 1 tsp. garlic salt
- ½ tsp. pepper
- 2 lbs. fresh asparagus, cut into 1-in. pieces
- 2 pouches (6.4 oz. each) light tuna in water
- 1½ cups shredded Colby cheese
- 1 cup multigrain snack chips, crushed
- 4 bacon strips, cooked and crumbled

1. Cook macaroni according to package directions for al dente; drain. Transfer to a 4- or 5-qt. greased slow cooker. Stir in soup, mushrooms, red pepper, onion, lemon juice, 1½ tsp. parsley, 1 tsp. paprika, garlic salt and pepper. Cook, covered, on low for 4 hours.

2. Stir in asparagus and tuna. Cook, covered, on low until the asparagus is crisp-tender, 1 hour longer. Serve with cheese, crushed chips and bacon. Sprinkle with the remaining 1½ tsp. parsley and ½ tsp. paprika.

1⅓ cups: 338 cal., 15g fat (6g sat. fat), 44mg chol., 1110mg sod., 30g carb. (5g sugars, 5g fiber), 22g pro.

SHRIMP MARINARA

This flavorful marinara sauce simmers for just a few hours. Right before mealtime, toss in the shrimp to cook quickly. Serve these saucy shrimp over hot spaghetti for a weeknight dish that feels dressed up.
—Sue Mackey, Jackson, WI

Prep: 30 min. • **Cook:** 3¼ hours
Makes: 6 servings

- 1 can (14½ oz.) Italian diced tomatoes, undrained
- 1 can (6 oz.) tomato paste
- ½ to 1 cup water
- 2 garlic cloves, minced
- 2 Tbsp. minced fresh parsley
- ½ tsp. salt
- 1 tsp. dried oregano
- ½ tsp. dried basil
- ¼ tsp. pepper
- 1 lb. uncooked shrimp (26-30 per lb.), peeled and deveined
- ¾ lb. spaghetti, cooked and drained
  Shredded Parmesan cheese, optional

1. In a 3-qt. slow cooker, combine the first 9 ingredients. Cover and cook on low for 3-4 hours.

2. Stir in shrimp. Cover and cook on high 15-25 minutes or just until the shrimp turn pink. Serve with spaghetti. Sprinkle with cheese if desired.

1 serving: 328 cal., 2g fat (0 sat. fat), 92mg chol., 527mg sod., 55g carb. (9g sugars, 3g fiber), 22g pro.

STEAMED MUSSELS WITH PEPPERS

Here's a worthy way to use your pressure cooker! Serve French bread along with the mussels to soak up the deliciously seasoned broth. If you like your food spicy, add the jalapeno seeds.
—*Taste of Home* Test Kitchen

Prep: 30 min. • **Cook:** 5 min.
Makes: 4 servings

- 2 lbs. fresh mussels, scrubbed and beards removed
- 2 Tbsp. olive oil
- 1 jalapeno pepper, seeded and chopped
- 3 garlic cloves, minced
- 1 bottle (8 oz.) clam juice
- ½ cup white wine or additional clam juice
- ⅓ cup chopped sweet red pepper
- 3 green onions, sliced
- ½ tsp. dried oregano
- 1 bay leaf
- 2 Tbsp. minced fresh parsley
- ¼ tsp. salt
- ¼ tsp. pepper
  French bread baguette, sliced, optional

1. Tap mussels; discard any that do not close. Set aside. Select saute setting on a 6-qt. electric pressure cooker. Adjust for medium heat; add oil. When oil is hot, cook and stir jalapeno until crisp-tender, 2-3 minutes. Add garlic; cook 1 minute longer. Press cancel. Stir in mussels, clam juice, wine, red pepper, green onions, oregano and bay leaf. Lock lid; close pressure-release valve. Adjust to pressure-cook on high for 2 minutes. Quick-release pressure.

2. Discard the bay leaf and any unopened mussels. Sprinkle with minced parsley, salt and pepper. Serve with baguette slices, if desired.

12 mussels: 293 cal., 12g fat (2g sat. fat), 65mg chol., 931mg sod., 12g carb. (1g sugars, 1g fiber), 28g pro.

SPICE TRADE BEANS & BULGUR

A rich blend of treasured spices turn nutritious bulgur and chickpeas into a tangy stew with just the right amount of heat. The hint of sweetness from the golden raisins makes the perfect accent.
— Faith Cromwell, San Francisco, CA

- -

Prep: 30 min. • **Cook:** 15 min.
Makes: 10 servings

3	Tbsp. canola oil, divided
1½	cups bulgur
2	medium onions, chopped
1	medium sweet red pepper, chopped
5	garlic cloves, minced
1	Tbsp. ground cumin
1	Tbsp. paprika
2	tsp. ground ginger
1	tsp. pepper
½	tsp. ground cinnamon
½	tsp. cayenne pepper
1	carton (32 oz.) vegetable broth
2	Tbsp. soy sauce
1	can (28 oz.) crushed tomatoes
1	can (14½ oz.) diced tomatoes, undrained
1	can (15 oz.) garbanzo beans or chickpeas, rinsed and drained
½	cup golden raisins
2	Tbsp. brown sugar
	Minced fresh cilantro, optional

1. Select saute setting on a 6-qt. electric pressure cooker. Adjust for medium heat; add 1 Tbsp. oil. When the oil is hot, cook and stir bulgur until lightly browned, 2-3 minutes. Remove from pressure cooker.
2. Heat remaining 2 Tbsp. oil in pressure cooker. Cook and stir the onions and red pepper until crisp-tender, 2-3 minutes. Add garlic and seasonings; cook 1 minute longer. Press cancel. Add broth, soy sauce and bulgur to pressure cooker.
3. Lock lid; close the pressure-release valve. Adjust to pressure-cook on low for 12 minutes. Quick-release pressure. Select the saute setting and adjust for low heat. Add tomatoes, beans, raisins and brown sugar; simmer, uncovered, until mixture is slightly thickened and heated through, about 10 minutes, stirring occasionally. If desired, sprinkle with cilantro.

1¼ cups: 245 cal., 6g fat (0 sat. fat), 0 chol., 752mg sod., 45g carb. (15g sugars, 8g fiber), 8g pro.

DID YOU KNOW?

For centuries, rich, flavorful spices such as cinnamon, cardamom, ginger and turmeric were traded along the Silk Road, the land route between India and Western Europe, through Central Asia and the Middle East. It was the search for alternate routes—by sea— that led Europeans to the Americas.

SLOW-COOKER STUFFED SHELLS

There's no need to precook the shells in this simple pasta dish. It's almost like magic to lift the lid and find such deliciousness ready to serve. Add garlic bread and you're golden!
—Sherry Day, Pinckney, MI

- -

Prep: 30 min. • **Cook:** 4 hours
Makes: 10 servings

- 1 carton (15 oz.) part-skim ricotta cheese
- 1 pkg. (10 oz.) frozen chopped spinach, thawed and squeezed dry
- 2½ cups shredded Italian cheese blend
- ½ cup diced red onion
- ½ tsp. garlic powder
- 2 tsp. dried basil
- ½ tsp. dried oregano
- ½ tsp. dried thyme
- 2 jars (24 oz. each) roasted garlic Parmesan pasta sauce
- 2 cups water
- 1 pkg. (12 oz.) jumbo pasta shells
  Optional: Additional shredded Italian cheese blend and sliced fresh basil

1. Mix first 8 ingredients (mixture will be stiff). In a greased 6-qt. slow cooker, mix 1 jar pasta sauce with water. Fill shells with ricotta mixture; layer in slow cooker. Top with remaining jar of pasta sauce.
2. Cook, covered, on low until pasta is tender, 4-5 hours. If desired, serve with additional cheese and fresh basil.
4 stuffed shells: 303 cal., 10g fat (6g sat. fat), 34mg chol., 377mg sod., 34g carb. (4g sugars, 3g fiber), 17g pro. **Diabetic exchanges:** 2 starch, 2 medium-fat meat.

PRESSURE-COOKER CLAM SAUCE

I serve this bright and fresh clam sauce often, usually with pasta. But it also makes a delectable hot dip for special get-togethers.
—Frances Pietsch, Flower Mound, TX

- -

Prep: 10 min. • **Cook:** 5 min.
Makes: 8 servings

- 4 Tbsp. butter
- 2 Tbsp. olive oil
- ½ cup finely chopped onion
- 8 oz. fresh mushrooms, chopped
- 2 garlic cloves, minced
- 2 cans (10 oz. each) whole baby clams
- ½ cup water
- ¼ cup sherry
- 2 tsp. lemon juice
- 1 bay leaf
- ¾ tsp. dried oregano
- ½ tsp. garlic salt
- ¼ tsp. white pepper
- ¼ tsp. Italian seasoning
- ¼ tsp. black pepper
- 2 Tbsp. chopped fresh parsley
  Hot cooked pasta
  Grated Parmesan cheese, optional

1. Select saute setting on a 6-qt. electric pressure cooker. Adjust for medium heat; add butter and oil. When hot, cook and stir onion for 2 minutes. Add mushrooms and garlic; cook 1 minute longer. Press cancel.
2. Drain clams, reserving liquid; coarsely chop. Add clams, reserved clam juice and the next 9 ingredients to pressure cooker. Lock lid; close pressure-release valve. Adjust to pressure-cook on high 2 minutes. Quick-release pressure.
3. Discard bay leaf; stir in parsley. Serve with pasta. If desired, serve with grated Parmesan cheese and additional lemon juice and parsley.
½ cup sauce: 138 cal., 10g fat (4g sat. fat), 40mg chol., 580mg sod., 5g carb. (1g sugars, 0 fiber), 7g pro.

CORNBREAD TOPPING

- 1 cup all-purpose flour
- 1 cup yellow cornmeal
- 1 Tbsp. sugar
- 1½ tsp. baking powder
- ½ tsp. salt
- 2 large eggs, lightly beaten
- 1¼ cups fat-free milk
- 1 can (8¼ oz.) cream-style corn
- 3 Tbsp. canola oil

1. In a large skillet, saute onion and green pepper in oil until tender. Add garlic; cook 1 minute longer. Transfer to a greased 5-qt. slow cooker.
2. Stir in the beans, tomatoes, tomato sauce, chili powder, pepper and pepper sauce. Cover and cook on high for 1 hour.
3. In a large bowl, combine the flour, cornmeal, sugar, baking powder and salt. Combine the eggs, milk, corn and oil; add to the dry ingredients and mix well. Spoon evenly over the bean mixture.
4. Cover and cook on high 2½-3 hours or until a toothpick inserted in the center of cornbread comes out clean.

1 serving: 367 cal., 9g fat (1g sat. fat), 54mg chol., 708mg sod., 59g carb. (10g sugars, 9g fiber), 14g pro.

TEST KITCHEN TIP

All slow cookers heat differently and some may cook at a lower temperature than others—so you may need to adjust the time to get your cornbread fully cooked.

CORNBREAD-TOPPED FRIJOLES

My family often requests this economical, slow-cooker favorite. It's loaded with fresh Southwestern flavors. One batch makes several servings—but it never lasts long at our house.
—Suzanne Caldwell, Artesia, NM

Prep: 20 min. • **Cook:** 3 hours
Makes: 8 servings

- 1 medium onion, chopped
- 1 medium green pepper, chopped
- 1 Tbsp. canola oil
- 2 garlic cloves, minced
- 1 can (16 oz.) kidney beans, rinsed and drained
- 1 can (15 oz.) pinto beans, rinsed and drained
- 1 can (14½ oz.) diced tomatoes, undrained
- 1 can (8 oz.) tomato sauce
- 1 tsp. chili powder
- ½ tsp. pepper
- ⅛ tsp. hot pepper sauce

PRESSURE-COOKER LENTIL STEW

With a little bit of heat from the chiles, wonderfully complex flavors from a variety of spices, and a smooth texture from the cream, this hearty vegetarian stew will satisfy even those who insist on meat!
—Michelle Collins, Suffolk, VA

- -

Prep: 45 min. • **Cook:** 15 min. + releasing
Makes: 8 servings (2¾ qt.)

- 2   Tbsp. canola oil
- 2   large onions, thinly sliced, divided
- 8   plum tomatoes, chopped
- 2   Tbsp. minced fresh gingerroot
- 3   garlic cloves, minced
- 2   tsp. ground coriander
- 1½ tsp. ground cumin
- ¼   tsp. cayenne pepper
- 3   cups vegetable broth
- 2   cups dried lentils, rinsed
- 2   cups water
- 1   can (4 oz.) chopped green chiles
- ¾   cup heavy whipping cream
- 2   Tbsp. butter

- 1   tsp. cumin seeds
- 6   cups hot cooked basmati
     or jasmine rice
     Optional: Sliced green onions or
     minced fresh cilantro

1. Select saute setting on a 6-qt. electric pressure cooker. Adjust for medium heat; add oil. When oil is hot, cook and stir half the onions until crisp-tender, 2-3 minutes. Add tomatoes, ginger and garlic, coriander, cumin and cayenne; cook and stir 1 minute longer. Press cancel. Stir in broth, lentils, water, green chiles and the remaining onion.
2. Lock lid; close pressure-release valve. Adjust to pressure-cook on high for 15 minutes. Let pressure release naturally. Just before serving, stir in cream. In a small skillet, heat butter over medium heat. Add cumin seeds; cook and stir until golden brown, 1-2 minutes. Add to lentil mixture.
3. Serve with rice. If desired, sprinkle with green onions or cilantro.
1⅓ cups stew with ¾ cup rice: 497 cal., 16g fat (8g sat. fat), 33mg chol., 345mg sod., 73g carb. (5g sugars, 8g fiber), 17g pro.

TOMATO-POACHED HALIBUT

This simple halibut with a bright burst of lemon comes together easily. Serve it with bread or, even better, try it with polenta or angel hair pasta.
—Danna Rogers, Westport, CT

- -

Prep: 15 min. • **Cook:** 5 min.
Makes: 4 servings

- 1   Tbsp. olive oil
- 2   poblano peppers, finely chopped
- 1   small onion, finely chopped
- 1   can (14½ oz.) fire-roasted
     diced tomatoes, undrained
- 1   can (14½ oz.) no-salt-added
     diced tomatoes, undrained
- ½   cup water
- ¼   cup chopped pitted green olives
- 3   garlic cloves, minced
- ¼   tsp. pepper
- ⅛   tsp. salt
- 4   halibut fillets (4 oz. each)
- ⅓   cup chopped fresh cilantro
- 4   lemon wedges
     Crusty whole grain bread, optional

1. Select saute setting on a 6-qt. electric pressure cooker. Adjust for medium heat; add oil. When oil is hot, cook and stir poblano peppers and onion until crisp-tender, 2-3 minutes. Press cancel. Stir in tomatoes, water, olives, garlic, pepper and salt. Top with the fillets.
2. Lock lid; close pressure-release valve. Adjust to pressure-cook on high for 3 minutes. Quick-release pressure. A thermometer inserted in fish should read at least 145°.
3. Sprinkle with cilantro. Serve with lemon wedges and, if desired, bread.
1 fillet with 1 cup sauce: 215 cal., 7g fat (1g sat. fat), 56mg chol., 614mg sod., 16g carb. (7g sugars, 3g fiber), 23g pro. **Diabetic exchanges:** 3 lean meat, 1 starch, ½ fat.

BUFFALO SHRIMP MAC & CHEESE

Rich, creamy and slightly spicy, this shrimp and pasta dish does it all. It's a nice new twist on popular Buffalo chicken dishes.
—Robin Haas, Cranston, RI

- -

Prep: 15 min. • **Cook:** 10 min.
Makes: 6 servings

- 2 cups 2% milk
- 1 cup half-and-half cream
- 1 Tbsp. unsalted butter
- 1 tsp. ground mustard
- ½ tsp. onion powder
- ¼ tsp. white pepper
- ¼ tsp. ground nutmeg
- 1½ cups uncooked elbow macaroni
- 2 cups shredded cheddar cheese
- 1 cup shredded Gouda or Swiss cheese
- ¾ lb. frozen cooked salad shrimp, thawed
- 1 cup crumbled blue cheese
- 2 Tbsp. Louisiana-style hot sauce
- 2 Tbsp. minced fresh chives
- 2 Tbsp. minced fresh parsley
  Additional Louisiana-style hot sauce, optional

1. In a 6-qt. electric pressure cooker, combine the first 7 ingredients; stir in macaroni. Lock lid; close pressure-release valve. Adjust to pressure-cook on high for 3 minutes. Allow pressure to naturally release for 4 minutes, then quick-release any remaining pressure.

2. Select saute setting, and adjust for medium heat. Stir in shredded cheeses, shrimp, blue cheese and hot sauce. Cook until heated through, 5-6 minutes. Just before serving, stir in chives, parsley and, if desired, additional hot sauce.

1 cup: 551 cal., 34g fat (20g sat. fat), 228mg chol., 1269mg sod., 22g carb. (7g sugars, 1g fiber), 38g pro.

CHICKPEA & POTATO CURRY

I make chana masala, the classic Indian dish, in my pressure cooker. It's quick work to brown the onion, ginger and garlic, and that really makes the sauce amazing.
—Anjana Devasahayam, San Antonio, TX

- -

Prep: 25 min. • **Cook:** 5 min. + releasing
Makes: 6 servings

1	Tbsp. canola oil
1	medium onion, chopped
2	garlic cloves, minced
2	tsp. minced fresh gingerroot
2	tsp. ground coriander
1	tsp. garam masala
1	tsp. chili powder
½	tsp. salt
½	tsp. ground cumin
¼	tsp. ground turmeric
2½	cups vegetable stock
2	cans (15 oz. each) chickpeas or garbanzo beans, rinsed and drained
1	can (15 oz.) crushed tomatoes
1	large baking potato, peeled and cut into ¾-in. cubes
1	Tbsp. lime juice
	Chopped fresh cilantro
	Hot cooked rice
	Optional: Sliced red onion and lime wedges

1. Select saute setting on a 6-qt. electric pressure cooker. Adjust for medium heat; add oil. When oil is hot, cook and stir onion until crisp-tender, 2-4 minutes. Add garlic, ginger and dry seasonings; cook and stir for 1 minute. Add stock to the pressure cooker. Cook 30 seconds, stirring to loosen the browned bits from pot. Press cancel. Stir in chickpeas, tomatoes and potato.

2. Lock lid; close pressure-release valve. Adjust to pressure-cook on high for 3 minutes. Let pressure release naturally for 10 minutes, then quick-release any remaining pressure.

3. Stir in lime juice; sprinkle with cilantro. Serve with rice and, if desired, red onion and lime wedges.

1¼ cups: 240 cal., 6g fat (0 sat. fat), 0 chol., 767mg sod., 42g carb. (8g sugars, 9g fiber), 8g pro.

Chickpeas are a smart way to add a dose of protein to a meatless main. They are also a good source of fiber, folate and vitamin B-6.

AFRICAN PEANUT SWEET POTATO STEW

When I was in college, my mom made an addicting sweet potato stew. I shared it with friends, and now all of us serve it to our own kids.
—Alexis Scatchell, Niles, IL

- -

Prep: 20 min. • **Cook:** 6 hours
Makes: 8 servings (2½ qt.)

- 1 can (28 oz.) diced tomatoes, undrained
- 1 cup fresh cilantro leaves
- ½ cup chunky peanut butter
- 3 garlic cloves, halved
- 2 tsp. ground cumin
- 1 tsp. salt
- ½ tsp. ground cinnamon
- ¼ tsp. smoked paprika
- 3 lbs. sweet potatoes (about 6 medium), peeled and cut into 1-in. pieces
- 1 can (15 oz.) garbanzo beans or chickpeas, rinsed and drained
- 1 cup water
- 8 cups chopped fresh kale
  Chopped peanuts and additional cilantro leaves, optional

1. Place the first 8 ingredients in a food processor; process until pureed. Transfer mixture to a 5-qt. slow cooker; stir in sweet potatoes, beans and water.

2. Cook, covered, on low for 6-8 hours or until the potatoes are tender, adding kale during the last 30 minutes. If desired, top individual servings with chopped peanuts and additional cilantro.

1¼ cups: 349 cal., 9g fat (1g sat. fat), 0 chol., 624mg sod., 60g carb. (23g sugars, 11g fiber), 10g pro.

PRESSURE-COOKER TUNA NOODLE CASSEROLE

We tweaked this family-friendly classic to work for the pressure cooker. Go for easy, wholesome and totally homemade!
—*Taste of Home* Test Kitchen

- -

Prep: 25 min. • **Cook:** 15 min.
Makes: 10 servings

- ¼ cup butter, cubed
- ½ lb. sliced fresh mushrooms
- 1 medium onion, chopped
- 1 medium sweet pepper, chopped
- 1 tsp. salt, divided
- 1 tsp. pepper, divided
- 2 garlic cloves, minced
- ¼ cup all-purpose flour
- 2 cups reduced-sodium chicken broth
- 2 cups half-and-half cream
- 4 cups (8 oz.) uncooked egg noodles
- 3 cans (5 oz. each) light tuna in water
- 2 Tbsp. lemon juice
- 2 cups shredded Monterey Jack cheese
- 2 cups frozen peas, thawed
- 2 cups crushed potato chips

1. Select saute setting on a 6-qt. electric pressure cooker and adjust for medium heat. Add butter. When melted, add the mushrooms, onion, sweet pepper, ½ tsp. salt and ½ tsp. pepper; cook and stir until tender, 6-8 minutes. Add garlic and cook 1 minute longer. Stir in flour until blended. Gradually whisk in broth. Bring to a boil, stirring constantly; cook and stir until thickened, 1-2 minutes. Stir in cream and noodles. Lock lid; close pressure-release valve. Adjust to pressure-cook on high for 3 minutes. Allow pressure to naturally release for 3 minutes, then quick-release any remaining pressure.

2. Meanwhile, in a small bowl, combine tuna, lemon juice and the remaining salt and pepper. Select saute setting and adjust for low heat. Stir cheese, tuna mixture and peas into the noodle mixture. Cook until heated through. Just before serving, sprinkle with potato chips.

1 serving: 393 cal., 21g fat (12g sat. fat), 84mg chol., 752mg sod., 28g carb. (5g sugars, 3g fiber), 22g pro.

RED CLAM SAUCE

This recipe tastes like an Italian restaurant specialty and cooks while you take care of other things. What a marvelous way to jazz up pasta sauce!
—JoAnn Brown, Latrobe, PA

Prep: 25 min. • **Cook:** 3 hours
Makes: 4 servings

1   medium onion, chopped
1   Tbsp. canola oil
2   garlic cloves, minced
2   cans (6½ oz. each) chopped clams, undrained
1   can (14½ oz.) diced tomatoes, undrained
1   can (6 oz.) tomato paste
¼   cup minced fresh parsley
1   bay leaf

1   tsp. sugar
1   tsp. dried basil
½   tsp. dried thyme
    Additional minced fresh parsley, optional
6   oz. linguine, cooked and drained

1. In a small skillet, saute onion in oil until tender. Add garlic; cook 1 minute longer.
2. Transfer to a 1½- or 2-qt. slow cooker. Stir in the clams, tomatoes, tomato paste, parsley, bay leaf, sugar, basil and thyme.
3. Cover and cook on low until heated through, 3-4 hours. Discard bay leaf. If desired, sprinkle with additional parsley. Serve with linguine.

Freeze option: Omit additional parsley. Cool before placing in a freezer container. Cover and freeze for up to 3 months. To use, thaw in the refrigerator overnight. Place in a large saucepan; heat through, stirring occasionally. Serve with linguine and, if desired, minced parsley.

1 cup sauce with ¾ cup cooked linguine: 305 cal., 5g fat (0 sat. fat), 15mg chol., 553mg sod., 53g carb. (14g sugars, 7g fiber), 15g pro.

TEST KITCHEN TIP

If you use a lot of parsley, buy three or four bunches at a time. Remove the stems and arrange the parsley loosely in a freezer container. Freeze overnight. Remove parsley to a cutting board. Use a rolling pin to crush the frozen parsley, then store it in freezer containers. You'll have fresh-tasting, pre-"chopped" parsley on hand at all times.

Dutch Oven
favorites

Beef

STOVETOP CHEESEBURGER PASTA

Cheeseburgers are delicious in any form, but I'm partial to this creamy pasta dish that seriously tastes just like the real thing. It's weeknight comfort in a bowl.
—Tracy Avis, Peterborough, ON

Takes: 30 min. • **Makes:** 8 servings

- 1 pkg. (16 oz.) penne pasta
- 1 lb. ground beef
- ¼ cup butter, cubed
- ½ cup all-purpose flour
- 2 cups 2% milk
- 1¼ cups beef broth
- 1 Tbsp. Worcestershire sauce
- 3 tsp. ground mustard
- 2 cans (14½ oz. each) diced tomatoes, drained
- 4 green onions, chopped
- 3 cups shredded Colby-Monterey Jack cheese, divided
- ⅔ cup grated Parmesan cheese, divided

1. Cook penne pasta according to package directions; drain.
2. Meanwhile, in a Dutch oven, cook and crumble beef over medium heat until no longer pink, 5-7 minutes. Remove from pot with a slotted spoon; pour off drippings.
3. In the same pot, melt butter over low heat; stir in flour until smooth. Cook and stir until lightly browned for 2-3 minutes (do not burn). Gradually whisk in the milk, broth, Worcestershire sauce and mustard. Bring to a boil, stirring constantly; cook and stir until thickened, 1-2 minutes. Stir in tomatoes; return to a boil. Reduce heat; simmer, covered, 5 minutes.
4. Stir in green onions, pasta and beef; heat through. Stir in half the cheeses until melted. Sprinkle with remaining cheese; remove from heat. Cover and let stand until melted.
1½ cups: 616 cal., 29g fat (17g sat. fat), 98mg chol., 727mg sod., 56g carb. (7g sugars, 3g fiber), 33g pro.

ONE-POT STUFFED PEPPER DINNER

Thick like chili and with plenty of stuffed pepper flavor, this dish will warm you up on chilly days.
—Charlotte Smith, McDonald, PA

Takes: 30 min. • **Makes:** 4 servings

- 1 lb. lean ground beef (90% lean)
- 3 medium green peppers, chopped (about 3 cups)
- 3 garlic cloves, minced
- 2 cans (14½ oz. each) Italian diced tomatoes, undrained
- 2 cups water
- 1 can (6 oz.) tomato paste
- 2 Tbsp. shredded Parmesan cheese
- ¼ tsp. pepper
- 1 cup uncooked instant rice
    Additional Parmesan cheese, optional

1. In a Dutch oven, cook and crumble beef with green peppers and garlic over medium-high heat until no longer pink and peppers are tender, 5-7 minutes; drain.
2. Stir in tomatoes, water, tomato paste, Parmesan cheese and pepper; bring to a boil. Stir in rice; remove from heat. Let stand, covered, for 5 minutes. If desired, sprinkle with additional cheese.
2 cups: 415 cal., 10g fat (4g sat. fat), 72mg chol., 790mg sod., 51g carb. (20g sugars, 5g fiber), 30g pro.

TEXAS TACO DIP PLATTER

When I'm entertaining, this colorful dish is my top menu choice. My friends can't resist the hearty appetizer topped with cheese, lettuce, tomatoes and olives.
—Kathy Young, Weatherford, TX

- -

Prep: 20 min. • **Cook:** 1½ hours
Makes: 20 servings

2 lbs. ground beef
1 large onion, chopped
1 can (14½ oz.) diced tomatoes, undrained
1 can (12 oz.) tomato paste
1 can (15 oz.) tomato puree
2 Tbsp. chili powder
1 tsp. ground cumin
½ tsp. garlic powder
2 tsp. salt
2 cans (15 oz. each) **Ranch Style beans** (pinto beans in seasoned tomato sauce)
1 pkg. (10½ oz.) corn chips
2 cups hot cooked rice
TOPPINGS
2 cups shredded cheddar cheese
1 medium onion, chopped
1 medium head iceberg lettuce, shredded
3 medium tomatoes, chopped
1 can (2¼ oz.) sliced ripe olives, drained
1 cup picante sauce, optional

1. In a Dutch oven, cook beef and onion over medium heat until meat is no longer pink; drain. Add next 7 ingredients; cover and simmer for 1½ hours.
2. Add beans and heat through. On a serving platter, layer the corn chips, rice, meat mixture, cheese, onion, lettuce, tomatoes and olives. If desired, serve with picante sauce.
1 serving: 522 cal., 24g fat (9g sat. fat), 56mg chol., 1200mg sod., 47g carb. (9g sugars, 8g fiber), 27g pro.

TEST KITCHEN TIP

Cooking spices in a bit of fat for a minute or two (known as blooming) helps take off the raw edges and encourages flavors to meld. After draining meat, try cooking it with seasonings for a minute before adding other ingredients. You can add sliced jalapenos or bell peppers, minced cilantro and/or chopped green onions if you crave a bit more flavor and color that pops.

STOVETOP ITALIAN MACARONI

I love how tasty this is and quick to prepare. I've shared it with many friends over the years. It makes a good vegetarian dish when made with meat substitute.
—Laila Zvejnieks, Stoney Creek, ON

- -

Takes: 25 min. • **Makes:** 5 servings

1   lb. ground beef
1   can (28 oz.) diced tomatoes, undrained
2   cups water
1   envelope onion soup mix
1   tsp. Italian seasoning
¼   tsp. crushed red pepper flakes, optional
2   cups uncooked elbow macaroni
½   cup grated Parmesan cheese
1   cup shredded part-skim mozzarella cheese

1. In a Dutch oven, cook ground beef over medium heat until no longer pink; drain. Add the tomatoes, water, soup mix, Italian seasoning and, if desired, pepper flakes. Bring to a boil. Stir in the macaroni. Reduce heat; cover and simmer for 8-9 minutes or until the macaroni is tender.

2. Remove from the heat; stir in Parmesan cheese. Sprinkle with mozzarella cheese. Cover and let stand for 2 minutes or until cheese is melted.

1⅓ cups: 410 cal., 17g fat (8g sat. fat), 76mg chol., 969mg sod., 34g carb. (7g sugars, 4g fiber), 30g pro.

OSSO BUCO

This dish can be assembled several hours ahead and put in the oven while the cook relaxes. I try to get shanks that are similar in size so they'll cook evenly, and usually plan on serving two shanks per person.
—Karen Jaffe, Short Hills, NJ

Prep: 30 min. • **Bake:** 2 hours
Makes: 6 servings

- ⅓ cup all-purpose flour
- 1 tsp. salt
- ½ tsp. pepp
- 6 veal shanks (2 in. thick)
- 5 Tbsp. olive oil
- 1 tsp. Italian seasoning
- ½ tsp. rubbed sage
- 2 medium carrots, sliced
- 1 medium onion, chopped
- 1 celery rib, cut in ½-in. slices
- 1 garlic clove, minced
- 1½ cups dry white wine or chicken broth
- 1 can (10½ oz.) condensed chicken broth, undiluted
- 2 Tbsp. tomato paste

GREMOLATA
- 2 garlic cloves, minced
- 1 to 2 Tbsp. minced fresh parsley
- 1 Tbsp. grated lemon zest

1. Preheat oven to 325°. Combine flour, salt and pepper; dredge meat. In a large skillet, brown meat in oil on all sides. Place the shanks in a single layer in a Dutch oven or oblong baking dish; sprinkle with Italian seasoning and sage. Combine the carrots, onion, celery and garlic; sprinkle over meat. In a small bowl, whisk together wine, broth and tomato paste. Pour over vegetables.
2. Cover and bake for 2 hours or until fork-tender. Just before serving, combine gremolata ingredients; sprinkle over each shank. Serve immediately.
1 serving: 413 cal., 22g fat (6g sat. fat), 111mg chol., 804mg sod., 13g carb. (3g sugars, 2g fiber), 30g pro.

BRAISED HANUKKAH BRISKET

My mother always used the most marbled cut of brisket she could find to give this recipe the most flavor. When she added the carrots to the pan, she threw in some potatoes, too. Expect this brisket to be even tastier the next day!
—Ellen Ruzinsky, Yorktown Heights, NY

Prep: 25 min. • **Cook:** 2¾ hours
Makes: 12 servings

- 2 Tbsp. canola oil
- 1 fresh beef brisket (4 to 5 lbs.)
- 3 celery ribs, cut into 1-in. pieces
- 3 large carrots, cut into ¼-in. slices
- 2 large onions, sliced
- 1 lb. medium fresh mushrooms
- ¾ cup cold water
- ¾ cup tomato sauce
- 3 Tbsp. Worcestershire sauce
- 1 Tbsp. prepared horseradish

1. In a Dutch oven, heat oil over medium heat. Brown the brisket on both sides. Remove from pot.
2. Add celery, carrots and onions to the same pot; cook and stir for 4-6 minutes or until crisp-tender. Stir in the remaining ingredients.
3. Return brisket to pot, fat side up. Bring mixture to a boil. Reduce heat; simmer, covered, 2½-3 hours or until the meat is tender. Remove the beef and vegetables; keep warm. Skim fat from the pan juices. If desired, thicken juices.
4. Cut brisket diagonally across the grain into thin slices. Serve with vegetables and pan juices.
Note: This recipe is made with a fresh beef brisket, not corned beef.
4 oz. cooked meat with ⅓ cup vegetables and ½ cup juices: 247 cal., 9g fat (3g sat. fat), 64mg chol., 189mg sod., 8g carb. (3g sugars, 2g fiber), 33g pro. **Diabetic exchanges:** 4 lean meat, 1 vegetable, ½ fat.

BEEF PAPRIKASH WITH FIRE-ROASTED TOMATOES

Beef cooked Hungarian style with paprika, peppers and tomatoes makes a marvelous Sunday dinner. We prefer it with kluski egg noodles, or try mashed potatoes.
—Gloria Bradley, Naperville, IL

- -

Prep: 15 min. • **Cook:** 1¾ hours
Makes: 8 servings

⅓ cup all-purpose flour
2 Tbsp. sweet Hungarian or regular paprika, divided
1¼ tsp. salt, divided
2 lbs. boneless beef chuck roast, cut into 1-in. pieces
2 Tbsp. canola oil, divided
1 large onion, chopped
1 small sweet red pepper, finely chopped

2 cans (8 oz. each) tomato sauce
1 can (14½ oz.) fire-roasted diced tomatoes, undrained
1 can (14½ oz.) beef broth
1 pkg. (16 oz.) kluski or other egg noodles
3 Tbsp. butter
Minced fresh parsley, optional

1. In a small bowl, mix flour, 1 Tbsp. paprika and ½ tsp. salt. Sprinkle over beef and toss to coat; shake off excess.
2. In a Dutch oven, heat 1 Tbsp. oil over medium heat. Brown the beef in batches, adding remaining oil as needed. Remove from pot with a slotted spoon, reserving drippings in pot.
3. Add onion and pepper to the drippings; cook and stir 4-5 minutes or until tender. Stir in tomato sauce, tomatoes, broth and the remaining 1 Tbsp. paprika and ¾ tsp. salt; bring to a boil. Reduce heat; simmer, covered, until beef is tender, 1½-2 hours.
4. Cook the noodles according to package directions. Drain; return to pot. Add butter and toss to coat. Serve with stew. If desired, sprinkle with parsley.

1 cup stew with ¾ cup cooked noodles: 534 cal., 21g fat (8g sat. fat), 133mg chol., 953mg sod., 51g carb. (5g sugars, 4g fiber), 33g pro.

Hungarian paprika is stronger than regular paprika, which comes from Spain. If you like your flavors a little bolder, and can't find Hungarian paprika, try adding a little cayenne pepper along with the paprika.

STOUT & SHIITAKE POT ROAST

A bit of stout beer, mushrooms and onions add excellent flavor to my pot roast. This one-dish wonder might taste even better when you serve up leftovers the next day!
—Madeleine Bessette, Coeur d'Alene, ID

- -

Prep: 30 min. • **Cook:** 1¾ hours
Makes: 6 servings

- 3 Tbsp. olive oil, divided
- 1 boneless beef chuck roast (2 to 3 lbs.)
- 2 medium onions, sliced
- 1 garlic clove, minced
- 1 bottle (12 oz.) stout or nonalcoholic beer
- ½ oz. dried shiitake mushrooms (about ½ cup)
- 1 Tbsp. brown sugar
- 1 tsp. Worcestershire sauce
- ½ tsp. dried savory
- 1 lb. red potatoes (about 8 small), cut into 1-in. pieces
- 2 medium carrots, sliced
- ½ cup water
- ½ tsp. salt
- ¼ tsp. pepper

1. In a Dutch oven, heat 1 Tbsp. oil over medium heat. Brown roast on all sides; remove from pot.
2. In same pot, heat the remaining oil. Add onions and garlic; cook and stir until tender. Add beer, stirring to loosen browned bits from pot. Stir in mushrooms, brown sugar, Worcestershire sauce and savory. Return roast to pot. Bring to a boil. Reduce heat; simmer, covered, for 1½ hours.
3. Stir in the remaining ingredients. Return to a boil. Reduce heat; simmer, covered, 15-25 minutes longer or until the meat and vegetables are tender. If desired, skim fat and thicken the cooking juices for gravy.
4 oz. cooked beef with 1 cup vegetables: 441 cal., 21g fat (7g sat. fat), 98mg chol., 293mg sod., 24g carb. (9g sugars, 3g fiber), 33g pro.

CREAMY BEEF & POTATOES

One of my husband's favorite childhood memories was eating his Grandma Barney's Tater Tot casserole. One day I started preparing it using O'Brien potatoes instead. Now I always make it this way.
—Heather Matthews, Keller, TX

- -

Takes: 20 min. • **Makes:** 4 servings

- 4 cups frozen O'Brien potatoes
- 1 Tbsp. water
- 1 lb. ground beef
- ½ tsp. salt
- ¼ tsp. pepper
- 2 cans (10¾ oz. each) condensed cream of mushroom soup, undiluted
- ⅔ cup 2% milk
- 2 cups shredded Colby-Monterey Jack cheese

1. Place potatoes and water in microwave-safe bowl. Microwave, covered, on high until tender, 8-10 minutes, stirring twice.
2. Meanwhile, in a Dutch oven, cook the beef over medium heat until no longer pink, breaking into crumbles, 6-8 minutes; drain and return to pot. Stir in salt and pepper. In a small bowl, whisk soup and milk until blended; add to the beef. Stir in potatoes. Sprinkle with cheese. Reduce heat to low; cook, covered, until cheese is melted.
1¾ cups: 664 cal., 38g fat (19g sat. fat), 130mg chol., 1851mg sod., 40g carb. (5g sugars, 6g fiber), 37g pro.

TEXAS TACOS

I created this recipe by combining a bunch of ingredients that my kids like. Once it's ready, I often keep the beef mixture warm in a slow cooker so the kids can quickly fill taco shells after an afternoon of rigorous soccer practice.
—Susan Scully, Mason, OH

- -

Takes: 30 min. • **Makes:** 10 servings

1½ lbs. lean ground beef (90% lean)
1 medium sweet red pepper, chopped
1 small onion, chopped
1 can (14½ oz.) diced tomatoes, drained
1⅓ cups frozen corn, thawed
1 can (8 oz.) tomato sauce
2 Tbsp. chili powder
½ tsp. salt
1 pkg. (8.8 oz.) ready-to-serve brown rice
20 taco shells, warmed
   Optional: Shredded lettuce, chopped fresh tomatoes and reduced-fat sour cream

1. In a Dutch oven, cook beef, red pepper and onion over medium heat until the beef is no longer pink and the vegetables are tender, breaking up beef into crumbles, 8-10 minutes. Drain.

2. Stir in tomatoes, corn, tomato sauce, chili powder and salt; bring to a boil. Add rice; heat through. Serve in taco shells with toppings of your choice.

2 tacos: 294 cal., 11g fat (4g sat. fat), 42mg chol., 420mg sod., 30g carb. (3g sugars, 3g fiber), 17g pro. **Diabetic exchanges:** 2 starch, 2 lean meat.

SPECIAL OCCASION BEEF BOURGUIGNON

I've enjoyed trying many rich and satisfying variations of boeuf bourguignon, including an intriguing peasant version that used beef cheeks and a rustic table wine. But this is my favorite take on the classic. To make this stew gluten-free, use white rice flour instead of all-purpose.
—Leo Cotnoir, Johnson City, NY

- -

Prep: 50 min. • **Bake:** 2 hours
Makes: 8 servings

- 4   bacon strips, chopped
- 1   beef sirloin tip roast (2 lbs.), cut into 1½-in. cubes and patted dry
- ¼   cup all-purpose flour
- ½   tsp. salt
- ½   tsp. pepper
- 1   Tbsp. canola oil
- 2   medium onions, chopped
- 2   medium carrots, coarsely chopped
- ½   lb. medium fresh mushrooms, quartered
- 4   garlic cloves, minced
- 1   Tbsp. tomato paste
- 2   cups dry red wine
- 1   cup beef stock
- 2   bay leaves
- ½   tsp. dried thyme
- 8   oz. uncooked egg noodles
      Minced fresh parsley

1. Preheat oven to 325°. In a Dutch oven, cook bacon over medium-low heat until crisp, stirring occasionally. Remove with a slotted spoon, reserving the drippings; drain on paper towels.

2. In batches, brown beef in the drippings over medium-high heat; remove from pot. Toss with flour, salt and pepper.

3. In the same pot, heat 1 Tbsp. oil over medium heat; saute onions, carrots and mushrooms until the onions are tender, 4-5 minutes. Add garlic and tomato paste; cook and stir 1 minute. Add wine and stock, stirring to loosen browned bits from pot. Add herbs, bacon and beef; bring to a boil.

4. Transfer to oven; bake, covered, until the meat is tender, 2-2¼ hours. Remove bay leaves.

5. To serve, cook noodles according to package directions; drain. Serve stew with noodles; sprinkle with parsley.

Freeze option: Freeze the cooled stew in freezer containers. To use, partially thaw in refrigerator overnight. Heat through in a saucepan, stirring occasionally and adding a little stock or broth if necessary.

⅔ cup stew with ⅔ cup noodles: 422 cal., 14g fat (4g sat. fat), 105mg chol., 357mg sod., 31g carb. (4g sugars, 2g fiber), 31g pro.

Diabetic exchanges: 4 lean meat, 2 fat, 1½ starch, 1 vegetable.

BOHEMIAN BEEF DINNER

When I was growing up, one of my favorite things to do was to help my mother in the kitchen while she prepared traditional Czech dishes like this. It makes a savory stick-to-your-ribs meal with beef and sauerkraut covered in a creamy sauce.
—Carl & Isobel Wanasek, Rogers, AR

Prep: 25 min. • **Cook:** 2 hours
Makes: 6 servings

- ¾ cups all-purpose flour
- 1 tsp. salt
- ¼ tsp. pepper
- 2 lbs. beef stew meat, cut into 1-in. cubes
- 2 Tbsp. canola oil
- 2 medium onions, chopped
- 1 garlic clove, minced
- 1 tsp. dill weed
- 1 tsp. caraway seeds
- 1 tsp. paprika
- ½ cup water
- 1 cup sour cream
- 2 cans (14 oz. each) sauerkraut, rinsed and well drained
  Additional paprika

1. In a large bowl or dish, combine flour, salt and pepper. Add beef and toss to coat. In a Dutch oven, brown the beef in oil in batches; drain. Add the onions, garlic, dill, caraway, paprika and water.
2. Cover and simmer for 2 hours or until the meat is tender, stirring occasionally.
3. Stir in sour cream; heat through but do not boil. Heat sauerkraut; drain and spoon onto a serving platter. Top with the beef mixture. Sprinkle with paprika.
1 serving: 442 cal., 22g fat (9g sat. fat), 121mg chol., 1321mg sod., 24g carb. (6g sugars, 5g fiber), 34g pro.

HEARTY VEGETABLE BEEF RAGOUT

This recipe is healthy yet satisfying, quick yet delicious. It's on the table in less than 30 minutes—and one that my children will gobble up! If you are not fond of kale, use baby spinach or chopped broccoli instead.
—Kim Van Dunk, Caldwell, NJ

Takes: 30 min. • **Makes:** 8 servings

- 4 cups uncooked whole wheat spiral pasta
- 1 lb. lean ground beef (90% lean)
- 1 large onion, chopped
- 3 garlic cloves, minced
- 2 cans (14½ oz. each) Italian diced tomatoes, undrained
- 1 jar (24 oz.) meatless spaghetti sauce
- 2 cups finely chopped fresh kale
- 1 pkg. (9 oz.) frozen peas, thawed
- ¾ tsp. garlic powder
- ¼ tsp. pepper
  Grated Parmesan cheese, optional

1. Cook pasta according to package directions; drain. Meanwhile, in a Dutch oven, cook beef, onion and garlic over medium heat until the beef is no longer pink, breaking up beef into crumbles, 6-8 minutes; drain and return to pot.
2. Stir in tomatoes, spaghetti sauce, kale, peas, garlic powder and pepper. Bring to a boil. Reduce heat; simmer, uncovered, until the kale is tender, 8-10 minutes. Stir the pasta into the sauce. If desired, serve with cheese.
1½ cups: 302 cal., 5g fat (2g sat. fat), 35mg chol., 837mg sod., 43g carb. (15g sugars, 7g fiber), 20g pro. **Diabetic exchanges:** 2 starch, 2 lean meat, 2 vegetable.

FAVORITE CORNED BEEF & CABBAGE

It may be the most famous dish to eat on St. Patrick's Day, but this Irish-American classic is a favorite at our table all year long.
—Evelyn Kenney, Trenton, NJ

Prep: 10 min. • **Cook:** 2¾ hours
Makes: 10 servings

- 1 corned beef brisket (about 4 lbs.) with spice packet
- 2 Tbsp. brown sugar
- 2 bay leaves
- 3½ lbs. small potatoes (10-15), peeled
- 8 medium carrots, halved crosswise
- 1 medium head cabbage, cut into wedges

HORSERADISH SAUCE
- 3 Tbsp. butter
- 2 Tbsp. all-purpose flour
- 1 to 1½ cups reserved cooking juices from corned beef
- 1 Tbsp. sugar
- 1 Tbsp. cider vinegar
- ¼ cup horseradish

MUSTARD SAUCE (OPTIONAL)
- 1 cup sour cream
- 2 Tbsp. Dijon mustard
- ¼ tsp. sugar

1. Place brisket, contents of the seasoning packet, brown sugar and bay leaves in a large Dutch oven or stockpot; cover with water. Bring to a boil. Reduce heat; simmer, covered, 2 hours.

2. Add potatoes and carrots; return to a boil. Reduce heat; simmer, covered, just until the beef and vegetables are tender, 30-40 minutes.

3. Add cabbage wedges to the pot; return to a boil. (If pot is too full, remove potatoes and carrots before adding cabbage; reheat before serving.) Reduce heat and simmer, covered, until the cabbage is tender, about 15 minutes. Remove vegetables and corned beef; keep warm.

4. For the horseradish sauce, strain and reserve 1½ cups cooking juices; skim fat from reserved juices. Discard remaining juices. In a small saucepan, melt butter over medium heat; stir in the flour until smooth. Gradually whisk in 1 cup reserved juices. Stir in sugar, vinegar and horseradish; bring to a boil, stirring constantly. Cook and stir until thickened. If desired, thin with additional juices. Season to taste with additional sugar, vinegar or horseradish.

5. For the mustard sauce, mix sour cream, Dijon mustard and sugar.

6. Cut beef across the grain into slices. Serve with vegetables, horseradish sauce and, if desired, mustard sauce.

1 serving (with horseradish sauce): 564 cal., 28g fat (10g sat. fat), 134mg chol., 1616mg sod., 50g carb. (11g sugars, 8g fiber), 29g pro.

STOVETOP ROOT VEGETABLE BEEF STEW

To me, the definition of cozy is a pot of tender beef simmering with sweet potatoes and parsnips. It doesn't get better than that!
—Beth Rossos, Estacada, OR

- -

Prep: 30 min. • **Cook:** 1¾ hours
Makes: 8 servings (2 qt.)

- ⅔ cup all-purpose flour
- 1½ tsp. salt, divided
- 1¼ tsp. pepper, divided
- 2 lbs. beef stew meat
- 4 Tbsp. olive oil
- ⅔ cup Burgundy wine
- 3 cups water
- 1 can (14½ oz.) stewed tomatoes
- 2 garlic cloves, minced
- 2 tsp. beef base
- ¼ tsp. dried thyme
- ¼ tsp. ground cinnamon
- ¼ tsp. crushed red pepper flakes
- 1 large sweet potato (about 1 lb.), peeled and coarsely chopped
- 2 medium carrots, coarsely chopped
- 1 medium onion, chopped
- 1 medium parsnip, peeled and coarsely chopped
  Sliced green onions, optional

1. In a shallow bowl, mix flour and 1 tsp. each salt and pepper. Add the beef, a few pieces at a time, and toss to coat; shake off excess.
2. In a Dutch oven, heat 2 Tbsp. oil over medium heat. Brown the beef in batches, adding additional oil as necessary. Remove with a slotted spoon. Add wine, stirring to loosen browned bits from pot.
3. Return beef to pot. Add water, tomatoes, garlic, beef base, thyme, cinnamon, pepper flakes and remaining salt and pepper; bring to a boil. Reduce heat; simmer, covered, 1¼ hours, stirring halfway through cooking.
4. Stir in the sweet potato, carrots, onion and parsnip. Cook, covered, 30-45 minutes longer or until the beef and vegetables are tender. If desired, sprinkle with sliced green onions before serving.

1 cup: 344 cal., 15g fat (4g sat. fat), 71mg chol., 696mg sod., 27g carb. (9g sugars, 3g fiber), 25g pro.

ITALIAN BEEF & SHELLS

I fix this supper when I'm pressed for time. It's as tasty as it is fast. Team it with salad, bread and fresh fruit for a healthy meal that really satisfies.
—Mike Tchou, Pepper Pike, OH

- -

Takes: 30 min. • **Makes:** 4 servings

- 1½ cups uncooked medium pasta shells
- 1 lb. lean ground beef (90% lean)
- 1 small onion, chopped
- 1 garlic clove, minced
- 1 jar (24 oz.) marinara sauce
- 1 small yellow summer squash, quartered and sliced
- 1 small zucchini, quartered and sliced
- ¼ cup dry red wine or reduced-sodium beef broth
- ½ tsp. salt
- ½ tsp. Italian seasoning
- ½ tsp. pepper

1. Cook pasta shells according to the package directions.
2. Meanwhile, in a Dutch oven, cook the beef, onion and garlic over medium heat until meat is no longer pink; drain. Stir in marinara sauce, squash, zucchini, wine and seasonings. Bring to a boil. Reduce heat; simmer, uncovered, until thickened, 10-15 minutes. Drain pasta; stir into the beef mixture and heat through.

1¾ cups: 396 cal., 10g fat (4g sat. fat), 71mg chol., 644mg sod., 45g carb. (16g sugars, 5g fiber), 29g pro. **Diabetic exchanges:** 3 starch, 3 lean meat.

SWEET BBQ MEATBALLS

These sauced-up meatballs have a distinctive Asian flair. If your family likes sweet-and-sour chicken, this beefy version is sure to hit the spot.
—*Taste of Home* Test Kitchen

- -

Takes: 25 min. • **Makes:** 6 servings

- 2 tsp. olive oil
- ½ lb. sliced fresh mushrooms
- 1 medium green pepper, cut into 1-in. pieces
- 1 medium onion, cut into 1-in. pieces
- 1 pkg. (12 oz.) frozen fully cooked Italian meatballs, thawed
- 1 bottle (18 oz.) barbecue sauce
- 1 jar (10 oz.) apricot preserves
- 1 cup unsweetened pineapple chunks
- ½ cup water
- ¾ tsp. ground mustard
- ⅛ tsp. ground allspice
  Hot cooked rice

1. In a Dutch oven, heat olive oil over medium-high heat. Add mushrooms, pepper and onion; cook and stir until tender, 7-9 minutes.

2. Stir in the meatballs, barbecue sauce, preserves, pineapple, water, mustard and allspice. Reduce heat to medium; cook and stir 6-8 minutes or until the meatballs are heated through. Serve with rice.

Freeze option: Freeze cooled meatball mixture in freezer containers. To use, partially thaw in refrigerator overnight. Heat through in a covered saucepan, stirring and adding a little water if necessary. Serve as directed.

1 cup: 512 cal., 16g fat (6g sat. fat), 27mg chol., 1507mg sod., 85g carb. (61g sugars, 3g fiber), 13g pro.

SHORT RIB TACOS

Whenever we go to Houston to visit family, we like to track down *cabeza*—or cow's head—which is cooked slowly, resulting in very tender meat that's excellent in tacos. Cabeza is hard to find in Seattle, so I use short ribs to replicate the texture. I like corn tortillas for these tacos and a quick pico de gallo to add some freshness to the rich, flavorful meat.
—Anai Yost, Bothell, WA

- -

Prep: 40 min. • **Bake:** 2½ hours
Makes: 6 servings

2	**Tbsp. canola oil**
6	**bone-in beef short ribs**
¼	**tsp. salt**
¼	**tsp. pepper**
2	**medium carrots, finely chopped**
1	**small yellow onion, finely chopped**
2	**Tbsp. baking cocoa**
1	**can (15 oz.) tomato sauce**
1	**bottle (12 oz.) dark beer or beef broth**
	Water, optional
12	**corn tortillas (6 in.), warmed**
¾	**cup pico de gallo**
¾	**cup queso fresco or crumbled feta cheese**

1. Preheat oven to 325°. In an ovenproof Dutch oven, heat oil over medium-high heat. Sprinkle beef with salt and pepper; brown in batches. Remove with tongs.
2. Reduce heat to medium. Add carrots and onion to the drippings; cook, stirring frequently, until starting to brown, 3-5 minutes. Add cocoa; toast, stirring frequently, until aromatic, 1-2 minutes. Add tomato sauce and beer, stirring to loosen the browned bits from pot. Bring to a boil; simmer for 2-3 minutes.
3. Return short ribs to pot; add water, if necessary, to cover. Bake, covered, until the meat is tender, 2½-3 hours. Remove from oven; drain, reserving juices. When cool enough to handle, remove ribs from pot and remove meat from bones; discard bones. Shred meat with 2 forks. Skim fat from the reserved juices. Return the meat and juices to pot; heat through. Serve on tortillas with pico de gallo and queso fresco.
2 tacos: 508 cal., 26g fat (9g sat. fat), 97mg chol., 557mg sod., 32g carb. (4g sugars, 6g fiber), 37g pro.

DID YOU KNOW?

Tender and flavorful, short ribs are the beef equivalent of pork spare ribs. What's sold as "boneless short ribs," isn't actually from the ribs, but from the shoulder (or chuck). If you're looking for a substitute for boneless short ribs, go with a chuck roast.

CORNED BEEF & CABBAGE CASSEROLE

Comic strip characters Maggie and Jiggs inspired me to serve this meal. Whenever Maggie asked Jiggs what he would like her to cook, he answered, "Corned beef and cabbage." My husband liked this meal, too, and I always enjoyed making it for potluck suppers and other gatherings.
—Daisy Lewis, Jasper, AL

Takes: 30 min. • **Makes:** 6 servings

- 1 medium head cabbage, shredded (about 8 cups)
- 1 small onion, chopped
- 1 cup water
- 1 can (15½ oz.) white hominy, rinsed and drained
- ¾ lb. thinly sliced deli corned beef, chopped
- ¼ tsp. salt
- ¼ tsp. pepper
- ¼ tsp. hot pepper sauce

In a large Dutch oven, combine cabbage, onion and water; bring to a boil. Reduce heat; cover and simmer for 15 minutes or until the cabbage is tender. Add remaining ingredients; simmer for 5 minutes.

1 serving: 157 cal., 4g fat (2g sat. fat), 37mg chol., 1198mg sod., 17g carb. (5g sugars, 5g fiber), 14g pro.

OLD-FASHIONED CABBAGE ROLLS

An abundance of dill in my garden led me to try this. My family liked the taste so much that from then on, I made my cabbage rolls with dill.
—Florence Krantz, Bismarck, ND

Prep: 25 min. • **Bake:** 1½ hours
Makes: 6 servings

- 1 medium head cabbage (3 lbs.)
- ½ lb. uncooked ground beef
- ½ lb. uncooked ground pork
- 1 can (15 oz.) tomato sauce, divided

- 1 small onion, chopped
- ½ cup uncooked long grain rice
- 1 Tbsp. dried parsley flakes
- ½ tsp. salt
- ½ tsp. snipped fresh dill or dill weed
- ⅛ tsp. cayenne pepper
- 1 can (14½ oz.) diced tomatoes, undrained
- ½ tsp. sugar

1. Preheat oven to 350°. Cook whole cabbage in boiling water just until the outer leaves pull away easily from head. Set aside 12 large leaves for rolls. In a small bowl, combine beef, pork, ½ cup tomato sauce, onion, rice, parsley, salt, dill and cayenne; mix well.

2. Cut out the thick vein from the bottom of each leaf, making a V-shaped cut. Place about ¼ cup meat mixture on a cabbage leaf; overlap cut ends of leaf. Fold in sides. Beginning from cut end, roll up. Repeat.

3. Slice the remaining cabbage; place in an ovenproof Dutch oven. Arrange the cabbage rolls seam side down over the sliced cabbage. Combine the tomatoes, sugar and remaining tomato sauce; pour over the rolls. Cover and bake for 1½ hours or until the cabbage rolls are tender.

2 rolls: 260 cal., 10g fat (4g sat. fat), 50mg chol., 694mg sod., 23g carb. (5g sugars, 3g fiber), 18g pro.

COMPANY POT ROAST

The aroma of this roast slowly cooking in the oven is absolutely mouthwatering. It gives the home such a cozy feeling, even on the chilliest winter days.
—Anita Osborne, Thomasburg, ON

- -

Prep: 20 min. • **Bake:** 2¾ hours
Makes: 6 servings

1 **boneless beef chuck roast (3 to 4 lbs.)**
2 **Tbsp. olive oil**
1 **cup sherry or beef broth**
½ **cup reduced-sodium soy sauce**
¼ **cup sugar**
2 **tsp. beef bouillon granules**
1 **cinnamon stick (3 in.)**

8 **medium carrots, cut into 2-in. pieces**
6 **medium potatoes, peeled and cut into 1½-in. pieces**
1 **medium onion, sliced**
2 **Tbsp. cornstarch**
2 **Tbsp. cold water**

1. Preheat oven to 325°. Brown roast in oil in a Dutch oven on all sides; drain. Combine the sherry, soy sauce, sugar, bouillon and cinnamon stick; pour over the roast.

2. Cover and bake for 2¾-3¼ hours or until the meat and vegetables are tender, adding the carrots, potatoes and onion during the last 30 minutes of cooking.

3. Remove roast and vegetables to a serving platter; keep warm. Combine cornstarch and water until smooth. Stir into pan. Bring to a boil; cook and stir for 2 minutes or until thickened. Serve with roast and vegetables.

6 oz. cooked meat with 2 cups vegetables and ¼ cup gravy: 713 cal., 26g fat (9g sat. fat), 148mg chol., 1437mg sod., 56g carb. (17g sugars, 5g fiber), 49g pro.

DID YOU KNOW?

Reheated pot roast has a tendency to be dry—to prevent that, use moist heat when reheating. Slice the meat and place it in a baking dish. Pour leftover pan juices over top, adding extra beef broth if needed to cover. Cover and bake at 325° only until heated through. This helps retain moisture.

Chicken & Turkey

ONE-POT SALSA CHICKEN

This stovetop recipe is a colorful and healthy main dish that can be on the table in just over an hour. The subtle, sweet-spicy flavor is a nice surprise.
—Ann Sheehy, Lawrence, MA

Prep: 20 min. • **Cook:** 45 min.
Makes: 6 servings

- 2 Tbsp. canola oil
- 2 lbs. boneless skinless chicken thighs, cut into 1-in. pieces
- 1 tsp. pepper
- ½ tsp. salt
- 2 medium sweet potatoes, peeled and chopped
- 1 jar (16 oz.) medium salsa
- 2 medium nectarines, peeled and chopped
- 2 Tbsp. Tajin seasoning
- 1 cup uncooked instant brown rice
- 1 cup water
- ¼ cup minced fresh parsley
  Minced fresh chives

1. In a Dutch oven, heat oil over medium-high heat. Sprinkle chicken with pepper and salt. Brown chicken in batches; return to pan. Add the sweet potatoes, salsa, nectarines and seasoning. Bring to a boil; reduce heat. Cover and simmer until the potatoes are almost tender, about 15 minutes.

2. Stir in rice and water; bring to a boil. Reduce heat. Cover and simmer until the potatoes are tender, about 10 minutes. Stir in parsley. Serve in bowls; sprinkle with chives.

1⅔ cups: 432 cal., 16g fat (3g sat. fat), 101mg chol., 1254mg sod., 39g carb. (13g sugars, 4g fiber), 31g pro.

> **TEST KITCHEN TIP**
>
> Tajin seasoning is a blend of lime, chili peppers and sea salt. Look for it in the spice aisle.

BUFFALO SLOPPY JOES

Lean ground turkey makes this a lighter sloppy joe than the standard ground beef version. A big splash of hot sauce and optional blue cheese provide that distinctive Buffalo-style flavor.
—Maria Regakis, Saugus, MA

Takes: 30 min. • **Makes:** 8 servings

- 2 lbs. extra-lean ground turkey
- 2 celery ribs, chopped
- 1 medium onion, chopped
- 1 medium carrot, grated
- 3 garlic cloves, minced
- 1 can (8 oz.) tomato sauce
- ½ cup chicken broth
- ¼ cup Louisiana-style hot sauce
- 2 Tbsp. brown sugar
- 2 Tbsp. red wine vinegar
- 1 Tbsp. Worcestershire sauce
- ¼ tsp. pepper
- 8 hamburger buns, split
  Crumbled blue cheese, optional

Cook the first 5 ingredients in a Dutch oven over medium heat until turkey is no longer pink. Stir in the tomato sauce, chicken broth, hot sauce, brown sugar, vinegar, Worcestershire sauce and pepper; heat through. Serve on buns. If desired, sprinkle with cheese.

1 sandwich: 279 cal., 3g fat (0 sat. fat), 45mg chol., 475mg sod., 30g carb. (9g sugars, 2g fiber), 33g pro. **Diabetic exchanges:** 4 lean meat, 2 starch.

HEARTY SAUSAGE & RICE

At the end of the day, who wants a stack of dishes to wash? That's why we love this entree: One pot. Minimal mess.
—*Taste of Home* Test Kitchen

Takes: 30 min. • **Makes:** 5 servings

1	**lb. Italian turkey sausage links, cut into ½-in. slices**
½	**lb. sliced fresh mushrooms**
1	**medium sweet yellow pepper, chopped**
1	**medium onion, chopped**
2	**tsp. olive oil**
1	**can (14½ oz.) diced tomatoes with mild green chiles, undrained**
2	**cups fresh baby spinach, coarsely chopped**
1½	**cups water**
1	**can (8 oz.) tomato sauce**
1	**tsp. dried oregano**
1	**tsp. chili powder**
½	**tsp. garlic salt**
2	**cups uncooked instant rice**

1. Cook sausage in a Dutch oven over medium heat until no longer pink; drain. Remove and keep warm. Saute the mushrooms, pepper and onion in oil in the same pot until tender.

2. Return sausage to the pot. Stir in the tomatoes, spinach, water, tomato sauce and seasonings.

3. Bring to a boil; cook for 2 minutes. Stir in rice. Remove from the heat; cover and let stand for 5-7 minutes or until rice is tender. Fluff with a fork.

1½ cups: 318 cal., 8g fat (2g sat. fat), 33mg chol., 1007mg sod., 45g carb. (6g sugars, 5g fiber), 16g pro.

CASSOULET FOR TODAY

Traditionally cooked for hours, this version of the rustic French cassoulet offers the same homey taste in less time. It's easy on the wallet, too.
—Virginia Anthony, Jacksonville, FL

- -

Prep: 45 min. • **Bake:** 50 min.
Makes: 6 servings

6	boneless skinless chicken thighs (about 1½ lbs.)
¼	tsp. salt
¼	tsp. coarsely ground pepper
3	tsp. olive oil, divided
1	large onion, chopped
1	garlic clove, minced
½	cup white wine or chicken broth
1	can (14½ oz.) diced tomatoes, drained
1	bay leaf
1	tsp. minced fresh rosemary or ¼ tsp. dried rosemary, crushed
1	tsp. minced fresh thyme or ¼ tsp. dried thyme
2	cans (15 oz. each) cannellini beans, rinsed and drained
¼	lb. smoked turkey kielbasa, chopped
3	bacon strips, cooked and crumbled

TOPPING

½	cup soft whole wheat bread crumbs
¼	cup minced fresh parsley
1	garlic clove, minced

1. Preheat oven to 325°. Sprinkle chicken with salt and pepper. In a broiler-safe Dutch oven, heat 2 tsp. oil over medium heat; brown chicken on both sides. Remove from pot.

2. In same pot, saute onion in the remaining oil over medium heat until crisp-tender. Add garlic; cook 1 minute. Add wine; bring to a boil, stirring to loosen browned bits from pot. Add tomatoes, herbs and chicken; return to a boil.

3. Transfer to oven; bake, covered, for 30 minutes. Stir in beans and kielbasa; bake, covered, until the chicken is tender, 20-25 minutes.

4. Remove from oven; preheat broiler. Discard bay leaf; stir in bacon. Toss bread crumbs with parsley and garlic; sprinkle over top. Place in oven so surface of cassoulet is 4-5 in. from heat; broil until crumbs are golden brown, 2-3 minutes.

Note: To make soft bread crumbs, tear the bread into pieces and place in a food processor or blender. Cover and pulse until crumbs form. One slice of bread yields ½ to ¾ cup crumbs.

1 serving: 394 cal., 14g fat (4g sat. fat), 91mg chol., 736mg sod., 29g carb. (4g sugars, 8g fiber), 33g pro. **Diabetic exchanges:** 4 lean meat, 2 starch, ½ fat.

TEST KITCHEN TIP

Adding pulses such as cannellini beans to a meat-based main dish bumps up the fiber and protein without adding saturated fat.

CHICKEN & BARLEY BOILED DINNER

I began putting this meal-in-one on my table because it's a nutritious way to satisfy the big appetites in my family. For a hearty home-style dinner, it's surprisingly easy to prepare. That's especially nice when I don't have a lot of time to spend in the kitchen.
—Susan Greeley, Morril, ME

Prep: 30 min. • **Cook:** 1¼ hours
Makes: 8 servings

- 2 broiler/fryer chickens (about 3 lbs. each), cut up and skin removed
- 3 Tbsp. canola oil
- 2 qt. chicken broth
- 1 cup uncooked brown rice
- ½ cup medium pearl barley
- 1 medium onion, chopped
- 2 bay leaves
- 1 tsp. salt
- ½ tsp. dried basil
- ¼ tsp. pepper
- 8 carrots, cut into 1-in. pieces
- 2½ cups frozen cut green beans
- 2 celery ribs, cut into 1-in. pieces

1. In a Dutch oven, brown chicken in oil. Remove chicken and set aside. Drain. In the same pot, combine the broth, rice, barley, onion, bay leaves, basil, salt and pepper; bring to a boil. Reduce heat.
2. Return chicken to the pot; cover and simmer for 45 minutes or until chicken juices run clear.
3. Stir in the carrots, beans and celery. Cook over medium heat for 30 minutes or until the grains are tender. Discard the bay leaves.
1 serving: 467 cal., 16g fat (3g sat. fat), 115mg chol., 1424mg sod., 38g carb. (6g sugars, 4g fiber), 42g pro.

CAZUELA

I learned to make *cazuela* while we were living in Chile for a few months. We grow extra butternut squash in our garden just for this recipe.
—Louise Schmid, Marshall, MN

Prep: 20 min. • **Cook:** 30 min.
Makes: 6 servings

- 6 chicken drumsticks or thighs
- 3 cups cubed peeled butternut squash (1-in. cubes)
- 6 small potatoes, peeled
- 6 pieces of fresh or frozen corn on the cob (2 in. each)
- 3 carrots, cut into 1-in. chunks
- 3 cans (14½ oz. each) chicken broth
  Hot cooked rice
  Hot pepper sauce to taste
  Salt and pepper to taste
  Minced fresh cilantro or parsley

Place the chicken, squash, potatoes, corn, carrots and broth in a Dutch oven or large soup kettle; bring to a boil. Reduce heat; cover and simmer for 25 minutes or until the chicken is done and the vegetables are tender. Serve over rice in a shallow soup bowl. Serve with hot pepper sauce, salt, pepper and cilantro or parsley.
1 serving: 416 cal., 8g fat (2g sat. fat), 52mg chol., 968mg sod., 67g carb. (12g sugars, 8g fiber), 23g pro.

1 habanero pepper, seeded and
  finely chopped
3 garlic cloves, minced
1 can (14½ oz.) fire-roasted
  diced tomatoes, drained
2 cups heavy whipping cream
½ cup shredded Italian cheese blend
⅓ cup chopped fresh basil

1. Cook pasta according to package directions; drain.
2. Meanwhile, heat 1 Tbsp. oil in a Dutch oven over medium-high heat. Add the chicken, 1 tsp. Italian seasoning, salt and pepper; saute until the meat is no longer pink, about 5 minutes. Remove from pot.
3. In the same pot, add onion, habanero pepper, garlic and the remaining Italian seasoning and oil; reduce heat to medium. Cook and stir until the onion is tender, about 5 minutes. Add tomatoes; cook and stir until slightly thickened, about 2 minutes. Stir in cream; bring to a boil. Add tortellini, chicken and cheese; heat through. Top with basil to serve.
1¼ cups: 488 cal., 31g fat (17g sat. fat), 126mg chol., 575mg sod., 30g carb. (5g sugars, 2g fiber), 22g pro.

TEST KITCHEN TIP

If you don't have fire-roasted diced tomatoes, use plain or try diced tomatoes flavored with basil, oregano and garlic.

CREAMY TOMATO BASIL TORTELLINI

A friend raved about a baked tortellini dish at a restaurant, so I wanted to try re-creating it for her at home. My stovetop version makes it weeknight-easy.
—Cyndy Gerken, Naples, FL

- -

Takes: 30 min. • **Makes:** 8 servings

1 pkg. (19 oz.) frozen
  cheese tortellini
2 Tbsp. olive oil, divided
1 lb. boneless skinless chicken
  breasts, cut into 1-in. cubes
2 tsp. Italian seasoning, divided
½ tsp. salt
¼ tsp. pepper
1 large onion, chopped

PEAR & TURKEY SAUSAGE RIGATONI

The sweet pear, salty sausage and creamy blue cheese make a wonderful combination in this one-pot supper. Now we don't have to go to an expensive restaurant to get an elegant meal.

—Debby Harden, Lansing, MI

Takes: 30 min. • **Makes:** 6 servings

- 8 oz. uncooked rigatoni or large tube pasta
- 2 Italian turkey sausage links (4 oz. each), casings removed
- 2 medium pears, sliced
- 2 cups fresh baby spinach
- ½ cup half-and-half cream
- ½ cup crumbled blue cheese, divided
  Toasted sliced almonds, optional

1. Cook rigatoni according to the package directions.

2. Meanwhile, in a Dutch oven, cook the sausage over medium heat until no longer pink, breaking into large crumbles, 6-8 minutes. Add pears; cook and stir until lightly browned, 3-5 minutes.

3. Drain pasta; add to the sausage mixture. Add spinach, cream and ¼ cup cheese; cook until the spinach is wilted, 3-4 minutes, stirring occasionally. Top with the remaining cheese. If desired, sprinkle with almonds.

Note: To toast nuts, bake in a shallow pan in a 350° oven for 5-10 minutes or cook in a skillet over low heat until lightly browned, stirring occasionally.

1⅓ cups: 273 cal., 9g fat (4g sat. fat), 32mg chol., 333mg sod., 37g carb. (7g sugars, 3g fiber), 13g pro. **Diabetic exchanges:** 2½ starch, 2 medium-fat meat.

TURKEY SHRIMP GUMBO

This slimmed-down version of gumbo tastes just as hearty as the classic version.
—Michael Williams, Westfield, New York

- -

Takes: 10 min. • **Cook:** 2 hours 5 min.

1   teaspoon salt
1   teaspoon pepper
1   teaspoon cayenne pepper
½   cup vegetable oil, divided
2   pounds uncooked skinless
      turkey breast, cubed
½   cup all-purpose flour
1   large onion, chopped
1   cup chopped celery
1   cup chopped sweet red pepper
4   garlic cloves, minced
4   cups chicken broth
2   cups sliced okra
4   green onions, sliced
10   ounces uncooked medium
      shrimp, peeled and deveined
5   cups hot cooked rice

1. In a small bowl, combine salt, pepper and cayenne pepper; sprinkle over turkey. Heat 2 Tbsp. oil In a Dutch oven and brown turkey, then remove with a slotted spoon. Add remaining oil and the flour, scraping the bottom of the pot to loosen any browned bits. Cook over medium-low heat for 25-30 minutes until dark brown in color, stirring frequently.

2. Add onion, celery, red pepper and garlic. Cook over medium heat until the vegetables are crisp-tender, 4-5 minutes. Gradually stir in the broth. Bring to a boil. Reduce heat; cover and simmer for 30 minutes. Return the turkey to pot; cover and simmer for 30-45 minutes or until turkey is tender. Add okra and green onions; simmer 10 minutes. Add shrimp; simmer until shrimp turn pink, 4-5 minutes. Serve over rice.

1 cup with ½ cup rice: 381 calories, 13g fat (2g saturated fat), 88mg cholesterol, 777mg sodium, 33g carbohydrate (3g sugars, 2g fiber), 30g protein.

TEST KITCHEN TIP

A roux is a mixture of fat (either oil or butter) and flour that thickens and adds flavor. In a traditional gumbo, the roux is ready when it's a rich brown color, which can take up to 30 minutes. Be sure to stir the roux while it's browning, preferably with a whisk; as it begins to darken, stir constantly.

CORN & CHICKEN DINNER

I grow most of the ingredients appearing in this dinner in my garden. There's something for every taste in this recipe. It would be great as a meal-in-one dish for a picnic or a family reunion.
—Doralee Pinkerton, Milford, IN

- -

Prep: 10 min. • **Cook:** 35 min.
Makes: 8 servings

- 3 lbs. chicken legs and thighs (about 8 pieces)
- ½ cup butter, divided
- 3 garlic cloves, minced, divided
- 3 ears fresh corn, husked, cleaned and cut into thirds
- ¼ cup water
- 2 tsp. dried tarragon, divided
- ½ tsp. salt
- ¼ tsp. pepper
- 2 medium zucchini, sliced into ½-in. pieces
- 2 tomatoes, seeded and cut into chunks

1. In a Dutch oven, cook chicken in 2 Tbsp. butter over medium heat until browned on each side. Add two-thirds of the garlic; cook 1 minute longer. Reduce heat; stir in corn and water. Sprinkle with 1 tsp. tarragon, salt and pepper. Cover; simmer 20-25 minutes or until a thermometer inserted in chicken reads 170°-175°.
2. Meanwhile, in a small saucepan, cook both the remaining garlic and tarragon in remaining butter for 1 minute; set aside.
3. Layer zucchini and tomatoes over the chicken mixture. Drizzle seasoned butter over all; cover and cook for 3-5 minutes or until heated through.
1 serving: 297 cal., 19g fat (9g sat. fat), 100mg chol., 331mg sod., 10g carb. (4g sugars, 2g fiber), 21g pro.

GRANDMA'S CAJUN CHICKEN & SPAGHETTI

I'm originally from Louisiana, where my grandma spoke Cajun French as she taught me how to make her spicy chicken spaghetti on an old wood stove.
—Brenda Melancon, McComb, MS

- -

Prep: 15 min. • **Cook:** 1¼ hours
Makes: 10 servings

- 1 broiler/fryer chicken (3 to 4 lbs.), cut up
- 1 to 1½ tsp. cayenne pepper
- ¾ tsp. salt
- 3 Tbsp. canola oil
- 1 pkg. (14 oz.) smoked sausage, sliced
- 1 large sweet onion, chopped
- 1 medium green pepper, chopped
- 1 celery rib, chopped
- 2 garlic cloves, minced
- 2 cans (14½ oz. each) diced tomatoes, undrained
- 1 can (14½ oz.) diced tomatoes with mild green chiles, undrained
- 1 pkg. (16 oz.) spaghetti

1. Sprinkle chicken with cayenne and salt. In a Dutch oven, heat oil over medium-high heat. Brown chicken in batches. Remove from pot.
2. Add sausage, onion, green pepper and celery to same pot; cook and stir over medium heat 3 minutes. Add garlic; cook 1 minute longer. Stir in tomatoes. Return chicken to pot; bring to a boil. Reduce heat; simmer, covered, until the chicken juices run clear, about 1 hour.
3. Cook spaghetti according to package directions. Remove chicken from pot. When cool enough to handle, remove meat from bones; discard skin and bones. Shred meat with 2 forks; return to pot. Bring to boil. Reduce heat; simmer, uncovered, until slightly thickened, 8-10 minutes. Skim fat. Drain spaghetti; serve with chicken mixture.
¾ cup chicken mixture with ¾ cup spaghetti: 550 cal., 26g fat (8g sat. fat), 89mg chol., 917mg sod., 45g carb. (8g sugars, 4g fiber), 33g pro.

CHICKEN PAPRIKASH

Some chicken paprikash recipes include vegetables like bell peppers and celery, but not my Grandmother Alta's. Hers was a simple combination of chicken, onions, garlic, paprika and sour cream.

—Lily Julow, Lawrenceville, GA

- -

Prep: 20 min. • **Cook:** 45 min.
Makes: 12 servings

2 broiler/fryer chickens (about 3½ to 4 lbs. each), cut into 8 pieces each
2 tsp. kosher salt
1 tsp. pepper
2 Tbsp. peanut oil or canola oil
2 medium onions, halved and sliced
2 large garlic cloves, chopped
3 Tbsp. all-purpose flour
1 Tbsp. sweet Hungarian paprika
2 cups hot chicken broth or water
1 cup sour cream
 Optional: Minced fresh parsley and additional sweet Hungarian paprika
 Hot cooked noodles or mashed potatoes, optional

1. Season chicken with kosher salt and pepper. In a Dutch oven, heat peanut oil over medium-high heat. Brown chicken in batches. Remove with a slotted spoon; drain and keep warm.
2. Reduce heat to medium-low. Add onions; cook, stirring to loosen browned bits from pot, until the onions begin to soften, 6-8 minutes. Add garlic; cook 1 minute longer.
3. Stir in flour and paprika; reduce heat to low. Cook until the paprika is fragrant, 3-5 minutes. Add broth; cook, stirring constantly, until smooth, 6-8 minutes. Return chicken to pot; simmer, covered, until a thermometer inserted into deepest part of thigh reads 170°, about 30 minutes. Transfer chicken to a serving platter.
4. Skim fat. Stir in sour cream; heat just until warmed through, 3-5 minutes (do not allow to boil). If desired, sprinkle with parsley and additional paprika. Serve with hot cooked noodles or mashed potatoes if desired.
1 serving: 422 cal., 26g fat (8g sat. fat), 127mg chol., 596mg sod., 5g carb. (2g sugars, 1g fiber), 40g pro.

Paprikash is traditionally made with sour cream, but you can use whole-milk yogurt or strained Greek yogurt instead.

APPLE CIDER CHICKEN & DUMPLINGS

I came up with this recipe one fall when I had an abundance of apple cider. Adding some to a down-home classic was a delectable decision.
—Margaret Sumner-Wichmann, Questa, NM

- -

Prep: 10 min. • **Bake:** 65 min.
Makes: 4 servings

- 8   **bone-in chicken thighs (3 lbs.), skin removed**
- 2   **Tbsp. butter**
- 1   **medium red onion, chopped**
- 1   **celery rib, chopped**
- 2   **Tbsp. minced fresh parsley**
    Salt and pepper to taste
- 3   **Tbsp. all-purpose flour**
- 3   **cups chicken broth**
- 1   **cup apple cider or juice**

DUMPLINGS
- 2   **cups all-purpose flour**
- 1   **Tbsp. baking powder**
- ½   **tsp. salt**
- 1   **Tbsp. cold butter**
- 1   **large egg, lightly beaten**
- ⅔   **cup whole milk**
    Additional minced fresh parsley, optional

1. In a Dutch oven, brown the chicken in butter; remove and set aside. In the same pot, combine onion, celery, parsley, salt and pepper; cook and stir until vegetables are tender. Sprinkle with flour and mix well. Add broth and cider. Bring to a boil; cook and stir until thickened, 2 minutes. Add chicken.
2. Cover; bake at 350° for 45-50 minutes. Increase heat to 425°.
3. For dumplings, combine the flour, baking powder and salt in a bowl; cut in butter until crumbly. Combine egg and milk; stir into dry ingredients just until moistened. Drop batter into 12 mounds onto hot broth.
4. Bake, uncovered, 10 minutes. Cover and bake until a toothpick inserted into a dumpling comes out clean, 10 minutes longer. Sprinkle with more minced parsley, if desired.

1 serving: 721 cal., 27g fat (11g sat. fat), 220mg chol., 1548mg sod., 65g carb. (12g sugars, 3g fiber), 50g pro.

Steam does the work when you cook dumplings on top of soup or stew, and dumplings must be surrounded by heat to cook evenly. Make sure the soup is boiling before adding the dumplings, and cover for either all or part of the cooking time.

ITALIAN RESTAURANT CHICKEN

While the chicken and sauce cook, I make pasta to serve with it. This tastes like a chef's special in a cozy Italian restaurant. Your family will be impressed!
—Patricia Nieh, Portola Valley, CA

- -

Prep: 25 min. • **Bake:** 50 min.
Makes: 6 servings

- 1   broiler/fryer chicken (3 lbs.), cut up and skin removed
- ½   tsp. salt
- ¼   tsp. pepper
- 2   Tbsp. olive oil
- 1   small onion, finely chopped
- ¼   cup finely chopped celery
- ¼   cup finely chopped carrot
- 3   garlic cloves, minced
- ½   cup dry red wine or reduced-sodium chicken broth
- 1   can (28 oz.) crushed tomatoes
- 1   bay leaf
- 1   tsp. minced fresh rosemary or ¼ tsp. dried rosemary, crushed
- ¼   cup minced fresh basil

1. Preheat oven to 325°. Sprinkle chicken pieces with salt and pepper. In an ovenproof Dutch oven, brown chicken in oil in batches. Remove and keep warm.

2. In the same pot, saute onion, celery, carrot and garlic in drippings until tender. Add red wine, stirring to loosen browned bits from pot. Stir in tomatoes, bay leaf, rosemary and chicken; bring to a boil.

3. Cover and bake for 50-60 minutes or until the juices run clear. Discard bay leaf; sprinkle with basil.

3 oz. cooked chicken with ⅔ cup sauce: 254 cal., 11g fat (2g sat. fat), 73mg chol., 442mg sod., 12g carb. (1g sugars, 3g fiber), 27g pro. **Diabetic exchanges:** 3 lean meat, 2 vegetable, 1 fat.

HEARTY JAMBALAYA

It's a pleasure to serve this meaty, satisfying jambalaya. It freezes nicely, so I can serve half and put the rest away for another day when time is tight.
—Mel Miller, Perkins, OK

- -

Prep: 25 min. • **Cook:** 10 min.
Makes: 8 servings

- 1 lb. smoked kielbasa or Polish sausage, cut into ½-in. slices
- 1 lb. boneless skinless chicken breasts, cubed
- 1 large onion, chopped
- ½ cup chopped celery
- ½ cup chopped green pepper
- 4 garlic cloves, minced
- 2 Tbsp. butter
- 1 can (14½ oz.) diced tomatoes, undrained
- 1 can (6 oz.) tomato paste
- ½ tsp. hot pepper sauce
- ¼ to ½ tsp. cayenne pepper
- ⅛ tsp. garlic powder
- ⅛ tsp. white pepper
- ⅛ tsp. pepper
- ½ lb. uncooked medium shrimp, peeled and deveined
  Hot cooked rice, optional

In a Dutch oven, saute sausage, chicken, onion, celery, green pepper and garlic in butter until chicken is browned. Stir in the tomatoes, tomato paste and seasonings. Bring to a boil. Reduce heat; cover and simmer 6-8 minutes or until chicken is no longer pink. Stir in shrimp; cover and simmer for 4 minutes or until the shrimp turn pink. Serve over rice if desired.

Freeze option: Freeze cooled jambalaya in freezer container. To use, partially thaw in refrigerator overnight. Heat in a saucepan, stirring occasionally; add water if necessary.
1 cup: 220 cal., 6g fat (3g sat. fat), 101mg chol., 675mg sod., 16g carb. (8g sugars, 3g fiber), 24g pro. **Diabetic exchanges:** 3 lean meat, 1 starch.

PORTOBELLO TURKEY BOLOGNESE

This sauce tastes better the longer it simmers, which allows the flavors to fully develop. In fact, it tastes best the second day after a night in the refrigerator.
—Darrell Kau, Eugene, OR

- -

Prep: 15 min. • **Cook:** 1¼ hours
Makes: 8 servings

- 1 Tbsp. olive oil
- 1½ lbs. lean ground turkey
- ½ lb. sliced baby portobello mushrooms
- 2 large onions, chopped
- 1 cup chopped carrots
- 6 garlic cloves, minced
- 1 can (14½ oz.) reduced-sodium beef broth
- 1 cup dry red wine or additional reduced-sodium beef broth
- 1 cup water
- 1 can (6 oz.) tomato paste
- ½ cup minced fresh basil
- 1 Tbsp. minced fresh oregano
- 2 tsp. minced fresh rosemary
- 2 tsp. fennel seed
- ¾ tsp. salt
- ½ tsp. crushed red pepper flakes
- ½ tsp. pepper
- 1 tsp. sugar
- 12 oz. uncooked penne
- ½ cup shredded Parmesan cheese

1. In a Dutch oven coated with cooking spray, heat oil over medium heat. Add turkey, mushrooms, onions, carrots and garlic; cook 10-12 minutes or until the turkey is no longer pink and the vegetables are tender.
2. Stir in broth, wine, water, tomato paste, herbs, seasonings and sugar; bring to a boil. Reduce heat; simmer, uncovered, 1 hour or until thickened, stirring occasionally.
3. Cook penne pasta according to package directions; drain. Serve with sauce. Sprinkle with cheese.
1 serving: 380 cal., 11g fat (3g sat. fat), 72mg chol., 508mg sod., 44g carb. (9g sugars, 5g fiber), 25g pro. **Diabetic exchanges:** 2 starch, 2 lean meat, 2 vegetable, 1 fat.

SUNDAY PAELLA

My adult children adore this recipe and look forward to eating it when they come to our house for lunch on Sundays. I do the prep work before leaving for church and cook it when I get home.
—Linda Rhoads, Lebanon, MO

Prep: 25 min. • **Cook:** 40 min.
Makes: 8 servings

- 1½ lbs. boneless skinless chicken breasts, cubed
- 3 Tbsp. canola oil
- 1 lb. smoked sausage, cut into ¼-in. slices
- 1 small onion, chopped
- 1½ cups uncooked long grain rice
- 2 tsp. Italian seasoning
- ¼ tsp. ground turmeric
- ¼ tsp. pepper
- 3 cups chicken broth
- 1½ lbs. uncooked medium shrimp, peeled and deveined
- 1 can (28 oz.) diced tomatoes, undrained
- 1½ cups frozen peas, thawed
- 1 Tbsp. sugar

1. In a Dutch oven, cook and stir chicken in oil over medium heat until no longer pink. Add sausage and onion; cook 3-4 minutes longer. Add the rice, Italian seasoning, turmeric and pepper; cook and stir for 3-4 minutes or until rice is lightly browned.
2. Add broth. Bring to a boil. Reduce heat; cover and simmer for 14-18 minutes or until the rice is almost tender. Stir in the shrimp, tomatoes, peas and sugar; cover and cook for 10-15 minutes or until the shrimp turn pink, stirring occasionally.
1½ cups: 570 cal., 24g fat (8g sat. fat), 190mg chol., 1309mg sod., 41g carb. (8g sugars, 4g fiber), 44g pro.

PAPRIKA CHICKEN STROGANOFF

Stroganoff is such a comfort food. While traditionally a beef dish, it can easily be adapted for other proteins, and it is just as delicious. With this creamy chicken stroganoff, I get to enjoy all the lovely sauciness with the benefits of the lighter white meat.

—Leo Lo, Norfolk, VA

- -

Prep: 20 min. • **Cook:** 30 min.
Makes: 6 servings

8	oz. uncooked wide egg noodles
1½	lbs. boneless skinless chicken breasts, cut into ½-in.-thick strips
2	tsp. paprika
1½	tsp. salt, divided
¾	tsp. pepper, divided
1	Tbsp. olive oil
1	lb. sliced baby portobello mushrooms
1	Tbsp. butter
1	large red onion, halved and sliced
3	garlic cloves, minced
1	cup dry white wine or chicken stock
1	cup chicken stock
1	Tbsp. Worcestershire sauce
1	Tbsp. Dijon mustard
1	cup creme fraiche or sour cream
1	Tbsp. minced fresh Italian parsley

1. Cook noodles according to package directions; drain.
2. Meanwhile, toss chicken with paprika, ½ tsp. salt and ¼ tsp. pepper. In a Dutch oven, heat oil over medium-high heat. In batches, saute the chicken strips until browned, 2-3 minutes. Remove from pot.
3. In the same pot, saute mushrooms in butter until lightly browned, 4-5 minutes. Add onion; cook and stir until softened, 3-4 minutes. Add garlic; cook and stir for 1 minute.
4. Add wine, stirring to loosen browned bits from pot. Add stock, Worcestershire sauce and mustard; bring to a boil. Cook, uncovered, until the liquid is reduced by half, 10-12 minutes. Stir in chicken; cook, uncovered, over medium-low until the chicken is no longer pink, 3-5 minutes.
5. Stir in creme fraiche, parsley and the remaining salt and pepper; remove from heat. Stir in noodles.

1⅔ cups: 505 cal., 24g fat (12g sat. fat), 133mg chol., 874mg sod., 35g carb. (4g sugars, 3g fiber), 33g pro.

TEST KITCHEN TIP

Creme fraiche is similar to sour cream but slightly thinner. It is not as sour as sour cream and is richer.

CREAMY BRAISED CHICKEN

A smooth, delicate cream sauce gives a special taste to tender chicken breasts accompanied by pearl onions and sauteed mushrooms. This dish is so rich-tasting, you'll want to serve it to company.
—Margaret Haugh Heilman, Houston, TX

Prep: 20 min. • **Cook:** 30 min.
Makes: 6 servings

- ½ lb. pearl onions
- 1 cup thinly sliced onion
- ½ cup thinly sliced carrot
- ½ cup thinly sliced celery
- 1 Tbsp. plus 2 tsp. butter, divided
- 6 boneless skinless chicken breast halves (4 oz. each)
- 1 cup chardonnay or other dry white wine or reduced-sodium chicken broth
- 1⅓ cups reduced-sodium chicken broth
- 1 Tbsp. minced fresh parsley
- 1 tsp. salt
- 1 tsp. dried thyme
- ⅛ tsp. white pepper
- 1 bay leaf
- 3 Tbsp. all-purpose flour
- ½ cup fat-free evaporated milk
- ½ lb. fresh mushrooms, quartered
  Additional minced fresh parsley, optional

1. In a Dutch oven, bring 6 cups water to a boil. Add pearl onions; boil for 3 minutes. Drain and rinse in cold water; peel and set aside. In the same pot, saute sliced onion, carrot and celery in 1 Tbsp. butter until tender. Remove vegetables; set aside.

2. Add chicken to pot; brown on both sides. Remove and keep warm. Add wine; simmer until reduced to ½ cup. Stir in broth and seasonings. Return chicken to pot; cover and simmer for 5 minutes or until the juices run clear. Remove chicken to a serving platter; keep warm.

3. Combine flour and milk until smooth; gradually stir into pot. Bring to a boil; cook and stir for 2 minutes or until thickened. Return vegetables to pot. Remove from the heat; cover and set aside.

4. In a nonstick skillet, saute pearl onions in the remaining butter until tender. Remove and set aside. In the same pan, saute mushrooms until tender. Add the onions and mushrooms to the serving platter.

Discard bay leaf from the sauce; spoon sauce over the chicken and vegetables. Sprinkle with additional minced parsley, if desired.

1 serving: 254 cal., 6g fat (3g sat. fat), 72mg chol., 647mg sod., 14g carb. (6g sugars, 1g fiber), 27g pro. **Diabetic exchanges:** 3 lean meat, 2 vegetable, ½ fat.

CHICKEN RIGGIES

Rigatoni cooked with cream and cream cheese spells comfort when combined with chicken marinated in sherry and garlic.
—Jackie Scanlan, Dayton, OH

- -

Prep: 30 min. + marinating • **Cook:** 15 min.
Makes: 12 servings

- ½ cup dry sherry
- 2 Tbsp. olive oil
- 3 garlic cloves, minced
- 1 tsp. dried oregano
- 2 lbs. boneless skinless chicken breasts, cubed

SAUCE

- 2 Tbsp. butter
- 1 each medium sweet red and green pepper, chopped
- 4 pickled hot cherry peppers, chopped
- 1 medium onion, chopped
- 2 garlic cloves, minced
- 1 cup dry sherry
- 2 cans (one 29 oz., one 15 oz.) tomato puree
- ¼ tsp. salt
- ⅛ tsp. pepper
- 2 pkg. (16 oz. each) uncooked rigatoni
- 1½ cups heavy whipping cream
- 6 oz. cream cheese, cut up
- 1½ cups grated Romano cheese

1. In a large bowl or dish, combine sherry, oil, garlic and oregano. Add chicken and turn to coat. Refrigerate 1 hour.

2. Drain chicken, discarding the marinade. Heat a Dutch oven over medium-high heat. Add chicken in batches; cook and stir until no longer pink. Remove from pot.

3. In the same pot, heat butter over medium-high heat. Add peppers, onion and garlic; cook and stir until tender. Add sherry; bring to a boil. Stir in tomato puree, salt and pepper; return to a boil. Reduce heat; simmer 8-10 minutes or until slightly thickened, stirring occasionally. Add the chicken; heat through.

4. Meanwhile, cook rigatoni according to package directions; drain.

5. In a small saucepan, combine cream and cream cheese over medium heat; cook and stir until blended. Add to chicken mixture; stir in Romano cheese.

6. Combine cooked pasta and sauce; toss to coat pasta with the sauce.

1¾ cups: 658 cal., 28g fat (15g sat. fat), 118mg chol., 514mg sod., 66g carb. (6g sugars, 4g fiber), 35g pro.

NEW ENGLAND BEAN & BOG CASSOULET

When I moved to New England, I embraced the local cuisine. My cassoulet with baked beans pays tribute to a French classic by giving it a distinctive New England spin.
—Devon Delaney, Westport, CT

- -

Prep: 15 min. • **Cook:** 35 min.
Makes: 8 servings (3½ qt.)

- 5 Tbsp. olive oil, divided
- 8 boneless skinless chicken thighs (about 2 lbs.)
- 1 pkg. (12 oz.) fully cooked Italian chicken sausage links, cut into ½-in. slices
- 4 shallots, finely chopped
- 2 tsp. minced fresh rosemary or ½ tsp. dried rosemary, crushed
- 2 tsp. minced fresh thyme or ½ tsp. dried thyme
- 1 can (28 oz.) fire-roasted diced tomatoes, undrained
- 1 can (16 oz.) baked beans
- 1 cup chicken broth
- ½ cup fresh or frozen cranberries
- 3 day-old croissants, cubed (about 6 cups)
- ½ tsp. lemon-pepper seasoning
- 2 Tbsp. minced fresh parsley

1. Preheat oven to 400°. In a Dutch oven, heat 2 Tbsp. oil over medium heat. In batches, brown chicken thighs on both sides; remove from pot, reserving the drippings. Add sausage; cook and stir until lightly browned. Remove from pot.

2. In the same pot, heat 1 Tbsp. oil over medium heat. Add the shallots, rosemary and thyme; cook and stir until the shallots are tender, 1-2 minutes. Stir in tomatoes, beans, broth and cranberries. Return chicken and sausage to pot; bring to a boil. Bake, covered, until the chicken is tender, 20-25 minutes.

3. Toss croissant pieces with the remaining oil; sprinkle with lemon pepper. Arrange over the chicken mixture. Bake, uncovered, until the croissants are golden brown, 12-15 minutes. Sprinkle with parsley.

1¾ cups: 500 cal., 26g fat (7g sat. fat), 127mg chol., 1050mg sod., 32g carb. (6g sugars, 5g fiber), 35g pro.

A "bog" is a low country stew, a hearty mixture of chicken and rice. In this version, beans take the place of rice, making it a southern classic by way of France and New England.

DELISH PESTO PASTA WITH CHICKEN MARSALA

This is my easy, go-to chicken and pasta recipe that's ready in less than 30 minutes—fabulous for a weeknight!
—Lorraine Stevenski, Land O' Lakes, FL

- -

Takes: 30 min. • **Makes:** 6 servings

- 4 cups uncooked penne pasta
- 2 Tbsp. olive oil, divided
- 2 lbs. boneless skinless chicken breasts, cut into thin strips, divided
- 3 garlic cloves, minced
- 2 tsp. grated lemon zest
- 1 cup Marsala wine
- 2 Tbsp. lemon juice
- 1 cup grated Parmesan cheese
- 1 cup 2% milk
- 1 envelope creamy pesto sauce mix
- 1 Tbsp. minced fresh basil
- 1 Tbsp. minced fresh parsley

1. Cook penne pasta according to package directions. In a Dutch oven, heat 1 Tbsp. olive oil over medium-high heat. Add half the chicken; cook and stir until no longer pink; remove from the pot. Repeat with the remaining oil and chicken; remove from pot.
2. Add garlic and lemon zest to the same pot; cook and stir for 30 seconds. Add wine and lemon juice, stirring to loosen browned bits from the pot. Bring to a boil; cook until liquid is reduced by half. Stir in the cheese, milk and sauce mix. Add chicken; cook until the sauce is slightly thickened.
3. Drain pasta; add to the chicken mixture and toss to combine. Sprinkle with herbs.
1¼ cups: 539 cal., 14g fat (4g sat. fat), 98mg chol., 622mg sod., 49g carb. (8g sugars, 2g fiber), 43g pro.

Other Options

CONFETTI PASTA

Our Christmas Eve tradition is to make a big pot of this linguine with red and green peppers and shrimp. We serve it with a snappy salad and garlic bread.
—Ellen Fiore, Montvale, NJ

Takes: 25 min. • Makes: 8 servings

- 1 pkg. (16 oz.) linguine
- 1 cup chopped sweet red pepper
- 1 cup chopped green pepper
- ⅓ cup chopped onion
- 3 garlic cloves, peeled and thinly sliced
- ¼ tsp. salt
- ¼ tsp. dried oregano
- ⅛ tsp. crushed red pepper flakes
- ⅛ tsp. pepper
- ¼ cup olive oil
- 2 lbs. peeled and deveined cooked shrimp (61-70 per lb.)
- ½ cup shredded Parmesan cheese

1. Cook linguine according to package directions. Meanwhile, in a Dutch oven, saute the peppers, onion, garlic and seasonings in oil until tender.
2. Add shrimp; cook and stir 2-3 minutes longer or until heated through. Drain linguine; toss with the shrimp mixture. Sprinkle with cheese.
1⅓ cups: 418 cal., 11g fat (2g sat. fat), 176mg chol., 331mg sod., 46g carb. (3g sugars, 3g fiber), 33g pro. Diabetic exchanges: 3 starch, 3 lean meat, 1½ fat.

To cook spaghetti without breaking it, carefully hold a bunch of spaghetti by one end and lower it into boiling water; ease it down into the water as it softens, pushing it around the edge of the pot. When the spaghetti is fully immersed, stir to separate strands.

CONTEST-WINNING NEW ENGLAND CLAM CHOWDER

In the Pacific Northwest, we dig our own razor clams and I grind them for chowder! Since these aren't readily available, canned clams are perfectly acceptable.
—Sandy Larson, Port Angeles, WA

Prep: 20 min. • Cook: 35 min.
Makes: 5 servings

- 4 center-cut bacon strips
- 2 celery ribs, chopped
- 1 large onion, chopped
- 1 garlic clove, minced
- 3 small potatoes, peeled and cubed
- 1 cup water
- 1 bottle (8 oz.) clam juice
- 3 tsp. reduced-sodium chicken bouillon granules
- ¼ tsp. white pepper
- ¼ tsp. dried thyme
- ⅓ cup all-purpose flour
- 2 cups fat-free half-and-half, divided
- 2 cans (6½ oz. each) chopped clams, undrained

1. In a Dutch oven, cook bacon strips over medium heat until crisp. Remove to paper towels to drain; set aside. Saute celery and onion in the drippings until tender. Add garlic; cook 1 minute longer. Stir in the potatoes, water, clam juice, bouillon, pepper and thyme. Bring to a boil. Reduce heat; simmer, uncovered, for 15-20 minutes or until the potatoes are tender.
2. In a small bowl, combine flour and 1 cup half-and-half until smooth. Gradually stir into soup. Bring to a boil; cook and stir for 1-2 minutes or until thickened.
3. Stir in chopped clams and remaining half-and-half; heat through (do not boil). Crumble the cooked bacon; sprinkle bacon over individual servings.
1⅓ cups: 260 cal., 4g fat (1g sat. fat), 22mg chol., 788mg sod., 39g carb. (9g sugars, 3g fiber), 13g pro.

PORK & APPLE SUPPER

Our part of upstate New York was settled by the Dutch, and this recipe originated there. This is also apple country, with at least 10 major orchards within a 15-mile radius of our home.
—Sharon Root, Wynantskill, NY

- -

Prep: 10 min. • **Cook:** 2 hours
Makes: 6 servings

1½	**lbs. boneless pork, cubed**
1	**Tbsp. canola oil**
4	**cups water**
1	**Tbsp. chicken bouillon granules**
1	**tsp. dried thyme**
¼	**tsp. pepper**
1	**bay leaf**
10	**to 12 small red potatoes (about 2 lbs.), quartered**
4	**medium tart apples, peeled and cut into wedges**
2	**Tbsp. cornstarch**
2	**Tbsp. cold water**

1. In a Dutch oven, brown pork cubes in oil. Add water, bouillon, thyme, pepper and bay leaf; bring to a boil. Reduce heat; cover and simmer until pork is tender, 1½-2 hours.

2. Add the potatoes; cover and cook for 15 minutes. Add apples; cover and cook for 10-12 minutes or until crisp-tender. Discard the bay leaf.

3. Combine cornstarch and cold water until smooth; stir into the pork mixture. Bring to a boil; cook and stir for 2 minutes or until thickened.

1¼ cups: 289 calories, 9g fat (3g sat. fat), 67mg chol., 473mg sod., 26g carb. (10g sugars, 3g fiber), 25g pro. **Diabetic exchanges:** 3 lean meat, 1½ starch, ½ fat.

SUMMER BOUNTY RATATOUILLE

The name says it all! Make use of your garden's surplus with this comforting dish. Originating from Nice, in the south of France, ratatouille is traditionally made with eggplant, tomatoes, onions, zucchini, garlic, bell peppers and various herbs. I highly recommend accompanying it with some freshly baked bread.

—Phyllis Jacques, Venice, FL

Prep: 20 min. + standing • **Cook:** 1 hour
Makes: 12 servings

- 1 large eggplant, peeled and cut into 1-in. cubes
- 1½ tsp. kosher salt, divided
- 3 Tbsp. olive oil
- 2 medium sweet red peppers, cut into ½-in. strips
- 2 medium onions, peeled and chopped
- 4 garlic cloves, minced
- ¼ cup tomato paste
- 1 Tbsp. herbes de Provence
- ½ tsp. pepper
- 3 cans (14½ oz. each) diced tomatoes, undrained
- 1½ cups water
- 4 medium zucchini, quartered lengthwise and sliced ½-in. thick
- ¼ cup chopped fresh basil
- 2 Tbsp. minced fresh rosemary
- 2 Tbsp. minced fresh parsley
- 2 French bread baguettes (10½ oz. each), cubed and toasted

1. Place eggplant in a colander over a plate; toss with 1 tsp. kosher salt. Let stand for 30 minutes. Rinse and drain well; pat dry.

2. In a Dutch oven, heat oil over medium-high heat; saute peppers and onions until tender, 8-10 minutes. Add garlic; cook and stir 1 minute. Stir in tomato paste, herbs de Provence, pepper, remaining salt, tomatoes and water. Add zucchini and eggplant; bring to a boil. Reduce heat; simmer, uncovered, until flavors are blended, 40-45 minutes, stirring occasionally.

3. Stir in fresh herbs. Serve over toasted baguette cubes.

Note: Look for herbes de Provence in the spice aisle.

1 cup ratatouille with 1 cup bread cubes: 205 cal., 4g fat (1g sat. fat), 0 chol., 542mg sod., 38g carb. (8g sugars, 6g fiber), 7g pro.

TEST KITCHEN TIP

Salting an eggplant draws out some of the moisture, giving the flesh a denser texture. This means it will give off less moisture and absorb less fat during cooking. Salting may cut some of the bitterness from an eggplant.

SOUTHWESTERN VEGETABLES & RICE

Short on time? Here's a spicy, satisfying supper that comes together in moments.
—*Taste of Home* Test Kitchen

- -

Takes: 20 min. • **Makes:** 4 servings

- 1 can (14½ oz.) fire-roasted diced tomatoes, undrained
- 1 pkg. (12 oz.) frozen vegetarian meat crumbles, thawed
- 1 pkg. (12 oz.) frozen southwestern corn, thawed
- 1 can (10¾ oz.) condensed tomato soup, undiluted
- 1 cup water
- 1 tsp. ground cumin
- ¼ tsp. salt
- 1 cup uncooked instant rice
- 1 cup shredded Monterey Jack cheese

In a Dutch oven, combine first 7 ingredients. Bring to a boil. Stir in rice. Remove from the heat; cover and let stand for 5-7 minutes or until rice is tender. Sprinkle with cheese.
1½ cups: 502 cal., 15g fat (6g sat. fat), 25mg chol., 1629mg sod., 62g carb. (16g sugars, 7g fiber), 29g pro.

MUSHROOM-BEAN BOURGUIGNON

In our family, boeuf bourguignon has been a staple for generations. I wanted a meatless alternative to our traditional favorite, so came up with this. All it needs is a French baguette!
—Sonya Labbe, West Hollywood, CA

- -

Prep: 15 min. • **Cook:** 1¼ hours
Makes: 10 servings (2½ qt.)

- 4 Tbsp. olive oil, divided
- 5 medium carrots, cut into 1-in. pieces
- 2 medium onions, halved and sliced
- 2 garlic cloves, minced
- 8 large portobello mushrooms, cut into 1-in. pieces
- 1 Tbsp. tomato paste
- 1 bottle (750 ml) dry red wine
- 2 cups mushroom broth or vegetable broth, divided
- 1 tsp. salt
- 1 tsp. minced fresh thyme or ½ tsp. dried thyme
- ½ tsp. pepper
- 2 cans (15½ oz. each) navy beans, rinsed and drained
- 1 pkg. (14.4 oz.) frozen pearl onions
- 3 Tbsp. all-purpose flour

1. In a Dutch oven, heat 2 Tbsp. olive oil over medium-high heat. Add carrots and onions; cook and stir 8-10 minutes or until the onions are tender. Add garlic; cook for 1 minute longer. Remove from pan.

2. In the same pan, heat 1 Tbsp. oil over medium-high heat. Add half the portobello mushrooms; cook and stir until lightly browned. Remove from pan; repeat with remaining oil and mushrooms.

3. Return the mushrooms to the pan. Add tomato paste; cook and stir 1 minute. Stir in wine, 1½ cups broth, salt, thyme, pepper and carrot mixture; bring to a boil. Reduce heat; simmer, covered, 25 minutes.

4. Add the beans and pearl onions; cook 30 minutes longer. In a small bowl, whisk flour and the remaining broth until smooth; stir into pan. Bring to a boil; cook and stir 2 minutes or until slightly thickened.

1 cup: 234 cal., 6g fat (1g sat. fat), 0 chol., 613mg sod., 33g carb. (6g sugars, 7g fiber), 9g pro. **Diabetic exchanges:** 2 starch, 2 vegetable, 1 lean meat, 1 fat.

CREOLE SHRIMP PASTA

Having grown up in Louisiana, we wait eagerly for the fresh Gulf shrimp season. Tossed with a spicy Creole sauce, this pasta dish pays homage to the bounty of the bayou.

—Melissa Cox, Bossier City, LA

Prep: 25 min. • **Cook:** 15 min.
Makes: 6 servings

- 1 pkg. (16 oz.) penne pasta
- 1 large red onion, finely chopped
- 3 Tbsp. butter
- 3 Tbsp. olive oil
- 3 garlic cloves, minced
- 1 lb. uncooked large shrimp, peeled and deveined
- 2 Tbsp. seafood seasoning
- ¼ cup heavy whipping cream
- 2 Tbsp. lemon juice
- 2 Tbsp. Worcestershire sauce
- 1 Tbsp. Cajun seasoning
- 1 Tbsp. Louisiana-style hot sauce
- ¼ tsp. pepper

1. Cook pasta according to the package directions. Meanwhile, in a Dutch oven, saute onion in butter and oil until tender. Add garlic; cook 1 minute longer. Sprinkle shrimp with seafood seasoning; add to pan.
2. Add and stir in the cream, lemon juice, Worcestershire sauce, Cajun seasoning, hot sauce and pepper. Drain the pasta, reserving ¾ cup cooking liquid. Add the reserved cooking liquid to pot. Cook and stir for 6-8 minutes or until shrimp turn pink. Add pasta and toss to coat.
1⅔ cups: 497 cal., 19g fat (7g sat. fat), 121mg chol., 1129mg sod., 60g carb. (4g sugars, 3g fiber), 23g pro.

BAHAMIAN PEAS & RICE

Ham, rice and veggies all in one bowl— so good on its own, but I often serve it up with deli potato salad or mac and cheese.
—Pamela Vitti Knowles, Hendersonville, NC

Prep: 15 min. • **Cook:** 50 min.
Makes: 14 servings

- 3 bacon strips, chopped
- 1 medium onion, chopped
- 1 celery rib, chopped
- ½ cup chopped green pepper
- 1 can (15 oz.) pigeon peas, drained
- 1 cup cubed fully cooked ham
- ¼ cup tomato paste
- 3 fresh thyme sprigs
- 1 tsp. salt
- ½ tsp. pepper
- 5½ cups water
- 1 can (13.66 oz.) coconut milk
- 3 cups uncooked brown rice

1. In a Dutch oven, cook the bacon over medium heat until crisp, stirring occasionally. Remove with a slotted spoon; drain on paper towels. Discard drippings, reserving 1 Tbsp.
2. Add onion, celery and green pepper to drippings; cook and stir over medium-high heat for 5-7 minutes or until tender. Stir in the pigeon peas, ham, tomato paste, thyme, salt and pepper.
3. Add water, coconut milk and cooked bacon; bring to a boil. Stir in rice. Reduce heat; cover and simmer for 45-50 minutes or until the rice is tender. Remove thyme sprigs before serving.
¾ cup: 304 cal., 11g fat (7g sat. fat), 10mg chol., 529mg sod., 44g carb. (2g sugars, 4g fiber), 10g pro.

Note: Wear disposable gloves when cutting hot peppers; the oils can burn skin. Avoid touching your face.

1 cup: 324 cal., 11g fat (5g sat. fat), 54mg chol., 1204mg sod., 47g carb. (16g sugars, 6g fiber), 10g pro.

VEG JAMBALAYA

This flavorful entree uses convenient canned beans in place of the meat— and never lets you leave hungry.
—Crystal Jo Bruns, Iliff, CO

- -

Prep: 10 min. • **Cook:** 30 min.
Makes: 6 servings

- 1   Tbsp. canola oil
- 1   medium green pepper, chopped
- 1   medium onion, chopped
- 1   celery rib, chopped
- 3   garlic cloves, minced
- 2   cups water
- 1   can (14½ oz.) diced tomatoes, undrained
- 1   can (8 oz.) tomato sauce
- ½   tsp. Italian seasoning
- ¼   tsp. salt
- ¼   tsp. crushed red pepper flakes
- ⅛   tsp. fennel seed, crushed
- 1   cup uncooked long grain rice
- 1   can (16 oz.) butter beans, rinsed and drained
- 1   can (16 oz.) red beans, rinsed and drained

1. In a Dutch oven, heat olive oil over medium-high heat. Add green pepper, onion and celery; cook and stir until tender. Add garlic; cook 1 minute longer.
2. Add the water, tomatoes, tomato sauce and the seasonings. Bring to a boil; stir in rice. Reduce heat; cover and simmer until liquid is absorbed and the rice is tender, 15-18 minutes. Stir in beans; heat through.
1⅓ cups: 281 cal., 3g fat (0 sat. fat), 0 chol., 796mg sod., 56g carb. (6g sugars, 9g fiber), 11g pro.

SWEET POTATO CHILI BAKE

I'm a vegetarian and wanted to develop some dishes that are a little heartier than traditional vegetarian fare. Here's one that I think is delicious!
—Jillian Tournoux, Massillon, OH

- -

Prep: 30 min. • **Bake:** 20 min.
Makes: 7 servings

- 2   cups cubed peeled sweet potato
- 1   medium sweet red pepper, chopped
- 1   Tbsp. olive oil
- 1   garlic clove, minced
- 1   can (28 oz.) diced tomatoes, undrained
- 2   cups vegetable broth
- 1   can (15 oz.) black beans, rinsed and drained
- 4½ tsp. brown sugar
- 3   tsp. chili powder
- 1   tsp. salt
- ½   tsp. pepper
- 1   pkg. (6½ oz.) cornbread/muffin mix
- ½   cup shredded cheddar cheese
  Optional: Sour cream, shredded cheddar cheese and chopped seeded jalapeno pepper

1. In a Dutch oven, saute the sweet potato and red pepper in oil until crisp-tender. Add garlic; cook 1 minute longer. Add tomatoes, broth, beans, brown sugar, chili powder, salt and pepper. Bring to a boil. Reduce heat; simmer, uncovered, 15-20 minutes or until the potatoes are tender.
2. Meanwhile, preheat the oven to 400°. Prepare cornbread batter according to package directions; stir in cheese. Drop by tablespoonfuls over chili.
3. Cover and bake until a toothpick inserted in center comes out clean, 18-20 minutes. Serve with toppings of your choice.

ONE-POT PORK & RICE

No one will suspect this filling entree goes easy on fat and calories. Green pepper and onion enhance the Spanish-style rice and tender chops, which are covered with diced tomatoes and gravy.
—Duna Stephens, Palisade, CO

- -

Prep: 20 min. • **Bake:** 1 hour
Makes: 6 servings

- 6   boneless pork loin chops
  (5 oz. each)
- 2   tsp. canola oil
- 1   cup uncooked long grain rice
- 1   large onion, sliced
- 1   large green pepper, sliced
- 1   envelope pork gravy mix
- 1   can (28 oz.) diced tomatoes, undrained
- 1½   cups water

1. Preheat oven to 350°. In a Dutch oven, brown the pork chops in oil on both sides; drain. Remove the chops from the pot and keep warm. Layer rice, onion and green pepper in pot; top with the pork chops.
2. Combine gravy mix, tomatoes and water; pour over the chops. Cover; bake for 1 hour or until a thermometer reads 160°.
1 serving: 391 cal., 10g fat (3g sat. fat), 83mg chol., 545mg sod., 40g carb. (0 sugars, 3g fiber), 33g pro. **Diabetic exchanges:** 3½ lean meat, 2 starch, 2 vegetable.

SUNDAY BEST STUFFED PORK CHOPS

When we're having our favorite stuffed pork chops for Sunday dinner, we pass around potatoes, a green salad and steamed broccoli on the side.
—Lorraine Smith, Carpenter, WY

Prep: 30 min. • **Cook:** 35 min.
Makes: 8 servings

- 1 pkg. (6 oz.) pork stuffing mix
- ¾ tsp. seasoned salt
- ½ tsp. garlic powder
- ½ tsp. coarsely ground pepper
- 1 can (10¾ oz.) condensed cream of mushroom soup, undiluted
- ¼ cup 2% milk
- 1 cup shredded smoked Gouda cheese
- 1 small apple, finely chopped
- ½ cup chopped pecans, toasted
- 8 boneless pork loin chops (6 oz. each)
- 2 Tbsp. olive oil, divided Minced fresh chives or parsley, optional

1. Prepare stuffing according to package directions; cool slightly. In a small bowl, mix seasonings. In another bowl, whisk soup and milk until blended.

2. Stir cheese, apple and pecans into the cooled stuffing. Cut a pocket horizontally in the thickest part of each chop. Fill with the stuffing mixture. Brush the outsides of the chops with 1 Tbsp. oil; sprinkle with the seasoning mixture.

3. In a Dutch oven, heat the remaining oil over medium heat. Stand pork chops in the pot, stuffing side up and spaced evenly. Pour the soup mixture around chops; bring to a boil. Reduce heat; simmer, covered, for 35-40 minutes or until the pork is no longer pink and a thermometer inserted in the stuffing reads 165°.

4. Remove from heat; let stand 5 minutes. Transfer chops to a serving dish. Spoon sauce over top. If desired, sprinkle with chives or parsley.

Note: To toast nuts, bake in a shallow pan in a 350° oven for 5-10 minutes or cook in a skillet over low heat until lightly browned, stirring occasionally.

1 stuffed pork chop with 3 Tbsp. sauce: 532 cal., 30g fat (11g sat. fat), 116mg chol., 973mg sod., 22g carb. (5 sugars, 2g fiber), 40g pro.

DIJON PORK CHOPS WITH CABBAGE & FENNEL

While I was living in Switzerland, my friends introduced me to an area renowned for cabbage, pork and potato dishes. I tried a cabbage and fennel combination and was amazed at how well they complemented each other. The juniper berries, an addition I learned after many years of cooking this recipe, add a special flavor to the cabbage.
—Grace Voltolina, Westport, CT

- -

Prep: 35 min. • **Bake:** 55 min.
Makes: 6 servings

- 1 small head green cabbage (about 1½ lbs.)
- 1 small head red cabbage (about 1½ lbs.)
- 4 Tbsp. whole grain Dijon mustard, divided
- 2 Tbsp. light brown sugar
- 3 tsp. kosher salt, divided
- 2½ tsp. pepper, divided
- 3 cups chicken stock
- 2 Tbsp. olive oil, divided
- 1 large onion, halved and thinly sliced
- 4 garlic cloves, thinly sliced
- 3 large Granny Smith apples, quartered
- 1 fennel bulb, cored and cut into ¼-in. slices
- 3 tsp. rubbed sage
- 6 center-cut pork rib chops (1 in. thick and 8 oz. each)
- 2 Tbsp. all-purpose flour

1. Preheat oven to 375°. Core and cut each cabbage into 6 wedges. In a bowl, mix 2 Tbsp. mustard, the brown sugar, 1½ tsp. salt, 1 tsp. pepper and the stock.
2. In a large Dutch oven, heat 1 Tbsp. oil over medium-high heat; saute onion until lightly browned, 4-6 minutes. Add garlic; cook and stir 1 minute. Remove from heat; add apples, fennel and cabbage. Pour the mustard mixture over top. Bake, covered, until the cabbage is tender, 45-60 minutes.

3. Meanwhile, mix sage and the remaining salt and pepper; rub onto both sides of pork chops. Dust with flour; shake off excess. In a large skillet, heat the remaining oil over medium-high heat. Brown chops in batches, 4-6 minutes per side; remove from pan.
4. Spread tops of pork chops with the remaining mustard; place over vegetables in the Dutch oven. Bake, uncovered, until a thermometer inserted in the pork reads 145°, 8-10 minutes.

1 pork chop with 2 cups vegetables:
435 cal., 16g fat (5g sat. fat), 72mg chol., 1533mg sod., 42g carb. (25g sugars, 10g fiber), 36g pro.

TEST KITCHEN TIP

We used a large Dutch oven to accommodate all the vegetables. The veggies will cook down, allowing room for the pork chops, which need to be cooked for just a short time after browning.

3. Shred pork with 2 forks. Return juices, onion and pork to Dutch oven. Stir in the barbecue sauce; heat through over medium heat, stirring occasionally.

⅔ cup pork mixture: 372 cal., 20g fat (7g sat. fat), 112mg chol., 466mg sod., 15g carb. (14g sugars, 1g fiber), 33g pro.

COUNTRY PORK & SAUERKRAUT

My mother and grandmother once ran a beanery for a train crew, which inspired a lot of my cooking. I adapted this recipe from one of theirs. The secret ingredient is the applesauce. When everything is cooked up, you wouldn't guess that it's in there, but the taste's just a bit sweeter.
—Donna Hellendrung, Minneapolis, MN

- -

Prep: 15 min. • **Bake:** 1½ hours
Makes: 4 servings

  2 **lbs. bone-in country-style pork ribs**
  1 **medium onion, chopped**
  1 **Tbsp. canola oil**
  1 **can (14 oz.) sauerkraut, undrained**
  1 **cup unsweetened applesauce**
  2 **Tbsp. brown sugar**
  2 **tsp. caraway seeds**
  1 **tsp. garlic powder**
  ½ **tsp. pepper**

1. Preheat oven to 350°. In a Dutch oven, cook ribs and onion in oil until the ribs are browned and onion is tender. Remove from the heat. Combine the remaining ingredients and pour over ribs.
2. Cover and bake for 1½-2 hours or until the ribs are tender.

1 serving: 477 cal., 24g fat (8g sat. fat), 130mg chol., 757mg sod., 23g carb. (15g sugars, 5g fiber), 41g pro.

DR SPICY BBQ PORK

I served this at my son's graduation party and kept it warm in a slow cooker after roasting it in the oven. The pork is superb by itself or piled high on rolls. For a classic combo, serve it with warm biscuits and coleslaw.
—Michelle Gauer, Spicer, MN

- -

Prep: 25 min. • **Bake:** 4 hours
Makes: 12 servings

  1 **boneless pork shoulder roast (5 to 7 lbs.)**
  1 **tsp. garlic powder**
  ½ **tsp. salt**
  ½ **tsp. freshly ground pepper**
  6 **chipotle peppers in adobo sauce, finely chopped (about ⅓ cup)**
  1 **large sweet onion, halved and sliced**
  2 **Tbsp. brown sugar**
  2 **cans (12 oz. each) Dr Pepper**
  1 **cup barbecue sauce**

1. Preheat oven to 325°. Sprinkle the roast with garlic powder, salt and pepper; rub with chipotle peppers. Place in a Dutch oven. Top with sweet onion; sprinkle with brown sugar. Pour Dr Pepper around the roast. Bake, covered, until the meat is tender, 4-4½ hours.
2. Remove roast; cool slightly. Strain cooking juices, reserving onion; skim fat from juices.

FIRE-ROASTED ZITI WITH SAUSAGE

We punch up our pasta with smoked sausage and fire-roasted tomato sauce. It's an easy recipe to switch up—use whatever noodles and spaghetti sauce are in your pantry.
—Jean Komlos, Plymouth, MI

- -

Takes: 30 min. • **Makes:** 8 servings

- 8 oz. uncooked ziti or rigatoni (about 3 cups)
- 1 can (28 oz.) Italian diced tomatoes, drained
- 1 jar (24 oz.) fire-roasted tomato and garlic pasta sauce
- 1 pkg. (16 oz.) smoked sausage, sliced
- 2 cups shredded part-skim mozzarella cheese, divided
- 1 cup 4% cottage cheese

1. In a Dutch oven, cook ziti according to the package directions for al dente. Drain; return to pot.
2. Add tomatoes, pasta sauce and sausage to the ziti; heat through over medium heat, stirring occasionally. Stir in 1 cup mozzarella cheese and cottage cheese. Sprinkle with the remaining mozzarella cheese. Cook, covered, for 2-5 minutes or until the cheese is melted.

1¼ cups: 463 cal., 23g fat (11g sat. fat), 66mg chol., 1634mg sod., 41g carb. (15g sugars, 3g fiber), 23g pro.

Once opened, wrap cheese in waxed paper, then again with a tight seal of plastic wrap or foil. Mozzarella cheese stored this way in the refrigerator will keep for several weeks. If mold develops, trim off the mold plus ½ inch extra of cheese. The rest of the cheese can be eaten.

SHRIMP & BROCCOLI BROWN RICE PAELLA

Years ago my husband and I were in France and came across an open market where a Spaniard was making paella in a skillet; we've been hooked ever since. I love to whip this up for a large group, but if the gathering is small, I know I can easily freeze leftovers for another time.
—Joni Hilton, Rocklin, CA

- -

Prep: 45 min. • **Cook:** 50 min.
Makes: 8 servings

- 1 Tbsp. olive oil
- 1 medium onion, chopped
- 1 medium sweet red pepper, chopped
- 1 cup sliced fresh mushrooms
- 2 cups uncooked long-grain brown rice
- 2 garlic cloves, minced
- 2 tsp. paprika
- ½ tsp. salt
- ½ tsp. cayenne pepper
- ¼ tsp. saffron threads
- 6 cups chicken stock
- 2 lbs. uncooked large shrimp, peeled and deveined
- 1½ cups fresh broccoli florets
- 1 cup frozen peas

1. In a Dutch oven, heat oil over medium-high heat. Add the onion, red pepper and mushrooms; cook and stir until tender, 6-8 minutes. Stir in the rice, garlic and seasonings; cook 1-2 minutes longer.
2. Stir in chicken stock; bring to a boil. Reduce heat; simmer, covered, or until liquid is absorbed and the rice is tender, 40-45 minutes. Add shrimp and broccoli; cook 8-10 minutes longer or until shrimp turn pink. Stir in peas; heat through.
Freeze option: Place cooled paella in freezer containers. To use, partially thaw in refrigerator overnight. Microwave, covered, on high in a microwave-safe dish until heated through, stirring gently and adding a little stock or water if necessary.

1½ cups: 331 cal., 5g fat (1g sat. fat), 138mg chol., 693mg sod., 44g carb. (4g sugars, 4g fiber), 27g pro. **Diabetic exchanges:** 3 lean meat, 2½ starch.

Skillet & Stovetop

favorites

Beef

DINNER IN A BAG

I get a head start on this family-pleasing dinner by assembling ready-to-grab pantry kits. I measure dry macaroni and the spice mixture into separate containers, storing them in a paper bag with canned tomatoes.
—Darlene Brenden, Salem, OR

- -

Prep: 5 min. • **Cook:** 25 min.
Makes: 4 servings

1	lb. ground beef
2	cans (14½ oz. each) stewed tomatoes
¼	cup dried minced onion
1	tsp. salt
1	tsp. chili powder
¼	to ½ tsp. pepper
¼	tsp. sugar
1	cup uncooked elbow macaroni

1. In a large skillet, cook beef over medium heat until no longer pink; drain. Add the tomatoes, seasonings and sugar; bring to a boil. Reduce heat and simmer for 5 minutes.
2. Stir in macaroni; cover and simmer for 15 minutes. Uncover; simmer until the macaroni is tender and sauce is thickened.
1 cup: 289 cal., 11g fat (5g sat. fat), 56mg chol., 858mg sod., 25g carb. (8g sugars, 2g fiber), 24g pro.

For each 14½-oz. can of stewed tomatoes, you can use use the same amount of home-canned tomatoes plus 3 Tbsp. finely chopped celery, 2 Tbsp. finely chopped onion, 1 Tbsp. finely chopped green pepper, ½ tsp. sugar and ⅛ tsp. salt.

ZUCCHINI BEEF SKILLET

This speedy summer recipe uses up those super abundant garden goodies: zucchini, tomatoes and green peppers.
—Becky Calder, Kingston, MO

- -

Takes: 30 min. • **Makes:** 4 servings

1	lb. ground beef
1	medium onion, chopped
1	small green pepper, chopped
2	tsp. chili powder
¾	tsp. salt
¼	tsp. pepper
3	medium zucchini, cut into ¾-in. cubes
2	large tomatoes, chopped
¼	cup water
1	cup uncooked instant rice
1	cup shredded cheddar cheese

1. In a large skillet, cook and crumble beef with onion and pepper over medium-high heat until no longer pink, 5-7 minutes; drain.
2. Stir in seasonings, vegetables, water and rice; bring to a boil. Reduce heat; simmer, covered, until rice is tender, 10-15 minutes. Sprinkle with cheese. Remove from heat; let stand until the cheese is melted.
2 cups: 470 cal., 24g fat (11g sat. fat), 98mg chol., 749mg sod., 33g carb. (8g sugars, 4g fiber), 32g pro.

EASY PEPPER STEAK

We live on the eastern edge of the Sand Hills in Nebraska, where most folks are ranchers—so delicious and satisfying meals are in big demand. This popular beef dish is tasty as well as colorful.
—Carolyn Butterfield, Atkinson, NE

- -

Prep: 10 min. • **Cook:** 55 min.
Makes: 4 servings

- 1 lb. beef top round steak, cut into ¼-in. x 2-in. strips
- 1 Tbsp. paprika
- 2 Tbsp. butter
- 1 can (10½ oz.) beef broth
- 2 garlic cloves, minced
- 2 medium green peppers, cut into strips
- 1 cup thinly sliced onion
- 2 Tbsp. cornstarch
- 2 Tbsp. soy sauce
- ⅓ cup cold water
- 2 fresh tomatoes, peeled and cut into wedges
  Cooked rice

1. Sprinkle meat with paprika. In a large skillet, melt butter over medium-high heat. Brown beef. Add broth and garlic. Simmer, covered, for 30 minutes. Add green peppers and onion. Cover and continue to simmer for 5 minutes.

2. Combine cornstarch, soy sauce and water; stir into meat mixture. Cook and stir until thickened. Gently stir in tomatoes and heat through. Serve over rice.

1 serving: 365 cal., 4g fat (1 sat. fat), 65mg chol., 465mg sod., 48g carb. (5 sugars, 4g fiber), 21g pro. **Diabetic exchanges:** 2½ lean meat, 1½ starch, 1½ vegetable, ½ fat.

BEEF TOSTADAS

Chipotle sauce gives meaty open-faced tacos just the right amount of heat to fire up a fiesta at the dinner table.
—*Taste of Home* Test Kitchen

Takes: 15 min. • **Makes:** 6 servings

1	lb. lean ground beef (90% lean)
1	cup chopped sweet red pepper
½	cup chili sauce
1	tsp. taco seasoning
¼	tsp. salt
¼	tsp. pepper
½	cup sour cream
3	tsp. chipotle sauce
6	tostada shells
3	cups shredded lettuce
1½	cups guacamole
1½	cups shredded Mexican cheese blend

1. In a large skillet, cook beef and red pepper over medium heat until the meat is no longer pink; drain. Stir in the chili sauce, taco seasoning, salt and pepper; heat through.

2. In a small bowl, combine sour cream and chipotle sauce. Layer each tostada with lettuce, meat mixture, guacamole, cheese and chipotle cream.

1 tostada: 460 cal., 30g fat (13g sat. fat), 75mg chol., 1040mg sod., 22g carb. (8g sugars, 6g fiber), 24g pro.

TEST KITCHEN TIP

Ground beef is often labeled using the cut of meat that it is ground from, such as ground chuck or ground round. If it's labeled ground beef, it comes from a combination of beef cuts. Ground beef can also be labeled according to the fat content of the ground mixture or the percentage of lean meat to fat, such as 85% or 90% lean. Select ground beef that is bright red and is in a tightly sealed package. Purchase all ground beef before the "sell by" date; use within 3-5 days of that date.

INSIDE-OUT STUFFED CABBAGE

Stuffed cabbage can be time-consuming to make, but this version is table-ready in just 30 minutes—with all the classic flavors, plus butternut squash.
—*Taste of Home* Test Kitchen

- -

Prep: 10 min. • **Cook:** 25 min.
Makes: 4 servings

- 1 lb. ground beef
- 2 cups cubed peeled butternut squash (about 12 oz.)
- 1 medium green pepper, chopped
- 1 envelope Lipton beefy onion soup mix
- 1 Tbsp. brown sugar
- 1 can (11½ oz.) Spicy Hot V8 juice
- 1 cup water
- 6 cups chopped cabbage (about 1 small head)
- ½ cup uncooked instant brown rice

1. In a Dutch oven, cook and crumble beef with squash and pepper over medium-high heat until no meat is longer pink; drain. Stir in the soup mix, brown sugar, V8 juice, water and cabbage; bring to a boil. Reduce heat; simmer, covered, until the cabbage is tender, 8-10 minutes, stirring occasionally.
2. Stir in rice; return to a boil. Simmer, covered, 5 minutes. Remove from heat; let stand, covered, until the rice is tender, about 5 minutes.
1½ cups: 382 cal., 15g fat (5g sat. fat), 70mg chol., 841mg sod., 40g carb. (13g sugars, 7g fiber), 25g pro.

GERMAN MEATBALLS

This is one of our favorite main dishes. Because we raise our own pork and beef, the meat we use is always freshly ground. For variety, these meatballs can be cooked with a sweet cream gravy or steamed with tomatoes. But we prefer them served over homemade sauerkraut.
—Iona Redemer, Calumet, OK

- -

Prep: 20 min. • **Cook:** 25 min.
Makes: 6 servings

- 1 lb. ground beef
- ½ lb. ground pork
- ½ cup finely chopped onion
- ¾ cup fine dry bread crumbs
- 1 Tbsp. snipped fresh parsley
- 1½ tsp. salt
- ⅛ tsp. pepper
- 1 tsp. Worcestershire sauce
- 1 large egg, beaten
- ½ cup 2% milk
- 2 to 3 Tbsp. vegetable oil
- 1 can (27 oz.) sauerkraut, undrained
- ⅓ to ½ cup water, optional
  Additional snipped parsley

In a bowl, combine first 10 ingredients; shape into 18 meatballs, 2 in. each. Heat the oil in a skillet; brown the meatballs. Remove meatballs and drain fat. Spoon sauerkraut into skillet; top with meatballs. Cover and simmer 15-20 minutes or until meatballs are cooked through, adding water if necessary. Sprinkle with parsley.
Freeze option: Freeze cooled meatball mixture in freezer containers. To use, partially thaw in refrigerator overnight. In a microwave-safe dish, cover and microwave on high until heated through, stirring gently.
3 meatballs: 376 cal., 22g fat (7g sat. fat), 114mg chol., 1636mg sod., 18g carb. (3g sugars, 4g fiber), 27g pro.

BEEF & BACON GNOCCHI SKILLET

This gnocchi dish tastes like bacon cheeseburgers. Go ahead and top it as you would a burger—with ketchup, mustard and pickles!
—Ashley Lecker, Green Bay, WI

Takes: 30 min. • **Makes:** 6 servings

- 1 pkg. (16 oz.) potato gnocchi
- 1¼ lbs. lean ground beef (90% lean)
- 1 medium onion, chopped
- 8 cooked bacon strips, crumbled and divided
- 1 cup water
- ½ cup heavy whipping cream
- 1 Tbsp. ketchup
- ¼ tsp. salt
- ¼ tsp. pepper
- 1½ cups shredded cheddar cheese
- ½ cup chopped tomatoes
- 2 green onions, sliced

1. Preheat broiler. Cook gnocchi according to the package directions; drain.
2. Meanwhile, in a large cast-iron or other ovenproof skillet, cook beef and onion, crumbling beef, over medium heat until no longer pink, 4-6 minutes. Drain.
3. Stir in half the bacon; add the gnocchi, water, cream and ketchup. Bring to a boil. Cook, stirring, over medium heat until the sauce has thickened, 3-4 minutes. Add salt and pepper. Sprinkle with cheese.
4. Broil 3-4 in. from heat until cheese has melted, 1-2 minutes. Top with tomatoes, green onions and the remaining bacon.
1 cup: 573 cal., 31g fat (16g sat. fat), 136mg chol., 961mg sod., 35g carb. (7g sugars, 2g fiber), 36g pro.

BEEFY HUEVOS RANCHEROS

This quick, easy and oh-so-tasty recipe works for breakfast, lunch or dinner and is great served with fruit or salad and flour tortillas.
—Sandra Leonard, Peculiar, MO

Prep: 15 min. • **Cook:** 20 min.
Makes: 6 servings

- 1 lb. lean ground beef (90% lean)
- 1 small onion, finely chopped
- 2 cans (14½ oz. each) diced tomatoes
- 1 cup frozen corn
- 1 can (4 oz.) chopped green chiles
- ½ tsp. salt
- 6 large eggs
- ¼ tsp. pepper
- 6 Tbsp. shredded cheddar cheese
- 6 flour tortillas (8 in.), warmed

Optional: Reduced-fat sour cream, guacamole, salsa and chopped green onions

1. In a large cast-iron or other heavy skillet, cook beef and onion over medium heat until the beef is no longer pink and onion is tender, breaking up beef into crumbles, 6-8 minutes. Drain and return to pan.
2. Drain tomatoes, reserving ½ cup liquid. Stir tomatoes, reserved liquid, corn, chiles and salt into the beef mixture; bring to a simmer. With the back of a spoon, make 6 wells in beef mixture; add an egg to each well. Sprinkle with pepper. Cook, covered, until whites are completely set, 5-7 minutes.
3. Sprinkle with cheese. Serve with tortillas and toppings as desired.
1 serving: 434 cal., 17g fat (6g sat. fat), 241mg chol., 879mg sod., 41g carb. (6g sugars, 5g fiber), 29g pro.

CHILI SKILLET

Like most farmers, my husband loves a good, hearty chili. With all the vegetables, cheese and meat in it, this dish makes a super supper—and it comes together in one skillet on top of the stove. I serve it frequently in fall and winter.
—Katherine Brown, Fredericktown, OH

- -

Prep: 15 min. • **Cook:** 40 min.
Makes: 4 servings

1	lb. ground beef
1	cup chopped onion
½	cup chopped green pepper
1	garlic clove, minced
1	can (16 oz.) kidney beans, rinsed and drained
1	cup tomato juice
½	cup water
4	tsp. chili powder
1	tsp. dried oregano
1	tsp. salt
½	cup uncooked long grain rice
1	cup canned or frozen corn
½	cup sliced ripe olives
1	cup shredded cheddar or Monterey Jack cheese Thinly sliced green onions, optional

1. In a large skillet over medium heat, cook beef, onion, pepper and garlic until the meat is no longer pink; drain. Add the next 7 ingredients; simmer, covered, until the rice is tender, about 25 minutes.

2. Stir in corn and olives; cover and cook 5 minutes more. Sprinkle with cheese; cook, covered, until the cheese is melted, about 5 more minutes. If desired, top with sliced green onions.

1 serving: 599 cal., 26g fat (11g sat. fat), 98mg chol., 1557mg sod., 54g carb. (9g sugars, 10g fiber), 38g pro.

MONGOLIAN BEEF

My family just loves this meal-in-one option, including my husband, a real meat-and-potatoes guy. The dish uses budget-friendly ingredients to offer big flavor in a small amount of time.
—Heather Blum, Coleman, WI

- -

Takes: 25 min. • **Makes:** 4 servings

1	Tbsp. cornstarch
¾	cup reduced-sodium chicken broth
2	Tbsp. reduced-sodium soy sauce
1	Tbsp. hoisin sauce
2	tsp. sesame oil
1	lb. beef top sirloin steak, cut into thin strips
1	Tbsp. olive oil, divided
5	green onions, cut into 1-in. pieces
2	cups hot cooked rice

1. In a small bowl, combine cornstarch and broth until smooth. Stir in the soy sauce, hoisin sauce and sesame oil; set aside. In a large nonstick skillet or wok, stir-fry the beef in 1½ tsp. hot olive oil until no longer pink. Remove and keep warm.

2. In the same skillet, stir-fry the onions in the remaining olive oil until crisp-tender, 3-4 minutes. Stir the cornstarch mixture and add it to the pan. Bring to a boil; cook and stir until thickened, about 2 minutes. Reduce heat; add beef and heat through. Serve with rice.

1 serving: 328 cal., 11g fat (3g sat. fat), 46mg chol., 529mg sod., 28g carb. (2g sugars, 1g fiber), 28g pro. **Diabetic exchanges:** 3 lean meat, 2 starch, 1 fat.

WASABI BEEF FAJITAS

Beef fajitas take on an Eastern spin with gingerroot, sesame oil and wasabi, a type of Japanese horseradish. You can find it in the Asian section at your supermarket.
—*Taste of Home* Test Kitchen

Takes: 20 min. • **Makes:** 8 servings

2	tsp. cornstarch
3	Tbsp. reduced-sodium soy sauce
2	tsp. prepared wasabi
2	tsp. minced fresh gingerroot
1	garlic clove, minced
2	Tbsp. sesame oil, divided
1	lb. uncooked beef stir-fry strips
12	green onions with tops, cut in half lengthwise
1	large sweet red pepper, julienned
8	flour tortillas (8 in.), warmed
1	cup coleslaw mix

1. In a small bowl, mix cornstarch, soy sauce, wasabi, ginger and garlic until blended. In a large skillet, heat 1 Tbsp. of oil over medium-high heat. Add beef; stir-fry 4-6 minutes or until no longer pink. Remove from pan.

2. Stir-fry green onions and red pepper in the remaining oil 2-3 minutes or until vegetables are crisp-tender.

3. Stir the cornstarch mixture and add to the pan. Bring to a boil; cook and stir for 1-2 minutes or until sauce is thickened. Return beef to pan; heat through. Serve with tortillas and coleslaw mix.

1 fajita: 287 cal., 9g fat (2g sat. fat), 23mg chol., 507mg sod., 32g carb. (2g sugars, 3g fiber), 17g pro. **Diabetic exchanges:** 2 starch, 2 lean meat, ½ fat.

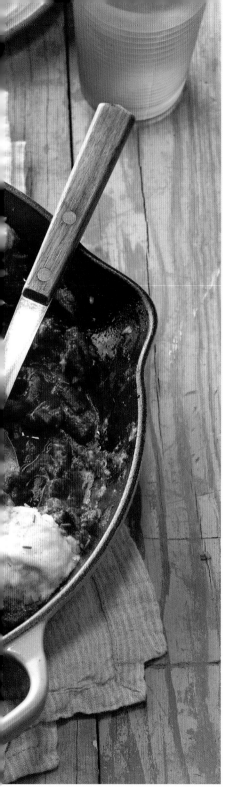

MEATBALL CHILI WITH DUMPLINGS

My family enjoys this delicious recipe—it's like a spicy meatball stew with dumplings!
—Sarah Yoder, Middlebury, IN

- -

Prep: 20 min. • **Cook:** 50 min.
Makes: 6 servings

- 1 **large egg, beaten**
- ¾ **cup finely chopped onion, divided**
- ¼ **cup dry bread crumbs or rolled oats**
- 5 **tsp. beef bouillon granules, divided**
- 3 **tsp. chili powder, divided**
- 1 **lb. ground beef**
- 3 **Tbsp. all-purpose flour**
- 1 **Tbsp. canola oil**
- 1 **can (28 oz.) diced tomatoes, undrained**
- 1 **garlic clove, minced**
- ½ **tsp. ground cumin**
- 1 **can (16 oz.) kidney beans, rinsed and drained**

CORNMEAL DUMPLINGS

- 1½ **cups biscuit/baking mix**
- ½ **cup yellow cornmeal**
- ⅔ **cup 2% milk**
  Minced chives, optional

1. In a large bowl, combine egg, ¼ cup onion, the bread crumbs, 3 tsp. bouillon and 1 tsp. chili powder; crumble beef over the mixture and mix well. Shape into twelve 1½-in. meatballs. Roll in flour.

2. Heat oil in a 12-in. cast-iron or other ovenproof skillet; brown meatballs. Drain on paper towels. Meanwhile, in a large saucepan, combine tomatoes, garlic and cumin with the remaining onion, bouillon and chili powder. Add meatballs. Cover and cook over low heat about 20 minutes. Stir in kidney beans.

3. Meanwhile, for dumplings, combine biscuit mix, cornmeal and milk. Drop by spoonfuls onto the chili; cook on low, uncovered, 10 minutes. Cover and cook until a toothpick inserted into a dumpling comes out clean, 10-12 minutes longer. If desired, sprinkle with minced chives.

1 serving: 475 cal., 16g fat (6g sat. fat), 76mg chol., 1523mg sod., 56g carb. (8g sugars, 7g fiber), 26g pro.

TEST KITCHEN TIP

If you want to reduce the amount of fat in your meatballs, try baking them instead of frying. Place on a rack in a broiler pan and bake in a 400° oven for 20 minutes. The rack will allow excess grease to drip away.

TACOS IN A BOWL

This easy skillet dish offers a tasty use for leftover taco meat. Garnish it with sour cream and salsa for southwestern flavor and top with crushed tortilla chips for a nice added crunch!
—Sue Schoening, Sheboygan, WI

Takes: 25 min. • **Makes:** 2 servings

- ½ lb. lean ground beef (90% lean)
- 2 Tbsp. finely chopped onion
- ¾ cup canned diced tomatoes, drained
- 2 Tbsp. taco seasoning
- 1 cup water
- 1 pkg. (3 oz.) ramen noodles
- ¼ cup shredded cheddar or Mexican cheese blend
  Crushed tortilla chips, optional

1. In a small skillet, cook beef and onion over medium heat until meat is no longer pink; drain. Stir in tomatoes, taco seasoning and water. Bring to a boil. Add ramen noodles (discard the seasoning packet or save for another use). Cook and stir until the noodles are tender, 3-5 minutes.
2. Spoon into serving bowls; sprinkle with cheese and tortilla chips if desired.
1 cup: 480 cal., 21g fat (10g sat. fat), 85mg chol., 1279mg sod., 40g carb. (3g sugars, 2g fiber), 30g pro.

SOUP-BOWL CABBAGE ROLLS

This fabulous alternative to traditional stuffed cabbage rolls is so handy for busy weeknights. It warms you up from head to toe.
—Terri Pearce, Houston, TX

Prep: 15 min. • **Cook:** 35 min.
Makes: 4 servings

- 1 lb. lean ground beef (90% lean)
- 1 garlic clove, minced
- 1 small head cabbage, chopped
- 2½ cups water
- ⅔ cup uncooked long grain rice
- 1 Tbsp. Worcestershire sauce
- 1 tsp. onion powder
- 1 tsp. dried basil
- ¼ tsp. cayenne pepper
- ¼ tsp. pepper
- 1 can (28 oz.) crushed tomatoes
- ½ tsp. salt
  Grated Parmesan cheese, optional

In a nonstick Dutch oven, cook ground beef and garlic over medium heat until meat is no longer pink; drain. Stir in next 8 ingredients; bring to a boil. Reduce heat; simmer, covered, until rice is tender, 25-30 minutes. Stir in tomatoes and salt; heat through. If desired, sprinkle with cheese.
2¼ cups: 397 cal., 9g fat (4g sat. fat), 56mg chol., 707mg sod., 51g carb. (6g sugars, 9g fiber), 30g pro.

1. In a large skillet, brown the ground beef with onion, garlic and curry; drain and discard the garlic. Stir in water, salt, sugar and pepper. Cover and simmer 15 minutes.
2. Add tomato and zucchini; cook just until heated through. Spoon the meat mixture into pita breads. If desired, serve with tzatziki sauce.

2 filled pita halves: 393 cal., 14g fat (5g sat. fat), 70mg chol., 665mg sod., 38g carb. (4g sugars, 3g fiber), 27g pro.

SKILLET BBQ BEEF POTPIE

Beef potpie is a classic comfort food, but who's got time to see it through? My crowd-pleaser is not only speedy but an excellent way to use leftover stuffing.
—Priscilla Yee, Concord, CA

Takes: 25 min. • **Makes:** 4 servings

- 1 lb. lean ground beef (90% lean)
- ⅓ cup thinly sliced green onions, divided
- 2 cups frozen mixed vegetables, thawed
- ½ cup salsa
- ½ cup barbecue sauce
- 3 cups cooked cornbread stuffing
- ½ cup shredded cheddar cheese
- ¼ cup chopped sweet red pepper

1. In a large skillet, cook beef and ¼ cup green onions over medium heat until beef is no longer pink, breaking into crumbles, 6-8 minutes; drain. Stir in mixed vegetables, salsa and barbecue sauce; cook, covered, over medium-low heat 4-5 minutes or until heated through.
2. Layer stuffing over the beef; sprinkle with cheese, red pepper and the remaining green onion. Cook, covered, 3-5 minutes longer or until heated through and cheese is melted.

1½ cups: 634 cal., 27g fat (9g sat. fat), 85mg chol., 1372mg sod., 62g carb. (19g sugars, 9g fiber), 33g pro.

CURRIED BEEF PITA POCKETS

If there's anyone in your family who thinks they won't like curry, serve this … they'll be a curry lover forever!
—Mary Ann Kosmas, Minneapolis, MN

Prep: 5 min. • **Cook:** 30 min.
Makes: 4 servings

- 1 lb. ground beef
- 1 medium onion, chopped
- 1 garlic clove, halved
- 1 Tbsp. curry powder
- ½ cup water
- ½ tsp. salt
- ½ tsp. sugar
- ¼ tsp. pepper
- 1 medium tomato, seeded and diced
- 1 medium zucchini, diced
- 8 pita pocket halves
   Refrigerated tzatziki sauce, optional

Freeze option: Prepare the beef mixture as directed but do not add sour cream. Freeze the cooled meat mixture in freezer containers. To use, partially thaw in the refrigerator overnight. Heat through in a large skillet, stirring occasionally and adding a little water if necessary. Stir in sour cream and proceed as directed.

1 serving: 448 cal., 20g fat (12g sat. fat), 80mg chol., 781mg sod., 45g carb. (8g sugars, 7g fiber), 24g pro.

TANGY SWEET & SOUR MEATBALLS

A tangy sauce, pineapple and green pepper transform premade meatballs into something special. Serve them over rice for a satisfying meal.
—Ruth Andrewson, Leavenworth, WA

Takes: 30 min. • **Makes:** 6 servings

- 1 can (20 oz.) pineapple chunks
- ⅓ cup water
- 3 Tbsp. vinegar
- 1 Tbsp. soy sauce
- ½ cup packed brown sugar
- 3 Tbsp. cornstarch
- 30 frozen fully cooked Italian meatballs (about 15 oz.)
- 1 large green pepper, cut into 1-in. pieces
   Hot cooked rice

Drain pineapple, reserving the juice. Set pineapple aside. Add water to the juice if needed to measure 1 cup; pour into a large skillet. Add ⅓ cup water, vinegar, soy sauce, brown sugar and cornstarch; stir until smooth. Cook over medium heat until thick, stirring constantly. Add the pineapple, meatballs and green pepper. Simmer, uncovered, until heated through, about 20 minutes. Serve with rice.

5 meatballs: 389 cal., 19g fat (8g sat. fat), 30mg chol., 682mg sod., 47g carb. (36g sugars, 2g fiber), 11g pro.

SKILLET SHEPHERD'S PIE

This is the best shepherd's pie I've ever tasted. It's very quick to make, and I usually have most—if not all—of the ingredients already on hand.
—Tirzah Sandt, San Diego, CA

Takes: 30 min. • **Makes:** 6 servings

- 1 lb. ground beef
- 1 cup chopped onion
- 2 cups frozen corn, thawed
- 2 cups frozen peas, thawed
- 2 Tbsp. ketchup
- 1 Tbsp. Worcestershire sauce
- 2 tsp. minced garlic
- 1 Tbsp. cornstarch
- 1 tsp. beef bouillon granules
- ½ cup cold water
- ½ cup sour cream
- 3½ cups mashed potatoes (prepared with milk and butter)
- ¾ cup shredded cheddar cheese

1. In a large skillet, cook beef and onion over medium heat until meat is no longer pink; drain. Stir in corn, peas, ketchup, Worcestershire sauce and garlic. Reduce heat to medium-low; cover and cook for 5 minutes.
2. Combine the cornstarch, bouillon and water until well blended; stir into the beef mixture. Bring to a boil over medium heat; cook and stir until thickened, 2 minutes. Stir in the sour cream and heat through (do not boil).
3. Spread the mashed potatoes over the top; sprinkle with cheese. Cover and cook until the potatoes are heated through and the cheese is melted.

STOVETOP GOULASH

I created this recipe after trying goulash at a local restaurant. The blend of spices gives it fabulous flavor, and it's so easy on a weeknight!

—Karen Schelert, Portland, OR

Takes: 25 min. • **Makes:** 4 servings

- 1 **lb. ground beef**
- 1 **pkg. (16 oz.) frozen mixed vegetables, thawed**
- 2 **cans (10¾ oz. each) condensed tomato soup, undiluted**
- 1 **cup water**
- 1 **small onion, chopped**
- 2 **tsp. Worcestershire sauce**
- 1 **tsp. garlic salt**
- 1 **tsp. chili powder**
- ½ **tsp. dried oregano**
- ½ **tsp. paprika**
- ⅛ **tsp. ground cinnamon**
- ⅛ **tsp. pepper**
- 1 **pkg. (24 oz.) refrigerated mashed potatoes**

1. Cook beef in a large skillet over medium heat until no longer pink; drain. Add mixed vegetables, tomato soup, water, onion, Worcestershire sauce and seasonings; bring to a boil. Reduce heat; simmer, uncovered, for 10 minutes or until slightly thickened.

2. Meanwhile, heat potatoes according to package directions. Serve with goulash.

1½ cups goulash with 1 cup potatoes: 605 cal., 22g fat (9g sat. fat), 92mg chol., 1425mg sod., 58g carb. (18g sugars, 8g fiber), 28g pro.

SPICY BEEF & PEPPER STIR-FRY

Think of this stir-fry as your chance to play with heat and spice. I balance the beef with coconut milk and a spritz of lime.
—Joy Zacharia, Clearwater, FL

- -

Prep: 20 min. + standing • **Cook:** 10 min.
Makes: 4 servings

- 1   lb. beef top sirloin steak, cut into thin strips
- 1   Tbsp. minced fresh gingerroot
- 3   garlic cloves, minced, divided
- ¼   tsp. pepper
- ¾   tsp. salt, divided
- 1   cup light coconut milk
- 2   Tbsp. sugar
- 1   Tbsp. Sriracha chili sauce
- ½   tsp. grated lime zest
- 2   Tbsp. lime juice
- 2   Tbsp. canola oil, divided
- 1   large sweet red pepper, cut into thin strips
- ½   medium red onion, thinly sliced
- 1   jalapeno pepper, seeded and thinly sliced
- 4   cups fresh baby spinach
- 2   green onions, thinly sliced
- 2   Tbsp. chopped fresh cilantro

1. In a large bowl, toss the beef with ginger, 2 garlic cloves, pepper and ½ tsp. salt; let stand 15 minutes. In a small bowl, whisk coconut milk, sugar, chili sauce, lime zest, lime juice and the remaining salt until blended; set aside.

2. In a large skillet or wok, heat 1 Tbsp. oil over medium-high heat. Add the beef and stir-fry until no longer pink, 2-3 minutes. Remove from pan.

3. Stir-fry red pepper, red onion, jalapeno and the remaining garlic in remaining oil just until the vegetables are crisp-tender, 2-3 minutes. Stir in coconut milk mixture; heat through. Add spinach and beef; cook until spinach is wilted and beef is heated through, stirring occasionally. Sprinkle with green onions and cilantro.

¾ cup: 312 cal., 16g fat (5g sat. fat), 46mg chol., 641mg sod., 15g carb. (10g sugars, 2g fiber), 26g pro. **Diabetic exchanges:** 3 lean meat, 2 fat, 1 vegetable, ½ starch.

TEST KITCHEN TIP

For a successful stir-fry, prepare all the ingredients before you begin. Cut all the vegetables the same size so they cook evenly. Select a wok or skillet that easily accommodates the volume of food—if the food is crowded in the pan, it will steam. If necessary, stir-fry the food in batches.

SKILLET STEAK SUPPER

With all of the ingredients cooked in one skillet, this steak dish couldn't be quicker to prepare, or easier to clean up after! The wine and mushroom sauce makes it extra special.

—Sandra Fisher, Missoula, MT

- -

Takes: 20 min. • **Makes:** 2 servings

- 1   beef top sirloin steak (¾ lb.)
- ½   tsp. salt, divided
- ½   tsp. pepper, divided
- 1   Tbsp. olive oil
- 1 to 2 Tbsp. butter
- ½   lb. sliced fresh mushrooms
- 2   Tbsp. white wine or chicken broth
- 3   Tbsp. chopped green onions
- 1   Tbsp. Worcestershire sauce
- 1   tsp. Dijon mustard

1. Sprinkle steak with ¼ tsp. each salt and pepper. In a skillet, heat oil over medium-high heat; cook steak to desired doneness (for medium-rare, a thermometer should read 135°; medium, 140°), 4-6 minutes per side. Remove from pan; keep warm.
2. In the same skillet, heat butter over medium-high heat; saute mushrooms until tender. Stir in wine; bring to a boil, stirring to loosen browned bits from pan. Stir in chopped green onions, Worcestershire sauce, mustard and the remaining salt and pepper. Cut steak in half; serve with the mushroom mixture.

1 serving: 368 cal., 20g fat (7g sat. fat), 85mg chol., 915mg sod., 6g carb. (3g sugars, 2g fiber), 40g pro.

PIEROGI BEEF SKILLET

Hearty and thick with beef, veggies and potatoes, this is a complete meal in one.
—*Taste of Home* Test Kitchen

- -

Takes: 25 min. • **Makes:** 4 servings

- 1   lb. ground beef
- ½   cup chopped onion
- ¼   cup all-purpose flour
- ½   tsp. Italian seasoning
- ½   tsp. pepper
- ⅛   tsp. salt
- 1   can (14½ oz.) beef broth
- 1   pkg. (16 oz.) frozen cheese and potato pierogi, thawed
- 2   cups frozen mixed vegetables (about 10 oz.), thawed and drained
- ½   cup shredded cheddar cheese

1. In a large cast-iron or other heavy skillet, cook and crumble beef with onion over medium heat until no longer pink, 5-7 minutes; drain, reserving 3 Tbsp. drippings. Stir in flour and seasonings until blended. Gradually stir in broth; bring to a boil. Cook and stir until thickened, 1-2 minutes.
2. Stir in pierogi and vegetables. Cook, uncovered, until heated through, about 5 minutes, stirring occasionally. Sprinkle with cheese.

1¾ cups: 654 cal., 31g fat (12g sat. fat), 102mg chol., 1157mg sod., 57g carb. (12g sugars, 7g fiber), 34g pro.

2. In the same skillet, heat the remaining oil over medium heat. Add onion; cook and stir 4-5 minutes or until tender. Add jalapeno and garlic; cook 2 minutes longer. Stir in salsa, cilantro, lime juice and pepper sauce; heat through.

3. Thinly slice the steak across the grain; stir into the onion mixture. Serve in tortillas; top as desired.

Note: Wear disposable gloves when cutting hot peppers; the oils can burn skin. Avoid touching your face.

2 tacos: 451 cal., 20g fat (7g sat. fat), 54mg chol., 884mg sod., 38g carb. (3g sugars, 4g fiber), 27g pro.

SKILLET BEEF & MACARONI

I found this recipe many years ago on a can label. My family loved it, and I always received compliments when I took the dish to potluck suppers. Since it's so easy to put together, it's a real timesaver for anyone with a busy schedule.
—Maxine Neuhauser, Arcadia, CA

Takes: 30 min. • **Makes:** 6 servings

- 1½ lb. ground beef
- ½ cup chopped onion
- 2 cans (8 oz. each) tomato sauce
- 1 cup water
- 1 pkg. (7 oz.) macaroni
- ½ cup chopped green pepper
- 2 Tbsp. Worcestershire sauce
- 1 tsp. salt
- ¼ tsp. pepper

In a large skillet over medium-high heat, cook beef and onion until the meat is no longer pink; drain. Stir in the remaining ingredients; bring to a boil. Reduce heat; simmer, covered, until macaroni is tender, stirring occasionally, 20-25 minutes. Add more water if needed.

1 cup: 317 cal., 11g fat (5g sat. fat), 56mg chol., 700mg sod., 29g carb. (3g sugars, 2g fiber), 25g pro.

CILANTRO BEEF TACOS

When I have leftover steak, it's time to make tacos. Set out bowls of toppings like lettuce, tomatoes, sour cream, avocado and salsa. That's a fiesta!
—Patti Rose, Tinley Park, IL

Takes: 30 min. • **Makes:** 4 servings

- 1 beef flank steak (1 lb.)
- ½ tsp. salt
- ¼ tsp. pepper
- 4 tsp. olive oil, divided
- 1 medium onion, halved and sliced
- 1 jalapeno pepper, seeded and finely chopped
- 1 garlic clove, minced
- ½ cup salsa
- ¼ cup minced fresh cilantro
- 2 tsp. lime juice
  Dash hot pepper sauce
- 8 flour tortillas (6 in.), warmed
  Optional: Salsa, cilantro, shredded lettuce and sour cream

1. Sprinkle the flank steak with salt and pepper. In a large skillet, heat 2 tsp. oil over medium-high heat. Add the steak; cook 5-7 minutes on each side or until the meat reaches desired doneness (for medium-rare, a thermometer should read 135°; medium, 140°; medium-well, 145°). Remove from pan.

Chicken

CHICKEN & GOAT CHEESE SKILLET

My husband was completely bowled over by this on-a-whim skillet meal. I can't wait to make it again!
—Ericka Barber, Eureka, CA

Takes: 20 min. • **Makes:** 2 servings

- ½ lb. boneless skinless chicken breasts, cut into 1-in. pieces
- ¼ tsp. salt
- ⅛ tsp. pepper
- 2 tsp. olive oil
- 1 cup cut fresh asparagus (1-in. pieces)
- 1 garlic clove, minced
- 3 plum tomatoes, chopped
- 3 Tbsp. 2% milk
- 2 Tbsp. herbed fresh goat cheese, crumbled
- Hot cooked rice or pasta
- Additional goat cheese, optional

1. Toss chicken with salt and pepper. In a large skillet, heat the oil over medium-high heat; saute chicken until no longer pink, 4-6 minutes. Remove from pan; keep warm.
2. Add asparagus to the skillet; cook and stir over medium-high heat for 1 minute. Add garlic; cook and stir 30 seconds. Stir in tomatoes, milk and 2 Tbsp. goat cheese; cook, covered, over medium heat until the cheese begins to melt, 2-3 minutes. Stir in the chicken. Serve with rice. If desired, top with additional goat cheese.

1½ cups chicken mixture: 251 cal., 11g fat (3g sat. fat), 74mg chol., 447mg sod., 8g carb. (5g sugars, 3g fiber), 29g pro. **Diabetic exchanges:** 4 lean meat, 2 fat, 1 vegetable.

ONE-PAN CHICKEN RICE CURRY

I've been loving the subtle spice from curry lately, so I incorporated it into this saucy chicken and rice dish. It's a one-pan meal that's become a go-to dinnertime favorite.
—Mary Lou Timpson, Colorado City, AZ

Takes: 30 min. • **Makes:** 4 servings

- 2 Tbsp. butter, divided
- 1 medium onion, halved and thinly sliced
- 2 Tbsp. all-purpose flour
- 3 tsp. curry powder
- ½ tsp. salt
- ½ tsp. pepper
- 1 lb. boneless skinless chicken breasts, cut into 1-in. pieces
- 1 can (14½ oz.) reduced-sodium chicken broth
- 1 cup uncooked Instant rice
- Chopped fresh cilantro leaves, optional

1. In a large nonstick skillet, heat 1 Tbsp. butter over medium-high heat; saute onion until tender and lightly browned, 3-5 minutes. Remove from pan.
2. In a bowl, mix flour and seasonings; toss with chicken. In the same skillet, heat the remaining butter over medium-high heat. Add the chicken; cook just until no longer pink, 4-6 minutes, turning occasionally.
3. Stir in broth and onion; bring to a boil. Stir in rice. Remove from heat; let stand, covered, 5 minutes (mixture will be saucy). If desired, sprinkle with cilantro.

1 cup: 300 cal., 9g fat (4g sat. fat), 78mg chol., 658mg sod., 27g carb. (2g sugars, 2g fiber), 27g pro. **Diabetic exchanges:** 3 lean meat, 2 starch, 1½ fat.

SAVORY BRAISED CHICKEN WITH VEGETABLES

Pick up a fresh baguette to serve with this hearty dish. You'll want it to soak up every last bit of savory veggie-laden broth!
—Michelle Collins, Lake Orion, MI

Prep: 15 min. • **Cook:** 40 min.
Makes: 6 servings

- ½ cup seasoned bread crumbs
- 6 boneless skinless chicken breast halves (4 oz. each)
- 2 Tbsp. olive oil
- 1 can (14½ oz.) beef broth
- 2 Tbsp. tomato paste
- 1 tsp. poultry seasoning
- ½ tsp. salt
- ½ tsp. pepper
- 1 lb. fresh baby carrots
- 1 lb. sliced fresh mushrooms
- 2 medium zucchini, sliced
  Sliced French bread baguette, optional

1. Place bread crumbs in a shallow bowl. Dip chicken breasts in the bread crumbs to coat both sides; shake off excess.
2. In a Dutch oven, heat oil over medium heat. Add the chicken in batches; cook 2-4 minutes on each side or until browned. Remove chicken from pan.
3. Add broth, tomato paste and seasonings to the same pan; cook over medium-high heat, stirring to loosen browned bits from pan. Add the vegetables and chicken; bring to a boil. Reduce heat; simmer, covered, 25-30 minutes or until vegetables are tender and a thermometer inserted in chicken reads 165°. If desired, serve with baguette.

1 chicken breast half with 1 cup vegetable mixture: 247 cal., 8g fat (1g sat. fat), 63mg chol., 703mg sod., 16g carb. (6g sugars, 3g fiber), 28g pro. **Diabetic exchanges:** 3 lean meat, 2 vegetable, 1 fat, ½ starch.

ROSEMARY CHICKEN WITH SPINACH & BEANS

With two young boys constantly on the go, I'm always looking for ways to simplify evening meals. This recipe uses just one skillet, making it a cinch to prepare dinner for a hungry family in half an hour.
—Sara Richardson, Littleton, CO

Takes: 30 min. • **Makes:** 4 servings

- 1 can (14½ oz.) stewed tomatoes
- 4 boneless skinless chicken breast halves (6 oz. each)
- 2 tsp. dried rosemary, crushed
- ½ tsp. salt
- ½ tsp. pepper
- 4 tsp. olive oil, divided
- 1 pkg. (6 oz.) fresh baby spinach
- 2 garlic cloves, minced
- 1 can (15 oz.) cannellini beans, rinsed and drained

1. Drain tomatoes, reserving the juice; coarsely chop tomatoes. Pound chicken with a meat mallet to ¼-in. thickness. Rub with rosemary, salt and pepper. In a large skillet, heat 2 tsp. oil over medium heat. Add chicken; cook 5-6 minutes on each side or until no longer pink. Remove and keep warm.
2. In same pan, heat the remaining oil over medium-high heat. Add spinach and garlic; cook and stir 2-3 minutes or until the spinach is wilted. Stir in beans, tomatoes and reserved juice; heat through. Serve with chicken.

1 chicken breast half with ¾ cup sauce: 348 cal., 9g fat (2g sat. fat), 94mg chol., 729mg sod., 25g carb. (5g sugars, 6g fiber), 41g pro. **Diabetic exchanges:** 5 lean meat, 2 vegetable, 1 starch, 1 fat.

TASTY TURKEY SKILLET

I like to use boxed rice and pasta mixes as the bases for quick meals. This colorful dish is simple to cook on the stovetop using a fried rice mix, tender turkey and convenient frozen vegetables.
—Betty Kleberger, Florissant, MO

- -

Prep: 10 min. • **Cook:** 35 min.
Makes: 4 servings

- 1 lb. turkey breast tenderloins, cut into ¼-in. strips
- 1 pkg. (6.2 oz.) fried rice mix
- 1 Tbsp. butter
- 2 cups water
- ⅛ tsp. cayenne pepper
- 1½ cups frozen corn, thawed
- 1 cup frozen broccoli cuts, thawed
- 2 Tbsp. chopped sweet red pepper, optional

1. In a skillet coated with cooking spray, cook turkey over medium heat until no longer pink; drain. Remove turkey from skillet and keep warm.

2. Set aside the seasoning packet from the rice. In the same skillet, saute rice in butter until lightly browned. Stir in the water, cayenne and contents of the seasoning packet.

3. Bring to a boil. Reduce heat; cover and simmer for 15 minutes. Stir in corn, broccoli, red pepper (if desired) and turkey. Return to a boil. Reduce heat; cover and simmer until the rice and vegetables are tender, 6-8 minutes.

1¼ cups: 351 cal., 6g fat (2g sat. fat), 53mg chol., 971mg sod., 43g carb. (4g sugars, 4g fiber), 35g pro.

GRECIAN CHICKEN

Caper, tomato and olive flavors whisk you away to the Greek isles in this easy skillet dish that's perfect for hectic weeknights.
—Jan Marler, Murchison, TX

Takes: 30 min. • **Makes:** 4 servings

3	tsp. olive oil, divided
1	lb. chicken tenderloins
2	medium tomatoes, sliced
1	cup sliced fresh mushrooms
½	cup chopped onion
1	Tbsp. capers, drained
1	Tbsp. lemon-pepper seasoning
1	Tbsp. salt-free Greek seasoning
1	medium garlic clove, minced
½	cup water
2	Tbsp. chopped ripe olives
	Hot cooked orzo pasta, optional

1. In a large skillet, heat 2 tsp. oil over medium heat. Add chicken; saute until no longer pink, 7-9 minutes. Remove and keep warm.
2. In same skillet, heat the remaining oil; add the next 6 ingredients. Cook and stir until onion is translucent, 2-3 minutes. Stir in garlic; cook 1 minute more. Add water; bring to a boil. Reduce heat and simmer, uncovered, until the vegetables are tender, 3-4 minutes. Return chicken to skillet; add olives. Simmer, uncovered, until the chicken is heated through, 2-3 minutes. If desired, serve with orzo.
1 serving: 172 cal., 5g fat (1g sat. fat), 56mg chol., 393mg sod., 6g carb. (3g sugars, 2g fiber), 28g pro. **Diabetic exchanges:** 3 lean meat, 1 vegetable, 1 fat.

CHICKEN THIGHS WITH SHALLOTS & SPINACH

What could be better than an entree that comes with its own creamy vegetable side? It makes an eye-catching presentation and goes together in no time flat for a healthy and delicious supper.
—Genna Johannes, Wrightstown, WI

Takes: 30 min. • **Makes:** 6 servings

6	boneless skinless chicken thighs (about 1½ lbs.)
½	tsp. seasoned salt
½	tsp. pepper
1½	tsp. olive oil
4	shallots, thinly sliced
⅓	cup white wine or reduced-sodium chicken broth
1	pkg. (10 oz.) fresh spinach, trimmed
¼	tsp. salt
¼	cup reduced-fat sour cream

1. Sprinkle chicken with seasoned salt and pepper. In a large nonstick skillet, heat oil over medium heat. Add the chicken; cook until a thermometer reads 170°, about 6 minutes on each side. Remove chicken from pan; keep warm.
2. In the same pan, cook and stir sliced shallots until tender. Add wine; bring to a boil. Cook until the wine is reduced by half. Add spinach and salt; cook and stir just until the spinach is wilted. Stir in the sour cream; serve with chicken.
Freeze option: Before adding sour cream, cool the chicken and spinach mixture. Freeze in freezer containers. To use, partially thaw in refrigerator overnight. Heat through slowly in a covered skillet, stirring occasionally, until a thermometer inserted in the chicken reads 170°. Stir in sour cream.
1 chicken thigh with ¼ cup spinach mixture: 223 cal., 10g fat (3g sat. fat), 77mg chol., 360mg sod., 7g carb. (2g sugars, 1g fiber), 23g pro. **Diabetic exchanges:** 3 lean meat, 1½ fat, 1 vegetable.

BULGUR JAMBALAYA

I like making this dish because it allows me to stay on track for my weight-loss target without giving up foods I love!
—Nicholas Monfre, Oak Ridge, NJ

Takes: 30 min. • **Makes:** 4 servings

- 8 oz. boneless skinless chicken breasts, cut into ¾-in. pieces
- 1 tsp. Cajun seasoning
- 2 tsp. olive oil
- 6 oz. smoked turkey sausage, sliced
- 1 medium sweet red pepper, diced
- 2 celery ribs, diced
- 1 small onion, chopped
- ½ cup no-salt-added tomato sauce
- 1 cup bulgur
- 1 cup reduced-sodium chicken broth
- ¾ cup water
- ¼ tsp. cayenne pepper, optional

1. Toss chicken with Cajun seasoning. In a large saucepan, heat oil over medium heat; saute chicken until browned, 2-3 minutes. Remove from pan.
2. In the same pan, saute sausage until browned, 1-2 minutes. Add red pepper, celery and onion; cook and stir 2 minutes. Stir in tomato sauce; cook 30 seconds. Stir in bulgur, broth, water, chicken and, if desired, cayenne; bring to a boil. Reduce heat; simmer, covered, until the bulgur is tender and the liquid is almost absorbed, about 10 minutes, stirring occasionally.
1 cup: 287 cal., 6g fat (2g sat. fat), 58mg chol., 751mg sod., 34g carb. (5g sugars, 6g fiber), 24g pro. **Diabetic exchanges:** 3 lean meat, 2 starch, ½ fat.

ISRAELI COUSCOUS & CHICKEN SAUSAGE SKILLET

Craving a plate full of comfort? This all-in-one skillet dinner is hearty, satisfying and a little bit different.
—Angela Spengler, Niceville, FL

Takes: 30 min. • **Makes:** 4 servings

- 2 tsp. olive oil
- 1 pkg. (12 oz.) fully cooked spinach and feta chicken sausage links or flavor of your choice, sliced
- 1 small onion, finely chopped
- 1 celery rib, finely chopped
- 1 garlic clove, minced
- 1 cup reduced-sodium chicken broth
- 1 cup water
- ¼ tsp. crushed red pepper flakes
- 1¼ cups uncooked pearl (Israeli) couscous
- 2 Tbsp. minced fresh parsley
- ¼ cup crumbled feta cheese, optional

1. In a large nonstick skillet, heat oil over medium-high heat. Add sausage, onion and celery; cook and stir 6-8 minutes or until the sausage is browned. Add garlic; cook 1 minute longer.
2. Stir in broth, water and pepper flakes; bring to a boil. Stir in couscous. Reduce heat; simmer, covered, 10-12 minutes or until liquid is absorbed. Remove from heat; let stand, covered, 5 minutes. Stir in parsley. If desired, sprinkle with feta cheese.
1 cup: 343 cal., 10g fat (3g sat. fat), 65mg chol., 694mg sod., 41g carb. (1g sugars, 1g fiber), 22g pro. **Diabetic exchanges:** 3 starch, 3 lean meat, ½ fat.

CHICKEN VEGGIE SKILLET

I concocted this chicken and veggie dish to use up extra mushrooms and asparagus. My husband raved over it and asked me to write it down because it's a keeper.
—Rebekah Beyer, Sabetha, KS

Takes: 30 min. • **Makes:** 6 servings

- 1½ lbs. boneless skinless chicken breasts, cut into ½-in. strips
- ½ tsp. salt
- ¼ tsp. pepper
- 6 tsp. olive oil, divided
- ½ lb. sliced fresh mushrooms
- 1 small onion, halved and sliced
- 2 garlic cloves, minced
- 1 lb. fresh asparagus, trimmed and cut into 1-in. pieces
- ½ cup sherry or chicken stock
- 2 Tbsp. cold butter, cubed

1. Sprinkle chicken strips with salt and pepper. In a large skillet, heat 1 tsp. olive oil over medium-high heat. Add half the chicken; cook and stir until no longer pink, 3-4 minutes. Remove from pan. Repeat with another 1 tsp. oil and the remaining chicken.
2. In the same pan, heat 2 tsp. oil. Add the mushrooms and onion; cook and stir for 2-3 minutes or until tender. Add garlic; cook 1 minute longer. Add to chicken.
3. Heat the remaining oil in the same pan. Add the asparagus; cook for 2-3 minutes or until crisp-tender. Add to the chicken and mushrooms.
4. Add sherry to skillet, stirring to loosen browned bits from pan. Bring to a boil; cook 1-2 minutes or until liquid is reduced to 2 Tbsp.. Return chicken and vegetables to pan; heat through. Remove from heat; stir in butter, 1 Tbsp. at a time.
1 cup: 228 cal., 11g fat (4g sat. fat), 73mg chol., 384mg sod., 6g carb. (2g sugars, 1g fiber), 25g pro. **Diabetic exchanges:** 3 lean meat, 2 fat, 1 vegetable.

SPANISH RICE WITH CHICKEN & PEAS

This dish reminds me of my wonderful family dinners growing up. My mom made this juicy chicken and rice for us every Wednesday, and now I make it for my family.
—Josee Lanzi, New Port Richey, FL

Prep: 15 min. • **Cook:** 30 min.
Makes: 6 servings

- 1 lb. boneless skinless chicken breasts, cut into 1½-in. pieces
- 1 Tbsp. all-purpose flour
- ½ tsp. pepper
- ½ tsp. salt, divided
- 4 tsp. plus 1 Tbsp. olive oil, divided
- 1 small sweet red pepper, chopped
- 1 small onion, chopped
- 1 celery rib, chopped
- 1½ cups uncooked long grain rice
- 1 tsp. ground cumin
- 1 tsp. chili powder
- 2¼ cups chicken broth
- 1 can (14½ oz.) diced tomatoes, undrained
- 1 cup frozen peas, thawed

1. In a small bowl, toss chicken with flour, pepper and ¼ tsp. salt. In a Dutch oven, heat 4 tsp. oil over medium-high heat. Brown chicken, stirring occasionally; remove from pan.
2. In the same pan, heat the remaining oil over medium heat. Add pepper, onion and celery; cook and stir until onion is tender, 2-4 minutes. Add rice, cumin, chili powder and the remaining salt; stir to coat rice. Stir in the remaining ingredients; bring to a boil. Reduce heat; simmer, covered, 10 minutes.
3. Place browned chicken over rice (do not stir in). Cook, covered, until the rice is tender and the chicken is cooked through, about 5 minutes longer.
1½ cups: 367 cal., 8g fat (1g sat. fat), 44mg chol., 755mg sod., 50g carb. (5g sugars, 4g fiber), 22g pro. **Diabetic exchanges:** 3 starch, 2 lean meat, 1 vegetable, 1 fat.

FLAVORFUL CHICKEN FAJITAS

This chicken fajita recipe is definitely on my weeknight dinner rotation. The marinated chicken in these wraps is mouthwatering. They go together in a snap and always get rave reviews!

—Julie Sterchi, Campbellsville, KY

- -

Prep: 20 min. + marinating • **Cook:** 10 min.
Makes: 6 servings

- 4 Tbsp. canola oil, divided
- 2 Tbsp. lemon juice
- 1½ tsp. seasoned salt
- 1½ tsp. dried oregano
- 1½ tsp. ground cumin
- 1 tsp. garlic powder
- ½ tsp. chili powder
- ½ tsp. paprika
- ½ tsp. crushed red pepper flakes, optional
- 1½ lbs. boneless skinless chicken breast, cut into thin strips
- ½ medium sweet red pepper, julienned
- ½ medium green pepper, julienned
- 4 green onions, thinly sliced
- ½ cup chopped onion
- 6 flour tortillas (8 in.), warmed
   Optional: Shredded cheddar cheese, taco sauce, salsa, guacamole and sour cream

1. In a large bowl, combine 2 Tbsp. oil, lemon juice and seasonings; add chicken. Turn to coat; cover. Refrigerate 1-4 hours.

2. In a large skillet, saute the peppers and onions in remaining oil until crisp-tender. Remove and keep warm.

3. Drain chicken, discarding marinade. In the same skillet, cook chicken strips over medium-high heat for 5-6 minutes or until no longer pink. Return pepper mixture to pan; heat through.

4. Spoon filling down the center of tortillas; fold in half. Serve with toppings as desired.

1 fajita: 369 cal., 15g fat (2g sat. fat), 63mg chol., 689mg sod., 30g carb. (2g sugars, 1g fiber), 28g pro. **Diabetic exchanges:** 3 lean meat, 2 starch, 2 fat.

DID YOU KNOW?

Oregano is used frequently in Latin American cuisine. Mexican oregano has a more citrusy, peppery bite than the sweeter Mediterranean oregano, but the flavors are similar and the two varieties can be used interchangeably.

COUSCOUS & SAUSAGE-STUFFED ACORN SQUASH

With a tiny apartment, zero counter space and only two people to feed, hefty meals are out. This acorn squash with couscous is just the right size. While the squash cooks in the microwave, the filling comes together in a skillet.
—Jessica Levinson, Nyack, NY

Takes: 25 min. • **Makes:** 2 servings

- 1 **medium acorn squash (about 1½ lbs.)**
- ¼ **tsp. salt**
- ¼ **tsp. pepper**
- 1 **Tbsp. olive oil**
- 1 **medium onion, chopped**
- 2 **fully cooked spinach and feta chicken sausage links (3 oz. each), sliced**
- ½ **cup chicken stock**
- ½ **cup uncooked couscous**
  Crumbled feta cheese, optional

1. Cut squash lengthwise in half; remove and discard seeds. Sprinkle squash with salt and pepper; place in a microwave-safe dish, cut side down. Microwave, covered, on high for 10-12 minutes or until tender.
2. Meanwhile, in a large skillet, heat oil over medium heat. Add onion; cook and stir 5-7 minutes or until tender and lightly browned. Add sliced sausage; cook and stir 2-3 minutes or until lightly browned.
3. Add chicken stock; bring to a boil. Stir in couscous. Remove from heat; let stand, covered, until stock is absorbed, about 5 minutes. Spoon over squash. If desired, top with feta cheese.
1 serving: 521 cal., 15g fat (4g sat. fat), 65mg chol., 979mg sod., 77g carb. (11g sugars, 8g fiber), 25g pro.

THAI CHICKEN PASTA SKILLET

This gorgeous Bangkok-style pasta has been a faithful standby for many years and always gets loads of praise. For a potluck, we double the recipe and make it ahead.
—Susan Ten Pas, Myrtle Creek, OR

Prep: 15 min. • **Cook:** 15 min.
Makes: 6 servings

- 6 oz. uncooked whole wheat spaghetti
- 2 tsp. canola oil
- 1 package (10 oz.) fresh sugar snap peas, trimmed and cut diagonally into strips
- 2 cups julienned carrots
- 2 cups shredded cooked chicken
- 1 cup Thai peanut sauce
- 1 medium cucumber, halved lengthwise, seeded and sliced diagonally
  Chopped fresh cilantro, optional

1. Cook spaghetti according to package directions; drain.

2. Meanwhile, in a large skillet, heat oil over medium-high heat. Add snap peas and carrots; stir-fry 6-8 minutes or until vegetables are crisp-tender. Add chicken, peanut sauce and spaghetti; heat through, tossing to combine.

3. Transfer to a serving plate. Top with cucumber and, if desired, cilantro.

1⅓ cups: 403 cal., 15g fat (3g sat. fat), 42mg chol., 432mg sod., 43g carb. (15g sugars, 6g fiber), 25g pro. **Diabetic exchanges:** 3 lean meat, 2½ starch, 2 fat, 1 vegetable.

CACCIATORE CHICKEN BREASTS

This easy recipe is my version of traditional chicken cacciatore. The tasty sauce and chicken can be served over rice or noodles. If you want to lower the sodium, use garlic powder instead of garlic salt.
—JoAnn McCauley, Dubuque, IA

Takes: 30 min. • **Makes:** 2 servings

- ½ medium onion, sliced and separated into rings
- ½ medium green pepper, sliced
- 1 Tbsp. olive oil
- 2 boneless skinless chicken breast halves (5 oz. each)
- ¾ cup canned stewed tomatoes
- 2 Tbsp. white wine or chicken broth
- ¼ tsp. garlic salt
- ¼ tsp. dried rosemary, crushed
- ⅛ tsp. pepper

1. In a large skillet, saute onion and green pepper in oil until crisp-tender. Remove and keep warm. Cook chicken over medium-high heat until juices run clear, 4-5 minutes on each side. Remove and set aside.

2. Add the tomatoes, wine, garlic salt, rosemary and pepper to the skillet. Stir in the onion mixture and heat through. Serve with chicken.

1 chicken breast half with ¾ cup sauce: 272 cal., 10g fat (2g sat. fat), 78mg chol., 462mg sod., 12g carb. (7g sugars, 2g fiber), 30g pro. **Diabetic exchanges:** 4 lean meat, 2 vegetable, 1½ fat.

TURKEY THYME RISOTTO

This satisfying risotto is a wonderful way to reinvent leftover turkey. I use Romano cheese, garlic and plenty of fresh mushrooms to create it.
—Sunny McDaniel, Cary, NC

Prep: 10 min. • **Cook:** 35 min.
Makes: 4 servings

2¾ to 3¼ cups reduced-sodium chicken broth
1 Tbsp. olive oil
2 cups sliced fresh mushrooms
1 small onion, chopped
1 garlic clove, minced
1 cup uncooked arborio rice
1 tsp. minced fresh thyme or ¼ tsp. dried thyme
½ cup white wine or additional broth
1½ cups cubed cooked turkey breast
2 Tbsp. shredded Romano cheese
¼ tsp. salt
¼ tsp. pepper

1. In a small saucepan, bring broth to a simmer; keep hot. In a large nonstick skillet, heat oil over medium-high heat; saute mushrooms, onion and garlic until tender, about 3 minutes. Add rice and thyme; cook and stir 2 minutes.
2. Stir in wine. Reduce heat to maintain a simmer; cook and stir until the wine is absorbed. Add the hot broth, ½ cup at a time, cooking and stirring after each addition until the broth has been absorbed. Continue until the rice is tender but firm to the bite, and the risotto is creamy. (This will take about 20 minutes.)
3. Add remaining ingredients; cook and stir until heated through. Serve immediately.
1 cup: 337 cal., 6g fat (2g sat. fat), 43mg chol., 651mg sod., 44g carb. (2g sugars, 1g fiber), 24g pro. **Diabetic exchanges:** 3 starch, 2 lean meat, ½ fat.

SUPER QUICK CHICKEN FRIED RICE

After my first child was born, I needed meals that were satisfying and fast. This dish is now part of our routine dinners.
—Alicia Gower, Auburn, NY

Takes: 30 min. • **Makes:** 6 servings

1 pkg. (12 oz.) frozen mixed vegetables
2 Tbsp. olive oil, divided
2 large eggs, lightly beaten
4 Tbsp. sesame oil, divided
3 pkg. (8.8 oz. each) ready-to-serve garden vegetable rice
1 rotisserie chicken, skin removed, shredded
¼ tsp. salt
¼ tsp. pepper

1. Prepare frozen vegetables according to package directions. Meanwhile, in a large skillet, heat 1 Tbsp. oil over medium-high heat. Pour in beaten eggs; cook and stir until thickened and no liquid egg remains. Remove from pan.
2. In the same skillet, heat 2 Tbsp. sesame oil and the remaining olive oil. Add rice; cook and stir until the rice begins to brown, 10-12 minutes.
3. Stir in chicken, salt and pepper. Add eggs and vegetables; heat through, breaking the eggs into small pieces and stirring to combine. Drizzle with remaining sesame oil.
1½ cups: 548 cal., 25g fat (5g sat. fat), 163mg chol., 934mg sod., 43g carb. (3g sugars, 3g fiber), 38g pro.

SPICY CHICKEN LETTUCE WRAPS

This is one of my go-to meals when I want a fun dinner. I love the spicy Asian flavors against the cool lettuce and the added crunch of peanuts and water chestnuts.
—Brittany Allyn, Mesa, AZ

Takes: 30 min. • **Makes:** 4 servings

- 1 **lb. chicken tenderloins, cut into ½-in. pieces**
- ⅛ **tsp. pepper**
- 2 **Tbsp. canola oil, divided**
- 1 **medium onion, finely chopped**
- 1 **small green pepper, finely chopped**
- 1 **small sweet red pepper, finely chopped**
- 1 **can (8 oz.) sliced water chestnuts, drained and finely chopped**
- 1 **can (4 oz.) mushroom stems and pieces, drained and finely chopped**
- 2 **garlic cloves, minced**
- ⅓ **cup stir-fry sauce**
- 1 **tsp. reduced-sodium soy sauce**
- 8 **Bibb or Boston lettuce leaves**
- ¼ **cup salted peanuts**
- 2 **tsp. minced fresh cilantro**

1. Sprinkle chicken with pepper. In a large skillet or wok, stir-fry chicken in 1 Tbsp. oil until no longer pink. Remove and set aside.
2. Stir-fry the onion and peppers in the remaining oil for 5 minutes. Add the water chestnuts, mushrooms and garlic; stir-fry 2-3 minutes longer or until the vegetables are crisp-tender. Add stir-fry sauce and soy sauce. Stir in the chicken; heat through.
3. Place ½ cup chicken mixture on each lettuce leaf; sprinkle each with 1½ tsp. peanuts and ¼ tsp. cilantro. Fold lettuce over filling.
Note: This recipe was tested with House of Tsang Saigon Sizzle Sauce.
2 each: 303 cal., 12g fat (1g sat. fat), 67mg chol., 981mg sod., 20g carb. (7g sugars, 4g fiber), 32g pro.

CHICKEN SAUSAGES WITH POLENTA

I get a kick out of serving this dish— everyone's always on time for dinner when they know it's on the menu.
—Angela Spengler, Niceville, FL

Takes: 30 min. • **Makes:** 6 servings

- 4 **tsp. olive oil, divided**
- 1 **tube (1 lb.) polenta, cut into ½-in. slices**
- 1 **each medium green, sweet red and yellow peppers, thinly sliced**
- 1 **medium onion, thinly sliced**
- 1 **pkg. (12 oz.) fully cooked Italian chicken sausage links, thinly sliced**
- ¼ **cup grated Parmesan cheese**
- 1 **Tbsp. minced fresh basil**

1. In a large nonstick skillet, heat 2 tsp. oil over medium heat. Add polenta; cook until golden brown, 9-11 minutes on each side. Keep warm.
2. Meanwhile, in another large skillet, heat the remaining oil over medium-high heat. Add peppers and onion; cook and stir until tender. Remove from pan.
3. Add sausages to the same pan; cook and stir for 4-5 minutes or until browned. Return the pepper mixture to pan; heat through. Serve with polenta; sprinkle with cheese and basil.
⅔ cup sausage mixture with 2 slices polenta: 212 cal., 9g fat (2g sat. fat), 46mg chol., 628mg sod., 19g carb. (4g sugars, 2g fiber), 13g pro. **Diabetic exchanges:** 2 lean meat, 1 starch, 1 vegetable, ½ fat.

CHICKEN BURRITO SKILLET

We love Mexican night at our house, and I love to re-create dishes from our favorite restaurants. This burrito-inspired dish is ready for the table in almost no time!
—Krista Marshall, Fort Wayne, IN

- -

Prep: 15 min. • **Cook:** 30 min.
Makes: 6 servings

- 1 lb. boneless skinless chicken breasts, cut into 1½-in. pieces
- ⅛ tsp. salt
- ⅛ tsp. pepper
- 2 Tbsp. olive oil, divided
- 1 cup uncooked long grain rice
- 1 can (15 oz.) black beans, rinsed and drained
- 1 can (14½ oz.) diced tomatoes, drained
- 1 tsp. ground cumin
- ½ tsp. onion powder
- ½ tsp. garlic powder
- ½ tsp. chili powder
- 2½ cups reduced-sodium chicken broth
- 1 cup shredded Mexican cheese blend
- 1 medium tomato, chopped
- 3 green onions, chopped

1. Toss chicken with salt and pepper. In a large cast-iron or other heavy skillet, heat 1 Tbsp. oil over medium-high heat; saute the chicken until browned, about 2 minutes. Remove from pan.

2. In the same pan, heat the remaining oil over medium-high heat; saute rice until lightly browned, 1-2 minutes. Stir in beans, canned tomatoes, seasonings and broth; bring to a boil. Place the chicken on top (do not stir into rice). Simmer, covered, until the rice is tender and the chicken is no longer pink, 20-25 minutes.

3. Remove from heat; sprinkle with cheese. Let stand, covered, until cheese is melted. Top with tomato and green onions.

1⅓ cups: 403 cal., 13g fat (4g sat. fat), 58mg chol., 690mg sod., 43g carb. (4g sugars, 5g fiber), 27g pro. **Diabetic exchanges:** 3 starch, 3 lean meat, 1½ fat.

TEST KITCHEN TIP

Any can of beans you have in your pantry will taste great in this recipe. We particularly like pintos and kidney beans here. Bump up the health factor by using brown rice instead of white.

DILLED CHICKEN & ASPARAGUS

If a delicious chicken and rice entree is what you're craving, look no further than this mild herb-flavored rice dish with tender asparagus.
—Mary Ann Marino, West Pittsburgh, PA

Takes: 30 min. • **Makes:** 2 servings

- ½ cup uncooked long grain rice
- 1 tsp. chicken bouillon granules
- 1½ cups water, divided
- 2 Tbsp. minced fresh parsley
- 1 Tbsp. lemon juice
- 2 tsp. olive oil
- 1½ tsp. dill weed
- ⅛ tsp. salt
- 9 fresh asparagus spears, cut into 2-in. pieces
- ½ lb. boneless skinless chicken breasts, cut into 1-in. cubes

1. In a small saucepan, bring rice, bouillon and 1 cup water to a boil. Reduce heat; cover and simmer for 15-18 minutes or until the liquid is absorbed and the rice is tender.

2. Meanwhile, combine parsley, lemon juice, oil, dill and salt; set aside. In a large nonstick skillet, bring the remaining water to a boil. Add the asparagus; cover and boil for 3 minutes. Drain and immediately place the asparagus in ice water. Drain and pat dry.

3. Coat the same skillet with cooking spray; saute chicken until juices run clear, then drain. Add the rice, asparagus and lemon mixture; toss to coat.

1¼ cups: 356 cal., 8g fat (2g sat. fat), 63mg chol., 371mg sod., 42g carb. (2g sugars, 2g fiber), 28g pro.

CHICKEN MARSALA WITH GORGONZOLA

Chicken topped with melting Gorgonzola is quick enough for weeknight cooking but also elegant enough for a dinner party. We live near the caves in Faribault, Minnesota, that are used to age the lovely AmaBlu Gorgonzola cheese, so this is a particular favorite for us.
—Jill Anderson, Sleepy Eye, MN

Prep: 10 min. • **Cook:** 30 min.
Makes: 4 servings

- 4   boneless skinless chicken breast halves (6 oz. each)
- ¼   tsp. plus ⅛ tsp. salt, divided
- ¼   tsp. pepper
- 3   Tbsp. olive oil, divided
- ½   lb. sliced baby portobello mushrooms
- 2   garlic cloves, minced
- 1   cup Marsala wine
- ⅔   cup heavy whipping cream
- ½   cup crumbled Gorgonzola cheese, divided
- 2   Tbsp. minced fresh parsley

1. Sprinkle the chicken with ¼ tsp. salt and pepper. In a large skillet, cook the chicken in 2 Tbsp. oil over medium heat for 6-8 minutes on each side or until a thermometer reads 165°. Remove and keep warm.
2. In the same skillet, saute mushrooms in remaining oil until tender. Add garlic; cook 1 minute.
3. Add wine, stirring to loosen browned bits from pan. Bring to a boil; cook until liquid is reduced by a third. Stir in cream and the remaining salt. Return to a boil; cook until slightly thickened.
4. Return chicken to pan; add ⅓ cup cheese. Cook until the cheese is melted. Sprinkle with remaining cheese; garnish with parsley.
1 serving: 514 cal., 33g fat (15g sat. fat), 161mg chol., 514mg sod., 8g carb. (3g sugars, 1g fiber), 40g pro.

STOVETOP TARRAGON CHICKEN

My oldest daughter can't get enough of the tarragon sauce in this dish. She uses biscuits to soak up every drop. My husband and I like it over mashed potatoes.
—Tina Westover, La Mesa, CA

Prep: 10 min. • **Cook:** 30 min.
Makes: 4 servings

- 4   boneless skinless chicken breast halves (5 oz. each)
- 2   tsp. paprika
- 1   Tbsp. olive oil
- 1   pkg. (10 oz.) julienned carrots
- ½   lb. sliced fresh mushrooms
- 2   cans (10¾ oz. each) reduced-fat reduced-sodium condensed cream of chicken soup, undiluted
- 3   tsp. dried tarragon
- 1   Tbsp. lemon juice
- 3   small zucchini, thinly sliced

1. Sprinkle chicken with paprika. In a Dutch oven, heat oil over medium heat. Cook chicken 2 minutes on each side or until lightly browned; remove from pan.
2. Add the carrots and mushrooms to the same pan; cook, covered, for 6-8 minutes or until carrots are crisp-tender, stirring occasionally.
3. In a small bowl, mix soup, tarragon and lemon juice until blended; pour over the vegetables. Return the chicken to pan. Bring to a boil; reduce heat to low. Cook, covered, 8 minutes.
4. Top with zucchini; cook, covered, for 6-8 minutes longer or until a thermometer inserted in the chicken reads 165° and the vegetables are tender.
1 chicken breast with 1 cup vegetables: 345 cal., 11g fat (3g sat. fat), 85mg chol., 649mg sod., 28g carb. (16g sugars, 5g fiber), 35g pro. **Diabetic exchanges:** 4 lean meat, 2 vegetable, 1 starch, 1 fat.

JERK CHICKEN WITH TROPICAL COUSCOUS

Caribbean cuisine brightens up our weeknights thanks to its bold colors and flavors. Done in less than 30 minutes, this chicken is one of my go-to easy meals.
—Jeanne Holt, Mendota Heights, MN

Takes: 25 min. • **Makes:** 4 servings

1 can (15.25 oz.) mixed tropical fruit
1 lb. boneless skinless chicken breasts, cut into 2½-in. strips
3 tsp. Caribbean jerk seasoning
1 Tbsp. olive oil
½ cup chopped sweet red pepper
1 Tbsp. finely chopped seeded jalapeno pepper
⅓ cup thinly sliced green onions (green portion only)
1½ cups reduced-sodium chicken broth
3 Tbsp. chopped fresh cilantro, divided
1 Tbsp. lime juice
¼ tsp. salt
1 cup uncooked whole wheat couscous
Lime wedges

1. Drain mixed fruit, reserving ¼ cup syrup. Chop fruit.

2. Toss the chicken with jerk seasoning. In a large cast-iron or other heavy skillet, heat oil over medium-high heat; saute chicken until no longer pink, 4-5 minutes. Remove from pan, reserving drippings.

3. In the same pan, saute peppers and green onions in the drippings for 2 minutes. Add the broth, 1 Tbsp. cilantro, lime juice, salt, reserved syrup and chopped fruit; bring to a boil. Stir in couscous; reduce heat to low. Place chicken on top; cook, covered, until liquid is absorbed and chicken is heated through, 3-4 minutes. Sprinkle with the remaining cilantro. Serve with lime wedges.

1½ cups: 411 cal., 7g fat (1g sat. fat), 63mg chol., 628mg sod., 57g carb. (19g sugars, 7g fiber), 31g pro.

DID YOU KNOW?

Jamaican jerk seasoning is traditionally a mix of chiles, thyme, spices (cinnamon, ginger, allspice, cloves, etc.), garlic and onions. It's usually applied as a dry blend for grilled meats, but can also be a marinade.

CHICKEN & VEGETABLE CURRY COUSCOUS

I find that a semi-homemade one-pot meal is the best way to get dinner done in a hurry. Use your family's favorite blend of frozen veggies and serve with toasted pita bread for smiles all around.
—Elizabeth Hokanson, Arborg, MB

Takes: 25 min. • **Makes:** 6 servings

- 1 Tbsp. butter
- 1 lb. boneless skinless chicken breasts, cut into strips
- 1 pkg. (16 oz.) frozen vegetable blend of your choice
- 1¼ cups water
- 1 pkg. (5.7 oz.) curry-flavored couscous mix
- ½ cup raisins

1. In a large nonstick skillet, heat butter over medium-high heat. Add chicken; cook and stir until no longer pink.

2. Add vegetable blend, water and contents of the couscous seasoning packet. Bring to a boil; stir in couscous and raisins. Remove from heat; let stand, covered, until water is absorbed, about 5 minutes. Fluff mixture with a fork.

1 cup: 273 cal., 4g fat (2g sat. fat), 47mg chol., 311mg sod., 39g carb. (9g sugars, 4g fiber), 21g pro. **Diabetic exchanges:** 2 starch, 2 lean meat, 1 vegetable, ½ fat.

CHICKEN ORZO SKILLET

Here's a great one-skillet supper that's colorful, healthy, filling and definitely special! The blend of spices, the touch of heat and the sophisticated flavor make this dish a must-try.
—Kellie Mulleavy, Lambertville, MI

Prep: 15 min. • **Cook:** 20 min.
Makes: 4 servings

- 1 lb. boneless skinless chicken breasts, cut into ½-in. strips
- 2 tsp. salt-free garlic seasoning blend
- 1 small onion, chopped
- 1 Tbsp. olive oil
- 1 garlic clove, minced
- 1 can (14½ oz.) diced tomatoes, undrained
- 1 pkg. (10 oz.) frozen chopped spinach, thawed and squeezed dry
- 1 cup reduced-sodium chicken broth
- ¾ cup uncooked orzo pasta
- 1 tsp. Italian seasoning
- ⅛ tsp. crushed red pepper flakes, optional
- ¼ cup grated Parmesan cheese, optional

1. Sprinkle the chicken strips with garlic seasoning blend. In a large cast-iron or other heavy skillet, saute the chicken and onion in oil until the chicken is no longer pink, 5-6 minutes. Add minced garlic; cook 1 minute longer.

2. Stir in tomatoes, spinach, broth, orzo, Italian seasoning and, if desired, pepper flakes. Bring to a boil; reduce heat. Cover and simmer until the orzo is tender and the liquid is absorbed, 15-20 minutes. If desired, sprinkle with cheese.

1¼ cups: 339 cal., 7g fat (1g sat. fat), 63mg chol., 384mg sod., 38g carb. (6g sugars, 5g fiber), 32g pro. **Diabetic exchanges:** 3 lean meat, 2 starch, 2 vegetable, ½ fat.

Pork

BARBECUE PORK & PENNE SKILLET

I'm the proud mother of wonderful and active children. Simple, delicious and quick meals like this are perfect for us to enjoy together after errands, school activities and soccer practice are over.
—Judy Armstrong, Prairieville, LA

Takes: 25 min. • **Makes:** 8 servings

- 1 pkg. (16 oz.) penne pasta
- 1 cup chopped sweet red pepper
- ¾ cup chopped onion
- 1 Tbsp. butter
- 1 Tbsp. olive oil
- 3 garlic cloves, minced
- 1 carton (16 oz.) refrigerated fully cooked barbecued shredded pork
- 1 can (14½ oz.) diced tomatoes with mild green chiles, undrained
- ½ cup beef broth
- 1 tsp. ground cumin
- 1 tsp. pepper
- ¼ tsp. salt
- 1¼ cups shredded cheddar cheese
- ¼ cup chopped green onions

1. Cook pasta according to the package directions. Meanwhile, in a large skillet, saute the red pepper and onion in butter and oil until tender. Add garlic; saute for 1 minute longer. Stir in shredded pork, tomatoes, broth, cumin, pepper and salt; heat through.

2. Drain pasta. Add the pasta and cheese to the pork mixture; stir until blended. Sprinkle with green onions.

Freeze option: Freeze cooled pasta mixture in freezer containers. To use, partially thaw in refrigerator overnight. Place in a greased shallow microwave-safe dish. Cover and microwave on high until heated through.

1¼ cups: 428 cal., 11g fat (6g sat. fat), 40mg chol., 903mg sod., 61g carb. (16g sugars, 4g fiber), 20g pro.

SKILLET ZUCCHINI & SAUSAGE

I lived on the Oregon coast for 20 years and had plenty of guests dropping by. I would often turn to this quick and easy dish, serving it up with skillet cornbread or garlic bread. Judging by the requests for the recipe, everyone loved it!
—LaBelle Doster, Vancouver, WA

Takes: 30 min. • **Makes:** 10 servings

- 2 Tbsp. vegetable oil
- ½ lb. fully cooked smoked Polish sausage, cut into ½-in. diagonal slices
- 1 cup chopped onion
- 1 cup sliced celery
- ½ cup chopped green pepper
- 1 garlic clove, minced
- ½ tsp. dried oregano
- ½ tsp. pepper
- 4 to 5 medium zucchini, sliced
- 4 to 5 medium tomatoes, coarsely chopped
  Herb seasoning blend to taste

Heat oil in a large skillet and lightly brown the sausage. Add onion, celery, green pepper, garlic, oregano and pepper. Cook and stir until the vegetables are almost tender. Add zucchini and tomatoes; cook and stir until the zucchini is just tender. Sprinkle with seasoning blend.

1 cup: 130 cal., 9g fat (3g sat. fat), 16mg chol., 211mg sod., 8g carb. (4g sugars, 2g fiber), 5g pro.

HAM STEAKS WITH GRUYERE, BACON & MUSHROOMS

This meat lover's breakfast has a big wow factor. The Gruyere, bacon and fresh mushrooms in the topping are a great combination.
—Lisa Speer, Palm Beach, FL

- -

Takes: 25 min. • **Makes:** 4 servings

- 2 Tbsp. butter
- ½ lb. sliced fresh mushrooms
- 1 shallot, finely chopped
- 2 garlic cloves, minced
- ⅛ tsp. coarsely ground pepper
- 1 fully cooked boneless ham steak (about 1 lb.), cut into 4 pieces
- 1 cup shredded Gruyere cheese
- 4 bacon strips, cooked and crumbled
- 1 Tbsp. minced fresh parsley, optional

1. In a large nonstick skillet, heat butter over medium-high heat. Add mushrooms and shallot; cook and stir 4-6 minutes or until tender. Add garlic and pepper; cook 1 minute longer. Remove from pan; keep warm. Wipe skillet clean.
2. In same skillet, cook ham over medium heat 3 minutes. Turn; sprinkle with cheese and bacon. Cook, covered, 2-4 minutes longer or until cheese is melted and ham is heated through. Serve with mushroom mixture. If desired, sprinkle with parsley.
1 serving: 352 cal., 22g fat (11g sat. fat), 113mg chol., 1576mg sod., 5g carb. (2g sugars, 1g fiber), 34g pro.

QUICK TACOS AL PASTOR

My husband and I tried pork and pineapple tacos at a truck stand in Hawaii. They were so tasty, I decided to make my own version at home.
—Lori McLain, Denton, TX

- -

Takes: 25 min. • **Makes:** 4 servings

- 1 pkg. (15 oz.) refrigerated pork roast au jus
- 1 cup well-drained unsweetened pineapple chunks, divided
- 1 Tbsp. canola oil
- ½ cup enchilada sauce
- 8 corn tortillas (6 in.), warmed
- ½ cup finely chopped onion
- ¼ cup chopped fresh cilantro
  Optional: Crumbled queso fresco, salsa verde and lime wedges

1. Coarsely shred pork, reserving juices. In a small bowl, crush half the pineapple with a fork.
2. In a large nonstick skillet, heat oil over medium-high heat. Add whole pineapple chunks; cook until lightly browned, 2-3 minutes, turning occasionally. Remove from pan.
3. Add the enchilada sauce and crushed pineapple to the same skillet; stir in the pork and the reserved juices. Cook over medium-high heat until liquid is evaporated, 4-6 minutes, stirring occasionally.
4. Serve in warm tortillas with pineapple chunks, onion and cilantro. If desired, top with cheese and salsa, and serve with lime wedges.
2 tacos: 317 cal., 11g fat (3g sat. fat), 57mg chol., 573mg sod., 36g carb. (12g sugars, 5g fiber), 24g pro. **Diabetic exchanges:** 3 lean meat, 2 starch, 1 fat.

MOM'S PAELLA

I enjoy cooking exotic foods, especially those that call for lots of rice. I often prepare this dish for special Sunday get-togethers, just like my mom did!
—Ena Quiggle, Goodhue, MN

- -

Prep: 10 min. • **Cook:** 40 min.
Makes: 6-8 servings

- 1½ cups cubed cooked chicken
- 1 cup cubed fully cooked ham
- ½ cup sliced fully cooked smoked sausage (¼-in. slices)
- 1 medium onion, chopped
- 1 small green pepper, chopped
- 4 Tbsp. olive oil, divided
- ¼ cup pimiento-stuffed olives, halved
- ½ cup raisins, optional
- 1 cup uncooked converted rice
- 2 garlic cloves, minced
- 3 tsp. ground turmeric
- 1½ tsp. curry powder
- 2¼ cups chicken broth
- 1½ cups frozen mixed vegetables

1. In a large skillet, saute the chicken, ham, sausage, onion and green pepper in 2 Tbsp. of oil for 3-5 minutes or until the onion is tender. Add olives and the raisins if desired. Cook 2-3 minutes longer or until heated through, stirring occasionally; remove the meat and vegetable mixture from pan and keep warm.
2. In the same skillet, saute rice in remaining oil for 2-3 minutes or until lightly browned. Stir in the garlic, turmeric and curry. Return the meat and vegetables to pan; toss lightly. Add broth and mixed vegetables; bring to a boil. Reduce heat; cover and simmer for 25-30 minutes or until the rice is tender.
1 cup: 258 cal., 14g fat (3g sat. fat), 39mg chol., 711mg sod., 19g carb. (3g sugars, 3g fiber), 15g pro.

PORK TENDERLOIN WITH THREE-BERRY SALSA

My husband came home from a work meeting where they'd served pork with a spicy blueberry salsa. He raved about how tasty it was, so I came up with my own rendition without seeing or tasting what he'd had. It took several tries, but this is the delicious result.

—Angie Phillips, Tarzana, CA

- -

Prep: 30 min. + standing • **Cook:** 25 min.
Makes: 6 servings

- 1¼ **cups fresh or frozen blackberries (about 6 oz.), thawed and drained**
- 1¼ **cups fresh or frozen raspberries (about 6 oz.), thawed and drained**
- 1 **cup fresh or frozen blueberries (about 6 oz.), thawed**
- 1 **medium sweet red pepper, finely chopped**
- 1 **jalapeno pepper, seeded and minced**
- ½ **medium red onion, finely chopped**
- ¼ **cup lime juice**
- 3 **Tbsp. minced fresh cilantro**
- ¼ **tsp. salt**

PORK

- 2 **pork tenderloins (¾ lb. each), cut into ¾-in. slices**
- 1 **tsp. salt**
- ½ **tsp. pepper**
- 2 **Tbsp. olive oil, divided**
- ½ **cup white wine or chicken broth**
- 2 **shallots, thinly sliced**
- ½ **cup chicken stock**

1. Place the first 5 ingredients in a bowl; toss lightly to combine. Reserve 1 cup berry mixture for sauce. For salsa, gently stir onion, lime juice, cilantro and salt into remaining mixture; let stand 30 minutes.
2. Meanwhile, sprinkle the pork with salt and pepper. In a large skillet, heat 1 Tbsp. oil over medium-high heat. Add half the pork and cook 2-4 minutes on each side until a thermometer inserted in the pork reads 145°. Remove from pan. Repeat with the remaining pork and oil.
3. In the same pan, add wine, shallots and the reserved berry mixture, stirring to loosen browned bits from pan. Bring to a boil; cook until liquid is reduced to 1 Tbsp., 4-6 minutes. Stir in stock; cook until shallots are tender, about 5 minutes longer, stirring occasionally. Return pork to pan; heat through. Serve with salsa.

3 oz. cooked pork with ⅔ cup salsa and 3 Tbsp. sauce: 239 cal., 9g fat (2g sat. fat), 64mg chol., 645mg sod., 15g carb. (7g sugars, 5g fiber), 25g pro.
Diabetic exchanges: 3 lean meat, ½ starch, ½ fruit.

HAM & SCALLOPED POTATOES

I fix this saucy skillet dish often, especially when I'm running late. It proves a dish doesn't have to be complicated to taste amazing—this easy, quick recipe won first prize in our local paper some years back.
—Emma Magielda, Amsterdam, NY

- -

Takes: 30 min. • **Makes:** 4 servings

- 4 medium potatoes, peeled and thinly sliced
- 2 Tbsp. butter
- ⅓ cup water
- ½ cup 2% milk
- 2 to 3 Tbsp. onion soup mix
- 3 Tbsp. minced fresh parsley
- 1 cup cubed Velveeta
- 1 cup cubed fully cooked ham

1. In a large skillet, cook the potatoes in butter until lightly browned. Add water; bring to a boil. Reduce heat; cover and simmer for 14-15 minutes or until the potatoes are tender.
2. Meanwhile in a small bowl, combine milk, soup mix and parsley; stir in cheese. Pour over the potatoes. Add ham; cook and stir gently over medium heat until the cheese is melted and the sauce is bubbly.

1 serving: 353 cal., 17g fat (10g sat. fat), 56mg chol., 1170mg sod., 36g carb. (6g sugars, 2g fiber), 16g pro.

SIMPLE SPARERIB & SAUERKRAUT SUPPER

Try a stout serving of old-fashioned goodness in one bowl. A little bit of everything makes a simple meal in one.
—Donna Harp, Cincinnati, OH

- -

Prep: 30 min. • **Cook:** 6 hours
Makes: 6 servings

- 1 lb. fingerling potatoes
- 1 medium onion, chopped
- 1 medium Granny Smith apple, peeled and chopped
- 3 slices thick-sliced bacon strips, cooked and crumbled
- 1 jar (16 oz.) sauerkraut, undrained
- 2 lbs. pork spareribs
- ½ tsp. salt
- ¼ tsp. pepper
- 1 Tbsp. vegetable oil
- 3 Tbsp. brown sugar
- ¼ tsp. caraway seeds
- ½ lb. smoked Polish sausage, cut into 1-in. slices
- 1 cup beer

1. Place the potatoes, onion, apple and bacon in a 6-qt. slow cooker. Drain the sauerkraut, reserving ⅓ cup liquid; add the sauerkraut and reserved liquid to slow cooker.
2. Cut spareribs into serving portions; sprinkle with salt and pepper. In a large skillet, heat oil over medium-high heat; brown ribs in batches. Transfer to the slow cooker; sprinkle with brown sugar and caraway seeds.
3. Add sausage; pour in beer. Cover and cook on low for 6-7 hours or until the ribs are tender.

1 serving: 590 cal., 37g fat (13g sat. fat), 118mg chol., 1285mg sod., 32g carb. (13g sugars, 4g fiber), 30g pro.

PORK CHOPS WITH TOMATO-BACON TOPPING

My husband and I collaborated on these pork chops with sun-dried tomatoes, bacon and rosemary. They're easy enough for any day of the week and fancy enough for special events.
—Trisha Klempel, Sidney, MT

Takes: 30 min. • **Makes:** 4 servings

- 4 thick-sliced bacon strips, chopped
- 4 boneless pork loin chops (6 oz. each)
- ½ tsp. salt
- ¼ tsp. pepper
- ¼ cup julienned oil-packed sun-dried tomatoes
- 2 Tbsp. brown sugar
- 2 tsp. minced fresh rosemary or ½ tsp. dried rosemary, crushed

1. Preheat broiler. In a large cast-iron or other ovenproof skillet, cook chopped bacon over medium heat until crisp, stirring occasionally. Remove with a slotted spoon; drain on paper towels.
2. Sprinkle pork chops with salt and pepper. Add chops to bacon drippings; cook until a thermometer reads 145°, 3-4 minutes on each side. Meanwhile, in a bowl, mix bacon, tomatoes, brown sugar and rosemary.
3. Spoon the tomato mixture over chops. Broil 3-4 in. from heat until brown sugar is melted, 1-2 minutes.
1 pork chop: 457 cal., 33g fat (12g sat. fat), 108mg chol., 636mg sod., 2g carb. (0 sugars, 0 fiber), 37g pro.

MEDITERRANEAN PORK & ORZO

On a really busy day, this meal-in-a-bowl is one of my top picks. It's quick to put together, leaving me a lot more time to relax at the table.
—Mary Relyea, Canastota, NY

Takes: 30 min. • **Makes:** 6 servings

- 1½ lbs. pork tenderloin
- 1 tsp. coarsely ground pepper
- 2 Tbsp. olive oil
- 3 qt. water
- 1¼ cups uncooked orzo pasta
- ¼ tsp. salt
- 1 pkg. (6 oz.) fresh baby spinach
- 1 cup grape tomatoes, halved
- ¾ cup crumbled feta cheese

1. Rub pork with pepper; cut into 1-in. cubes. In a large nonstick skillet, heat oil over medium heat. Add pork; cook and stir 8-10 minutes or until no longer pink.
2. Meanwhile, in a Dutch oven, bring water to a boil. Stir in the orzo and salt; cook, uncovered, 8 minutes. Stir in spinach; cook 45-60 seconds longer or until the orzo is tender and the spinach is wilted. Drain.
3. Add tomatoes to pork and heat through. Stir in the orzo mixture and cheese.
1⅓ cups: 372 cal., 11g fat (4g sat. fat), 71mg chol., 306mg sod., 34g carb. (2g sugars, 3g fiber), 31g pro. **Diabetic exchanges:** 3 lean meat, 2 starch, 1 vegetable, 1 fat.

CREAMY PAPRIKA PORK

When I was little, I would often ask my mom to make "favorite meat." She knew that I was requesting this homey pork recipe. It's been in my family for more than 30 years and it's still a favorite!
—Alexandra Barnett, Forest, VA

- -

Takes: 30 min. • **Makes:** 4 servings

- 1   pork tenderloin (1 lb.), cut into 1-in. cubes
- 1   tsp. all-purpose flour
- 4   tsp. paprika
- ¾   tsp. salt
- ¼   tsp. pepper
- 1   Tbsp. butter
- ¾   cup heavy whipping cream
  Hot cooked egg noodles or rice
  Minced fresh parsley, optional

1. Toss pork with flour and seasonings. In a large skillet, heat butter over medium heat; saute the pork until lightly browned, 4-5 minutes.
2. Add the cream; bring to a boil, stirring to loosen browned bits from pan. Cook, uncovered, until cream is slightly thickened, 5-7 minutes.
3. Serve with noodles. If desired, sprinkle with parsley.

¾ cup pork mixture: 320 cal., 23g fat (14g sat. fat), 122mg chol., 524mg sod., 3g carb. (1g sugars, 1g fiber), 24g pro.

TEST KITCHEN TIP

For a spicy kick, substitute hot paprika for sweet. Always store paprika in the refrigerator to keep its flavor fresh.

JUST PEACHY PORK TENDERLOIN

I had a pork tenderloin and some ripe peaches and decided to put them together. The results proved irresistible! This fresh entree tastes like summer.
—Julia Gosliga, Addison, VT

- -

Takes: 20 min. • **Makes:** 4 servings

- 1   lb. pork tenderloin, cut into 12 slices
- ½   tsp. salt
- ¼   tsp. pepper
- 2   tsp. olive oil
- 4   medium peaches, peeled and sliced
- 1   Tbsp. lemon juice
- ¼   cup peach preserves

1. Flatten each tenderloin slice to ¼-in. thickness. Sprinkle with salt and pepper. In a large nonstick skillet over medium heat, cook the pork in oil until tender. Remove and keep warm.
2. Add the peaches and lemon juice, stirring to loosen any browned bits from the pan. Cook and stir until the peaches are tender, 3-4 minutes. Stir in the pork and preserves; heat through.

1 serving: 241 cal., 6g fat (2g sat. fat), 63mg chol., 340mg sod., 23g carb. (20g sugars, 2g fiber), 23g pro. **Diabetic exchanges:** 3 lean meat, 1 fruit, ½ starch, ½ fat.

 ASPARAGUS HAM DINNER

I've been making this light meal for my family for years now, and it's always well received. With asparagus, tomato, pasta and chunks of ham, it's a tempting blend of tastes and textures.

—Rhonda Zavodny, David City, NE

- -

Takes: 25 min. • **Makes:** 6 servings

2	cups uncooked corkscrew or spiral pasta
¾	lb. fresh asparagus, cut into 1-in. pieces
1	medium sweet yellow pepper, julienned
1	Tbsp. olive oil
6	medium tomatoes, diced
6	oz. boneless fully cooked ham, cubed
¼	cup minced fresh parsley
½	tsp. salt
½	tsp. dried oregano
½	tsp. dried basil
⅛	to ¼ tsp. cayenne pepper
¼	cup shredded Parmesan cheese

Cook pasta according to the package directions. Meanwhile, in a large cast-iron or other heavy skillet, saute the asparagus and yellow pepper in oil until crisp-tender. Add tomatoes and ham; heat through. Drain pasta; add to the vegetable mixture. Stir in the parsley and seasonings. Sprinkle with cheese.

1⅓ cups: 204 cal., 5g fat (1g sat. fat), 17mg chol., 561mg sod., 29g carb. (5g sugars, 3g fiber), 12g pro. **Diabetic exchanges:** 1½ starch, 1 lean meat, 1 vegetable, ½ fat.

APPLE-TOPPED HAM STEAK

Sweet apples combine nicely with tangy mustard in this dish to create a luscious topping for skillet-fried ham steak. I especially like to serve this to guests in the fall, when apples are at their best.
—Eleanor Chore, Athena, OR

- -

Takes: 30 min. • **Makes:** 8 servings

- 4 fully cooked boneless ham steaks (8 oz. each)
- 1 cup chopped onion
- 3 cups apple juice
- 2 tsp. Dijon mustard
- 2 medium green apples, thinly sliced
- 2 medium red apples, thinly sliced
- 2 Tbsp. cornstarch
- ¼ cup cold water
- 1 Tbsp. minced fresh sage or 1 tsp. rubbed sage
- ¼ tsp. pepper

1. In a large skillet coated with cooking spray, brown ham steaks in batches over medium heat; remove and keep warm.
2. In the same skillet, saute onion until tender. Stir in apple juice and mustard; bring to a boil. Add apples. Reduce heat; cover and simmer for 4 minutes or until the apples are tender.
3. Combine cornstarch and water until smooth; stir into the apple juice mixture. Bring to a boil; cook and stir for 2 minutes. Stir in sage and pepper. Return steaks to skillet; heat through.
1 serving: 219 cal., 4g fat (1g sat. fat), 58mg chol., 1213mg sod., 25g carb. (18g sugars, 2g fiber), 21g pro.

PORK CHOPS & PIEROGIES

The Polish dumplings are traditionally served as a meal, with applesauce or sour cream. This meal in one is a different way to use pierogi.
—Greta Igl, Menomonee Falls, WI

- -

Takes: 25 min. • **Makes:** 2 servings

- 8 frozen potato and onion pierogi
- 2 bone-in pork loin chops (¾ in. thick)
- ½ tsp. salt, divided
- ½ tsp. pepper, divided
- 4 Tbsp. butter, divided
- 1 medium sweet onion, sliced and separated into rings
- 1 medium Golden Delicious apple, cut into ¼-in. slices
- ¼ cup sugar
- ¼ cup cider vinegar

1. Cook pierogi according to package directions. Meanwhile, sprinkle pork chops with ¼ tsp. salt and ¼ tsp. pepper. In a large skillet, cook chops in 2 Tbsp. butter over medium heat until juices run clear; remove and keep warm.
2. In the same skillet, saute onion in the remaining butter for 3 minutes. Add apple; saute until almost tender. Stir in sugar, vinegar, and remaining salt and pepper. Bring to a boil. Reduce heat; simmer, uncovered, for 5 minutes. Drain pierogi. Add chops and pierogi to skillet; stir to coat.
1 serving: 730 cal., 33g fat (18g sat. fat), 154mg chol., 1207mg sod., 72g carb. (45g sugars, 5g fiber), 36g pro.

1 medium green pepper,
  cut into strips
¾ cup pineapple tidbits
  Optional: Hot cooked rice,
  chow mein noodles or
  crispy wonton strips

1. In a small bowl, combine cornstarch and pineapple juice until smooth. Stir in cranberry and barbecue sauces; set aside.
2. In a large skillet, stir-fry pork in oil until meat is no longer pink, 3 minutes. Sprinkle with salt and pepper. Remove from the pan and keep warm.
3. Add green pepper and pineapple to pan; stir-fry for 2 minutes. Stir the cornstarch mixture and add to skillet. Bring to a boil. Cook and stir until thickened, 2 minutes. Add pork; heat through. Serve with rice, noodles or wonton strips if desired.
Freeze option: Place the cooled mixture in freezer containers. To use, partially thaw in refrigerator overnight. Heat through slowly in a covered skillet, stirring occasionally and adding a little water if necessary.
1¼ cups: 268 cal., 7g fat (2g sat. fat), 63mg chol., 444mg sod., 28g carb. (19g sugars, 1g fiber), 23g pro.

TEST KITCHEN TIP

If you're not a fan of green peppers, snow peas make a great substitute in any dish that calls for them—stir-fries, omelets, tomato sauces, vegetable soup and even pizza!

CRANBERRY SWEET & SOUR PORK

This fresh and unexpected take on the beloved Asian-style dish is sure to cause a stir at the dinner table!
—Gert Snyder, West Montrose, ON

- -

Takes: 20 min. • **Makes:** 6 servings

1   Tbsp. cornstarch
½   cup unsweetened pineapple juice
1   cup whole-berry cranberry sauce
½   cup barbecue sauce
1½ lbs. pork tenderloin, cut into
     ½-in. cubes
1   Tbsp. canola oil
½   tsp. salt
¼   tsp. pepper

PORK TENDERLOIN FAJITAS

This simple recipe offers loads of taste appeal. Sizzling pork tenderloin and veggies are coated with a zippy cilantro mixture and tucked into tortillas for a fun take on taco night.
—Rachel Hozey, Pensacola, FL

- -

Takes: 25 min. • **Makes:** 4 servings

- ¼ cup minced fresh cilantro
- ½ tsp. garlic powder
- ½ tsp. chili powder
- ½ tsp. ground cumin
- 1 pork tenderloin (1 lb.), thinly sliced
- 1 Tbsp. canola oil
- 1 small onion, sliced and separated into rings
- 1 medium green pepper, julienned
- 4 flour tortillas (8 in.), warmed
  Optional: Shredded cheddar cheese, sour cream

1. In a small bowl, combine cilantro, garlic powder, chili powder and cumin; set aside. In a large skillet, saute pork in oil until no longer pink. Add onion and green pepper; cook until vegetables are crisp-tender.
2. Sprinkle with seasoning mixture; toss to coat. Spoon onto tortillas; serve with cheese and sour cream if desired.
1 fajita: 327 cal., 11g fat (2g sat. fat), 63mg chol., 299mg sod., 29g carb. (2g sugars, 1g fiber), 28g pro. **Diabetic exchanges:** 3 lean meat, 1½ starch, 1 vegetable, ½ fat.

HASH BROWN PORK SKILLET

Add potatoes and veggies to leftover pork tenderloin for an easy, creamy weeknight supper that's ready in minutes!
—*Taste of Home* Test Kitchen

- -

Takes: 25 min. • **Makes:** 6 servings

- 4 cups frozen O'Brien potatoes, thawed
- 1 cup chopped onion
- 1 cup chopped green pepper
- 2 Tbsp. butter
- 2 cups shredded cooked pork
- 2 tsp. chicken bouillon granules
- ¼ tsp. pepper
- 2 tsp. all-purpose flour
- ½ cup 2% milk
- ¾ cup shredded cheddar cheese

1. In a large cast-iron or other heavy skillet, cook the potatoes, onion and green pepper in butter over medium heat until almost tender. Stir in pork, bouillon and pepper; heat through.
2. In a small bowl, combine the flour and milk until smooth; add to skillet. Cook on medium-low heat until mixture is thickened, stirring frequently, 4-5 minutes.
3. Sprinkle with cheese. Remove from heat; cover and let stand until cheese is melted.
1 cup: 286 cal., 13g fat (7g sat. fat), 70mg chol., 449mg sod., 22g carb. (4g sugars, 3g fiber), 19g pro.

JIFFY GROUND PORK SKILLET

Some people call it dinner hour, but many of us call it rush hour. Slow down with this so-simple meal. The only thing you'll have left over is time to share with your family at the table.

—Brigitte Schaller, Flemington, MO

Takes: 30 min. • **Makes:** 5 servings

1½ cups uncooked penne pasta
1 lb. ground pork
½ cup chopped onion
1 can (14½ oz.) stewed tomatoes, undrained
1 can (8 oz.) tomato sauce
1 tsp. Italian seasoning
1 medium zucchini, cut into ¼-in. slices

1. Cook pasta according to the package directions. Meanwhile, in a large skillet, cook pork and onion over medium heat until the meat is no longer pink; drain. Add the tomatoes, tomato sauce and Italian seasoning. Bring to a boil. Reduce heat; cover and cook for 5 minutes to allow the flavors to blend.
2. Drain pasta; add to the skillet. Stir in zucchini. Cook, covered, 3-5 minutes or until the zucchini is crisp-tender.
Freeze option: Transfer individual portions of the cooled pasta mixture to freezer containers. To use, partially thaw in refrigerator overnight. Heat through in a saucepan, stirring occasionally; add a little tomato sauce if necessary.
1⅓ cups: 317 cal., 14g fat (5g sat. fat), 61mg chol., 408mg sod., 27g carb. (7g sugars, 2g fiber), 21g pro.

GINGER PORK STIR-FRY

An easy homemade stir-fry sauce is the perfect base for this weeknight dish. It comes together quickly, creating a skillet of tender pork infused with Asian flavors.
—Adeline Russell, Hartford, WI

- -

Takes: 20 min. • **Makes:** 4 servings

  2 Tbsp. cornstarch
  1 cup beef broth
  3 Tbsp. soy sauce
  1 Tbsp. sugar
1½ tsp. ground ginger
  ½ tsp. garlic powder
  ½ tsp. crushed red pepper flakes
  1 pork tenderloin (1 lb.), cut into 2-in. strips
  2 Tbsp. canola oil, divided
  1 pkg. (16 oz.) frozen sugar snap stir-fry vegetable blend, thawed
    Hot cooked rice
    Minced fresh cilantro, optional

1. In a small bowl, combine cornstarch and broth until smooth. Stir in the soy sauce, sugar, ginger, garlic powder and pepper flakes; set aside.
2. In a wok or large skillet, stir-fry pork in 1 Tbsp. oil until juices run clear. Remove and keep warm. In the same pan, stir-fry the vegetables in remaining oil until crisp-tender.
3. Stir the broth mixture and add to the vegetables. Bring to a boil; cook and stir for 1 minute or until thickened. Return pork to the pan; heat through. Serve with rice and, if desired, sprinkle with cilantro.
1 cup: 278 cal., 11g fat (2g sat. fat), 63mg chol., 958mg sod., 16g carb. (7g sugars, 4g fiber), 27g pro.
Ginger-Orange Pork Stir-Fry: Omit the first 7 ingredients. Combine 1 Tbsp. cornstarch with 1 cup orange juice and 2 Tbsp. soy sauce until smooth. Stir in 2 minced garlic cloves and ¾ tsp. ground ginger. Proceed as recipe directs.

PORK WITH SWEET POTATOES

With sweet potatoes, dried cranberries and apple slices, this pork dish is especially popular during fall and winter. Your family will love not only the taste, but also the colorful medley of ingredients.
—Mary Relyea, Canastota, NY

- -

Prep: 20 min. • **Cook:** 20 min.
Makes: 4 servings

½ cup all-purpose flour
½ tsp. salt
¼ tsp. pepper
 1 pork tenderloin (about 1 lb.)
 1 Tbsp. canola oil
 2 medium sweet potatoes (about 1 lb.), peeled and cubed
½ cup dried cranberries
 1 can (14½ oz.) reduced-sodium chicken broth
 1 Tbsp. Dijon mustard
 1 medium apple, sliced
 4 green onions, chopped

1. In a shallow bowl, mix the flour, salt and pepper. Cut tenderloin into 12 slices; pound each with a meat mallet to ¼-in. thickness. Dip each slice in the flour mixture to coat both sides; shake off excess.
2. In a large skillet coated with cooking spray, heat oil over medium-high heat; brown pork in batches. Remove from pan.
3. Add the sweet potatoes, cranberries and broth to the same pan. Bring to a boil. Reduce heat; simmer, covered, 4-6 minutes or until the potatoes are almost tender. Stir in mustard.
4. Return the pork to pan; add apple and green onions. Return to a boil. Reduce heat; simmer, covered, 4-6 minutes or until the pork and sweet potatoes are tender.
3 slices pork with 1 cup potato mixture: 315 cal., 8g fat (2g sat. fat), 63mg chol., 513mg sod., 36g carb. (20g sugars, 4g fiber), 26g pro. **Diabetic exchanges:** 3 lean meat, 2½ starch, ½ fat.

PEAR PORK CHOPS & CORNBREAD STUFFING

You'll be tempted to eat this main dish straight out of the pan. But save some for your guests! It's sure to wow them at the dinner table.
—*Taste of Home* Test Kitchen

- -

Takes: 30 min. • **Makes:** 4 servings

- 1 pkg. (6 oz.) cornbread stuffing mix
- 4 boneless pork loin chops (6 oz. each)
- ½ tsp. pepper
- ¼ tsp. salt
- 2 Tbsp. butter
- 2 medium pears, chopped
- 1 medium sweet red pepper, chopped
- 2 green onions, thinly sliced

1. Prepare the stuffing mix according to package directions. Meanwhile, sprinkle pork chops with pepper and salt. In a large skillet, brown chops in butter. Sprinkle with pears and red pepper.

2. Top with stuffing and onions. Cook, uncovered, over medium heat until a thermometer inserted in the pork reads 145°, 8-10 minutes.

1 pork chop with ¾ cup stuffing mixture: 603 cal., 28g fat (14g sat. fat), 127mg chol., 1094mg sod., 47g carb. (14g sugars, 5g fiber), 38g pro.

PORK PANCIT

A dear friend gave me a pork recipe so tempting that we never have leftovers. Try it with chicken, sausage or Spam, too.
—Priscilla Gilbert, Indian Harbour Beach, FL

- -

Takes: 30 min. • **Makes:** 6 servings

- 8 oz. uncooked vermicelli or angel hair pasta
- 1 lb. boneless pork loin chops (½ in. thick), cut into thin strips
- 3 Tbsp. canola oil, divided
- 4 garlic cloves, minced
- 1½ tsp. salt, divided
- 1 medium onion, halved and thinly sliced
- 2½ cups shredded cabbage
- 1 medium carrot, julienned
- 1 cup fresh snow peas
- ¼ tsp. pepper

1. Break vermicelli in half; cook according to package directions. Drain.

2. Meanwhile, in a bowl, toss pork with 2 Tbsp. oil, garlic and ½ tsp. salt. Place a large skillet over medium-high heat. Add half the pork mixture; stir-fry 2-3 minutes or until browned. Remove from pan. Repeat with the remaining pork mixture.

3. In same skillet, heat the remaining oil over medium-high heat. Add onion; stir-fry 1-2 minutes or until tender. Add remaining vegetables; stir-fry 3-5 minutes or until crisp-tender. Stir in pepper and remaining salt. Return pork to pan. Add the vermicelli; heat through, tossing to combine.

1⅓ cups: 326 cal., 12g fat (2g sat. fat), 36mg chol., 627mg sod., 34g carb. (3g sugars, 3g fiber), 21g pro. **Diabetic exchanges:** 2 starch, 2 lean meat, 1 vegetable, 1 fat.

PORK MEDALLIONS WITH SAUTEED APPLES

This down-home supper takes advantage of the classic pairing of pork and apples. Instead of chops, I use the tenderloin—I really like that the lean cut of meat is tender and juicy, but healthy, too.
—Clara Coulson Minney, Washington Court House, OH

Takes: 30 min. • **Makes:** 4 servings

- 2 tsp. cornstarch
- ⅔ cup reduced-sodium chicken broth
- ¼ cup apple juice
- 1 Tbsp. butter
- 2 medium apples, thinly sliced
- 2 green onions, sliced
- 1 garlic clove, minced
- ¾ tsp. dried thyme
- ½ tsp. paprika
- ¼ tsp. salt
- ¼ tsp. pepper
- 1 lb. pork tenderloin, cut into 1-in. slices

1. Preheat broiler. In a small bowl, mix cornstarch, broth and apple juice. In a nonstick skillet, heat butter over medium-high heat. Add apples, green onions and garlic; cook and stir 2-3 minutes or until the apples are crisp-tender. Stir the cornstarch mixture and add to the pan. Bring to a boil; cook and stir 1-2 minutes or until thickened. Keep warm.
2. Mix thyme, paprika, salt and pepper. Pound pork slices with a meat mallet to ½-in. thickness; sprinkle both sides with seasonings.
3. Place pork on a broiler pan. Broil 3 in. from heat 3-4 minutes on each side or until a thermometer reads 145°. Let stand 5 minutes before serving. Serve with apples.

3 oz. cooked pork with ½ cup apples: 251 cal., 10g fat (4g sat. fat), 85mg chol., 335mg sod., 15g carb. (10g sugars, 3g fiber), 25g pro. **Diabetic exchanges:** 3 lean meat, 1 fruit, ½ fat.

TROPICAL SWEET & SPICY PORK TENDERLOIN

When we crave something sweet and spicy, pork tenderloin cooked with chipotle, barbecue sauce and pineapple really delivers.
—Cyndy Gerken, Naples, FL

Takes: 30 min. • **Makes:** 4 servings

- 1 pork tenderloin (1 lb.), cut into 1-in. cubes
- ¼ tsp. salt
- ¼ tsp. pepper
- 2 Tbsp. olive oil
- 1 medium onion, chopped
- 1 medium green pepper, chopped
- 3 garlic cloves, minced
- 1 cup chicken stock
- 1 can (20 oz.) pineapple tidbits, drained
- 1 cup honey barbecue sauce
- ½ cup packed brown sugar
- 2 finely chopped chipotle peppers plus 2 tsp. adobo sauce
- 2 Tbsp. reduced-sodium soy sauce
  Hot cooked rice

1. Sprinkle pork with salt and pepper. In a large skillet, heat oil over medium-high heat. Add the pork; cook until browned, 4-6 minutes. Remove.
2. In the same skillet, cook onion and pepper until softened, 2-4 minutes. Add garlic; cook 1 minute. Return the pork to pan; stir in chicken stock. Cook, covered, until the pork is tender, about 5 minutes.
3. Stir in the next 5 ingredients; simmer, uncovered, until the sauce is thickened, about 5 minutes. Serve with rice.
1½ cups: 539 cal., 11g fat (2g sat. fat), 64mg chol., 1374mg sod., 82g carb. (72g sugars, 2g fiber), 25g pro.

Seafood &
Meatless

BLACK BEAN BURRITOS

My neighbor and I discovered these fabulous low-fat burritos a few years ago. On nights my husband or I have a meeting, we can have a satisfying supper on the table in minutes.
—Angela Studebaker, Goshen, IN

Takes: 10 min. • **Makes:** 4 servings

- 1 Tbsp. canola oil
- 3 Tbsp. chopped onion
- 3 Tbsp. chopped green pepper
- 1 can (15 oz.) black beans, rinsed and drained
- 4 flour tortillas (8 in.), warmed
- 1 cup shredded Mexican cheese blend
- 1 medium tomato, chopped
- 1 cup shredded lettuce
   Optional: Salsa, sour cream, minced fresh cilantro and cubed avocado

1. In a nonstick skillet, heat oil over medium heat; saute onion and green pepper until tender. Stir in beans; heat through.
2. Spoon about ½ cup vegetable mixture off center on each tortilla. Sprinkle with cheese, tomato and lettuce. Fold the sides and ends of the tortilla over filling and roll up. Serve with optional toppings as desired.
1 burrito: 395 cal., 16g fat (6g sat. fat), 25mg chol., 610mg sod., 46g carb. (2g sugars, 7g fiber), 16g pro. **Diabetic exchanges:** 2½ starch, 1 lean meat, 1 vegetable, 1 fat.

You can use corn tortillas for these burritos if you like; just be sure to steam them so they stay pliable. Wrap a stack in a damp paper towel and microwave for about 30 seconds.

THAI SCALLOP SAUTE

Just open a bottle of Thai peanut sauce to give this seafood stir-fry some serious authenticity.
—*Taste of Home* Test Kitchen

Prep: 15 min. • **Cook:** 20 min.
Makes: 4 servings

- 3 tsp. olive oil, divided
- 1½ lbs. sea scallops
- 2 cups fresh broccoli florets
- 2 medium onions, halved and sliced
- 1 medium zucchini, sliced
- 4 small carrots, sliced
- ¼ cup Thai peanut sauce
- ¼ tsp. salt
   Hot cooked rice
   Lime wedges, optional

1. In a large skillet, heat 1 tsp. oil over medium-high heat. Add half the scallops; stir-fry until firm and opaque. Remove from pan. Repeat with an additional 1 tsp. oil and the remaining scallops.
2. In the same skillet, heat the remaining oil over medium-high heat. Add vegetables; stir-fry until crisp-tender, 7-9 minutes. Stir in peanut sauce and salt. Return the scallops to pan; heat through. Serve with rice and, if desired, lime wedges.
1½ cups: 268 cal., 8g fat (1g sat. fat), 41mg chol., 1000mg sod., 24g carb. (10g sugars, 4g fiber), 25g pro.

SHRIMP WITH WARM GERMAN-STYLE COLESLAW

We love anything that's tangy or bacony. With fennel and tarragon, this is a super savory dish. I use the medley from Minute Rice if I don't have time to make my own.
—Ann Sheehy, Lawrence, MA

Takes: 30 min. • **Makes:** 4 servings

- 6 bacon strips
- 2 Tbsp. canola oil, divided
- 3 cups finely shredded green cabbage
- ½ cup finely shredded carrot (1 medium carrot)
- 1 cup finely shredded red cabbage, optional
- ½ cup finely shredded fennel bulb, optional
- 6 green onions, finely chopped
- 3 Tbsp. minced fresh parsley
- 2 Tbsp. minced fresh tarragon or 2 tsp. dried tarragon
- ¼ tsp. salt
- ⅛ tsp. pepper
- ¼ cup red wine vinegar
- 1 lb. uncooked shrimp (26-30 per lb.), peeled and deveined
- 3 cups hot cooked rice or multigrain medley

1. In a large skillet, cook bacon strips over medium heat until crisp. Remove to paper towels. Pour off the drippings, reserving 2 Tbsp.; discard the rest. Crumble bacon.

2. In same skillet, heat 1 Tbsp. drippings with 1 Tbsp. oil over medium heat. Add green cabbage and carrot and, if desired, red cabbage and fennel; cook and stir until the vegetables are just tender, 1-2 minutes. Remove to a bowl. Stir in green onions, parsley, tarragon, salt and pepper; toss with vinegar. Keep warm.

3. Add the remaining drippings and the remaining oil to skillet. Add shrimp; cook and stir over medium heat until the shrimp turn pink, 2-3 minutes. Remove from heat.

4. To serve, spoon rice and coleslaw into soup bowls. Top with shrimp; sprinkle with crumbled bacon.

1 serving: 472 cal., 20g fat (5g sat. fat), 156mg chol., 546mg sod., 44g carb. (2g sugars, 3g fiber), 28g pro.

TEST KITCHEN TIP

While a little red cabbage adds a nice pop of color to this dish, it's fine to go all-green instead. And if you have a chive plant, feel free to use ½ cup chopped chives in place of the green onions.

SMOKED SALMON QUESADILLAS WITH CREAMY CHIPOTLE SAUCE

These quesadillas taste extra special, but they take just minutes to make. A fresh burst of chopped fresh cilantro is the perfect finishing touch.

—Daniel Shemtob, Irvine, CA

- -

Takes: 25 min.
Makes: 3 servings (⅔ cup sauce)

- ½ cup creme fraiche or sour cream
- 2 Tbsp. minced chipotle peppers in adobo sauce
- 2 Tbsp. lime juice
- ⅛ tsp. salt
- ⅛ tsp. pepper

QUESADILLAS
- ¼ cup cream cheese, softened
- 2 oz. fresh goat cheese
- 3 flour tortillas (8 in.)
- 3 oz. smoked salmon or lox, chopped
- ¼ cup finely chopped shallots
- ¼ cup finely chopped roasted sweet red pepper
- Coarsely chopped fresh cilantro

1. In a small bowl, mix first 5 ingredients. In another bowl, mix the cream cheese and goat cheese until blended; spread over the tortillas. Top half of each with the salmon, shallots and red pepper; fold the tortilla over the filling.

2. Place quesadillas on a greased griddle. Cook over medium heat until tortillas are lightly browned and the cheeses are melted, 1-2 minutes on each side. Serve with sauce; top with cilantro.

1 quesadilla with 3 Tbsp. sauce: 453 cal., 28g fat (16g sat. fat), 74mg chol., 1118mg sod., 33g carb. (2g sugars, 0 fiber), 15g pro.

SPRING PILAF WITH SALMON & ASPARAGUS

Celebrate the very best of spring in one fabulous dish! Fresh asparagus, carrots, lemon and chives perfectly complement leftover cooked salmon in this simple, sensational entree.
—Steve Westphal, Wind Lake, WI

Prep: 15 min. • **Cook:** 30 min.
Makes: 4 servings

- 2 medium carrots, sliced
- 1 medium sweet yellow pepper, chopped
- ¼ cup butter
- 1½ cups uncooked long grain rice
- 4 cups reduced-sodium chicken broth
- ½ tsp. salt
- ¼ tsp. pepper
- 2½ cups cut fresh asparagus (1-in. pieces)
- 12 oz. fully cooked salmon chunks
- 2 Tbsp. lemon juice
- 2 Tbsp. minced fresh chives, divided
- 1 tsp. grated lemon zest

1. Saute carrots and yellow pepper in butter in a large saucepan until crisp-tender. Add rice; cook and stir for 1 minute or until lightly toasted.
2. Stir in the broth, salt and pepper. Bring to a boil. Reduce heat; cover and simmer for 20 minutes. Stir in asparagus. Cook, uncovered, 3-4 minutes longer or until the rice is tender.
3. Stir in the salmon, lemon juice, 1 Tbsp. chives and the lemon zest; heat through. Fluff with a fork. Sprinkle with remaining minced chives.
2 cups: 568 cal., 21g fat (9g sat. fat), 80mg chol., 1023mg sod., 65g carb. (5g sugars, 4g fiber), 27g pro.

SHRIMP & CORN STIR-FRY

I make this seafood stir-fry at summer's end when my garden is producing plenty of tomatoes, squash, garlic and corn. My family loves it over rice.
—Lindsay Honn, Huntingdon, PA

Takes: 20 min. • **Makes:** 4 servings

- 2 Tbsp. olive oil
- 2 small yellow summer squash, sliced
- 1 small onion, chopped
- 1 lb. uncooked shrimp (26-30 per lb.), peeled and deveined
- 1½ cups fresh or frozen corn, thawed
- 1 cup chopped tomatoes
- 4 garlic cloves, minced
- ½ tsp. salt
- ¼ tsp. pepper
- ¼ tsp. crushed red pepper flakes, optional
- ¼ cup chopped fresh basil
  Hot cooked brown rice, optional

1. In a large skillet, heat oil over medium-high heat. Add squash and onion; stir-fry until squash is crisp-tender, 2-3 minutes.
2. Add next 6 ingredients and, if desired, pepper flakes; stir-fry until the shrimp turn pink, 3-4 minutes longer. Top with basil. Serve with rice if desired.
1 serving: 239 cal., 9g fat (1g sat. fat), 138mg chol., 443mg sod., 19g carb. (8g sugars, 3g fiber), 22g pro. **Diabetic exchanges:** 3 lean meat, 1½ fat, 1 starch, 1 vegetable.

SHRIMP & VEGETABLE BOIL

When my children were small, they liked picking out the ingredients for making this supper. When there's no shrimp on hand, we use crab or chicken.
—Joyce Guth, Mohnton, PA

- -

Prep: 20 min. • **Cook:** 30 min.
Makes: 6 servings

- 4 cups water
- 4 cups chicken broth
- 2 tsp. salt
- 2 tsp. ground nutmeg
- ½ tsp. sugar
- 2 lbs. red potatoes (about 8 medium), cut into wedges
- 1 medium head cauliflower, broken into florets
- 2 large onions, quartered
- 3 medium carrots, sliced
- 1 lb. fresh peas, shelled (about 1 cup)
- 2 lbs. uncooked shell-on shrimp (26-30 per lb.), deveined
- 6 oz. fresh baby spinach (about 8 cups)
- 1 Tbsp. minced fresh parsley
     Salt and pepper to taste

1. In a stockpot, combine the first 5 ingredients; add potatoes, cauliflower, onions, carrots and peas. Bring to a boil. Reduce heat; simmer, uncovered, until the vegetables are tender, 12-15 minutes.
2. Stir in the shrimp and spinach; cook 3-5 minutes longer or until the shrimp turn pink. Drain; transfer to a serving bowl. Sprinkle with parsley; season with salt and pepper.

2⅔ cups: 367 cal., 3g fat (1g sat. fat), 185mg chol., 721mg sod., 50g carb. (12g sugars, 11g fiber), 35g pro. **Diabetic exchanges:** 4 lean meat, 3 starch.

COD WITH HEARTY TOMATO SAUCE

My father made up this sweet, flavorful recipe for my mother when he took over the cooking. We serve it with whole wheat pasta or brown rice.
—Ann Marie Eberhart, Gig Harbor, WA

- -

Takes: 30 min. • **Makes:** 4 servings

- 2 cans (14½ oz. each) diced tomatoes with basil, oregano and garlic, undrained
- 4 cod fillets (6 oz. each)
- 2 Tbsp. olive oil, divided
- 2 medium onions, halved and thinly sliced (about 1½ cups)
- ½ tsp. dried oregano
- ¼ tsp. pepper
- ¼ tsp. crushed red pepper flakes
     Hot cooked whole wheat pasta
     Minced fresh parsley, optional

1. Place tomatoes in a blender. Cover and process until pureed.
2. Pat fish dry with paper towels. In a large skillet, heat 1 Tbsp. oil over medium-high heat. Add cod fillets; cook until the surface of the fish begins to color, 2-4 minutes on each side. Remove from pan.
3. In the same skillet, heat the remaining oil over medium-high heat. Add onions; cook and stir until tender, 2-4 minutes. Stir in the seasonings and pureed tomatoes; bring to a boil. Add the cod fillets; return just to a boil, spooning the sauce over top of fish. Reduce heat; simmer, uncovered, until the fish just begins to flake easily with a fork, 5-7 minutes. Serve with pasta. If desired, sprinkle with parsley.

1 fillet with ¾ cup sauce: 271 cal., 8g fat (1g sat. fat), 65mg chol., 746mg sod., 17g carb. (9g sugars, 4g fiber), 29g pro. **Diabetic exchanges:** 3 lean meat, 2 vegetable, 1½ fat.

VEGETARIAN LINGUINE
Looking for a tasty alternative to the usual meat-and-potatoes meals? Try this colorful pasta dish. My oldest son came up with the scrumptious supper that takes advantage of fresh mushrooms, zucchini and other vegetables as well as basil and provolone.
—Jane Bone, Cape Coral, FL

Takes: 30 min. • **Makes:** 6 servings

- 6 oz. uncooked linguine
- 2 Tbsp. butter
- 1 Tbsp. olive oil
- 2 medium zucchini, thinly sliced
- ½ lb. fresh mushrooms, sliced
- 1 large tomato, chopped
- 2 green onions, chopped
- 1 garlic clove, minced
- ½ tsp. salt
- ¼ tsp. pepper
- 1 cup shredded provolone cheese
- 3 Tbsp. shredded Parmesan cheese
- 2 tsp. minced fresh basil

Cook linguine according to package directions. Meanwhile, in a large skillet, heat butter and oil over medium heat. Add zucchini and mushrooms; saute 3-5 minutes. Add tomato, onions, garlic and seasonings. Reduce heat; simmer, covered, about 3 minutes. Drain linguine; add to the vegetable mixture. Sprinkle with cheeses and basil. Toss to coat.
1½ cups: 260 cal., 13g fat (7g sat. fat), 25mg chol., 444mg sod., 26g carb. (3g sugars, 2g fiber), 12g pro. **Diabetic exchanges:** 1½ starch, 1½ fat, 1 medium-fat meat, 1 vegetable.

QUICK ITALIAN VEGGIE SKILLET
When you don't know what to serve, Italian flavors are a good starting point! This snappy rice dish is sure to please.
—Sonya Labbe, West Hollywood, CA

Takes: 25 min. • **Makes:** 4 servings

- 1 can (15 oz.) no-salt-added garbanzo beans or chickpeas, rinsed and drained
- 1 can (15 oz.) no-salt-added cannellini beans, rinsed and drained
- 1 can (14½ oz.) no-salt-added stewed tomatoes, undrained
- 1 cup vegetable broth
- ¾ cup uncooked instant rice
- 1 tsp. Italian seasoning
- ¼ tsp. crushed red pepper flakes, optional
- 1 cup marinara sauce
- ¼ cup grated Parmesan cheese Minced fresh basil

In a large skillet, combine first 6 ingredients and, if desired, pepper flakes; bring to a boil. Reduce heat; simmer, covered, until rice is tender, 7-9 minutes. Stir in marinara sauce; heat through, stirring occasionally. Top with cheese and basil.
1⅓ cups: 342 cal., 4g fat (1g sat. fat), 6mg chol., 660mg sod., 59g carb. (10g sugars, 11g fiber), 16g pro.

CAULIFLOWER & TOFU CURRY

Cauliflower, garbanzo beans and tofu are subtle on their own, but together they make an awesome base for curry. We have this recipe weekly because one of us is always craving it.
—Patrick McGilvray, Cincinnati, OH

Takes: 30 min. • **Makes:** 6 servings

- 1 Tbsp. olive oil
- 2 medium carrots, sliced
- 1 medium onion, chopped
- 3 tsp. curry powder
- ¼ tsp. salt
- ¼ tsp. pepper
- 1 small head cauliflower, broken into florets (about 3 cups)
- 1 can (14½ oz.) fire-roasted crushed tomatoes
- 1 pkg. (14 oz.) extra-firm tofu, drained and cut into ½-in. cubes
- 1 cup vegetable broth
- 1 can (15 oz.) garbanzo beans or chickpeas, rinsed and drained
- 1 can (13.66 oz.) coconut milk
- 1 cup frozen peas
  Hot cooked rice
  Chopped fresh cilantro

1. In a 6-qt. stockpot, heat oil over medium-high heat. Add the carrots and onion; cook and stir until the onion is tender, 4-5 minutes. Stir in seasonings.
2. Add cauliflower, tomatoes, tofu and broth; bring to a boil. Reduce heat; simmer, covered, 10 minutes. Stir in garbanzo beans, coconut milk and peas; return to a boil. Reduce heat to medium; cook, uncovered, stirring occasionally, until slightly thickened and the cauliflower is tender, 5-7 minutes. Serve with rice. Sprinkle with cilantro.
1⅓ cups: 338 cal., 21g fat (13g sat. fat), 0 chol., 528mg sod., 29g carb. (9g sugars, 7g fiber), 13g pro.

SHRIMP RISOTTO

This delightful main dish will add elegance to family meals. Instant rice makes it come together quickly for a special dinner any day of the week.
—*Taste of Home* Test Kitchen

Takes: 30 min. • **Makes:** 4 servings

- 1 small onion, chopped
- 2 Tbsp. butter
- 1¾ cups uncooked instant rice
- 2 garlic cloves, minced
- ½ tsp. dried basil
- ¼ tsp. pepper
- 2 cans (14½ oz. each) chicken broth
- 1 lb. peeled and deveined cooked medium shrimp
- 2 cups fresh baby spinach, coarsely chopped
- 1 cup frozen corn, thawed
- 1 plum tomato, chopped
- ¼ cup grated Parmesan cheese
- 2 Tbsp. 2% milk

1. In a large skillet, saute onion in butter until tender. Add rice, garlic, basil and pepper; cook 2 minutes longer. Stir in 1 can broth. Cook and stir until most of the liquid is absorbed.
2. Add the remaining broth, ½ cup at a time, stirring constantly. Allow the liquid to absorb between additions. Cook until the risotto is creamy and the rice is tender.
3. Add the remaining ingredients; cook and stir until the spinach is wilted and the shrimp are heated through.
1⅓ cups: 420 cal., 10g fat (5g sat. fat), 197mg chol., 1196mg sod., 49g carb. (3g sugars, 3g fiber), 32g pro.

BLACKENED TILAPIA WITH ZUCCHINI NOODLES

I love quick and bright meals like this one-skillet wonder. Homemade pico de gallo is easy to make the night before.
—Tammy Brownlow, Dallas, TX

- -

Takes: 30 min. • **Makes:** 4 servings

- 2 **large zucchini (about 1½ lbs.)**
- 1½ tsp. **ground cumin**
- ¾ tsp. **salt, divided**
- ½ tsp. **smoked paprika**
- ½ tsp. **pepper**
- ¼ tsp **garlic powder**
- 4 **tilapia fillets (6 oz. each)**
- 2 tsp. **olive oil**
- 2 **garlic cloves, minced**
- 1 cup **pico de gallo**

1. Trim ends of zucchini. Using a spiralizer, cut the zucchini into thin strands.
2. Mix cumin, ½ tsp. salt, smoked paprika, pepper and garlic powder; sprinkle the seasonings generously onto both sides of tilapia. In a large nonstick skillet, heat oil over medium-high heat. In batches, cook the tilapia until fish just begins to flake easily with a fork, 2-3 minutes per side. Remove from pan; keep warm.
3. In the same pan, cook the zucchini with garlic over medium-high heat until slightly softened, 1-2 minutes, tossing constantly with tongs (do not overcook). Sprinkle with the remaining salt. Serve with tilapia and pico de gallo.

Note: If you don't have a spiralizer, you can cut the zucchini into ribbons using a vegetable peeler. Saute as directed, increasing time as necessary.

1 serving: 203 cal., 4g fat (1g sat. fat), 83mg chol., 522mg sod., 8g carb. (5g sugars, 2g fiber), 34g pro. **Diabetic exchanges:** 5 lean meat, 1 vegetable, ½ fat.

SHRIMP & FETA SKILLET

My friend's feisty Italian grandmother, Gemma, makes a dish similar to my shrimp with tomatoes. When I make it, I think of Gemma and smile while stirring.
—Celeste Ehrenberg, Topeka, KS

- -

Takes: 25 min. • **Makes:** 4 servings

- 2 cans (14½ oz. each) diced tomatoes with basil, oregano and garlic, undrained
- 2 tsp. garlic powder
- 2 tsp. dried basil
- 1¼ lbs. uncooked shrimp (31-40 per lb.), peeled and deveined
- 1 cup crumbled feta cheese
   Crusty whole grain bread, optional

1. In a large skillet, combine tomatoes, garlic powder and basil; bring to a boil. Reduce heat; simmer, uncovered, 4-6 minutes or until slightly thickened.
2. Add shrimp; cook and stir 3-4 minutes or until the shrimp turn pink. Sprinkle feta over shrimp; serve with bread if desired.
1¼ cups: 261 cal., 6g fat (3g sat. fat), 187mg chol., 1092mg sod., 15g carb. (7g sugars, 5g fiber), 30g pro.

COCONUT-GINGER CHICKPEAS & TOMATOES

This is my go-to quick dish. When you add tomatoes, you can also toss in some chopped green peppers to make it even more colorful.
—Mala Udayamurthy, San Jose, CA

- -

Takes: 30 min. • **Makes:** 6 servings

- 2 Tbsp. canola oil
- 2 medium onions, chopped (about 1⅓ cups)
- 3 large tomatoes, seeded and chopped (about 2 cups)
- 1 jalapeno pepper, seeded and chopped
- 1 Tbsp. minced fresh gingerroot
- 2 cans (15 oz. each) chickpeas or garbanzo beans, rinsed and drained
- ¼ cup water
- 1 tsp. salt
- 1 cup light coconut milk
- 3 Tbsp. minced fresh cilantro
- 4½ cups hot cooked brown rice
   Additional minced fresh cilantro, optional

1. In a large skillet, heat canola oil over medium-high heat. Add chopped onions; cook and stir until crisp-tender. Add the tomatoes, jalapeno and ginger; cook and stir 2-3 minutes longer or until tender.

2. Stir in chickpeas, water and salt; bring to a boil. Reduce heat; simmer, uncovered, 4-5 minutes or until the liquid is almost evaporated. Remove from heat and stir in coconut milk and cilantro.
3. Serve with rice; sprinkle with additional cilantro if desired.
Note: Wear disposable gloves when cutting hot peppers; the oils can burn skin. Avoid touching your face.
⅔ cup chickpea mixture with ¾ cup rice: 402 cal., 12g fat (3g sat. fat), 0 chol., 590mg sod., 65g carb. (10g sugars, 10g fiber), 11g pro.

onion mixture to pan; heat through. Serve with tortillas, salsa and sour cream mixture.

2 fajitas with ¼ cup sour cream mixture and 2 Tbsp. salsa: 418 cal., 13g fat (1g sat. fat), 147mg chol., 962mg sod., 44g carb. (8g sugars, 2g fiber), 29g pro.

TASTY LENTIL TACOS

My husband has to watch his cholesterol. This is a dish I found that's healthy for him and yummy for our five children.
—Michelle Thomas, Bangor, ME

- -

Prep: 15 min. • **Cook:** 40 min.
Makes: 6 servings

1	tsp. canola oil
1	medium onion, finely chopped
1	garlic clove, minced
1	cup dried lentils, rinsed
1	Tbsp. chili powder
2	tsp. ground cumin
1	tsp. dried oregano
2½	cups vegetable or reduced-sodium chicken broth
1	cup salsa
12	taco shells
1½	cups shredded lettuce
1	cup chopped fresh tomatoes
1½	cups shredded reduced-fat cheddar cheese
6	Tbsp. fat-free sour cream

1. In a large nonstick skillet, heat oil over medium heat; saute onion and garlic until tender. Add lentils and seasonings; cook and stir 1 minute. Stir in broth; bring to a boil. Reduce heat; simmer, covered, until the lentils are tender, 25-30 minutes.
2. Uncover and cook until thickened, 6-8 minutes, stirring occasionally. Mash the lentils slightly; stir in salsa and heat through. Serve in taco shells. Top with remaining ingredients.

2 tacos: 365 cal., 12g fat (5g sat. fat), 21mg chol., 777mg sod., 44g carb. (5g sugars, 6g fiber), 19g pro. **Diabetic exchanges:** 2½ starch, 2 lean meat, 1 vegetable, 1 fat.

SHRIMP FAJITAS

My husband and I have both lost a lot of weight recently and we're always looking for tasty, less filling meals. Busy parents would love this dish as much as we do because it's so quick and easy.
—Charlene Chambers, Ormond Beach, FL

- -

Takes: 30 min. • **Makes:** 4 servings

1	lb. uncooked medium shrimp, peeled and deveined
4	Tbsp. minced fresh cilantro, divided
1	Tbsp. plus 2 tsp. olive oil, divided
3	tsp. Caribbean jerk seasoning
⅛	tsp. chili powder
⅛	tsp. ground cumin
1	cup fat-free sour cream
1	large onion, halved and thinly sliced
1	medium sweet red pepper, cut into thin strips
1	medium green pepper, cut into thin strips
8	flour tortillas (6 in.), warmed
½	cup salsa

1. In a large bowl, toss shrimp with 2 Tbsp. cilantro, 1 Tbsp. oil and spices; let stand 10 minutes. Meanwhile, in a small bowl, mix sour cream and the remaining cilantro.
2. In a large nonstick skillet, heat 1 tsp. oil over medium-high heat. Add onion and peppers; cook and stir until crisp-tender. Remove from pan.
3. In the same pan, heat remaining oil over medium-high heat. Add shrimp; cook and stir until the shrimp turn pink. Return the

APPLE & SWEET
POTATO QUINOA

APPLE & SWEET POTATO QUINOA

When feeding three hungry boys, I rely on quick, filling and tasty meals. My boys weren't big quinoa fans, but the sweet potatoes and apples won them over.
—Cheryl Beadle, Plymouth, MI

Takes: 30 min. • **Makes:** 6 servings

- 2¼ cups chicken or vegetable stock
- 1 cup quinoa, rinsed
- 2 Tbsp. canola oil
- 2 lbs. sweet potatoes (about 3 medium), peeled and cut into ½-in. pieces
- 2 shallots, finely chopped
- 3 medium Gala or Honeycrisp apples, cut into ¼-in. slices
- ½ cup white wine or additional stock
- ½ tsp. salt
- 1 can (15 oz.) black beans, rinsed and drained

1. In a large saucepan, combine stock and quinoa; bring to a boil. Reduce heat; simmer, covered, 15-20 minutes or until the liquid is almost absorbed. Remove from heat.
2. Meanwhile, in a 6-qt. stockpot, heat oil over medium heat. Add sweet potatoes and shallots; cook and stir 5 minutes. Add apples; cook and stir 6-8 minutes longer until the potatoes and apples are tender.
3. Stir in wine and salt. Bring to a boil; cook, uncovered, until the wine is evaporated, about 1 minute. Stir in black beans and quinoa; heat through.
1⅓ cups: 423 cal., 7g fat (1g sat. fat), 0 chol., 541mg sod., 76g carb. (23g sugars, 10g fiber), 12g pro.

SPICY TILAPIA RICE BOWL

I love eating well, and tilapia is a staple in my kitchen. Fresh vegetables are always good but take more prep time, so I like the frozen veggie blend here.
—Rosalin Johnson, Tupelo, MS

Takes: 30 min. • **Makes:** 4 servings

- 4 tilapia fillets (4 oz. each)
- 1¼ tsp. Cajun seasoning
- 3 Tbsp. olive oil, divided
- 1 medium yellow summer squash, halved lengthwise and sliced
- 1 pkg. (16 oz.) frozen pepper and onion stir-fry blend
- 1 can (14½ oz.) diced tomatoes, drained
- 1 envelope fajita seasoning mix
- 1 can (15 oz.) black beans, rinsed and drained
- ⅛ tsp. salt
- ⅛ tsp. pepper
- 3 cups hot cooked brown rice
  Optional: Cubed avocado, sour cream, salsa

1. Sprinkle fillets with Cajun seasoning. In a large skillet, heat 2 Tbsp. oil over medium heat. Add fillets; cook until fish just begins to flake easily with a fork, 4-6 minutes on each side. Remove and keep warm. Wipe pan clean.
2. In the same skillet, heat the remaining oil. Add squash; cook and stir 3 minutes. Add stir-fry blend and tomatoes; cook until the vegetables are tender, 6-8 minutes longer. Stir in fajita seasoning mix; cook and stir until slightly thickened, 1-2 minutes longer.
3. In a small bowl, mix beans, salt and pepper. Divide rice among 4 serving bowls; layer with beans, vegetables and fillets. If desired, serve with toppings.
1 serving: 538 cal., 13g fat (2g sat. fat), 55mg chol., 1365mg sod., 71g carb. (11g sugars, 10g fiber), 33g pro.

EASY CHANA MASALA

I love this quick, healthy Indian-inspired dish so much I always make sure to have the ingredients stocked in my pantry. It always makes weeknights feel a little more special.

—Janeen Judah, Houston, TX

Takes: 30 min. • **Makes:** 4 servings

- 1 Tbsp. canola oil
- ½ cup finely chopped onion
- 1 Tbsp. minced fresh gingerroot
- 2 garlic cloves, minced
- 1 jalapeno pepper, seeded and finely chopped, optional
- ½ tsp. salt
- 1 tsp. garam masala
- ½ tsp. ground coriander
- ½ tsp. ground cumin
- 1 can (15 oz.) diced tomatoes, undrained
- 1 can (15 oz.) garbanzo beans or chickpeas, rinsed and drained
- 3 cups hot cooked brown rice
- ¼ cup plain yogurt
  Minced fresh cilantro

1. In a large skillet, heat oil over medium heat. Add onion, ginger, garlic and, if desired, jalapeno; cook and stir until the onion is softened and lightly browned, 4-5 minutes. Add salt and spices; cook and stir for 1 minute.

2. Stir in tomatoes and garbanzo beans; bring to a boil. Reduce heat; simmer, covered, until the flavors are blended, 12-15 minutes, stirring occasionally. Serve with rice. Top with yogurt and cilantro.

Freeze option: Freeze cooled garbanzo bean mixture in freezer containers. To use, partially thaw in refrigerator overnight. Heat through in a saucepan, stirring occasionally and adding a little water if necessary.

¾ cup chickpea mixture with ¾ cup rice: 359 cal., 8g fat (1g sat. fat), 2mg chol., 616mg sod., 64g carb. (8g sugars, 9g fiber), 10g pro.

DID YOU KNOW?

This is a quick version of a popular Indian and Pakistani dish. In Indian cuisine, *chana* refers to the chickpeas.

TILAPIA WITH SAUTEED SPINACH

You'll love this delicious restaurant-quality meal fit for guests. And because it's all cooked in the same skillet, cleanup won't be a chore at all!
—*Taste of Home* Test Kitchen

Prep: 20 min. • **Cook:** 15 min.
Makes: 4 servings

- 1 **large egg, lightly beaten**
- ½ **cup dry bread crumbs**
- 1 **tsp. Italian seasoning**
- ¾ **tsp. salt, divided**
- ¼ **tsp. garlic powder**
- ¼ **tsp. paprika**
- 4 **tilapia fillets (6 oz. each)**
- 4 **Tbsp. olive oil, divided**
- 1 **small onion, chopped**
- 1 **garlic clove, minced**
- 5 **cups fresh baby spinach**
- ⅛ **tsp. crushed red pepper flakes**
- ⅛ **tsp. pepper**
- ¼ **cup chopped walnuts, toasted**

1. Place egg in a shallow bowl. In another shallow bowl, combine the bread crumbs, Italian seasoning, ½ tsp. salt, garlic powder and paprika. Dip fillets in the egg, then the bread crumb mixture.

2. In a large skillet, cook fillets in 3 Tbsp. oil over medium heat for 4-5 minutes on each side or until golden brown and the fish flakes easily with a fork. Remove and keep warm.

3. In the same skillet, saute onion in the remaining oil until tender. Add garlic; cook 1 minute longer. Stir in the spinach, pepper flakes, pepper and remaining salt. Cook and stir for 3-4 minutes or until the spinach is wilted. Serve with fillets; sprinkle individual servings with walnuts.

1 fillet with ¼ cup spinach and 1 Tbsp. walnuts : 362 cal., 21g fat (3g sat. fat), 115mg chol., 446mg sod., 9g carb. (1g sugars, 2g fiber), 37g pro.

MEDITERRANEAN SPINACH & BEANS

If you want to take this dish from meatless to vegetarian, just use soy sauce instead of Worcestershire. I like it warm or cold.
—Becky Cuba, Spotsylvania, VA

- -

Takes: 30 min. • **Makes:** 4 servings

- 1 Tbsp. olive oil
- 1 small onion, chopped
- 2 garlic cloves, minced
- 1 can (14½ oz.) no-salt-added diced tomatoes, undrained
- 2 Tbsp. Worcestershire sauce
- ¼ tsp. salt
- ¼ tsp. pepper
- ⅛ tsp. crushed red pepper flakes
- 1 can (15 oz.) cannellini beans, rinsed and drained
- 1 can (14 oz.) water-packed artichoke hearts, rinsed, drained and quartered
- 6 oz. fresh baby spinach (about 8 cups)
  Additional olive oil, optional

1. In a 12-in. skillet, heat oil over medium-high heat; saute onion until tender, 3-5 minutes. Add garlic; cook and stir 1 minute. Stir in tomatoes, Worcestershire sauce and seasonings; bring to a boil. Reduce heat; simmer, uncovered, until liquid is almost evaporated, 6-8 minutes.
2. Add the beans, artichoke hearts and spinach; cook and stir until the spinach is wilted, 3-5 minutes. If desired, drizzle with additional oil.

1½ cups: 187 cal., 4g fat (1g sat. fat), 0 chol., 650mg sod., 30g carb. (4g sugars, 6g fiber), 8g pro. **Diabetic exchanges:** 1 starch, 1 lean meat, 2 vegetable, 1 fat.

SCALLOPS WITH WILTED SPINACH

Two of my favorite foods are bacon and seafood. Here, I combine them with white wine, shallots and baby spinach. Serve with crusty bread to soak up the tasty broth!
—Deborah Williams, Peoria, AZ

- -

Takes: 25 min. • **Makes:** 4 servings

- 4 bacon strips, chopped
- 12 sea scallops (about 1½ lbs.), side muscles removed
- 2 shallots, finely chopped
- ½ cup white wine or chicken broth
- 8 cups fresh baby spinach (about 8 oz.)

1. In a large nonstick skillet, cook bacon over medium heat until crisp, stirring occasionally. Remove with a slotted spoon; drain on paper towels. Reserve 2 Tbsp. drippings; discard the rest or save for future use. Wipe the skillet clean if necessary.
2. Pat scallops dry with paper towels. In the same skillet, heat 1 Tbsp. drippings over medium-high heat. Add scallops; cook until golden brown and firm, 2-3 minutes on each side. Remove from pan; keep warm.
3. Heat the remaining drippings in same pan over medium-high heat. Add shallots; cook and stir until tender, 2-3 minutes. Add wine; bring to a boil, stirring to loosen browned bits from pan. Add spinach; cook and stir until wilted, 1-2 minutes. Stir in bacon. Serve with scallops.

3 scallops with ½ cup spinach mixture: 247 cal., 11g fat (4g sat. fat), 56mg chol., 964mg sod., 12g carb. (1g sugars, 1g fiber), 26g pro.

1 serving: 307 cal., 12g fat (2g sat. fat), 124mg chol., 606mg sod., 15g carb. (9g sugars, 3g fiber), 35g pro. **Diabetic exchanges:** 4 lean meat, 3 vegetable, 2 fat.

CILANTRO SHRIMP & RICE
I created this one-dish wonder for my son, who has the pickiest palate. The aroma of fresh herbs is so appetizing—even my son can't resist!
—Nibedita Das, Fort Worth, TX

- -

Takes: 30 min. • **Makes:** 8 servings

- 2 pkg. (8½ oz. each) ready-to-serve basmati rice
- 2 Tbsp. olive oil
- 2 cups frozen corn, thawed
- 2 medium zucchini, quartered and sliced
- 1 large sweet red pepper, chopped
- ½ tsp. crushed red pepper flakes
- 3 garlic cloves, minced
- 1 lb. peeled and deveined cooked large shrimp, tails removed
- ½ cup chopped fresh cilantro
- 1 Tbsp. grated lime zest
- 2 Tbsp. lime juice
- ¾ tsp. salt
  Lime wedges, optional

1. Prepare basmati rice according to the package directions.
2. Meanwhile, in a large skillet, heat oil over medium-high heat. Add the corn, zucchini, red pepper and pepper flakes; cook and stir 3-5 minutes or until zucchini is crisp-tender. Add garlic; cook 1 minute longer. Add the shrimp; cook and stir 3-5 minutes or until heated through.
3. Stir in rice, cilantro, lime zest, lime juice and salt. If desired, serve with lime wedges.
1½ cups: 243 cal., 6g fat (1g sat. fat), 86mg chol., 324mg sod., 28g carb. (3g sugars, 3g fiber), 16g pro. **Diabetic exchanges:** 2 lean meat, 1½ starch, ½ fat.

MAHI MAHI & VEGGIE SKILLET
Cooking mahi mahi with a mix of vegetables may seem complex, but I developed a skillet recipe to bring out the wow factor without the hassle and fuss.
—Solomon Wang, Arlington, TX

- -

Takes: 30 min. • **Makes:** 4 servings

- 3 Tbsp. olive oil, divided
- 4 mahi mahi or salmon fillets (6 oz. each)
- 3 medium sweet red peppers, cut into thick strips
- ½ lb. sliced baby portobello mushrooms
- 1 large sweet onion, cut into thick rings and separated
- ⅓ cup lemon juice
- ¾ tsp. salt, divided
- ½ tsp. pepper
- ¼ cup minced fresh chives
- ⅓ cup pine nuts, optional

1. In a large skillet, heat 2 Tbsp. oil over medium-high heat. Add fillets; cook for 4-5 minutes on each side or until the fish just begins to flake easily with a fork. Remove from pan.
2. Add the remaining oil, red peppers, mushrooms, onion rings, lemon juice and ¼ tsp. salt. Cover and cook over medium heat until vegetables are tender, stirring occasionally, 6-8 minutes.
3. Place fish over vegetables; sprinkle with pepper and remaining salt. Cook, covered, 2 minutes longer or until heated through. Sprinkle with chives and, if desired, pine nuts before serving.

2. Stir in beans and corn; heat through. Top with cheese and cilantro.

1½ cups: 333 cal., 8g fat (2g sat. fat), 8mg chol., 699mg sod., 50g carb. (5g sugars, 9g fiber), 15g pro. **Diabetic exchanges:** 3 starch, 1 lean meat, 1 fat.

COD WITH SWEET PEPPERS
This quick and delicious dish is a family favorite. I like to use three or four different colors of peppers.
—Judy Grebetz, Racine, WI

Takes: 25 min. • **Makes:** 4 servings

- 1 medium onion, halved and sliced
- 1 cup reduced-sodium chicken broth
- 1 Tbsp. lemon juice
- 3 garlic cloves, minced
- 1½ tsp. dried oregano
- ½ tsp. grated lemon zest
- ¼ tsp. salt
- 4 cod fillets (6 oz. each)
- ¾ cup julienned green pepper
- ¾ cup julienned sweet red pepper
- 2½ tsp. cornstarch
- 1 Tbsp. cold water
- 1 medium lemon, halved and sliced

1. In a large nonstick skillet, combine the first 7 ingredients. Bring to a boil. Reduce heat; cover and simmer until onion slices are tender, 6-8 minutes.

2. Arrange fish and peppers over the onion mixture. Cover and simmer until the fish flakes easily with a fork and the peppers are tender, 6-9 minutes. Remove fish and vegetables and keep warm.

3. Combine cornstarch and water until smooth; gradually stir into the pan juices. Bring to a boil; cook and stir until thickened, about 2 minutes. Spoon over the fish fillets and vegetables. Serve with lemon.

1 fillet with ⅓ cup pepper mixture: 168 cal., 1g fat (0 sat. fat), 65mg chol., 398mg sod., 10g carb. (4g sugars, 2g fiber), 29g pro. **Diabetic exchanges:** 4 lean meat, 1 vegetable.

BLACK BEAN QUINOA BOWLS
Did you know that quinoa is a seed? This recipe tastes so good, you'd never guess it was the healthy main-dish equivalent of eating straight spinach!
—Laura Lewis, Boulder, CO

Prep: 15 min. • **Cook:** 30 min.
Makes: 4 servings

- 1 Tbsp. olive oil
- 2 cups sliced baby portobello mushrooms
- 1 medium onion, chopped
- 3 garlic cloves, minced
- ¾ cup quinoa, rinsed
- 1 tsp. ground cumin
- ⅛ tsp. cayenne pepper
- ⅛ tsp. pepper
- 1½ cups vegetable broth
- 1 medium zucchini, halved and thinly sliced
- 1 can (15 oz.) black beans, rinsed and drained
- 1 cup frozen corn (about 5 oz.)
- ½ cup crumbled feta cheese Minced fresh cilantro

1. In a large saucepan, heat oil over medium-high heat; saute mushrooms and onion until tender and lightly browned, 4-6 minutes. Add garlic; cook and stir for 1 minute. Stir in the quinoa, seasonings and broth; bring to a boil. Reduce heat; simmer, covered, 15 minutes. Stir in zucchini; cook, covered, until crisp-tender, about 5 minutes.

Sheet Pan
Pan *favorites*

Chicken & Turkey

SHEET-PAN LEMON GARLIC CHICKEN

Everyone needs an easy meal sometimes. This one is a perfect example of a dish that is not only simple but also delicious—and it's guaranteed to please the whole family.
—Andrea Potischman, Menlo Park, CA

- -

Prep: 20 min. + marinating • **Bake:** 40 min.
Makes: 6 servings

¼	cup olive oil
2	Tbsp. lemon juice
3	garlic cloves, minced
1½	tsp. minced fresh thyme or ¾ tsp. dried thyme
1	tsp. salt
½	tsp. minced fresh rosemary or ¼ tsp. dried rosemary, crushed
¼	tsp. pepper
6	bone-in chicken thighs
6	chicken drumsticks
1	lb. baby red potatoes, halved
1	medium lemon, sliced
2	Tbsp. minced fresh parsley

1. Preheat oven to 425°. In a small bowl, whisk the first 7 ingredients until blended. Pour ¼ cup marinade into a large bowl or shallow dish. Add the chicken and turn to coat. Refrigerate 30 minutes. Cover and refrigerate remaining marinade.
2. Drain chicken, discarding any remaining marinade in bowl. Place the chicken in a 15x10x1-in. baking pan; add potatoes in a single layer. Drizzle reserved marinade over potatoes; top with lemon slices. Bake until a thermometer reads 170°-175° and potatoes are tender, 40-45 minutes. If desired, broil chicken 3-4 in. from heat until deep golden brown, about 3-4 minutes. Sprinkle with parsley before serving.

1 chicken thigh and 1 chicken leg with ½ cup potatoes: 483 cal., 29g fat (7g sat. fat), 128mg chol., 507mg sod., 15g carb. (1g sugars, 1g fiber), 39g pro.

TURKEY LATTICE PIE

With its beautiful crust, this cheesy baked dish is as eye-catching as it is tasty. It's easy to make, too, since it calls for ready to go crescent roll dough.
—Lorraine Naig, Emmetsburg, IA

- -

Prep: 20 min. • **Bake:** 20 min.
Makes: 12 servings

3	tubes (8 oz. each) refrigerated crescent rolls
4	cups cubed cooked turkey
1½	cups shredded cheddar or Swiss cheese
3	cups frozen chopped broccoli, thawed and drained
1	can (10¾ oz.) condensed cream of chicken soup, undiluted
1⅓	cups whole milk
2	Tbsp. Dijon mustard
1	Tbsp. dried minced onion
½	tsp. salt
	Dash pepper
1	large egg, lightly beaten

1. Preheat oven to 375°. Unroll 2 tubes of crescent roll dough and separate into rectangles. Place the rectangles in an ungreased 15x10x1-in. baking pan. Press onto bottom and ¼ in. up the sides of pan to form a crust, sealing seams and perforations. Bake for 5-7 minutes or until crust is light golden brown.
2. Meanwhile, in a large bowl, combine the turkey, cheese, broccoli, soup, milk, mustard, onion, salt and pepper. Spoon over crust.
3. Unroll the remaining dough; divide into rectangles. Seal perforations. Cut each rectangle into four 1-in. strips. Using the strips, make a lattice design on top of the turkey mixture. Brush with the egg. Bake 17-22 minutes longer or until the top crust is golden brown and the filling is bubbly.

1 piece: 396 cal., 20g fat (4g sat. fat), 81mg chol., 934mg sod., 30g carb. (8g sugars, 2g fiber), 24g pro.

PAN-ROASTED CHICKEN & VEGETABLES

This one-dish meal tastes as if it took hours of hands-on time to put together, but the simple ingredients can be prepared in minutes. The rosemary gives it a rich flavor, and the meat juices cook the veggies to perfection. So easy!
—Sherri Melotik, Oak Creek, WI

- -

Prep: 15 min. • **Bake:** 45 min.
Makes: 6 servings

2	**lbs. red potatoes (about 6 medium), cut into ¾-in. pieces**
1	**large onion, coarsely chopped**
2	**Tbsp. olive oil**
3	**garlic cloves, minced**
1¼	**tsp. salt, divided**
1	**tsp. dried rosemary, crushed, divided**
¾	**tsp. pepper, divided**
½	**tsp. paprika**
6	**bone-in chicken thighs (about 2¼ lbs.), skin removed**
6	**cups fresh baby spinach (about 6 oz.)**

1. Preheat oven to 425°. In a large bowl, combine potatoes, onion, oil, garlic, ¾ tsp. salt, ½ tsp. rosemary and ½ tsp. pepper; toss to coat. Transfer to a 15x10x1-in. baking pan coated with cooking spray.
2. In a small bowl, mix paprika and the remaining salt, rosemary and pepper. Sprinkle chicken with the paprika mixture; arrange over the vegetables. Roast until a thermometer inserted in the chicken reads 170°-175° and vegetables are just tender, 35-40 minutes.
3. Remove chicken to a serving platter; keep warm. Top the vegetables with spinach. Roast until the vegetables are tender and spinach is wilted, 8-10 minutes longer. Stir vegetables to combine; serve with chicken.

1 chicken thigh with 1 cup vegetables:
357 cal., 14g fat (3g sat. fat), 87mg chol., 597mg sod., 28g carb. (3g sugars, 4g fiber), 28g pro. **Diabetic exchanges:** 4 lean meat, 1½ starch, 1 vegetable, 1 fat.

TEST KITCHEN TIP

Prepare your sheet-pan meal the night before, then just bring it to room temperature and pop it in the preheated oven to bake it. This actually helps to deeply flavor the chicken. A win-win!

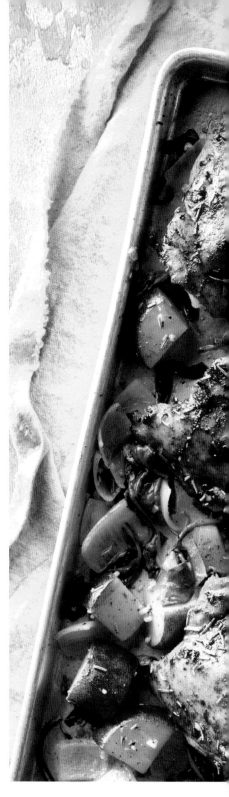

TARA'S SPANISH CHICKEN

The simple flavors of this dish instantly take me back to my Grandma's house. She knew a million ways to cook a chicken, but this is definitely my favorite. I'll often make a pot of long grain white rice and toss together all of the ingredients and juice from the cooked chicken, fresh from the oven. To round out the meal, serve with a salad.
—Tara Imig, Fort Worth, TX

Prep: 25 min. • **Bake:** 55 min.
Makes: 6 servings

- 1 broiler/fryer chicken (3 to 4 lbs.), cut up
- 1 large sweet red pepper, sliced
- 1 medium lemon, sliced
- ¼ cup sliced pimiento-stuffed olives
- 2 Tbsp. capers, drained
- ¼ cup olive oil
- 2 Tbsp. dried oregano
- 1 Tbsp. smoked paprika
- 1 tsp. salt
- ½ tsp. pepper

1. Preheat oven to 350°. Place the first 5 ingredients in a large bowl. Combine the remaining ingredients; drizzle over chicken mixture. Toss to coat. Transfer to a 15x10x1-in. baking pan.

2. Bake, uncovered, until chicken juices run clear, 55-60 minutes.

4 oz. cooked chicken: 402 cal., 27g fat (6g sat. fat), 104mg chol., 673mg sod., 5g carb. (2g sugars, 2g fiber), 34g pro.

CHICKEN VEGGIE FAJITAS

My family loves the spicy flavor of these fajitas. They make an excellent weeknight meal since they're so fast to fix!
—Eleanor Martens, Rosenort, MB

Takes: 20 min. • **Makes:** 4 servings

- 3 Tbsp. lemon juice
- 1 Tbsp. soy sauce
- 1 Tbsp. Worcestershire sauce
- 2 tsp. canola oil
- 1 garlic clove, minced
- ½ tsp. ground cumin
- ½ tsp. dried oregano
- ¾ lb. boneless skinless chicken breasts, cut into ½-in. strips
- 1 small onion, sliced and separated into rings
- ½ each medium green, sweet red and yellow pepper, julienned
- 4 flour tortillas (6 in.), warmed Shredded cheddar cheese, optional

1. In a bowl, combine the first 7 ingredients. Place the chicken and vegetables in a single layer in a greased 15x10x1-in. baking pan; drizzle with ¼ cup lemon juice mixture. Broil 4-6 in. from the heat for 4 minutes.
2. Turn the chicken and vegetables; drizzle with remaining lemon juice mixture. Broil 4 minutes longer or until the chicken juices run clear. Serve on tortillas with shredded cheese, if desired.
1 fajita: 231 cal., 7g fat (1g sat. fat), 47mg chol., 460mg sod., 20g carb. (3g sugars, 1g fiber), 21g pro.

CHILI-STUFFED POBLANO PEPPERS

After exploring some Mexican restaurants, my husband and I teamed up to figure out how to make chiles rellenos at home!
—Lorrie Grabczynski, Commerce Township, MI

Takes: 30 min. • **Makes:** 4 servings

- 1 lb. lean ground turkey (93% lean)
- 1 can (15 oz.) chili without beans
- ¼ tsp. salt
- 1½ cups shredded Mexican cheese blend, divided
- 1 medium tomato, finely chopped
- 4 green onions, chopped
- 4 large poblano peppers
- 1 Tbsp. olive oil

1. Preheat the broiler. In a large skillet over medium heat, cook turkey, crumbling meat, until no longer pink, 5-7 minutes; drain. Add chili and salt; heat through. Stir in ½ cup cheese, tomato and green onions.
2. Meanwhile, cut peppers lengthwise in half; remove seeds. Place on a foil-lined 15x10x1-in. baking pan, cut side down; brush with oil. Broil 4 in. from heat until skins blister, about 5 minutes.
3. With tongs, turn the peppers. Fill with the turkey mixture; sprinkle with remaining cheese. Broil until the cheese is melted, 1-2 minutes longer.
Note: Wear disposable gloves when cutting hot peppers; the oils can burn skin. Avoid touching your face.
2 stuffed pepper halves: 496 cal., 30g fat (11g sat. fat), 134mg chol., 913mg sod., 17g carb. (5g sugars, 4g fiber), 40g pro.

GARLICKY CHICKEN DINNER

Bone-in chicken brings extra flavor to this beautiful dish, which is enhanced by garlic, herbs, lemon and hearty vegetables.
—Shannon Norris, Cudahy, WI

- -

Prep: 25 min. • **Bake:** 45 min.
Makes: 8 servings

1¼ lbs. small red potatoes, quartered
4   medium carrots, cut into
    ½-in. slices
1   medium red onion, cut into
    thin wedges
1   Tbsp. olive oil
6   garlic cloves, minced
2   tsp. minced fresh thyme, divided
1½ tsp. salt, divided
1   tsp. pepper, divided
1   tsp. paprika
4   chicken drumsticks
4   bone-in chicken thighs
1   small lemon, sliced
1   pkg. (5 oz.) fresh spinach

1. Preheat oven to 425°. In a large bowl, combine the potatoes, carrots, onion, oil, garlic, 1 tsp. thyme, ¾ tsp. salt and ½ tsp. pepper; toss to coat. Transfer the mixture to a 15x10x1-in. baking pan coated with cooking spray.

2. In a small bowl, mix paprika and the remaining thyme, salt and pepper. Sprinkle chicken with paprika mixture; arrange over vegetables. Top with lemon slices. Roast until a thermometer inserted in chicken reads 170°-175° and vegetables are just tender, 35-40 minutes.

3. Remove chicken to a serving platter; keep warm. Top vegetables with spinach. Roast until vegetables are tender and spinach is wilted, 8-10 minutes longer. Stir vegetables to combine; serve with chicken.

1 piece chicken with 1 cup vegetables: 264 cal., 12g fat (3g sat. fat), 64mg chol., 548mg sod., 18g carb. (3g sugars, 3g fiber), 21g pro.
Diabetic exchanges: 3 medium-fat meat, 1 starch, 1 vegetable, ½ fat.

DID YOU KNOW?

You can use boneless skinless chicken in some recipes that call for bone-in. If you do, however, it will take more work to keep the chicken moist, and cooking time will be reduced. Start testing the temperature of boneless chicken at least 20 minutes before the time stated in a recipe for bone-in.

PARMESAN CHICKEN WITH ARTICHOKE HEARTS

I've liked the chicken and artichoke combo for a long time, and eventually I decided to come up with my own lemony twist. With all the praise it gets, this dinner is so much fun to serve and even more fun to eat.
—Carly Giles, Hoquiam, WA

Prep: 20 min. • **Bake:** 20 min.
Makes: 4 servings

- 4   boneless skinless chicken breast halves (6 oz. each)
- 3   tsp. olive oil, divided
- 1   tsp. dried rosemary, crushed
- ½   tsp. dried thyme
- ½   tsp. pepper
- 2   cans (14 oz. each) water-packed artichoke hearts, drained and quartered
- 1   medium onion, coarsely chopped
- ½   cup white wine or reduced-sodium chicken broth
- 2   garlic cloves, chopped
- ¼   cup shredded Parmesan cheese
- 1   lemon, cut into 8 slices
- 2   green onions, thinly sliced

1. Preheat oven to 375°. Place chicken in a 15x10x1-in. baking pan coated with cooking spray; drizzle with 1½ tsp. oil. In a small bowl, mix rosemary, thyme and pepper; sprinkle half over the chicken.
2. In a large bowl, combine the artichoke hearts, onion, wine, garlic, the remaining oil and the remaining herb mixture; toss to coat. Arrange around chicken. Sprinkle chicken with cheese; top with lemon slices.
3. Roast until a thermometer inserted in chicken reads 165°, 20-25 minutes. Sprinkle with green onions.

1 chicken breast half with ¾ cup artichoke mixture: 339 cal., 9g fat (3g sat. fat), 98mg chol., 667mg sod., 18g carb. (2g sugars, 1g fiber), 42g pro. **Diabetic exchanges:** 5 lean meat, 1 vegetable, 1 fat, ½ starch.

HOISIN SRIRACHA SHEET-PAN CHICKEN

This dinner's simplicity and convenience makes it extra awesome. Switch up which veggies you use throughout the year—the spicy-sweet sauce is good on all of them!
—Julie Peterson, Crofton, MD

Prep: 20 min. • **Bake:** 40 min.
Makes: 4 servings

- ⅓   cup hoisin sauce
- ⅓   cup reduced-sodium soy sauce
- 2   Tbsp. maple syrup
- 2   Tbsp. Sriracha chili sauce
- 1   Tbsp. rice vinegar
- 2   tsp. sesame oil
- 2   garlic cloves, minced
- ½   tsp. minced fresh gingerroot
- 4   bone-in chicken thighs (6 oz. each)
- ¼   tsp. salt
- ¼   tsp. pepper
- 1   medium sweet potato, cut into ¾-in. cubes
- 2   Tbsp. olive oil, divided
- 4   cups fresh cauliflowerets
- 1   medium sweet red pepper, cut into ¾-in. pieces
     Sesame seeds, optional

1. Preheat oven to 400°. Whisk together the first 8 ingredients. Set aside.
2. Sprinkle both sides of chicken with salt and pepper. Place chicken and sweet potato in a single layer in a foil-lined 15x10x1-in. baking pan. Drizzle with 1 Tbsp. olive oil and a third of hoisin mixture; toss to coat.
3. Bake for 15 minutes; turn chicken and potatoes. Add cauliflower and red pepper; drizzle with another third of the hoisin mixture and the remaining olive oil. Bake until a thermometer inserted in chicken reads 170°-175°, about 25 minutes longer. Drizzle with remaining sauce. If desired, sprinkle with sesame seeds.

1 serving: 490 cal., 24g fat (5g sat. fat), 81mg chol., 1665mg sod., 40g carb. (23g sugars, 5g fiber), 28g pro.

TURKEY-STUFFED BELL PEPPERS

This light meal is especially great for those with a lactose allergy—it's so tasty you may not even notice it's not real cheddar! If you don't have a dietary restriction, feel free to use real cheddar. Serve with a refreshing salad or a side of rice.
—Judy Hand-Truitt, Birmingham, AL

- -

Prep: 30 min. • **Bake:** 20 min.
Makes: 5 servings

- 5 medium green, red or yellow peppers
- 2 tsp. olive oil
- 1¼ lbs. extra-lean ground turkey (99% lean)
- 1 large onion, chopped
- 1 garlic clove, minced
- 2 tsp. ground cumin
- 1 tsp. Italian seasoning
- ½ tsp. salt
- ½ tsp. pepper
- 2 medium tomatoes, finely chopped
- 1¾ cups shredded cheddar-flavored lactose-free or other cheese
- 1½ cups soft bread crumbs
- ¼ tsp. paprika

1. Preheat oven to 325°. Cut the peppers lengthwise in half; remove seeds. Place in a 15x10x1-in. pan coated with cooking spray.
2. In a large skillet, heat oil over medium-high heat. Cook and crumble turkey with onion, garlic and seasonings over medium-high heat until the meat is no longer pink, 6-8 minutes. Cool slightly. Stir in tomatoes, cheese and bread crumbs.
3. Fill peppers with the turkey mixture. Sprinkle with paprika. Bake, uncovered, until heated through and peppers are tender, 20-25 minutes.

2 stuffed pepper halves: 323 cal., 10g fat (0 sat. fat), 45mg chol., 771mg sod., 20g carb. (6g sugars, 4g fiber), 40g pro.
Diabetic exchanges: 5 lean meat, 2 vegetable, 1 starch, ½ fat.

SHEET-PAN PINEAPPLE CHICKEN FAJITAS

Try this Tex-Mex classic with a tropical twist for a sweet new flavor combination in your fajitas. My family loves them!
—Nancy Heishman, Las Vegas, NV

Prep: 20 min. • **Cook:** 20 min.
Makes: 6 servings

2	Tbsp. coconut oil, melted
3	tsp. chili powder
2	tsp. ground cumin
1	tsp. garlic powder
¾	tsp. kosher salt
1½	lbs. chicken tenderloins, halved lengthwise
1	large red or sweet onion, halved and sliced (about 2 cups)
1	large sweet red pepper, cut into ½-in. strips
1	large green pepper, cut into ½-in. strips
1	Tbsp. minced seeded jalapeno pepper
2	cans (8 oz. each) unsweetened pineapple tidbits, drained
2	Tbsp. honey
2	Tbsp. lime juice
12	corn tortillas (6 in.), warmed
	Optional toppings: Pico de gallo, sour cream, shredded Mexican cheese blend and sliced avocado
	Lime wedges, optional

1. Preheat oven to 425°. In a large bowl, mix first 5 ingredients; stir in chicken. Add the onion, peppers, pineapple, honey and lime juice; toss to combine. Spread evenly in 2 greased 15x10x1-in. baking pans.
2. Roast for 10 minutes, rotating the pans halfway through cooking. Remove the pans from oven; preheat broiler.
3. Broil the chicken mixture, one pan at a time, 3-4 in. from heat until the vegetables are lightly browned and chicken is no longer pink, 3-5 minutes. Serve in tortillas, with toppings and lime wedges as desired.
Note: Wear disposable gloves when cutting hot peppers; the oils can burn skin. Avoid touching your face.
2 fajitas: 359 cal., 8g fat (4g sat. fat), 56mg chol., 372mg sod., 45g carb. (19g sugars, 6g fiber), 31g pro. **Diabetic exchanges:** 3 starch, 3 lean meat, 1 fat.

Don't let the extra juice from canned pineapple go to waste! You can use it to coat apple slices and keep them white and fresh. Or add it to a pitcher of orange juice for a little extra tropical flavor.

HERB-BRINED CORNISH GAME HENS

Instead of a turkey or a big roast, why not serve individual Cornish game hens at your next holiday or special-occasion gathering? The hens cook in a fraction of the time, and their tenderness and herb-buttered flavor is guaranteed to impress all of your guests.
—Shannon Norris, Cudahy, WI

Prep: 35 min. + chilling
Bake: 35 min. + standing • **Makes:** 8 servings

- ⅔ cup kosher salt
- ¼ cup packed brown sugar
- 12 whole peppercorns
- 5 fresh sage leaves
- 2 garlic cloves
- 1 fresh thyme sprig
- 1 fresh rosemary sprig
- 1 qt. water
- 1½ qt. cold water
- 2 large turkey-size oven roasting bags
- 4 Cornish game hens (20 oz. each)

HERB BUTTER

- 14 whole peppercorns
- 2 garlic cloves
- ¾ cup butter, softened
- 3 Tbsp. plus 1 tsp. olive oil, divided
- ⅓ cup packed fresh parsley sprigs
- 3 Tbsp. fresh sage leaves
- 1 Tbsp. fresh rosemary leaves
- 2 Tbsp. fresh thyme leaves
- 2 lbs. fresh Brussels sprouts, trimmed and halved
- 2 small red onions, cut into wedges
- ½ tsp. kosher salt
- ½ tsp. coarsely ground pepper

1. In a saucepan, combine the salt, brown sugar, peppercorns, sage, garlic, thyme, rosemary and 1 qt. water. Bring to a boil. Cook and stir until the salt and sugar are dissolved. Remove from heat. Add cold water to cool brine to room temperature.
2. Place a turkey-size oven roasting bag inside a second roasting bag; add hens. Carefully pour cooled brine into bag.
Squeeze out as much air as possible; seal bags and turn to coat. Place in a roasting pan. Refrigerate for 1-2 hours, turning occasionally. Drain and discard the brine; pat hens dry.
3. Place the peppercorns and garlic in a food processor; cover and pulse until coarsely chopped. Add the butter, 3 Tbsp. olive oil and herbs; cover and process until smooth. With fingers, carefully loosen skin from hens; rub half of the butter mixture under skin. Secure skin to the underside of the breast with toothpicks; tie drumsticks together. Rub the remaining butter mixture over skin.

4. Preheat oven to 450°. In a 15x10x1-in. baking pan, toss the Brussels sprouts and onions with remaining olive oil, salt and pepper. Arrange in a single layer. Place hens, breast side up, on top of the vegetables. Bake until thermometer inserted in breast reads 165°, 35-40 minutes. Cover loosely with foil if hens brown too quickly.
5. Remove hens and vegetables to a serving platter; cover and let stand for 10 minutes before carving.
1 serving: 592 cal., 39g fat (16g sat. fat), 199mg chol., 474mg sod., 12g carb. (3g sugars, 4g fiber), 49g pro.

SHEET-PAN CHICKEN PARMESAN

This recipe gives you saucy chicken, melty mozzarella and crisp-tender broccoli, all in one pan. What could be better?
—Becky Hardin, St. Peters, MO

- -

Prep: 15 min. • **Bake:** 25 min.
Makes: 4 servings

- 1 large egg
- ½ cup panko (Japanese) bread crumbs
- ½ cup grated Parmesan cheese
- ½ tsp. salt
- 1 tsp. pepper
- 1 tsp. garlic powder
- 4 boneless skinless chicken breast halves (6 oz. each)

Olive oil-flavored cooking spray
- 4 cups fresh or frozen broccoli florets (about 10 oz.)
- 1 cup marinara sauce
- 1 cup shredded mozzarella cheese
- ¼ cup minced fresh basil, optional

1. Preheat oven to 400°. Lightly coat a 15x10x1-in. baking pan with cooking spray.
2. In a shallow bowl, whisk the egg. In a separate shallow bowl, stir together next 5 ingredients. Dip chicken breast in egg; allow the excess to drip off. Then dip in the crumb mixture, patting to help the coating adhere. Repeat with the remaining chicken. Place chicken breasts in the center third of the baking pan. Spritz with cooking spray.
3. Bake for 10 minutes. Remove from oven. Spread broccoli in a single layer along both sides of sheet pan (if broccoli is frozen, break pieces apart). Return to oven; bake 10 minutes longer. Remove from oven.
4. Preheat broiler. Spread marinara sauce over chicken; top with shredded cheese. Broil chicken and broccoli 3-4 in. from heat until cheese is golden brown and vegetables are tender, 3-5 minutes. If desired, sprinkle with fresh basil.

1 serving: 504 cal., 17g fat (7g sat. fat), 147mg chol., 1151mg sod., 27g carb. (10g sugars, 8g fiber), 52g pro.

TEST KITCHEN TIP

Before shredding soft cheese like mozzarella, put it in the freezer for about 30 minutes. This makes it easier to shred and keeps it from sticking to the grater.

Other Options

SAUSAGE & PEPPER SHEET-PAN SANDWICHES

This yummy meal was always on the table when I was growing up, but I discovered an easier way to recreate it. Here's my secret: Just grab a sheet pan and the ingredients, then let the oven do the work!
—Debbie Glasscock, Conway, AR

Prep: 20 min. • **Bake:** 35 min.
Makes: 6 servings

- 1 lb. uncooked sweet Italian turkey sausage links, roughly chopped
- 3 medium sweet red peppers, seeded and sliced
- 1 large onion, halved and sliced
- 1 Tbsp. olive oil
- 6 hot dog buns, split
- 6 slices provolone cheese

1. Preheat oven to 375°. Place the sausage pieces in a 15x10x1-in. sheet pan, arranging peppers and onions around sausage. Drizzle olive oil over sausage and vegetables; bake, stirring mixture after 15 minutes, until the sausage is no longer pink and vegetables are tender, 30-35 minutes.
2. During last 5 minutes of baking, arrange buns cut side up in a second sheet pan; top each bun bottom with a cheese slice. Bake until buns are golden brown and cheese is melted. Spoon sausage and pepper mixture onto bun bottoms. Replace tops.

1 sandwich: 315 cal., 15g fat (5g sat. fat), 43mg chol., 672mg sod., 28g carb. (7g sugars, 2g fiber), 18g pro.

 ## CRISPY DILL TILAPIA

Every week, I try to serve a new dish that tastes as good as it is good for your health. With its delicious fresh dill and crisp panko crust, this mild tilapia recipe is one of my favorite creations.
—Tamara Huron, New Market, AL

Takes: 20 min. • **Makes:** 4 servings

- 1 cup panko (Japanese) bread crumbs
- 2 Tbsp. olive oil
- 2 Tbsp. snipped fresh dill
- ¼ tsp. salt
- ⅛ tsp. pepper
- 4 tilapia fillets (6 oz. each)
- 1 Tbsp. lemon juice
  Lemon wedges

1. Preheat oven to 400°. Toss together the first 5 ingredients.
2. Place tilapia in a 15x10x1-in. baking pan coated with cooking spray; brush with lemon juice. Top with the crumb mixture, patting to help adhere.
3. Bake, uncovered, on an upper oven rack until fish just begins to flake easily with fork, 12-15 minutes. Serve with lemon wedges.

1 fillet: 256 cal., 9g fat (2g sat. fat), 83mg chol., 251mg sod., 10g carb. (1g sugars, 1g fiber), 34g pro. **Diabetic exchanges:** 5 lean meat, 1½ fat, ½ starch.

SLICED HAM WITH ROASTED VEGETABLES

To prepare this colorful and zesty meal, I "shop" in my backyard for the oranges—picked from our own tree—and fresh veggies that spark this ham's beloved flavor. It's my family's favorite main dish.
—Margaret Pache, Mesa, AZ

Prep: 10 min. • **Bake:** 35 min.
Makes: 6 servings

Cooking spray
6 medium potatoes, peeled and cubed
5 medium carrots, sliced
1 medium turnip, peeled and cubed
1 large onion, cut into thin wedges
6 slices (4 to 6 oz. each) fully cooked ham, halved
¼ cup thawed orange juice concentrate
2 Tbsp. brown sugar
1 tsp. prepared horseradish
1 tsp. grated orange zest
Coarsely ground pepper

1. Preheat the oven to 425°. Grease two 15x10x1-in. baking pans with cooking spray. Add potatoes, carrots, turnip and onion; generously coat with cooking spray. Bake, uncovered, until tender, 25-30 minutes.

2. Arrange ham slices over the vegetables. In a bowl, combine concentrate, brown sugar, horseradish and orange zest. Spoon over ham and vegetables. Bake until the ham is heated through, about 10 minutes longer. Sprinkle with pepper.

1 serving: 375 cal., 5g fat (1g sat. fat), 71mg chol., 1179mg sod., 55g carb. (15g sugars, 7g fiber), 31g pro.

MINI MEAT LOAF SHEET-PAN MEAL

I grew up with this recipe for meat loaf, but decided to adapt it to mini loaves that would bake more quickly. No matter the loaf's size, the sauce is always going to be a hit. I added potatoes and asparagus to even out the meal, but you can use green beans instead of asparagus. Just increase their cooking time to 20 minutes.
—Deanne Johnson, Reading, PA

- -

Prep: 35 min. • **Bake:** 40 min. + standing
Makes: 6 servings

- 2   large eggs, lightly beaten
- 1   cup tomato juice
- ¾   cup quick-cooking oats
- ¼   cup finely chopped onion
- ½   tsp. salt
- 1½   lbs. lean ground beef (90% lean)
- ¼   cup ketchup
- 3   Tbsp. brown sugar
- 1   tsp. prepared mustard
- ¼   tsp. ground nutmeg
- 3   large potatoes, peeled and cut into ½-in. pieces
- 3   Tbsp. olive oil, divided
- ½   tsp. garlic salt, divided
- ¼   tsp. pepper, divided
- 1   lb. fresh asparagus, trimmed and halved

1. Preheat oven to 425°. In a large bowl, combine the eggs, tomato juice, oats, onion and salt. Add the beef; mix lightly but thoroughly. Shape into six 4x2½-in. loaves; place on a 15x10x1-in. baking pan or large shallow roasting pan. Combine ketchup, brown sugar, mustard and nutmeg; brush mixture over the loaves.
2. Combine potatoes with 2 Tbsp. oil, ¼ tsp. garlic salt and ⅛ tsp. pepper; toss to coat. Add to pan in single layer. Bake 25 minutes.
3. Combine asparagus with the remaining 1 Tbsp. oil, ¼ tsp. garlic salt and ⅛ tsp. pepper; toss to coat. Add to pan. Bake until a thermometer inserted into meat loaves reads 160° and vegetables are tender, about 15-20 minutes. Let stand for 5-10 minutes before serving.

1 meat loaf with 1¼ cups vegetables: 460 cal., 19g fat (5g sat. fat), 133mg chol., 690mg sod., 45g carb. (13g sugars, 3g fiber), 29g pro.

Make the most of your meat loaf leftovers! Crumble and use in spaghetti, chili and tacos, or as an extra topping on pizzas. You can also cut leftovers into cubes and fry them in oil, with cubes of boiled potatoes, until browned. Serve with ketchup and dill pickles.

BACON, LETTUCE & TOMATO PIZZA

I bring together two all-time favorite dishes in this fun recipe. I took the mouthwatering mashup to a ladies' lunch and was met with lots of oohs and aahs.
—Bonnie Hawkins, Elkhorn, WI

Takes: 30 min. • **Makes:** 6 servings

- 1 tube (13.8 oz.) refrigerated pizza crust
- 2 Tbsp. olive oil
- 2 Tbsp. grated Parmesan cheese
- 1 tsp. garlic salt
- ½ cup mayonnaise
- 2 tsp. ranch dip mix
- 4 cups shredded romaine
- 3 to 4 plum tomatoes, chopped
- ½ lb. bacon strips, cooked and crumbled

1. Preheat oven to 425°. Unroll and press dough onto bottom of a greased 15x10x1-in. baking pan. Brush with oil; top with cheese and garlic salt. Bake until golden brown, 15-18 minutes; cool slightly.
2. Meanwhile, combine mayonnaise and ranch mix. Spread over the pizza crust; top with lettuce, tomatoes and bacon.
1 piece: 389 cal., 23g fat (5g sat. fat), 16mg chol., 1236mg sod., 34g carb. (5g sugars, 2g fiber), 11g pro.

SMOKED SAUSAGE & VEGGIE SHEET-PAN SUPPER

This fast-to-fix dish is delicious, and it can easily be doubled for last-minute dinner guests. Cook it in the oven or on the grill, and add veggies of your choice.
—Judy Batson, Tampa, FL

Takes: 30 min. • **Makes:** 4 servings

- 1 pkg. (13½ oz.) smoked sausage, cut into ½-in. slices
- 8 fresh Brussels sprouts, thinly sliced
- 1 large sweet onion, halved and sliced
- 1 medium yellow summer squash, halved and sliced
- 1 medium zucchini, halved and sliced
- 1 medium sweet yellow pepper, chopped
- 1 medium green pepper, chopped
- 1 medium tomato, chopped
- ¾ cup sliced fresh mushrooms
- ½ cup Greek vinaigrette

Preheat oven to 400°. Place the first 9 ingredients into a greased 15x10x1-in. baking pan. Drizzle with vinaigrette; toss to coat. Bake, uncovered, 15 minutes. Remove pan from oven; preheat broiler. Broil the sausage mixture 3-4 in. from heat until the vegetables are lightly browned, 3-4 minutes.
2 cups: 491 cal., 37g fat (13g sat. fat), 64mg chol., 1430mg sod., 22g carb. (13g sugars, 5g fiber), 18g pro.

4 **boneless pork loin chops**
   (1 in. thick and about 6 oz. each)
2 **tsp. southwest seasoning**

1. Preheat oven to 425°. Line a 15x10x1-in. baking pan with foil; brush with 2 tsp. oil.
2. In a large bowl, toss the potatoes with 1 Tbsp. oil. Place in 1 section of prepared baking pan. In same bowl, toss asparagus with 1 Tbsp. olive oil; place in another section of pan. Sprinkle salt and pepper over the potatoes and asparagus.
3. In the same bowl, toss apple with 1 tsp. olive oil. In a small bowl, mix brown sugar, cinnamon and ginger; sprinkle over the apples and toss to coat. Transfer to a different section of the same pan.
4. Brush pork chops with the remaining oil; sprinkle both sides with southwest seasoning. Place chops in the remaining section of pan. Bake until a thermometer inserted in pork reads 145° and potatoes and apples are tender, 20-25 minutes. Let stand 5 minutes before serving.
1 serving: 486 cal., 23g fat (5g sat. fat), 82mg chol., 447mg sod., 32g carb. (10g sugars, 5g fiber), 37g pro.

Potatoes and apples make a good team! Storing potatoes with a couple of apples can help keep them from sprouting. For a sweet and savory side using both ingredients, season diced potatoes with chopped fresh aromatic herbs like thyme, rosemary or sage. Then cook the potatoes with apples, kale and onion.

PORK & ASPARAGUS SHEET-PAN DINNER

When time is of the essence, it's so nice to have a quick, easy meal idea in your back pocket. Not only is this one tasty, but you can also clean it up in a flash.
—Joan Hallford, North Richland Hills, TX

- -

Prep: 20 min. • **Bake:** 20 min.
Makes: 4 servings

¼ **cup olive oil, divided**
3 **cups diced new potatoes**
3 **cups cut fresh asparagus**
   (1-in. pieces)
¼ **tsp. salt**
¼ **tsp. pepper**
1 **large gala or Honeycrisp apple,**
   peeled and cut into 1-in. wedges
2 **tsp. brown sugar**
1 **tsp. ground cinnamon**
¼ **tsp. ground ginger**

MEDITERRANEAN TILAPIA

I recently became a fan of tilapia. Its mellow taste makes it easy to top with my favorite ingredients. Plus, it's low in calories and fat. What's not to love?
—Robin Brenneman, Hilliard, OH

Takes: 20 min. • Makes: 6 servings

- 6 tilapia fillets (6 oz. each)
- 1 cup canned Italian diced tomatoes
- ½ cup water-packed artichoke hearts, chopped
- ½ cup sliced ripe olives
- ½ cup crumbled feta cheese

Preheat oven to 400°. Place the fillets in a 15x10x1-in. baking pan coated with cooking spray. Top with tomatoes, artichoke hearts, olives and cheese. Bake, uncovered, until fish flakes easily with a fork, 15-20 minutes.
1 fillet: 197 cal., 4g fat (2g sat. fat), 88mg chol., 446mg sod., 5g carb. (2g sugars, 1g fiber), 34g pro. **Diabetic exchanges:** 5 lean meat, ½ fat.
Italian Tilapia: Follow method as directed, but top fillets with 1 cup canned diced tomatoes with roasted garlic, ½ cup each julienned roasted sweet red pepper, sliced fresh mushrooms and diced fresh mozzarella, and ½ tsp. dried basil.
Southwest Tilapia: Follow method as directed, but top fillets with 1 cup canned diced tomatoes with mild green chiles, ½ cup each cubed avocado, frozen corn (thawed), cubed cheddar, and ½ tsp. dried cilantro.

SOUTHERN HASH BROWNS & HAM SHEET-PAN BAKE

There's nothing better on a busy weeknight than breakfast for dinner, especially when you can use a sheet pan to make it. In this recipe, yummy hash browns and ham are tossed with a special sauce that's sweet, tangy and irresistible. Add on a few eggs and freshly chopped scallions, and voila! Breakfast—or dinner—is served.
—Colleen Delawder, Herndon, VA

Prep: 15 min. • Bake: 35 min.
Makes: 4 servings

- 1 pkg. (20 oz.) refrigerated shredded hash brown potatoes
- 3 Tbsp. olive oil
- ½ tsp. salt
- ½ tsp. pepper
- ¼ cup apple jelly
- ¼ cup apricot preserves
- 1 Tbsp. horseradish sauce
- 1 tsp. Dijon mustard
- ¼ tsp. garlic powder
- ¼ tsp. onion powder
- 2 cups cubed fully cooked ham
- 4 large eggs, room temperature
- 2 green onions, finely chopped

1. Preheat oven to 400°. Place potatoes in a greased 15x10x1-in. baking pan. Drizzle with oil; sprinkle with salt and pepper. Toss to coat. Bake until edges are golden brown, 25-30 minutes.
2. In a small bowl, combine jelly, preserves, horseradish sauce, Dijon mustard, garlic powder and onion powder. Pour over the potatoes; add ham. Toss to coat.
3. With the back of a spoon, make 4 wells in the potato mixture. Break an egg in each well. Bake until egg whites are completely set and yolks begin to thicken but are not hard, 10-12 minutes. Sprinkle with green onions and additional pepper.
1 serving: 483 cal., 19g fat (4g sat. fat), 228mg chol., 1340mg sod., 55g carb. (23g sugars, 3g fiber), 24g pro.

AVOCADO CRAB BOATS

These boats are great with tortilla chips, beans or rice. You can also cover them, pack them on ice, and take them to a picnic or potluck. Straight from the oven or cold, they're always delicious.
—Frances Benthin, Scio, OR

- -

Takes: 20 min. • **Makes:** 8 servings

5	medium ripe avocados, peeled and halved
½	cup mayonnaise
2	Tbsp. lemon juice
2	cans (6 oz. each) lump crabmeat, drained
¼	cup chopped fresh cilantro, divided
2	Tbsp. minced chives
1	serrano pepper, seeded and minced
1	Tbsp. capers, drained
¼	tsp. pepper
1	cup shredded pepper jack cheese
½	tsp. paprika
	Lemon wedges

1. Preheat broiler. Place 2 avocado halves in a large bowl; mash lightly with a fork. Add mayonnaise and lemon juice; mix until well blended. Stir in the crab, 3 Tbsp. cilantro, chives, serrano pepper, capers and pepper. Spoon into the remaining avocado halves.
2. Transfer to a 15x10x1-in. baking pan. Sprinkle with cheese and paprika. Broil 4-5 in. from heat until the cheese is melted, 3-5 minutes. Sprinkle with the remaining cilantro; serve with lemon wedges.
Note: Wear disposable gloves when cutting hot peppers; the oils can burn skin. Avoid touching your face.
1 filled avocado half: 325 cal., 28g fat (6g sat. fat), 57mg chol., 427mg sod., 8g carb. (0 sugars, 6g fiber), 13g pro.

ROASTED KIELBASA & VEGETABLES

I like this dish featuring kielbasa and veggies for two reasons: It's so hearty, and it's a one-pan meal. That's definitely a win-win dinner!

—Marietta Slater, Justin, TX

- -

Prep: 20 min. • **Bake:** 40 min.
Makes: 6 servings

- 3 medium sweet potatoes, peeled and cut into 1-in. pieces
- 1 large sweet onion, cut into 1-in. pieces
- 4 medium carrots, cut into 1-in. pieces
- 2 Tbsp. olive oil
- 1 lb. smoked kielbasa or Polish sausage, halved and cut into 1-in. pieces
- 1 medium yellow summer squash, cut into 1-in. pieces
- 1 medium zucchini, cut into 1-in. pieces
- ¼ tsp. salt
- ¼ tsp. pepper
  Dijon mustard, optional

1. Preheat oven to 400°. Divide sweet potatoes, onion and carrots between 2 greased 15x10x1-in. baking pans. Drizzle with oil; toss to coat. Roast 25 minutes, stirring occasionally.
2. Add kielbasa, squash and zucchini to pans; sprinkle with salt and pepper. Roast until vegetables are tender, 15-20 minutes longer. Transfer to a serving bowl; toss to combine. If desired, serve with mustard.
1⅔ cups: 378 cal., 25g fat (8g sat. fat), 51mg chol., 954mg sod., 26g carb. (12g sugars, 4g fiber), 13g pro.

ORANGE-GLAZED PORK WITH SWEET POTATOES

When it's chilly outside, I like to roast pork tenderloin with sweet potatoes, apples and an orange. The sweetness and spices make any evening cozy.

—Danielle Lee Boyles, Weston, WI

- -

Prep: 20 min. • **Bake:** 55 min. + standing
Makes: 6 servings

- 1 lb. sweet potatoes (about 2 medium)
- 2 medium apples
- 1 medium orange
- 1 tsp. salt
- ½ tsp. pepper
- 1 cup orange juice
- 2 Tbsp. brown sugar
- 2 tsp. cornstarch
- 1 tsp. ground cinnamon
- 1 tsp. ground ginger
- 2 pork tenderloins (about 1 lb. each)

1. Preheat oven to 350°. Peel the sweet potatoes; core apples. Cut potatoes, apples and orange crosswise into ¼-in.-thick slices. Arrange in a foil-lined 15x10x1-in. baking pan coated with cooking spray; sprinkle with salt and pepper. Roast 10 minutes.
2. Meanwhile, in a microwave-safe bowl, mix the orange juice, brown sugar, cornstarch, cinnamon and ginger. Microwave, covered, on high, stirring every 30 seconds until thickened, 1-2 minutes. Stir until smooth.
3. Place the pork over the sweet potato mixture; drizzle with orange juice mixture. Roast until a thermometer inserted in pork reads 145° and the sweet potatoes and apples are tender, 45-55 minutes longer. Remove from oven; tent with foil. Let stand 10 minutes before slicing.
4 oz. cooked pork with about 1 cup sweet potato mixture: 325 cal., 5g fat (2g sat. fat), 85mg chol., 467mg sod., 36g carb. (21g sugars, 3g fiber), 32g pro.
Diabetic exchanges: 4 lean meat, 2 starch.

ROASTED CURRIED CHICKPEAS & CAULIFLOWER

When there's not much time to cook, try roasting potatoes and cauliflower with chickpeas for a tasty, warm-you-up dinner. Add chicken or tofu if you'd like.
—Pam Correll, Brockport, PA

Prep: 15 min. • **Bake:** 30 min.
Makes: 4 servings

- 2 lbs. potatoes (about 4 medium), peeled and cut into ½-in. cubes
- 1 small head cauliflower, broken into florets (about 3 cups)
- 1 can (15 oz.) chickpeas or garbanzo beans, rinsed and drained
- 3 Tbsp. olive oil
- 2 tsp. curry powder
- ¾ tsp. salt
- ¼ tsp. pepper
- 3 Tbsp. minced fresh cilantro or parsley

1. Preheat oven to 400°. Place the first 7 ingredients in a large bowl; toss to coat. Transfer to a 15x10x1-in. baking pan coated with cooking spray.
2. Roast until the vegetables are tender, 30-35 minutes, stirring occasionally. Sprinkle with cilantro.
1½ cups: 339 cal., 13g fat (2g sat. fat), 0 chol., 605mg sod., 51g carb. (6g sugars, 8g fiber), 8g pro. **Diabetic exchanges:** 3 starch, 2 fat, 1 vegetable, 1 lean meat.

COD & ASPARAGUS BAKE

The lemon pulls this flavorful and healthy dish together. You can also use grated Parmesan cheese instead of Romano.
—Thomas Faglon, Somerset, NJ

Takes: 30 min. • **Makes:** 4 servings

- 4 cod fillets (4 oz. each)
- 1 lb. fresh thin asparagus, trimmed
- 1 pint cherry tomatoes, halved
- 2 Tbsp. lemon juice
- 1½ tsp. grated lemon zest
- ¼ cup grated Romano cheese

1. Preheat oven to 375°. Place cod and asparagus in a 15x10x1-in. baking pan brushed with oil. Add the tomatoes, cut sides down. Brush fish with lemon juice; sprinkle with lemon zest. Sprinkle fish and vegetables with Romano cheese. Bake until the fish just begins to flake easily with a fork, about 12 minutes.
2. Remove pan from oven; preheat broiler. Broil the cod mixture 3-4 in. from heat until vegetables are lightly browned, 2-3 minutes.
1 serving: 141 cal., 3g fat (2g sat. fat), 45mg chol., 184mg sod., 6g carb. (3g sugars, 2g fiber), 23g pro. **Diabetic exchanges:** 3 lean meat, 1 vegetable.

½ tsp. pepper
2 tilapia fillets (6 oz. each)
2 tsp. minced fresh tarragon or
   ½ tsp. dried tarragon
⅛ tsp. salt
1 Tbsp. butter, softened
   Optional: Lemon wedges and
      tartar sauce

1. Preheat oven to 450°. Line a 15x10x1-in. baking pan with foil; grease foil.
2. In a bowl, combine the first 5 ingredients. Add melted butter, garlic salt and pepper; toss to coat. Place vegetables in a single layer in prepared pan; bake until potatoes are tender, about 20 minutes.
3. Remove from oven; preheat broiler. Arrange vegetables on one side of the sheet pan. Add fish to the other side. Sprinkle the fillets with tarragon and salt; dot with softened butter. Broil 4-5 in. from heat until the fish flakes easily with a fork, about 5 minutes. If desired, serve with lemon wedges and tartar sauce.
1 serving: 555 cal., 20g fat (12g sat. fat), 129mg chol., 892mg sod., 56g carb. (8g sugars, 8g fiber), 41g pro.

DID YOU KNOW?

Sugar snap peas are rich in vitamin C, which boosts the immune system, helps prevent cardiovascular disease and even repairs sun-damaged skin cells. Sugar snap peas are also a good source of lutein and zeaxanthin, two carotenoids that can reduce the risk of chronic eye diseases.

SHEET-PAN TILAPIA & VEGETABLE MEDLEY

Unlike some one-pan dinners that require some precooking in a skillet or pot, this one with fish and spring veggies uses just the sheet pan, period.
—Judy Batson, Tampa, FL

- -

Prep: 15 min. • **Bake:** 25 min.
Makes: 2 servings

2 medium Yukon Gold potatoes, cut into wedges
3 large fresh Brussels sprouts, thinly sliced
3 large radishes, thinly sliced
1 cup fresh sugar snap peas, cut into ½-in. pieces
1 small carrot, thinly sliced
2 Tbsp. butter, melted
½ tsp. garlic salt

LEMON-DIJON PORK SHEET-PAN SUPPER

On my busiest nights, I look for recipes that require minimal effort while still delivering delicious results. This supper has become one of my favorites, not only because of its bright flavors, but also its speedy cleanup!
—Elisabeth Larsen, Pleasant Grove, UT

- -

Prep: 20 min. • **Bake:** 20 min.
Makes: 4 servings

- 4 tsp. Dijon mustard
- 2 tsp. grated lemon zest
- 1 garlic clove, minced
- ½ tsp. salt
- 2 Tbsp. canola oil
- 1½ lbs. sweet potatoes (about 3 medium), cut into ½-in. cubes
- 1 lb. fresh Brussels sprouts (about 4 cups), quartered
- 4 boneless pork loin chops (6 oz. each)
  Coarsely ground pepper, optional

1. Preheat oven to 425°. In a large bowl, mix the first 4 ingredients; gradually whisk in oil. Remove 1 Tbsp. mixture for brushing pork. Add vegetables to the remaining mixture; toss to coat.
2. Place the pork chops and vegetables in a 15x10x1-in. pan coated with cooking spray. Brush chops with the reserved mustard mixture. Roast 10 minutes.
3. Turn chops and stir vegetables; roast until a thermometer inserted in the pork reads 145° and the vegetables are tender, 10-15 minutes longer. If desired, sprinkle with coarsely ground pepper. Let stand for 5 minutes before serving.

1 pork chop with 1¼ cups vegetables: 516 cal., 17g fat (4g sat. fat), 82mg chol., 505mg sod., 51g carb. (19g sugars, 9g fiber), 39g pro. **Diabetic exchanges:** 5 lean meat, 3 starch, 1½ fat, 1 vegetable.

SHEET-PAN CHIPOTLE-LIME SHRIMP BAKE

I make this seafood dinner when we have company over because it tastes incredible, and it takes very little effort to throw it all together. Use asparagus, broccolini or a mix of the two—the dish will impress your family and guests no matter what.
—Colleen Delawder, Herndon, VA

- -

Prep: 10 min. • **Bake:** 40 min.
Makes: 4 servings

- 1½ lbs. baby red potatoes, cut into ¾-in. cubes
- 1 Tbsp. extra virgin olive oil
- ¾ tsp. sea salt, divided
- 3 medium limes
- ¼ cup unsalted butter, melted
- 1 tsp. ground chipotle pepper
- ½ lb. fresh asparagus, trimmed
- ½ lb. Broccolini or broccoli, cut into small florets
- 1 lb. uncooked shrimp (16-20 per lb.), peeled and deveined
- 2 Tbsp. minced fresh cilantro

1. Preheat oven to 400°. Place the potatoes in a greased 15x10x1-in. baking pan; drizzle with olive oil. Sprinkle with ¼ tsp. sea salt; stir mixture to combine. Bake 30 minutes. Meanwhile, squeeze ⅓ cup juice from limes, reserving fruit. Combine lime juice, melted butter, chipotle and remaining sea salt.
2. Remove sheet pan from oven; stir the potatoes. Arrange asparagus, Broccolini, shrimp and the reserved limes on top of the potatoes. Pour the lime juice mixture over the vegetables and shrimp.
3. Bake until the shrimp turn pink and the vegetables are tender, about 10 minutes. Sprinkle with cilantro.

1 serving: 394 cal., 17g fat (8g sat. fat), 168mg chol., 535mg sod., 41g carb. (4g sugars, 6g fiber), 25g pro.

Pizza & Pasta *favorites*

Pizza

ARTICHOKE CHICKEN PESTO PIZZA

Garlicky pesto perfectly complements the mild flavor of artichoke and tender chicken.
—Trisha Kruse, Eagle, ID

- -

Takes: 15 min. • **Makes:** 8 slices

- 1 prebaked 12-in. pizza crust
- ½ cup prepared pesto
- 2 cups cubed cooked chicken breast
- 2 jars (6½ oz. each) marinated artichoke hearts, drained
- 2 cups shredded part-skim mozzarella cheese
   Grated Parmesan cheese and minced fresh basil, optional

Preheat oven to 425°. Place crust on an ungreased 12-in. pizza pan. Spread with pesto. Arrange chicken and artichokes over top; sprinkle with cheese. Bake until golden brown, 10-12 minutes. If desired, top with Parmesan cheese and minced fresh basil.

1 slice: 381 cal., 20g fat (6g sat. fat), 45mg chol., 880mg sod., 28g carb. (2g sugars, 4g fiber), 23g pro.

DEEP-DISH SAUSAGE PIZZA

My grandma made the tastiest meals for us when we stayed the night at her farm. Her wonderful pizza, covered with cheese and full of fragrant herbs in the crust, smelled heavenly when fresh from the oven. Now I make the same beloved pizza for my family.
—Michele Madden,
Washington Court House, OH

- -

Prep: 30 min. + rising
Bake: 30 min. + standing • **Makes:** 8 slices

- 1 pkg. (¼ oz.) active dry yeast
- ⅔ cup warm water (110° to 115°)
- 1¾ to 2 cups all-purpose flour
- ¼ cup vegetable oil
- 1 tsp. each dried oregano, basil and marjoram
- ½ tsp. garlic salt
- ½ tsp. onion salt

TOPPINGS
- 4 cups shredded part-skim mozzarella cheese, divided
- 2 medium green peppers, chopped
- 1 large onion, chopped
- ½ tsp. each dried oregano, basil and marjoram
- 1 Tbsp. olive oil
- 1 cup grated Parmesan cheese
- 1 lb. bulk pork sausage, cooked and drained
- 1 can (28 oz.) diced tomatoes, well drained
- 2 oz. sliced pepperoni

1. In a large bowl, dissolve the dry yeast in warm water. Add 1 cup flour, oil and crust seasonings; beat until smooth. Add enough remaining flour to form a soft dough.
2. Turn onto a floured surface; knead until smooth and elastic, 6-8 minutes. Place in a greased bowl; turn once to grease top. Cover and let rise in a warm place until doubled, about 1 hour.
3. Preheat oven to 400°. Punch dough down; roll out into a 15-in. circle. Transfer to a well-greased 12-in. heavy ovenproof skillet or round baking pan; let dough drape over edges. Sprinkle with 1 cup mozzarella.
4. In a skillet, saute green peppers, onion and topping seasonings in oil until tender; drain. Layer half the mixture over crust. Layer with half each of the Parmesan, sausage and tomatoes. Sprinkle with 2 cups mozzarella. Repeat layers. Fold the crust to form an edge.
5. Bake for 20 minutes. Top with pepperoni and the remaining mozzarella. Bake until the crust is browned, 10-15 minutes longer. Let stand for 10 minutes before slicing.

1 slice: 548 cal., 34g fat (14g sat. fat), 68mg chol., 1135mg sod., 32g carb. (8g sugars, 4g fiber), 27g pro.

BARBECUE CHICKEN PIZZA

My husband and I are big fans of barbecue chicken and pizza, so I make this yummy creation often. To take it up a notch, I add other toppings we love, including smoky bacon and creamy Gorgonzola. My mouth starts to water just thinking about it!
—Megan Crow, Lincoln, NE

- -

Prep: 30 min. • **Bake:** 15 min.
Makes: 8 servings

- 2 **Tbsp. olive oil**
- 1 **medium red onion, sliced**
- 1 **tube (13.8 oz.) refrigerated pizza crust**
- ¾ **cup barbecue sauce**
- 2 **cups shredded cooked chicken breast**
- 6 **bacon strips, cooked and crumbled**
- ¼ **cup crumbled Gorgonzola cheese**
- 2 **jalapeno peppers, seeded and minced**
- 1 **tsp. paprika**
- 1 **tsp. garlic powder**
- 2 **cups shredded part-skim mozzarella cheese**

1. Preheat oven to 425°. In a large skillet, heat oil over medium heat. Add the onion; cook and stir 4-6 minutes or until softened. Reduce heat to medium-low; cook for 20-25 minutes or until the onion is deep golden brown, stirring occasionally.
2. Unroll dough for crust, pressing onto the bottom and ½ in. up the sides of a greased 15x10x1-in. baking pan. Bake 8 minutes.
3. Spread barbecue sauce over the dough; top with chicken, cooked onion, bacon, Gorgonzola cheese and jalapenos. Sprinkle with paprika and garlic powder; top with mozzarella cheese. Bake 8-10 minutes or until crust is golden and cheese is melted.

Freeze option: Bake crust as directed; cool. Top with all the ingredients as directed; securely wrap and freeze unbaked pizza. To use, unwrap pizza; bake as directed, increasing time as necessary.

Note: Wear disposable gloves when cutting hot peppers; the oils can burn skin. Avoid touching your face.

1 piece: 354 cal., 15g fat (5g sat. fat), 53mg chol., 851mg sod., 29g carb. (7g sugars, 2g fiber), 25g pro.

TEST KITCHEN TIP

For a thicker, sweeter spin on barbecue sauce, mash McIntosh or Gala apples and blend them with your favorite bottled barbecue sauce in a food processor. Use wherever you would use regular barbecue sauce.

GAME-NIGHT NACHO PIZZA

Some like it hot with jalapenos; others like it cool with a dollop of sour cream. But one thing's for sure: This is "nacho" ordinary pizza night!
—Jamie Jones, Madison, GA

Takes: 20 min. • **Makes:** 6 servings

1   prebaked 12-in. pizza crust
1   Tbsp. olive oil
1   cup refried beans
1   cup refrigerated fully cooked barbecued shredded beef
½   cup chopped seeded tomatoes
½   cup pickled jalapeno slices
1   cup shredded Colby-Monterey Jack cheese
    Optional toppings: Shredded lettuce, sour cream and salsa

1. Preheat oven to 450°. Place crust on an ungreased pizza pan. Brush with oil. Spread beans over crust. Top with beef, tomatoes, jalapenos and cheese.

2. Bake 10-15 minutes or until cheese is melted. Serve with lettuce, sour cream and salsa if desired.

1 serving: 370 cal., 13g fat (5g sat. fat), 30mg chol., 1103mg sod., 46g carb. (6g sugars, 3g fiber), 18g pro.

CHILI DOG PIZZA

My girls love it when I make this mash-up pizza with hot dogs and chili. The bonus: It's a marvelous way to use up leftover chili.
—Jennifer Stowell, Deep River, IA

Takes: 25 min. • **Makes:** 8 servings

- 1   **tube (11 oz.) refrigerated thin pizza crust**
- ½   **cup yellow mustard**
- 1   **can (15 oz.) chili with beans**
- 6   **hot dogs, sliced**
- 2   **cups shredded cheddar cheese**
     Chopped onion and sweet pickle relish, optional

1. Preheat oven to 425°. Unroll and press dough into bottom of a greased 15x10x1-in. baking pan. Bake until edges are lightly browned, 5-7 minutes.

2. Spread with mustard; top with chili, hot dogs and cheese. Bake until crust is golden and cheese is melted, 10-15 minutes. If desired, sprinkle with onion and relish.

1 piece: 404 cal., 25g fat (11g sat. fat), 54mg chol., 1113mg sod., 28g carb. (4g sugars, 3g fiber), 18g pro.

SPINACH-PESTO WHITE PIZZA

When my kids were younger, I had to get creative so they would eat their veggies. Because pesto is already green, I figured it'd make the perfect disguise for spinach. The pizza gained a following right away, and now it's one of my favorite recipes!
—Janet Burbach, North Platte, NE

Takes: 30 min. • **Makes:** 6 servings

- 1   **tsp. olive oil**
- 3   **cups fresh baby spinach**
- ¼   **cup plus 1 Tbsp. prepared pesto, divided**
- 1   **pkg. (6 oz.) ready-to-use grilled chicken breast strips**
- 1   **prebaked 12-in. pizza crust**
- 2   **cups shredded part-skim mozzarella cheese**
- 5   **bacon strips, cooked and crumbled**
- ½   **cup part-skim ricotta cheese**
- ¼   **cup shredded Parmesan cheese**

1. Preheat oven to 450°. In a large skillet, heat oil over medium-high heat. Add spinach; cook and stir just until wilted. Remove from heat; stir in ¼ cup pesto. In a small bowl, toss chicken strips with the remaining pesto.

2. Place crust on an ungreased baking sheet. Spread with the spinach mixture; top with chicken, mozzarella cheese and bacon. Drop ricotta cheese by rounded teaspoonfuls over top; sprinkle with Parmesan cheese. Bake 8-10 minutes or until the cheese is melted.

1 slice: 453 cal., 22g fat (8g sat. fat), 52mg chol., 956mg sod., 35g carb. (3g sugars, 2g fiber), 30g pro.

2. Place baguette halves on a baking sheet, cut side up; sprinkle with half the cheese and ½ cup basil. Top with mushroom mixture, tomatoes and the remaining mozzarella cheese.

3. Bake 10-15 minutes or until the cheese is melted. Sprinkle with remaining basil. Cut each half into 3 portions.

1 piece: 260 cal., 7g fat (4g sat. fat), 18mg chol., 614mg sod., 36g carb. (5g sugars, 3g fiber), 13g pro. **Diabetic exchanges:** 2 starch, 1 vegetable, 1 medium-fat meat.

GREEK SAUSAGE PITA PIZZAS

I turned my favorite sandwich into a pizza, tzatziki sauce and all. It's great for a casual lunch or dinner, but keep it in mind when you're having company over, too.
—Marion McNeill, Mayfield Heights, OH

Takes: 30 min. • **Makes:** 4 servings

- 1 pkg. (19 oz.) Italian sausage links, casings removed
- 2 garlic cloves, minced
- 4 whole pita breads
- 2 plum tomatoes, seeded and chopped
- 1 medium ripe avocado, peeled and cubed
- ½ cup crumbled feta cheese
- 1 small cucumber, sliced
- ½ cup refrigerated tzatziki sauce

1. Preheat oven to 350°. In a large skillet, cook sausage and garlic over medium heat 6-8 minutes or until no longer pink, breaking up the sausage into large crumbles; drain.

2. Meanwhile, place whole pita breads on ungreased baking sheets. Bake 3-4 minutes each side or until browned and almost crisp.

3. Top pita breads with the sausage mixture, tomatoes, avocado and cheese. Bake for 3-4 minutes longer or until heated through. Top with sliced cucumbers; drizzle with the tzatziki sauce.

1 pizza: 632 cal., 40g fat (12g sat. fat), 85mg chol., 1336mg sod., 43g carb. (3g sugars, 5g fiber), 25g pro.

MUSHROOM CAPRESE PIZZA

When my tomatoes ripen all at once, I like to use them up in simple recipes like this one. Cheesy baguette pizzas, served with a salad, are ideal for lunch—and they make standout appetizers for any party.
—Lorraine Caland, Shuniah, ON

Prep: 25 min. • **Bake:** 10 min.
Makes: 6 servings

- 2 tsp. olive oil
- 8 oz. sliced fresh mushrooms
- 2 medium onions, halved and sliced
- 2 garlic cloves, minced
- ½ tsp. Italian seasoning
- ¼ tsp. salt
  Dash pepper
- 1 French bread baguette (10½ oz.), halved lengthwise
- 1½ cups shredded part-skim mozzarella cheese
- ¾ cup thinly sliced fresh basil leaves, divided
- 3 medium tomatoes, sliced

1. Preheat oven to 400°. In a large skillet, heat oil over medium-high heat; saute the mushrooms and onions until tender. Add garlic, Italian seasoning, salt and pepper; cook and stir 1 minute.

3. Remove flatbreads from grill. Layer grilled sides with sauce, sausage, cheeses and basil. Return to grill; cook, covered, until cheese is melted, 2-3 minutes longer.

1 pizza: 808 cal., 56g fat (19g sat. fat), 112mg chol., 1996mg sod., 41g carb. (9g sugars, 3g fiber), 34g pro.

BACON & SPINACH PIZZA

Our go-to pizza is a snap to make using packaged pizza crust and ready-to-serve bacon. Best of all, the kids don't even mind the spinach on top!
—Annette Riva, Naperville, IL

Takes: 20 min. • **Makes:** 6 servings

- 1 prebaked 12-in. pizza crust
- ⅓ cup pizza sauce
- 1 cup shaved Parmesan cheese
- 2 cups fresh baby spinach, thinly sliced
- 8 ready-to-serve fully cooked bacon strips, cut into 1-in. pieces

Preheat oven to 450°. Place crust on an ungreased baking sheet. Spread with sauce; top with ½ cup cheese, spinach and bacon. Sprinkle with remaining cheese. Bake until cheese is melted, 8-10 minutes.

1 slice: 269 cal., 10g fat (4g sat. fat), 10mg chol., 726mg sod., 31g carb. (2g sugars, 2g fiber), 15g pro. **Diabetic exchanges:** 2 starch, 2 medium-fat meat.

If you need only a small amount of an ingredient, don't forget to check out the grocery store salad bar! You may find fresh spinach, chicken or bacon strips, cheese and nuts are cheaper there than elsewhere in the store.

GRILLED SAUSAGE-BASIL PIZZAS

These easy little pizzas are a wonderful change of pace from the classic cookout menu. Set out bowls of various toppings, and let everyone go crazy!
—Lisa Speer, Palm Beach, FL

Takes: 30 min. • **Makes:** 4 servings

- 4 Italian sausage links (4 oz. each)
- 4 naan flatbreads or whole pita breads
- ¼ cup olive oil
- 1 cup tomato basil pasta sauce
- 2 cups shredded part-skim mozzarella cheese
- ½ cup grated Parmesan cheese
- ½ cup thinly sliced fresh basil

1. Grill sausages, covered, over medium heat until a thermometer reads 160°, 10-12 minutes, turning occasionally. Cut into ¼-in. slices.
2. Brush both sides of flatbreads with oil. Grill the flatbreads, covered, over medium heat until the bottoms are lightly browned, 2-3 minutes.

SHRIMP & CRAB PIZZA

When my siblings and I were growing up, my mother often made us this amazing pizza with shrimp and crab. Now my kids ask for it, and the tradition continues.
—Danielle Woodward, Colorado Springs, CO

Takes: 30 min. • **Makes:** 6 servings

- ½ lb. uncooked shrimp (61-70 per lb.), peeled and deveined
- 1 cup water
- 2 Tbsp. lemon juice
- 1 Tbsp. butter
- 1¾ cups sliced fresh mushrooms
- 1 small onion, chopped
- 1 small sweet red pepper, cut into strips
- 1 garlic clove, minced
- ¼ tsp. salt
- 1¼ cups coarsely chopped imitation crabmeat (about ½ lb.)
- 1 prebaked 12-in. pizza crust
- ⅓ cup Alfredo sauce
- 2 cups shredded part-skim mozzarella cheese

1. Preheat oven to 450°. In a small bowl, combine shrimp, water and lemon juice. Let stand 10 minutes.
2. Meanwhile, in a large skillet, heat butter over medium-high heat. Add mushrooms, onion and pepper; cook and stir until tender, 4-5 minutes. Add garlic and salt; cook 1 minute longer.
3. Drain the shrimp, discarding liquid. Add shrimp and crab to pan; cook and stir 1-2 minutes longer or until the shrimp turn pink.
4. Place crust on an ungreased 12-in. pizza pan or baking sheet; spread with Alfredo sauce. Spoon shrimp mixture over sauce; sprinkle with cheese. Bake 8-10 minutes or until crust is golden and cheese is melted.
1 slice: 403 cal., 15g fat (7g sat. fat), 84mg chol., 1014mg sod., 40g carb. (4g sugars, 2g fiber), 27g pro.

GRILLED VEGGIE TORTILLAS

Your garden's bounty will be put to good use in this delightful pizzalike entree. After this recipe was so well received, I made a copy, put it in a protective sleeve and stored it in a binder, so I could make it again and again.
—Sharon Delaney-Chronis, South Milwaukee, WI

Takes: 25 min. • **Makes:** 4 servings

- 1 medium zucchini, cut lengthwise into ½-in. slices
- 1 yellow summer squash, cut lengthwise into ½-in. slices
- 1 small sweet red pepper, cut in half
- 2 Tbsp. olive oil, divided
- ½ tsp. salt
- 1 large tomato, chopped
- ¼ cup reduced-fat mayonnaise
- 2 Tbsp. prepared pesto
- 1 Tbsp. minced fresh basil
- 1 Tbsp. minced fresh oregano
- 4 whole wheat tortillas (8 in.)
- 1 cup shredded part-skim mozzarella cheese

1. Brush the zucchini, summer squash and red pepper with 1 Tbsp. oil. Sprinkle with salt. Grill vegetables over medium heat for 4-5 minutes on each side or until tender. Cut into ½-in. cubes and place in a small bowl; stir in tomato.
2. Combine mayonnaise, pesto, basil and oregano; set aside. Brush both sides of the tortillas with the remaining oil. Grill, uncovered, over medium heat 2-3 minutes or until puffed.
3. Remove tortillas from grill. Spread grilled sides with sauce; top with the vegetable mixture. Sprinkle with cheese. Grill, covered, for 2-3 minutes or until the cheese is melted.
1 pizza: 390 cal., 23g fat (6g sat. fat), 24mg chol., 785mg sod., 31g carb. (6g sugars, 4g fiber), 14g pro. **Diabetic exchanges:** 3 fat, 1½ starch, 1 medium-fat meat, 1 vegetable.

MEATBALL PIZZA

I always keep meatballs and pizza crusts in the freezer so I can make this specialty at a moment's notice. Add a tossed salad and you have a delicious dinner.
—Mary Humeniuk-Smith, Perry Hall, MD

Takes: 25 min. • **Makes:** 8 servings

- 1 prebaked 12-in. pizza crust
- 1 can (8 oz.) pizza sauce
- 1 tsp. garlic powder
- 1 tsp. Italian seasoning
- ¼ cup grated Parmesan cheese
- 1 small onion, halved and sliced
- 12 frozen fully cooked Italian meatballs (½ oz. each), thawed and halved
- 1 cup shredded part-skim mozzarella cheese
- 1 cup shredded cheddar cheese

1. Preheat oven to 350°. Place crust on an ungreased 12-in. pizza pan or baking sheet.
2. Spread sauce over crust; sprinkle with garlic powder, Italian seasoning and Parmesan cheese. Top with onion and meatballs; sprinkle with the remaining cheeses. Bake until the cheese is melted, 12-17 minutes.

1 serving: 321 cal., 16g fat (8g sat. fat), 36mg chol., 755mg sod., 28g carb. (3g sugars, 2g fiber), 17g pro.

CHICKEN FLORENTINE PIZZA

On pizza night, we like to switch things up with this chicken and spinach version. One taste of the ricotta cheese base and you won't miss traditional sauce one bit.
—Pam Corder, Monroe, LA

- -

Takes: 25 min. • **Makes:** 8 servings

- 1 tsp. Italian seasoning
- ½ tsp. garlic powder
- 3 cups cooked chicken breasts (about 1 lb.), cubed
- 1 cup whole-milk ricotta cheese
- 1 prebaked 12-in. pizza crust
- 1 pkg. (10 oz.) frozen chopped spinach, thawed and squeezed dry
- 2 Tbsp. oil-packed sun-dried tomatoes, drained and chopped
- ½ cup shredded fresh mozzarella cheese
- ¼ cup grated Parmesan cheese

Preheat oven to 425°. Stir together Italian seasoning and garlic powder; toss with chicken. Spread ricotta cheese on pizza crust. Top with chicken, spinach and tomatoes. Sprinkle with mozzarella and Parmesan cheese. Bake until crust is golden and the cheese is melted, 10-15 minutes.

1 slice: 311 cal., 11g fat (5g sat. fat), 65mg chol., 423mg sod., 26g carb. (3g sugars, 2g fiber), 28g pro.

STEAK & BLUE CHEESE PIZZA

Even my husband who doesn't normally like blue cheese adores this scrumptious pizza! If time allows, cook the onion until it's rich and caramelized for an unbeatable flavor.
—Kadija Bridgewater, Boca Raton, FL

- -

Takes: 30 min. • **Makes:** 6 servings

- ½ lb. beef top sirloin steak, thinly sliced
- ¼ tsp. salt
- ¼ tsp. pepper
- 2 Tbsp. olive oil, divided
- 2 cups sliced baby portobello mushrooms
- 1 large onion, sliced
- ½ cup heavy whipping cream
- ¼ cup crumbled blue cheese
- 1 prebaked 12-in. pizza crust
- 2 tsp. minced fresh parsley

1. Preheat oven to 450°. Sprinkle beef with salt and pepper. In a large skillet, heat 1 Tbsp. oil over medium heat. Add beef and mushrooms; cook until the beef is no longer pink, 3-4 minutes. Remove from pan.

2. Cook onion in the remaining oil until tender, 2-3 minutes. Add cream and blue cheese; cook until slightly thickened, 3-5 minutes longer.

3. Place crust on a 12-in. pizza pan or baking sheet. Spread with the cream mixture; top with the beef mixture. Sprinkle with parsley. Bake until the sauce is bubbly and the crust is lightly browned, 10-12 minutes.

1 slice: 365 cal., 19g fat (8g sat. fat), 47mg chol., 535mg sod., 33g carb. (3g sugars, 2g fiber), 18g pro.

PIZZA ON THE GRILL

I make pizza at least once a week, and this is one of my favorites during grilling season. The barbecue flavor mingling with the cheese tastes delicious.
—Lisa Boettcher, Columbus, WI

Prep: 30 min. + resting • **Grill:** 10 min.
Makes: 4 servings

- 1 pkg. (¼ oz.) active dry yeast
- 1 cup warm water (110° to 115°)
- 2 Tbsp. canola oil
- 2 tsp. sugar
- 1 tsp. baking soda
- 1 tsp. salt
- 2¾ to 3 cups all-purpose flour

TOPPINGS
- 2 cups cubed cooked chicken
- ½ to ¾ cup barbecue sauce
- ½ cup julienned green pepper
- 2 cups shredded Monterey Jack cheese

1. In a large bowl, dissolve yeast in water. Add the oil, sugar, baking soda, salt and 2 cups flour. Stir in enough of the remaining flour to form a soft dough.
2. Turn dough onto a floured surface; knead until smooth and elastic, 6-8 minutes. Cover and let rest for 10 minutes.
3. On a floured surface, roll dough into a 13-in. circle. Transfer to a greased 12-in. pizza pan. Build up edges slightly.
4. Grill, covered, over medium heat for 5 minutes. Remove from grill. Combine chicken and barbecue sauce; spread over the crust. Sprinkle with green pepper and cheese. Grill, covered, 5-10 minutes longer or until the crust is golden and the cheese is melted.
1 slice: 757 cal., 31g fat (13g sat. fat), 113mg chol., 1525mg sod., 73g carb. (8g sugars, 3g fiber), 44g pro.

CHICKEN PARMESAN PIZZA

This is a big winner for home cooks—quick and easy to make, and a favorite among even the pickiest of eaters. It's handy for a busy weeknight dinner or a kids party.
—Karen Wittmeier, Parkland, FL

Prep: 25 min. • **Bake:** 15 min.
Makes: 6 servings

- 8 frozen breaded chicken tenders
- 1 loaf (1 lb.) frozen pizza dough, thawed
- ½ cup marinara sauce
- ¼ tsp. garlic powder
- 2 cups (8 oz.) shredded part-skim mozzarella cheese
- ¼ cup shredded Parmesan cheese
- 2 Tbsp. thinly sliced fresh basil

1. Bake chicken tenders according to package directions. Remove from oven; increase oven setting to 450°.
2. Meanwhile, grease a 12-in. pizza pan. Roll dough to fit pan. In a small bowl, mix marinara sauce and garlic powder; spread over the dough.
3. Cut chicken into 1-in. pieces. Top pizza with chicken and mozzarella cheese. Bake on a lower oven rack for 12-15 minutes or until crust is golden brown and cheese is melted. Sprinkle with Parmesan cheese and basil.
1 slice: 440 cal., 17g fat (6g sat. fat), 35mg chol., 774mg sod., 48g carb. (4g sugars, 3g fiber), 23g pro.

GRILLED FLATBREAD VEGGIE PIZZA

At our house, we love to pile veggies onto flatbread for a fun way to eat healthier. This is a go-to recipe for weeknights, but you can easily switch it up by adding meats or different veggies.
—Darla Andrews, Schertz, TX

Takes: 25 min. • **Makes:** 4 servings

- 1 Tbsp. butter
- ½ lb. sliced baby portobello mushrooms
- 1 large green pepper, julienned
- 4 cups fresh baby spinach (about 4 oz.)
- ¼ tsp. salt
- ⅛ tsp. pepper
- 2 naan flatbreads or 4 whole pita breads
- 2 Tbsp. olive oil
- ¼ cup prepared pesto
- 2 plum tomatoes, sliced
- 2 cups shredded part-skim mozzarella cheese

1. In a large skillet, heat butter over medium-high heat. Add mushrooms and green pepper; cook and stir 5-7 minutes or until tender. Add the spinach, salt and pepper; cook and stir 2-3 minutes or until the spinach is wilted.
2. Brush both sides of flatbreads with oil. Grill the flatbreads, covered, over medium heat for 2-3 minutes on 1 side or until lightly browned.
3. Remove flatbreads from grill. Spread grilled sides with pesto; top with the vegetable mixture, tomatoes and cheese. Return to grill; cook, covered, 2-3 minutes longer or until the cheese is melted. Cut pizzas in half before serving.
½ pizza: 426 cal., 28g fat (11g sat. fat), 47mg chol., 1005mg sod., 25g carb. (6g sugars, 3g fiber), 20g pro.

CHEESE & MUSHROOM SKILLET PIZZA

This Italian skillet recipe is an awesome way to use up extra spaghetti sauce at the end of the week. It's a perfect choice for your next Friday pizza night.
—Clare Butler, Little Elm, TX

Takes: 30 min. • **Makes:** 4 servings

- 1 cup all-purpose flour
- 2 tsp. baking powder
- 1 tsp. dried oregano
- ½ tsp. salt
- 6 Tbsp. water
- 2 Tbsp. plus 1 tsp. olive oil, divided
- ½ cup pizza sauce
- 25 slices pepperoni
- 1 jar (4½ oz.) sliced mushrooms, drained
- 1 can (2¼ oz.) sliced ripe olives, drained
- 1 cup shredded part-skim mozzarella cheese

1. Preheat broiler. In a small bowl, whisk flour, baking powder, oregano and salt. Stir in water and 2 Tbsp. olive oil to form a soft dough. Turn onto a floured surface; knead 6-8 times. Roll into a 12-in. circle.
2. Brush bottom of a 12-in. ovenproof skillet with the remaining oil; heat over medium-high. Cook dough 2-3 minutes on each side or until golden brown. Remove from heat. Spread with pizza sauce and top with the pepperoni, mushrooms, olives and cheese.
3. Broil 3-4 in. from heat 3-5 minutes or until cheese is melted.
1 slice: 374 cal., 22g fat (7g sat. fat), 30mg chol., 1284mg sod., 31g carb. (3g sugars, 3g fiber), 14g pro.

BREADSTICK PIZZA

Make Monday fun-day with a hassle-free homemade pizza featuring refrigerated breadsticks as the crust. If you're feeding kids, slice pieces into small strips and let them dip each strip into marinara sauce. They'll love it!

—Mary Hankins, Kansas City, MO

- -

Prep: 25 min. • **Bake:** 20 min.
Makes: 12 servings

2	tubes (11 oz. each) refrigerated breadsticks
½	lb. sliced fresh mushrooms
2	medium green peppers, chopped
1	medium onion, chopped
1½	tsp. Italian seasoning, divided
4	tsp. olive oil, divided
1½	cups shredded cheddar cheese, divided
5	oz. Canadian bacon, chopped
1½	cups shredded part-skim mozzarella cheese
	Marinara sauce

1. Preheat oven to 350°. Unroll breadsticks into a greased 15x10x1-in. baking pan. Press onto bottom and up sides of pan; pinch the seams to seal. Bake until set, 6-8 minutes.

2. Meanwhile, in a large skillet, saute the mushrooms, peppers, onion and 1 tsp. Italian seasoning in 2 tsp. oil until vegetables are crisp-tender; drain.

3. Brush crust with remaining oil. Sprinkle with ¾ cup cheddar cheese; top with the vegetable mixture and Canadian bacon. Combine mozzarella cheese and remaining cheddar cheese; sprinkle over top. Sprinkle with the remaining Italian seasoning.

4. Bake until cheese is melted and crust is golden brown, 20-25 minutes. Serve with marinara sauce.

Freeze option: Bake crust as directed, add toppings and cool. Securely wrap and freeze unbaked pizza. To use, unwrap pizza; bake as directed, increasing time as necessary.

1 piece: 267 cal., 11g fat (6g sat. fat), 27mg chol., 638mg sod., 29g carb. (5g sugars, 2g fiber), 13g pro.

DID YOU KNOW?

American bacon comes from the belly of a pig, but Canadian bacon is cut from the loin—that's why Canadian bacon is much leaner and comes in rounded slices rather than strips. To substitute for Canadian bacon, use your favorite deli meat rather than American bacon.

GARLIC & HERB STEAK PIZZA

We crave pizza that's fast to fix, cheesy and original. This one with steak and veggies is for folks who like their pies with everything on top—and you can always add more!
—Jade Fears, Grand Ridge, FL

Takes: 30 min. • **Makes:** 6 servings

1   **beef top sirloin steak (¾ in. thick and 1 lb.)**
¾   **tsp. salt**
¾   **tsp. pepper**
1   **Tbsp. olive oil**
1   **prebaked 12-in. thin pizza crust**
½   **cup garlic-herb spreadable cheese (about 3 oz.)**
2   **cups chopped fresh spinach**
1   **cup sliced red onion**
1   **cup sliced fresh mushrooms**
1½   **cups shredded part-skim mozzarella cheese**

1. Preheat oven to 450°. Season the steak with salt and pepper. In a large skillet, heat oil over medium heat. Add steak; cook 5-6 minutes each side or until a thermometer reads 145° for medium-rare doneness. Remove from pan.
2. Meanwhile, place the pizza crust on an ungreased baking sheet; spread with garlic-herb cheese. Top with the spinach and onion.
3. Cut the steak into slices; arrange on the pizza. Top with mushrooms and cheese. Bake 8-10 minutes or until the cheese is melted. Cut pizza into 12 pieces.

1 serving: 440 cal., 23g fat (11g sat. fat), 72mg chol., 926mg sod., 29g carb. (3g sugars, 2g fiber), 30g pro.

MOZZARELLA CORNBREAD PIZZA

My sons like pizza, but not takeout, so I pull out my trusty baking pan frequently to make this cornbread pizza with veggies in the crust. Adjust toppings to your liking.
—Mary Leverette, Columbia, SC

Prep: 25 min. + standing • **Bake:** 20 min.
Makes: 10 servings

- 3 cups shredded zucchini
- 1 tsp. salt, divided
- 2 pkg. (8½ oz. each) cornbread/muffin mix
- 3 large eggs, lightly beaten
- ¼ tsp. pepper

TOPPINGS

- 1 jar (14 oz.) pizza sauce
- ¾ cup chopped sweet red or green pepper
- 1 can (2¼ oz.) sliced ripe olives, drained
- 4 green onions, chopped
- ⅓ cup coarsely chopped fresh basil
- 1 Tbsp. minced fresh oregano or 1 tsp. dried oregano
- 3 cups shredded part-skim mozzarella cheese

1. Preheat oven to 450°. Place zucchini in a colander over a bowl; sprinkle with ¾ tsp. salt and toss. Let stand 15 minutes.
2. Press zucchini and blot dry with paper towels; transfer to a large bowl. Add cornbread mixes, eggs, pepper and the remaining salt; stir until blended. Spread evenly into a greased 15x10x1-in. baking pan. Bake until lightly browned, 8-10 minutes. Reduce oven setting to 350°.
3. Spread pizza sauce over the crust. Top with red pepper, olives and green onions. Sprinkle with herbs and cheese. Bake until the cheese is melted, 12-15 minutes.
1 piece: 366 cal., 15g fat (6g sat. fat), 79mg chol., 912mg sod., 42g carb. (14g sugars, 5g fiber), 15g pro.

EGGPLANT FLATBREAD PIZZAS

I loved to make these back in my home cooking days. Now I'm a chef!
—Christine Wendland, Browns Mills, NJ

Takes: 30 min. • **Makes:** 4 servings

- 3 Tbsp. olive oil, divided
- 2½ cups cubed eggplant (½ in.)
- 1 small onion, halved and thinly sliced
- ½ tsp. salt
- ⅛ tsp. pepper
- 1 garlic clove, minced
- 2 naan flatbreads
- ½ cup part-skim ricotta cheese
- 1 tsp. dried oregano
- ½ cup roasted garlic tomato sauce
- ½ cup loosely packed basil leaves
- 1 cup shredded part-skim mozzarella cheese
- 2 Tbsp. grated Parmesan cheese Sliced fresh basil, optional

1. Preheat oven to 400°. In a large skillet, heat 1 Tbsp. oil over medium-high heat; saute eggplant and onion with salt and pepper until the eggplant begins to soften, 4-5 minutes. Stir in the garlic; remove from heat.
2. Place naan on a baking sheet. Spread with ricotta cheese; sprinkle with oregano. Spread with tomato sauce. Top with the eggplant mixture and whole basil leaves. Sprinkle with mozzarella and Parmesan cheeses; drizzle with the remaining oil.
3. Bake until the crust is golden brown and cheese is melted, 12-15 minutes. If desired, top with sliced basil.
Note: Roasted garlic tomato sauce may be replaced with any flavored tomato sauce or a meatless pasta sauce.
½ pizza: 340 cal., 21g fat (7g sat. fat), 32mg chol., 996mg sod., 25g carb. (5g sugars, 3g fiber), 14g pro.

1. Preheat oven to 425°. Unroll dough into a greased 15x10x1-in. baking pan; flatten dough and build up edges slightly. Bake 10-12 minutes or until lightly browned.

2. Meanwhile, saute mushrooms and onion in butter in a large skillet until tender. Add garlic; cook 1 minute longer. Stir in Alfredo sauce and thyme. Spread over crust. Top with spinach, sausage and cheese.

3. Bake for 10-15 minutes or until the crust is lightly browned and the cheese is melted.

1 piece: 288 cal., 14g fat (8g sat. fat), 56mg chol., 706mg sod., 24g carb. (3g sugars, 2g fiber), 16g pro.

CHICKEN THAI PIZZA

I make this recipe for my friends on a girls night filled with fun and laughter. It's simple to make but is full of flavor.
—Kimberly Knuppenburg, Menomonee Falls, WI

- -

Takes: 25 min. • **Makes:** 6 servings

- 1 prebaked 12-in. pizza crust
- ⅔ cup Thai peanut sauce
- 2 Tbsp. reduced-sodium soy sauce
- 2 Tbsp. creamy peanut butter
- 1 cup shredded cooked chicken breast
- 1 cup shredded part-skim mozzarella cheese
- 3 green onions, chopped
- ½ cup bean sprouts
- ½ cup shredded carrot

1. Preheat oven to 400°. Place the crust on an ungreased 12-in. pizza pan or baking sheet. In a small bowl, combine the peanut sauce, soy sauce and peanut butter. Add chicken; toss to coat. Spread chicken mixture over crust; sprinkle with cheese and onions.

2. Bake for 10-12 minutes or until the cheese is melted. Top with bean sprouts and carrot.

1 slice: 361 cal., 15g fat (4g sat. fat), 29mg chol., 1183mg sod., 35g carb. (4g sugars, 3g fiber), 23g pro.

SMOKED GOUDA SPINACH PIZZA

You can make this yummy pizza in hardly any time, thanks to a refrigerated crust and some store-bought Alfredo sauce. My daughter created it as an appetizer, but we love it for a main course, too. Leftovers pack beautifully for a workday lunch.
—Marie Hattrup, Sonoma, CA

- -

Takes: 30 min. • **Makes:** 10 servings

- 1 tube (13.8 oz.) refrigerated pizza crust
- ½ lb. sliced fresh mushrooms
- 1 small red onion, chopped
- 2 Tbsp. butter
- 2 garlic cloves, minced
- 1 cup Alfredo sauce
- ½ tsp. dried thyme
- 1 pkg. (6 oz.) fresh baby spinach
- ½ lb. fully cooked Italian chicken sausage links, sliced
- 2 cups shredded smoked Gouda cheese

3. Remove from heat. Top each naan with basil and Romano; cut into thirds.

2 pieces: 391 cal., 24g fat (9g sat. fat), 51mg chol., 1276mg sod., 25g carb. (4g sugars, 1g fiber), 20g pro.

REUBEN PIZZA

Fridays are pizza nights at our house, and we do a lot of experimenting so we don't have the same old thing every week. This pizza was a fantastic discovery! With only five ingredients, it's a snap to whip up...and it tastes just like a Reuben sandwich.
—Nicole German, Hutchinson, MN

- -

Takes: 25 min. • **Makes:** 6 servings

1	prebaked 12-in. pizza crust
⅔	cup Thousand Island salad dressing
½	lb. sliced deli corned beef, cut into strips
1	can (14 oz.) sauerkraut, rinsed and well drained
2	cups shredded Swiss cheese

Preheat oven to 400°. Place crust on an ungreased or parchment-lined baking sheet. Spread with salad dressing. Top with corned beef, sauerkraut and cheese. Bake until the cheese is melted, 12-15 minutes.

1 slice: 480 cal., 27g fat (10g sat. fat), 57mg chol., 1527mg sod., 36g carb. (6g sugars, 3g fiber), 23g pro.

Before adding sauerkraut to a dish, use a potato ricer to squeeze out the excess juice. Then you won't have to worry about soggy sandwiches or pizza, and you'll retain all its flavor.

GRILLED ZUCCHINI & PESTO PIZZA

When camping in the great outdoors, we use this amazing recipe to surprise our friends who don't think it's possible to make a standout pizza in the backwoods. This one certainly proves our point.
—Jesse Arriaga, Reno, NV

- -

Takes: 20 min. • **Makes:** 6 servings

4	naan flatbreads
½	cup prepared pesto
2	cups shredded part-skim mozzarella cheese
1	medium zucchini, thinly sliced
1	small red onion, thinly sliced
¼	lb. thinly sliced hard salami, chopped
½	cup fresh basil leaves, thinly sliced
¼	cup grated Romano cheese

1. Over each naan, spread 2 Tbsp. pesto; top with ½ cup mozzarella and one-fourth each of the zucchini, onion and salami.

2. Grill, covered, over medium-low heat until the mozzarella has melted and the vegetables are tender, 4-6 minutes. Rotate naan halfway through grilling for an evenly browned crust.

TANDOORI SPICED CHICKEN PITA PIZZA WITH GREEK YOGURT & CILANTRO

My family and I are big picnickers, and I'm always looking for new dishes to take along and enjoy on our outings. The incredible flavors at our favorite Indian restaurant inspired these mini pizzas.
—Angela Spengler, Niceville, FL

- -

Takes: 25 min. • **Makes:** 4 servings

- 1 cup plain Greek yogurt, divided
- 2 Tbsp. chopped fresh cilantro
- ½ tsp. ground coriander
- ½ tsp. ground cumin
- ½ tsp. ground ginger
- ½ tsp. ground turmeric
- ½ tsp. paprika
- ½ tsp. cayenne pepper
- ¾ lb. boneless skinless chicken breasts, cut into ½-in.-thick strips
- 4 whole wheat pita breads (6 in.)
- ⅔ cup crumbled feta cheese
- ⅓ cup chopped seeded tomato
- ⅓ cup chopped fresh Italian parsley

1. For sauce, mix ½ cup yogurt and cilantro. In a large bowl, mix spices and the remaining yogurt; stir in chicken to coat.
2. Place chicken on an oiled grill rack over medium heat; grill, covered, until no longer pink, 2-3 minutes per side. Grill pita breads until warmed, about 1 minute per side.
3. Spread the pitas with sauce. Top with chicken strips, cheese, tomato and parsley.
1 pizza: 380 cal., 12g fat (6g sat. fat), 72mg chol., 598mg sod., 41g carb. (5g sugars, 5g fiber), 29g pro. **Diabetic exchanges:** 3 lean meat, 2½ starch.

PEPPERY PIZZA LOAVES

I often take these French bread pizzas to church picnics or potluck suppers, and there's never a crumb left! When I fix them for just the two of us, I freeze halves in foil to enjoy later.
—Lou Stasny, Poplarville, MS

- -

Prep: 20 min. • **Bake:** 20 min.
Makes: 12 servings

- 1½ lbs. ground beef
- ½ tsp. garlic powder
- ½ tsp. salt
- 2 loaves (8 oz. each) French bread, halved lengthwise
- 1 jar (8 oz.) process cheese sauce
- 1 can (4 oz.) mushroom stems and pieces, drained
- 1 cup chopped green onions
- 1 can (4 oz.) sliced jalapenos, drained
- 1 can (8 oz.) tomato sauce
- ½ cup grated Parmesan cheese
- 4 cups shredded part-skim mozzarella cheese

1. Preheat oven to 350°. In a large skillet, cook beef over medium heat until no longer pink; drain. Stir in garlic powder and salt.
2. Place each bread half on a large piece of heavy-duty foil. Spread with cheese sauce. Top with beef mixture, mushrooms, onions and jalapenos. Drizzle with tomato sauce. Top with Parmesan and mozzarella cheeses.
3. Bake for 10-15 minutes or until golden brown. Serve warm.
Freeze option: Wrap and freeze loaves. To use, unwrap loaves and thaw on baking sheets in the refrigerator. Bake at 350° for 18 minutes or until the cheese is melted. Freeze for up to 3 months.
1 piece: 323 cal., 19g fat (11g sat. fat), 71mg chol., 907mg sod., 15g carb. (2g sugars, 1g fiber), 23g pro.

CHICKEN PIZZA

Your family will never guess this fun twist on typical pizza uses up leftover pesto. Loaded with chicken and black beans, hearty slices will fill them up fast.
—*Taste of Home* Test Kitchen

Takes: 30 min. • Makes: 6 servings

- 1 **lb. boneless skinless chicken breasts, cut into 1-in. pieces**
- 1 **Tbsp. olive oil**
- 1 **prebaked 12-in. pizza crust**
- ¼ **cup prepared pesto**
- 1 **large tomato, chopped**
- ½ **cup canned black beans, rinsed and drained**
- 1 **cup shredded part-skim mozzarella cheese**
- ½ **cup shredded Parmesan cheese**

1. Preheat oven to 400°. In a large skillet, cook chicken in oil over medium heat for 10-15 minutes or until no longer pink.
2. Place the crust on a lightly greased 12-in. pizza pan. Spread with pesto; top with the chicken, tomato, beans and cheeses. Bake 10-12 minutes or until cheese is melted.

Freeze option: Securely wrap and freeze unbaked pizza. To use, unwrap pizza; bake as directed, increasing time as necessary.

1 serving: 431 cal., 18g fat (6g sat. fat), 65mg chol., 692mg sod., 35g carb. (1g sugars, 1g fiber), 32g pro.

RICH CHICKEN ALFREDO PIZZA

After a busy day, settle in for this appetizing homemade pizza. With a prebaked crust and simple Alfredo, it's easy and delicious.
—Tammy Hanks, Gainsville, FL

Prep: 30 min. • **Bake:** 15 min.
Makes: 8 servings

- 2½ tsp. butter
- 1 garlic clove, minced
- 1½ cups heavy whipping cream
- 3 Tbsp. grated Parmesan cheese
- ½ tsp. salt
- ¼ tsp. pepper
- 1 Tbsp. minced fresh parsley
- 1 prebaked 12-in. thin pizza crust
- 1 cup cubed cooked chicken breast
- 1 cup thinly sliced baby portobello mushrooms
- 1 cup fresh baby spinach
- 2 cups shredded part-skim mozzarella cheese

1. Preheat oven to 450°. In a small saucepan over medium heat, melt butter. Add garlic; cook and stir for 1 minute. Add cream; cook until liquid is reduced by half, 15-20 minutes. Add Parmesan cheese, salt and pepper; cook and stir until thickened. Remove from heat; stir in parsley. Cool slightly.
2. Place the crust on an ungreased baking sheet; spread with the cream mixture. Top with chicken, mushrooms, spinach and mozzarella cheese. Bake 15-20 minutes or until the cheese is melted and the crust is golden brown.
1 slice: 391 cal., 26g fat (15g sat. fat), 87mg chol., 612mg sod., 21g carb. (3g sugars, 1g fiber), 18g pro.

CRANBERRY, BRIE & TURKEY PIZZA

While we were traveling in New Zealand, my husband and I discovered turkey pizza. We came up with our own version for a creative way to use leftovers.
—Kristin Stone, Little Elm, TX

Takes: 25 min. • **Makes:** 6 servings

- 1 prebaked 12-in. pizza crust
- 1 cup whole-berry cranberry sauce
- 1 tsp. grated orange zest
- 2 cups shredded part-skim mozzarella cheese
- 1 cup coarsely shredded cooked turkey
- ½ small red onion, thinly sliced
- 4 oz. Brie cheese, cubed
- 1 Tbsp. minced fresh rosemary

1. Preheat oven to 450°. Place crust on an ungreased baking sheet.
2. In a small bowl, mix cranberry sauce and orange zest; spread over crust. Top with mozzarella cheese, turkey, onion and Brie cheese; sprinkle with rosemary. Bake 10-12 minutes or until cheese is melted.
1 slice: 456 cal., 17g fat (9g sat. fat), 67mg chol., 768mg sod., 49g carb. (14g sugars, 2g fiber), 27g pro.

1 large onion, chopped
½ tsp. coarsely ground pepper
¼ tsp. celery seed
2 garlic cloves, minced
1 cup pizza sauce
¼ tsp. Louisiana-style hot sauce
1 large green pepper, thinly sliced

1. Preheat oven to 425°. Place crust on an ungreased baking sheet. Brush with 1½ tsp. oil; sprinkle with ½ cup mozzarella cheese. Set aside. Combine lemon juice and ½ tsp. Creole seasoning. Add shrimp; toss to coat.
2. In a small skillet, heat the remaining oil over medium heat. Add onion, pepper, celery seed and the remaining Creole seasoning; saute until onion is tender. Add garlic; cook 1 minute longer. Stir in pizza sauce and hot sauce. Remove from heat.
3. Drain shrimp. Spread the sauce mixture over crust. Top with the shrimp and green pepper; sprinkle with remaining cheese. Bake until the shrimp turn pink and cheese is melted, 25-30 minutes.
Note: The following mix of spices may be substituted for 1 tsp. Creole seasoning: ¼ tsp. each salt, garlic powder and paprika and a pinch each dried thyme, ground cumin and cayenne pepper.
1 piece: 378 cal., 13g fat (4g sat. fat), 110mg chol., 969mg sod., 39g carb. (6g sugars, 3g fiber), 27g pro.

TEST KITCHEN TIP

There are several kinds of Louisiana-style hot sauce, and each packs a punch. We used just a touch, but feel free to shake on more. In the mood for pasta? Try tossing the toppings with hot cooked fettuccine instead.

CREOLE SHRIMP PIZZA
The flavors and heat of Creole cuisine blend extraordinarily well in this hearty pizza with a crispy crust.
—Robin Haas, Cranston, RI

Prep: 15 min. • **Bake:** 25 min.
Makes: 6 servings

1 prebaked 12-in. pizza crust
1 Tbsp. olive oil, divided
1½ cups shredded part-skim mozzarella cheese, divided
1 Tbsp. lemon juice
1½ tsp. reduced-sodium Creole seasoning, divided
1 lb. uncooked shrimp (31-40 per lb.), peeled and deveined

Pasta

GREEK PASTA TOSS

My husband and I developed this bright, colorful pasta dish by tossing in favorite Greek ingredients like olives, feta cheese and sun-dried tomatoes. Try it with shrimp or chicken, too!
—Terri Gilson, Calgary, AB

Takes: 30 min. • **Makes:** 4 servings

- 3 cups uncooked whole wheat spiral pasta (about 7 oz.)
- ¾ lb. Italian turkey sausage links, casings removed
- 2 garlic cloves, minced
- 4 oz. fresh baby spinach (about 5 cups)
- ½ cup pitted Greek olives, halved
- ⅓ cup julienned oil-packed sun-dried tomatoes, drained and chopped
- ¼ cup crumbled feta cheese
  Lemon wedges, optional

1. In a 6-qt. stockpot, cook pasta according to package directions. Drain; return to pot.
2. Meanwhile, in a large skillet, cook and coarsely crumble turkey sausage over medium high heat until no longer pink, 4-6 minutes. Add garlic; cook and stir for 1 minute. Add to pasta.
3. Stir in the spinach, olives and tomatoes; heat through, allowing the spinach to wilt slightly. Stir in cheese. If desired, serve with lemon wedges.

2 cups: 335 cal., 13g fat (3g sat. fat), 35mg chol., 742mg sod., 36g carb. (1g sugars, 6g fiber), 19g pro. **Diabetic exchanges:** 2 starch, 2 lean meat, 2 fat, 1 vegetable.

Turkey or chicken sausage is an excellent substitute for beef or pork sausages, such as chorizo and kielbasa, whenever you're looking to cut back on saturated fat.

BACON CHEESEBURGER PASTA

The dishes I cook up most frequently are kid-friendly and easy to reheat because my husband works long hours, and he often eats later than our children. We especially love this pasta for its simple deliciousness.
—Melissa Stevens, Elk River, MN

Takes: 30 min. • **Makes:** 6 servings

- 8 oz. uncooked penne pasta
- 1 lb. ground beef
- 6 bacon strips, diced
- 1 can (10¾ oz.) condensed tomato soup, undiluted
- ½ cup water
- 1 cup shredded cheddar cheese
  Optional: Barbecue sauce and prepared mustard

1. Cook pasta according to the package directions. Meanwhile, in a large skillet, cook beef over medium heat until no longer pink; drain and set aside.
2. In the same skillet, cook bacon until crisp; remove with a slotted spoon to paper towels to drain. Discard the drippings. Add the pasta to the skillet. Stir in soup, water, beef and bacon; heat through.
3. Remove from the heat and sprinkle with cheese. Cover and let stand 2-3 minutes or until the cheese is melted. Serve with barbecue sauce and mustard if desired.

1 serving: 389 cal., 16g fat (8g sat. fat), 62mg chol., 565mg sod., 36g carb. (5g sugars, 2g fiber), 25g pro.

ITALIAN PASTA BAKE

I make this whenever I need to take a dish to share at a family gathering or a neighborhood potluck. Fresh tomatoes add a nice touch that's missing from most other meat and pasta casseroles.
—Karla Johnson, East Helena, MT

Prep: 40 min. • **Bake:** 25 min.
Makes: 8 servings

- 2   lbs. ground beef
- 1   large onion, chopped
- 2   garlic cloves, minced
- 1   jar (24 oz.) spaghetti sauce
- 1   can (14½ oz.) diced tomatoes, undrained
- 1   can (4 oz.) mushroom stems and pieces, drained
- 1   tsp. Italian seasoning
- 3   cups uncooked medium pasta shells
- 3   plum tomatoes, sliced
- ¾   cup shredded provolone cheese
- ¾   cup shredded part-skim mozzarella cheese

1. In a large skillet, cook beef and onion over medium heat until no longer pink. Add the garlic; cook 1 minute longer. Drain. Stir in the spaghetti sauce, diced tomatoes, mushrooms and Italian seasoning. Bring to a boil. Reduce heat; simmer, uncovered, about 20 minutes.

2. Meanwhile, preheat oven to 350°. Cook pasta according to the package directions; drain. Add to the beef mixture and gently stir in sliced tomatoes.

3. Transfer to an ungreased 13x9-in. baking dish. Sprinkle with cheeses. Bake 25-30 minutes or until bubbly and heated through.

1½ cups: 489 cal., 20g fat (8g sat. fat), 80mg chol., 702mg sod., 45g carb. (10g sugars, 5g fiber), 32g pro.

CHICKEN BROCCOLI SHELLS

This cheesy entree is a make-ahead dream. Once you have it assembled, all that's left to do is pop it in the oven when company arrives! I round out the meal with a tossed salad and warm bread.
—Karen Jagger, Columbia City, IN

Prep: 15 min. • **Bake:** 30 min.
Makes: 7 servings

- 1 jar (16 oz.) Alfredo sauce
- 2 cups frozen chopped broccoli, thawed
- 2 cups diced cooked chicken
- 1 cup shredded cheddar cheese
- ¼ cup shredded Parmesan cheese
- 21 jumbo pasta shells, cooked and drained

Preheat oven to 350°. In a large bowl, combine the Alfredo sauce, broccoli, chicken and cheeses. Spoon into pasta shells. Place in a greased 13x9-in. baking dish. Cover and bake for 30-35 minutes or until heated through.
Freeze option: Cover and freeze the unbaked casserole. To use, partially thaw in refrigerator overnight. Remove from refrigerator 30 minutes before baking. Preheat oven to 350°. Bake casserole as directed, increasing time as necessary to heat through and for a thermometer inserted in center to read 165°.
3 shells: 355 cal., 16g fat (9g sat. fat), 72mg chol., 453mg sod., 28g carb. (2g sugars, 2g fiber), 24g pro.

SHRIMP ARTICHOKE PASTA

This light pasta looks as if it came straight from an Italian restaurant. When I'm in a rush, I use jarred tomato sauce and omit the tomatoes and seasonings. You can also fix this ahead and reheat it for convenience.
—Nancy Deans, Acton, ME

Takes: 30 min. • **Makes:** 6 servings

- 9 oz. uncooked linguine
- 2 Tbsp. olive oil
- 1 cup sliced fresh mushrooms
- 1 lb. uncooked medium shrimp, peeled and deveined
- 3 medium tomatoes, chopped
- 1 can (14 oz.) water-packed artichoke hearts, rinsed, drained and halved
- 1 can (6 oz.) pitted ripe olives, drained and halved
- 2 garlic cloves, minced
- 1 tsp. dried oregano
- ½ tsp. salt
- ½ tsp. dried basil
- ⅛ tsp. pepper

1. Cook linguine according to the package directions. Meanwhile, in a large skillet, heat oil over medium-high heat. Add the mushrooms; cook and stir 4 minutes. Add the remaining ingredients; cook and stir 5 minutes or until the shrimp turn pink.
2. Drain linguine; serve with shrimp mixture.
1 serving: 328 cal., 9g fat (1g sat. fat), 112mg chol., 748mg sod., 41g carb. (4g sugars, 3g fiber), 21g pro. **Diabetic exchanges:** 2 starch, 2 lean meat, 1½ fat, 1 vegetable.

PORCINI MAC & CHEESE

This tasty dish was inspired by a mushroom mac and cheese I had at a local restaurant. The pumpkin ale adds a warm, comforting fall flavor that might even make it better than the original!
—Laura Davis, Chincoteague, VA

Prep: 30 min. + standing • **Bake:** 35 min.
Makes: 6 servings

- 1 pkg. (1 oz.) dried porcini mushrooms
- 1 cup boiling water
- 1 pkg. (16 oz.) small pasta shells
- 6 Tbsp. butter, cubed
- 1 cup chopped baby portobello mushrooms
- 1 shallot, finely chopped
- 1 garlic clove, minced
- 3 Tbsp. all-purpose flour
- 2½ cups 2% milk
- ½ cup pumpkin or amber ale
- 2 cups shredded sharp white cheddar cheese
- 1 cup shredded fontina cheese
- 1 tsp. salt
- 1 cup soft bread crumbs

1. Preheat oven to 350°. In a small bowl, combine dried mushrooms and boiling water; let stand 15-20 minutes or until mushrooms are softened. Remove with a slotted spoon; rinse and finely chop, then set aside. Discard liquid. Cook pasta shells according to package directions for al dente.

2. Meanwhile, in a Dutch oven, heat butter over medium-high heat. Add portobello mushrooms and shallot; cook and stir 2-3 minutes or until tender. Add the garlic; cook 1 minute longer. Stir in flour until blended; gradually stir in milk and beer. Bring to a boil, stirring constantly; cook and stir 3-4 minutes or until slightly thickened. Stir in cheeses, salt and the reserved porcini mushrooms.

3. Drain pasta; add to mushroom mixture and toss to combine. Transfer to a greased 13x9-in. baking dish. Top with soft bread crumbs. Bake, uncovered, 35-40 minutes or until golden brown.

Note: To make soft bread crumbs, tear bread into pieces and place in a food processor or blender. Cover and pulse until crumbs form. One slice of bread yields ½-¾ cup crumbs.

1½ cups: 723 cal., 33g fat (19g sat. fat), 97mg chol., 968mg sod., 74g carb. (9g sugars, 4g fiber), 30g pro.

SHRIMP TORTELLINI PASTA TOSS

No matter how you toss 'em up, shrimp and herbs play nicely with vegetables of your choice in a steaming bowl of yummy pasta, making this an all-seasons favorite.
—*Taste of Home* Test Kitchen

- -

Takes: 20 min. • **Makes:** 4 servings

1 pkg. (9 oz.) refrigerated cheese tortellini
1 cup frozen peas
3 Tbsp. olive oil, divided
1 lb. uncooked shrimp (31-40 per lb.), peeled and deveined
2 garlic cloves, minced
¼ tsp. salt
¼ tsp. dried thyme
¼ tsp. pepper

1. Cook tortellini according to the package directions, adding peas during the last 5 minutes of cooking.

2. Meanwhile, in a large nonstick skillet, heat 2 Tbsp. oil over medium-high heat. Add the shrimp; cook and stir 2 minutes. Add garlic; cook 1-2 minutes longer or until the shrimp turn pink.

3. Drain the tortellini mixture; add to skillet. Stir in salt, thyme, pepper and remaining oil; toss to coat.

1¼ cups: 413 cal., 17g fat (4g sat. fat), 165mg chol., 559mg sod., 36g carb. (4g sugars, 3g fiber), 29g pro. **Diabetic exchanges:** 4 lean meat, 2 starch, 2 fat.

Shrimp Asparagus Fettuccine: Bring 4 qt. water to a boil. Add 9 oz. refrigerated fettuccine and 1 cup cut fresh asparagus. Boil 2-3 minutes or until the pasta is tender. Proceed with recipe as written, but replace thyme with ¾ tsp. dried basil.

1½ cups: 379 cal., 13g fat (2g sat. fat), 138mg chol., 411mg sod., 37g carb., 3g fiber, 27g pro. **Diabetic exchanges:** 3 lean meat, 2½ starch, 2 fat.

Soy Shrimp with Rice Noodles: Cook 8.8 oz. thin rice noodles according to the package directions, adding 1 cup frozen shelled edamame during the last 4 minutes of cooking. Proceed with recipe as written, but replace thyme with ¼ cup reduced-sodium soy sauce and omit salt.

1½ cups: 444 cal., 14g fat (2g sat. fat), 138mg chol., 744mg sod., 50g carb., 2g fiber, 26g pro. **Diabetic exchanges:** 3 starch, 3 lean meat, 2 fat.

MAKE-AHEAD LASAGNA

This dish is an old standby when I'm short on time and expecting guests for dinner. It's a flavorful combination of several easy lasagna recipes I have tried over the years.
—Mary Grimm, Williamsburg, IA

Prep: 35 min. + chilling
Bake: 55 min. + standing
Makes: 12 servings

- 1 lb. ground beef
- 1 lb. bulk hot Italian sausage
- 2 cups marinara sauce
- 1 can (15 oz.) pizza sauce
- 2 large eggs, lightly beaten
- 1 carton (15 oz.) whole-milk ricotta cheese
- ½ cup grated Parmesan cheese
- 1 Tbsp. dried parsley flakes
- ½ tsp. pepper
- 12 no-cook lasagna noodles
- 4 cups shredded part-skim mozzarella cheese

1. In a large skillet, cook and crumble beef and sausage over medium-high heat until no longer pink; drain. Stir in the marinara and pizza sauces. In a bowl, mix the eggs, ricotta cheese, Parmesan cheese, parsley and pepper.
2. Spread 1 cup meat sauce into a greased 13x9-in. baking dish. Layer with 4 noodles, half the ricotta cheese mixture, 1 cup meat sauce and 1 cup mozzarella cheese. Repeat layers. Top with the remaining noodles, meat sauce and mozzarella cheese. Refrigerate, covered, 8 hours or overnight.
3. Preheat oven to 375°. Remove lasagna from refrigerator while oven heats. Bake, covered, 45 minutes. Uncover and bake until cheese is melted, 10-15 minutes more. Let stand 10 minutes before cutting.
1 piece: 462 cal., 27g fat (12g sat. fat), 117mg chol., 931mg sod., 26g carb. (7g sugars, 2g fiber), 30g pro.

VEGETARIAN PAD THAI

Here's my version of pad Thai loaded with crisp, colorful vegetables and zesty flavor. Give these fresh and simple noodles a twirl.
—Colleen Doucette, Truro, NS

Takes: 30 min. • **Makes:** 4 servings

- 6 oz. uncooked thick rice noodles
- 2 Tbsp. packed brown sugar
- 3 Tbsp. reduced-sodium soy sauce
- 4 tsp. rice vinegar
- 2 tsp. lime juice
- 2 tsp. olive oil
- 3 medium carrots, shredded
- 1 medium sweet red pepper, cut into thin strips
- 4 green onions, chopped
- 3 garlic cloves, minced
- 4 large eggs, lightly beaten
- 2 cups bean sprouts
- ⅓ cup chopped fresh cilantro
  Chopped peanuts, optional
  Lime wedges

1. Prepare noodles according to package directions. Drain; rinse well and drain again. In a small bowl, mix together brown sugar, soy sauce, vinegar and lime juice.
2. In a large nonstick skillet, heat oil over medium-high heat; stir-fry carrots and pepper until crisp-tender, 3-4 minutes. Add green onions and garlic; cook and stir 2 minutes. Remove from pan.
3. Reduce heat to medium. Pour eggs into the same pan; cook and stir until no liquid egg remains. Stir in the carrot mixture, noodles and sauce mixture; heat through. Add the bean sprouts; toss to combine. Top with cilantro and, if desired, peanuts. Serve with lime wedges.
1¼ cups: 339 cal., 8g fat (2g sat. fat), 186mg chol., 701mg sod., 55g carb. (15g sugars, 4g fiber), 12g pro.

ANGEL HAIR PASTA WITH SAUSAGE & SPINACH

You won't miss the marinara sauce once you taste this pasta, which gets its flavor from comforting chicken broth. The Italian sausage simmers away, without much work on your part, until it's time to add noodles. My husband likes this dish so much that I make it twice a week!
—Daphine Smith, Baytown, TX

Takes: 30 min. • **Makes:** 4 servings

- 4   Italian sausage links (4 oz. each), sliced
- 1   medium onion, chopped
- 2   garlic cloves, minced
- 2   tsp. olive oil
- 2   cans (14½ oz. each) chicken broth
- 8   oz. uncooked angel hair pasta, broken in half
- 2   pkg. (9 oz. each) fresh spinach, trimmed and coarsely chopped
- 2   Tbsp. all-purpose flour
- ¼   tsp. pepper
- ⅓   cup heavy whipping cream

1. In a Dutch oven, cook sausage, onion and garlic in oil over medium heat until the meat is no longer pink; drain. Add broth; bring to a boil. Add pasta; cook for 3 minutes, stirring frequently.

2. Gradually add spinach. Cook and stir 2-3 minutes or until the pasta is tender and the spinach is wilted. In a small bowl, combine the flour, pepper and cream until smooth; gradually stir into pasta mixture. Bring to a boil; cook and stir 1-2 minutes or until thickened.

1½ cups: 563 cal., 26g fat (10g sat. fat), 77mg chol., 1546mg sod., 57g carb. (6g sugars, 6g fiber), 25g pro.

ONE-SKILLET LASAGNA

This is hands-down one of the best skillet lasagna recipes our testing panel has ever tasted. With classic flavors and cheesy layers, it's definitely kid-friendly.
—*Taste of Home* Test Kitchen

- -

Takes: 30 min. • **Makes:** 6 servings

¾ lb. ground beef
2 garlic cloves, minced
1 can (14½ oz.) diced tomatoes with basil, oregano and garlic, undrained
2 jars (14 oz. each) spaghetti sauce
⅔ cup condensed cream of onion soup, undiluted
2 large eggs, lightly beaten
1¼ cups 1% cottage cheese
¾ tsp. Italian seasoning
9 no-cook lasagna noodles
½ cup shredded Colby-Monterey Jack cheese
½ cup shredded part-skim mozzarella cheese

1. In a large skillet, cook beef and garlic over medium heat until meat is no longer pink; drain. Stir in tomatoes and spaghetti sauce; heat through. Transfer to a large bowl.
2. In a small bowl, combine the soup, eggs, cottage cheese and Italian seasoning.
3. Return 1 cup meat sauce to the skillet; spread evenly. Layer with 1 cup cottage cheese mixture, 1½ cups meat sauce and half the noodles, breaking to fit. Repeat layers of cottage cheese mixture, meat sauce and noodles. Top with the remaining meat sauce. Bring to a boil. Reduce heat; cover and simmer 15-17 minutes or until the noodles are tender.
4. Remove from the heat. Sprinkle with shredded cheeses; cover and let stand for 2 minutes or until melted.
1 serving: 478 cal., 20g fat (8g sat. fat), 128mg chol., 1552mg sod., 43g carb. (15g sugars, 4g fiber), 31g pro.

CHARD & BACON LINGUINE

When Swiss chard is in season, I like to use it every way I can, and that includes stirring it into this breezy linguine. When you're time-limited, this dish keeps life simple.
—Diane Nemitz, Ludington, MI

- -

Takes: 30 min. • **Makes:** 4 servings

8 oz. uncooked whole wheat linguine
4 bacon strips, chopped
4 garlic cloves, minced
½ cup reduced-sodium chicken broth
½ cup dry white wine or additional chicken broth
¼ tsp. salt
6 cups chopped Swiss chard (about 6 oz.)
⅓ cup shredded Parmesan cheese

1. Cook linguine according to the package directions; drain. Meanwhile, in a large skillet, cook bacon over medium heat until crisp, stirring occasionally. Add garlic; cook 1 minute longer.
2. Add broth, wine, salt and Swiss chard to the skillet; bring to a boil. Cook and stir 4-5 minutes or until the chard is tender.
3. Add linguine; heat through, tossing to combine. Sprinkle with cheese.
1 cup: 353 cal., 14g fat (5g sat. fat), 23mg chol., 633mg sod., 47g carb. (2g sugars, 7g fiber), 14g pro. **Diabetic exchanges:** 3 starch, 1 medium-fat meat, 1 vegetable.

PASTA & BROCCOLI SAUSAGE SIMMER

I created this meal when trying to use up a large head of broccoli. My family requests it at least once a week, which is handy because we always have the ingredients.
—Lisa Montgomery, Elmira, ON

- -

Takes: 30 min. • **Makes:** 8 servings

- 3   cups uncooked spiral pasta
- 2   lbs. smoked kielbasa or Polish sausage, cut into ¼-in. slices
- 2   medium bunches broccoli, cut into florets
- 1   cup sliced red onion
- 2   cans (14½ oz. each) diced tomatoes, undrained
- 2   Tbsp. minced fresh basil or 2 tsp. dried basil
- 2   Tbsp. minced fresh parsley or 2 tsp. dried parsley flakes
- 2   tsp. sugar

1. Cook spiral pasta according to the package directions.
2. Meanwhile, in a Dutch oven, saute sausage, broccoli and onion until the broccoli is crisp-tender, 5-6 minutes.
3. Add tomatoes, basil, parsley and sugar. Cover and simmer for 10 minutes. Drain pasta; stir into the sausage mixture.

1 serving: 544 cal., 32g fat (11g sat. fat), 76mg chol., 1395mg sod., 42g carb. (9g sugars, 8g fiber), 25g pro.

ONE-PAN TUSCAN RAVIOLI

Sometimes I use garbanzo beans instead of cannellini beans, grated Asiago cheese or Provolone instead of Parmesan, and only zucchini if I don't have eggplant. That's what I love about this dish—it's so flexible!
—Sonya Labbe, West Hollywood, CA

- -

Takes: 25 min. • **Makes:** 4 servings

- 1   Tbsp. olive oil
- 2   cups cubed eggplant (½ in.)
- 1   can (14½ oz.) Italian diced tomatoes, undrained
- 1   can (14½ oz.) reduced-sodium chicken broth
- 1   medium zucchini, halved lengthwise and cut into ½-in. slices
- 1   pkg. (9 oz.) refrigerated cheese ravioli
- 1   can (15 oz.) cannellini beans, rinsed and drained
     Shredded Parmesan cheese
     Thinly sliced fresh basil

1. In a large skillet, heat oil over medium heat; saute eggplant until lightly browned, 2-3 minutes.
2. Stir in tomatoes, broth and zucchini; bring to a boil. Add ravioli; cook, uncovered, over medium heat until the ravioli are tender, 7-9 minutes, stirring occasionally. Stir in beans; heat through. Sprinkle with cheese and fresh basil.

1½ cups: 376 cal., 10g fat (4g sat. fat), 36mg chol., 1096mg sod., 56g carb. (11g sugars, 8g fiber), 16g pro.

ONE-PAN ROTINI WITH TOMATO CREAM SAUCE

I make one-pan recipes all the time, and my family proclaimed this dish a winner. (Bonus: It also makes for easy cleanup.) Serve with bread to dip into the sauce.
—Angela Lively, Conroe, TX

Prep: 15 min. • **Cook:** 30 min.
Makes: 6 servings

1   lb. lean ground beef (90% lean)
1   medium onion, chopped
2   garlic cloves, minced
1   tsp. Italian seasoning
½   tsp. pepper
¼   tsp. salt
2   cups beef stock
1   can (14½ oz.) fire-roasted diced tomatoes, undrained
2   cups uncooked spiral pasta
1   cup frozen peas
1   cup heavy whipping cream
½   cup grated Parmesan cheese

1. In a large skillet, cook beef and onion over medium heat until beef is no longer pink and onion is tender, breaking up beef into crumbles, 5-10 minutes; drain. Add garlic, Italian seasoning, pepper and salt; cook 1 minute longer. Add stock and tomatoes; bring to a boil. Add pasta and peas; reduce heat. Simmer, covered, until the pasta is tender, 10-12 minutes.
2. Gradually stir in cream and cheese; heat through (do not allow to boil).

1 cup: 443 cal., 23g fat (13g sat. fat), 98mg chol., 646mg sod., 33g carb. (6g sugars, 3g fiber), 25g pro.

TEST KITCHEN TIP

Even if all the noodles aren't completely submerged in liquid when added to the pan, they will still cook through. For an extra boost of flavor, stir in cooked sausage of your choice and serve with additional cheese.

CAJUN CHICKEN & PASTA

This kicked-up pasta dish is a family favorite and my most requested recipe. Best of all, it's easy to adapt, too. Substitute shrimp for the chicken, add your favorite veggies and adjust the spice level to your family's taste—the possibilities are endless!
—Dolly Kragel, Sloan, IA

- -

Prep: 10 min. + standing • **Cook:** 35 min.
Makes: 6 servings

- 1 lb. boneless skinless chicken breasts, cut into 2x½-in. strips
- 3 tsp. Cajun seasoning
- 8 oz. uncooked penne pasta (about 2⅓ cups)
- 2 Tbsp. butter, divided
- 1 small sweet red pepper, diced
- 1 small green pepper, diced
- ½ cup sliced fresh mushrooms
- 4 green onions, chopped
- 1 cup heavy whipping cream
- ½ tsp. salt
- ¼ tsp. dried basil
- ¼ tsp. lemon-pepper seasoning
- ¼ tsp. garlic powder
  Pepper to taste
  Chopped plum tomatoes
  Minced fresh basil
  Shredded Parmesan cheese

1. Toss chicken with Cajun seasoning; let stand 15 minutes. Cook pasta according to the package directions; drain.
2. In a large skillet, heat 1 Tbsp. butter over medium-high heat; saute chicken until no longer pink, 5-6 minutes. Remove from pan.
3. In same pan, heat the remaining butter over medium-high heat; saute peppers, mushrooms and green onions until peppers are crisp-tender, 6-8 minutes. Stir in cream and seasonings; bring to a boil. Cook and stir until slightly thickened, 4-6 minutes. Stir in pasta and chicken; heat through. Top with tomatoes and basil. Sprinkle with cheese.

1 serving: 398 cal., 21g fat (12g sat. fat), 97mg chol., 357mg sod., 31g carb. (4g sugars, 2g fiber), 22g pro.

CURRIED SHRIMP PASTA

This light and spicy dish comes together so easily. My favorite pasta to use is angel hair, but spaghetti works as well if that's what you have on hand.
—Thomas Faglon, Somerset, NJ

- -

Takes: 25 min. • **Makes:** 4 servings

- 8 oz. uncooked angel hair pasta
- 8 oz. fresh sugar snap peas (about 2 cups), halved diagonally
- 2 Tbsp. olive oil
- 1 lb. uncooked shrimp (26-30 per lb.), peeled and deveined
- 3 tsp. curry powder
- 1 tsp. ground cumin
- ¾ tsp. salt
- 6 green onions, diagonally sliced

1. Cook pasta according to the package directions, adding snap peas during last 1-2 minutes of cooking. Drain, reserving ½ cup pasta water.
2. In a large skillet, heat oil over medium-high heat; saute shrimp 2 minutes. Add the seasonings and green onions; cook and stir until the shrimp turn pink, 1-2 minutes. Add pasta and peas; heat through, tossing to combine and adding the reserved pasta water if desired.

1⅓ cups: 404 cal., 10g fat (1g sat. fat), 138mg chol., 588mg sod., 50g carb. (4g sugars, 5g fiber), 28g pro. **Diabetic exchanges:** 3 starch, 3 lean meat, 1½ fat.

SPICY SHRIMP & PENNE PASTA

I created this creamy pasta dish when I needed to use up some marinara. Red pepper flakes give it a little heat, which my family loves. It's super versatile, so try it with chicken or stir in fresh basil, too.
—Lorri Stout, Gaithersburg, MD

Takes: 30 min. • **Makes:** 6 servings

- 3 cups uncooked penne pasta (about 12 oz.)
- 1 Tbsp. butter
- 1 Tbsp. olive oil
- 2 lbs. uncooked shrimp (31-40 per lb.), peeled and deveined
- ½ tsp. crushed red pepper flakes
- 1 jar (24 oz.) marinara sauce
- ¾ cup half-and-half cream
- 4 cups chopped fresh spinach

1. In a 6-qt. stockpot, cook penne pasta according to the package directions; drain and return to pot.
2. In a large skillet, heat half the butter and half the oil over medium-high heat. Saute half the shrimp with ¼ tsp. pepper flakes until the shrimp turn pink, 3-5 minutes; remove from pan. Repeat with remaining butter, oil, shrimp and pepper flakes.
3. In same pan, heat marinara sauce and cream just to a boil over medium heat, stirring to blend. Stir in spinach until wilted; add to pasta. Stir in shrimp; heat through.

1⅔ cups: 395 cal., 12g fat (4g sat. fat), 206mg chol., 702mg sod., 38g carb. (9g sugars, 4g fiber), 33g pro. **Diabetic exchanges:** 4 lean meat, 2 starch, 1 vegetable, 1 fat.

SPINACH-BASIL LASAGNA

In the kitchen, my husband and I like to use classic ingredients in new ways. I came up with this lasagna one day and haven't made another type since. We love it!
—Charlotte Gehle, Brownstown, MI

- -

Prep: 20 min. • **Bake:** 45 min.
Makes: 9 servings

- 1 large egg, lightly beaten
- 2 cups reduced-fat ricotta cheese
- 4 oz. crumbled feta cheese
- ¼ cup grated Parmesan cheese
- ¼ cup chopped fresh basil
- 2 garlic cloves, minced
- ¼ tsp. pepper
- 1 jar (24 oz.) pasta sauce
- 9 no-cook lasagna noodles
- 3 cups fresh baby spinach
- 2 cups shredded part-skim mozzarella cheese

1. Preheat oven to 350°. In a bowl, mix egg, cheeses, basil, garlic and pepper.
2. Spread ½ cup pasta sauce into a greased 13x9-in. baking dish. Layer with 3 noodles, ¾ cup ricotta mixture, 1 cup spinach, ½ cup mozzarella cheese and ⅔ cup sauce. Repeat layers twice. Sprinkle with the remaining mozzarella cheese.
3. Bake, covered, 35 minutes. Uncover and bake until heated through and the cheese is melted, 10-15 minutes. Let stand 5 minutes before serving.
Freeze option: Cover and freeze unbaked lasagna. To use, partially thaw in refrigerator overnight. Remove from the refrigerator 30 minutes before baking. Preheat oven to 350°. Bake the lasagna as directed, increasing time as necessary to heat through and for a thermometer inserted in center to read 165°.
1 piece: 292 cal., 12g fat (6g sat. fat), 59mg chol., 677mg sod., 27g carb. (10g sugars, 3g fiber), 18g pro. **Diabetic exchanges:** 2 starch, 2 medium-fat meat.

PEANUT GINGER PASTA

To get the luscious flavor of Thai cuisine, combine ginger, basil, lime and peanut butter in a sauce for linguine. It's so good that we've never had leftovers.
—Allil Binder, Spokane, WA

- -

Takes: 30 min. • **Makes:** 4 servings

- 2½ tsp. grated lime zest
- ¼ cup lime juice
- 2 Tbsp. reduced-sodium soy sauce
- 2 tsp. water
- 1 tsp. sesame oil
- ⅓ cup creamy peanut butter
- 2½ tsp. minced fresh gingerroot
- 2 garlic cloves, minced
- ¼ tsp. salt
- ¼ tsp. pepper
- 8 oz. uncooked whole wheat linguine
- 2 cups small fresh broccoli florets
- 2 medium carrots, grated
- 1 medium sweet red pepper, julienned
- 2 green onions, chopped
- 2 Tbsp. minced fresh basil

1. Place the first 10 ingredients in a blender; cover and process until blended. Cook linguine according to package directions, adding broccoli during the last 5 minutes of cooking; drain.
2. Transfer the linguine and broccoli to a large bowl. Add the remaining ingredients. Add the peanut butter mixture and toss to combine.
2 cups: 365 cal., 13g fat (2g sat. fat), 0 chol., 567mg sod., 57g carb. (6g sugars, 10g fiber), 14g pro.

THREE-CHEESE MEATBALL MOSTACCIOLI

When my husband travels for work, I make a special dinner for my kids to keep their minds off missing Daddy. This tasty mostaccioli is meatball magic.
—Jennifer Gilbert, Brighton, MI

Prep: 15 min. • **Bake:** 35 min.
Makes: 10 servings

- 1 pkg. (16 oz.) mostaccioli
- 2 large eggs, lightly beaten
- 1 carton (15 oz.) part-skim ricotta cheese
- 1 lb. ground beef
- 1 medium onion, chopped
- 1 Tbsp. brown sugar
- 1 Tbsp. Italian seasoning
- 1 tsp. garlic powder
- ¼ tsp. pepper
- 2 jars (24 oz. each) pasta sauce with meat
- ½ cup grated Romano cheese
- 1 pkg. (12 oz.) frozen fully cooked Italian meatballs, thawed
- ¾ cup shaved Parmesan cheese
    Optional: Minced fresh parsley or fresh baby arugula

1. Preheat oven to 350°. Cook mostaccioli according to the package directions for al dente; drain. Meanwhile, in a small bowl, mix eggs and ricotta cheese.
2. In a 6-qt. stockpot, cook beef and onion 6-8 minutes or until beef is no longer pink, breaking up beef into crumbles; drain. Stir in brown sugar and seasonings. Add pasta sauce and mostaccioli; toss to combine.
3. Transfer half the pasta mixture to a greased 13x9-in. baking dish. Layer with ricotta mixture and the remaining pasta mixture; sprinkle with Romano cheese. Top with meatballs and Parmesan cheese.
4. Bake, uncovered, 35-40 minutes or until heated through. If desired, top with parsley.
1⅓ cups: 541 cal., 23g fat (11g sat. fat), 105mg chol., 1335mg sod., 55g carb. (13g sugars, 5g fiber), 34g pro.

EASY ASIAN BEEF & NOODLES

Years ago, I created this tasty dish on a whim to feed my hungry teenagers. It has since become a dinnertime staple, and now two of my grandchildren make it in their own kitchens.
—Judy Batson, Tampa, FL

Takes: 25 min. • **Makes:** 4 servings

- 1 beef top sirloin steak (1 lb.), cut into ¼-in.-thick strips
- 6 Tbsp. reduced-sodium teriyaki sauce, divided
- 8 oz. uncooked whole grain thin spaghetti
- 2 Tbsp. canola oil, divided
- 3 cups broccoli coleslaw mix
- 1 medium onion, halved and thinly sliced
    Chopped fresh cilantro, optional

1. Toss beef with 2 Tbsp. teriyaki sauce. Cook spaghetti according to the package directions; drain.
2. In a large skillet, heat 1 Tbsp. oil over medium-high heat; stir-fry beef strips until browned, 1-3 minutes. Remove from pan.
3. In same skillet, heat the remaining oil over medium-high heat; stir-fry coleslaw mix and onion until crisp-tender, 3-5 minutes. Add spaghetti and the remaining teriyaki sauce; toss and heat through. Stir in the beef. If desired, sprinkle with cilantro.
2 cups: 462 cal., 13g fat (2g sat. fat), 46mg chol., 546mg sod., 52g carb. (9g sugars, 8g fiber), 35g pro.

ONE-POT BACON CHEESEBURGER PASTA

When the weather's too chilly to grill burgers, I whip up a big pot of this cheesy pasta. Believe it or not, it tastes just like a bacon cheeseburger, and it's much easier for my young children to enjoy.
—Carly Terrell, Granbury, TX

- -

Prep: 15 min. • **Cook:** 35 min.
Makes: 12 servings

8 bacon strips, chopped
2 lbs. ground beef
½ large red onion, chopped
12 oz. uncooked spiral pasta
4 cups chicken broth
2 cans (15 oz. each) crushed tomatoes
1 can (8 oz.) tomato sauce
1 cup water
¼ cup ketchup
3 Tbsp. prepared mustard
2 Tbsp. Worcestershire sauce
¼ tsp. salt
¼ tsp. pepper
2 cups shredded cheddar cheese, divided
⅓ cup chopped dill pickle
   Optional: Chopped tomatoes, shredded lettuce, sliced pickles and sliced red onion

1. In a 6-qt. stockpot, cook bacon over medium heat, stirring occasionally, until crisp, 6-8 minutes. Remove bacon with a slotted spoon; drain on paper towels. Discard the drippings.

2. In the same pot, cook the ground beef and onion over medium heat until the meat is no longer pink, breaking into crumbles, 6-8 minutes; drain. Add next 10 ingredients; bring to a boil. Reduce heat; simmer, covered, until the pasta is al dente, stirring occasionally, about 10 minutes.

3. Stir in 1 cup cheese, pickle and bacon; cook and stir until cheese is melted. Serve with remaining cheese and, if desired, tomatoes, lettuce, pickles and red onions.

1⅓ cups: 390 cal., 18g fat (8g sat. fat), 73mg chol., 1023mg sod., 31g carb. (7g sugars, 3g fiber), 25g pro.

TEST KITCHEN TIP

Take the extra time and shred cheese from a block for this recipe; it will stir in with a smoother texture than preshredded cheese. Use Dijon mustard to give this dish a little bit of a grown-up taste.

SHRIMP PUTTANESCA

I throw together these bold ingredients for a feisty seafood pasta. It doesn't take a lot of work to create a truly impressive result.
—Lynda Balslev, Sausalito, CA

Takes: 30 min. • **Makes:** 4 servings

- 2 Tbsp. olive oil, divided
- 1 lb. uncooked shrimp (31-40 per lb.), peeled and deveined
- ¾ to 1 tsp. crushed red pepper flakes, divided
- ¼ tsp. salt
- 1 small onion, chopped
- 2 to 3 anchovy fillets, finely chopped
- 3 garlic cloves, minced
- 2 cups grape tomatoes or small cherry tomatoes
- ½ cup dry white wine or vegetable broth
- ⅓ cup pitted Greek olives, coarsely chopped
- 2 tsp. drained capers
  Sugar to taste
  Chopped fresh Italian parsley
  Hot cooked spaghetti, optional

1. In a large skillet, heat 1 Tbsp. oil; saute shrimp with ½ tsp. pepper flakes until the shrimp turn pink, 2-3 minutes. Stir in salt; remove from pan.
2. In same pan, heat the remaining oil over medium heat; saute onion until tender, about 2 minutes. Add anchovies, garlic and remaining pepper flakes; cook and stir until fragrant, about 1 minute. Stir in tomatoes, wine, olives and capers; bring to a boil. Reduce heat; simmer, uncovered, until the tomatoes are softened and the mixture is thickened, 8-10 minutes.
3. Stir in shrimp. Add sugar to taste; sprinkle with parsley. If desired, serve with spaghetti.
1 cup shrimp mixture: 228 cal., 12g fat (2g sat. fat), 140mg chol., 579mg sod., 8g carb. (3g sugars, 1g fiber), 20g pro.

SAUSAGE SPAGHETTI SPIRALS

My family often requests this casserole with hearty chunks of sausage and green pepper. The recipe makes a big pan, so it's a perfect bring-along for gatherings.
—Carol Carolton, Wheaton, IL

Prep: 15 min. • **Bake:** 30 min.
Makes: 6 servings

- 1 lb. bulk Italian sausage
- 1 medium green pepper, chopped
- 5 cups spiral pasta, cooked and drained
- 1 jar (24 oz.) spaghetti sauce
- 1½ cups shredded part-skim mozzarella cheese

1. Preheat oven to 350°. In a large skillet, cook Italian sausage and chopped green pepper over medium heat until the meat is no longer pink; drain. Stir in pasta and spaghetti sauce.
2. Transfer to a greased 13x9-in. baking dish. Cover and bake 25 minutes. Uncover; sprinkle with cheese. Bake 5-10 minutes longer or until the cheese is melted.
1 serving: 592 cal., 24g fat (9g sat. fat), 59mg chol., 1071mg sod., 67g carb. (12g sugars, 5g fiber), 26g pro.

ITALIAN SAUSAGE ORZO

This light dish is perfect for any night of the week, and tastes even better than it looks! If you have leftover sauteed mushrooms or other vegetables, toss them in as well.
—Lisa Speer, Palm Beach, FL

Prep: 15 min. • **Cook:** 25 min.
Makes: 6 servings

8	cups water
3	tsp. reduced-sodium chicken bouillon granules
1½	cups uncooked whole wheat orzo pasta (about 8 oz.)
1	pkg. (19½ oz.) Italian turkey sausage links, casings removed
½	cup chopped sweet onion
2	garlic cloves, minced
3	plum tomatoes, chopped
½	cup chopped roasted sweet red pepper
⅛	tsp. salt
⅛	tsp. pepper
⅛	tsp. crushed red pepper flakes
⅓	cup chopped fresh basil
¼	cup grated Parmesan cheese

1. In a large saucepan, bring water and bouillon to a boil. Stir in orzo; return to a boil. Cook until al dente, 8-10 minutes. Drain the orzo, reserving ¾ cup cooking liquid.

2. In a large skillet coated with cooking spray, cook and crumble sausage with onion and garlic over medium heat until no longer pink, 6-8 minutes. Stir in tomatoes, roasted pepper, salt, pepper, pepper flakes and the orzo. Heat through over medium-low heat; stir in reserved cooking liquid to moisten if desired. Remove from heat; stir in fresh basil and Parmesan cheese.

1 cup: 265 cal., 7g fat (2g sat. fat), 37mg chol., 623mg sod., 32g carb. (2g sugars, 7g fiber), 16g pro. **Diabetic exchanges:** 2 starch, 2 lean meat.

GNOCCHI WITH WHITE BEANS

Here's one of those no-fuss recipes you can toss together and cook in one skillet. Ideal for a busy weeknight, it's also good with crumbled Italian chicken sausage if you need to please meat lovers.
—Juli Meyers, Hinesville, GA

- -

Takes: 30 min. • **Makes:** 6 servings

- 1 Tbsp. olive oil
- 1 medium onion, chopped
- 2 garlic cloves, minced
- 1 pkg. (16 oz.) potato gnocchi
- 1 can (15 oz.) cannellini beans, rinsed and drained
- 1 can (14½ oz.) Italian diced tomatoes, undrained
- 1 pkg. (6 oz.) fresh baby spinach
- ¼ tsp. pepper
- ½ cup shredded part-skim mozzarella cheese
- 3 Tbsp. grated Parmesan cheese

1. In a large skillet, heat oil over medium-high heat. Add onion; cook and stir until tender. Add garlic; cook 1 minute longer. Add gnocchi; cook and stir 5-6 minutes or until golden brown. Stir in beans, tomatoes, spinach and pepper; heat through.
2. Sprinkle with cheeses; cover and remove from heat. Let stand 3-4 minutes or until cheese is melted.
Note: Look for potato gnocchi in the pasta or frozen foods section.
1 cup: 307 cal., 6g fat (2g sat. fat), 13mg chol., 789mg sod., 50g carb. (10g sugars, 6g fiber), 13g pro.

TURKEY SPAGHETTI CASSEROLE

My mom made this creamy spaghetti when I was growing up. Whenever I have any leftover chicken or turkey, I look forward to preparing this simple, tasty dinner.
—Casandra Hetrick, Lindsey, OH

- -

Prep: 30 min. • **Bake:** 1¼ hours
Makes: 6 servings

- 1 medium onion, chopped
- 1 medium carrot, chopped
- 1 celery rib, chopped
- ⅓ cup sliced fresh mushrooms
- 1 Tbsp. butter
- 2½ cups reduced-sodium chicken broth
- 1 can (10¾ oz.) reduced-fat reduced-sodium condensed cream of mushroom soup, undiluted
- ¼ tsp. salt
- ¼ tsp. pepper
- 2½ cups cubed cooked turkey breast
- 6 oz. uncooked spaghetti, broken into 2-in. pieces
- ½ cup shredded reduced-fat Colby-Monterey Jack cheese
- ½ tsp. paprika

1. In a small skillet, saute the vegetables in butter until tender. In a large bowl, combine the broth, soup, salt and pepper.
2. In a 2½-qt. baking dish coated with cooking spray, layer the turkey, spaghetti and vegetable mixture. Pour broth mixture over the top.
3. Cover and bake at 350° for 70-80 minutes or until spaghetti is tender, stirring once. Uncover; sprinkle with cheese and paprika. Bake 5-10 minutes longer or until cheese is melted.
1 cup: 284 cal., 6g fat (3g sat. fat), 62mg chol., 702mg sod., 30g carb. (4g sugars, 3g fiber), 26g pro. **Diabetic exchanges:** 3 lean meat, 1½ starch, 1 vegetable, ½ fat.

MUSHROOM PENNE BAKE

This is an easy, hearty and delicious meal that will hit the spot anytime, but especially on a chilly evening! Its cheesy goodness will have you going back for seconds. Serve with salad and garlic bread.
—Sue Aschemeier, Defiance, OH

- -

Prep: 25 min. • **Bake:** 25 min.
Makes: 8 servings

- 1 pkg. (12 oz.) whole wheat penne pasta
- 1 Tbsp. olive oil
- 1 lb. sliced baby portobello mushrooms
- 2 garlic cloves, minced
- 1 jar (24 oz.) marinara sauce
- 1 tsp. Italian seasoning
- ½ tsp. salt
- 2 cups reduced-fat ricotta cheese
- 1 cup shredded part-skim mozzarella cheese, divided
- ½ cup grated Parmesan cheese

1. Preheat oven to 350°. In a 6-qt. stockpot, cook pasta according to package directions. Drain and return to pot; cool slightly.
2. In a large skillet, heat oil over medium-high heat; saute mushrooms until tender, 4-6 minutes. Add garlic; cook 1 minute. Stir in marinara sauce and seasonings. Spread half the mushroom mixture into a 13x9-in. baking dish coated with cooking spray.
3. Stir ricotta cheese and ½ cup mozzarella cheese into the pasta; spoon over the mushroom mixture in the baking dish. Spread the remaining mushroom mixture over the pasta layer.
4. Sprinkle with the remaining mozzarella and Parmesan cheese. Bake, uncovered, until bubbly, 25-30 minutes.
1 cup: 353 cal., 11g fat (4g sat. fat), 30mg chol., 748mg sod., 44g carb. (10g sugars, 7g fiber), 20g pro. **Diabetic exchanges:** 3 starch, 2 lean meat, 1 fat.

ONE-POT SPAGHETTI DINNER

All you need is one pot to make this meal that features a simple homemade sauce. Allspice adds a unique taste, but you can substitute Italian seasoning if you prefer.
—Carol Benzel-Schmidt, Stanwood, WA

- -

Prep: 10 min. • **Cook:** 25 min.
Makes: 4 servings

- 1 lb. lean ground beef (90% lean)
- 1¾ cups sliced fresh mushrooms
- 3 cups tomato juice
- 1 can (14½ oz.) no-salt-added diced tomatoes, drained
- 1 can (8 oz.) no-salt-added tomato sauce
- 1 Tbsp. dried minced onion
- ½ tsp. salt
- ½ tsp. garlic powder
- ½ tsp. ground mustard
- ¼ tsp. pepper
- ⅛ tsp. ground allspice
- ⅛ tsp. ground mace, optional
- 6 oz. uncooked multigrain spaghetti, broken into pieces
  Optional: Fresh mozzarella cheese pearls or shaved Parmesan cheese

1. In a Dutch oven, cook the beef and mushrooms over medium heat until the meat is no longer pink; drain. Add tomato juice, tomatoes, tomato sauce, onion and seasonings.
2. Bring to a boil. Stir in the spaghetti. Simmer, covered, 12-15 minutes or until the spaghetti is tender. If desired, serve with cheese.
1½ cups: 414 cal., 10g fat (4g sat. fat), 71mg chol., 925mg sod., 48g carb. (15g sugars, 6g fiber), 33g pro.

FARMERS MARKET PASTA

When we moved into our house, little did we know that we had purchased a wild asparagus patch along with it! Twenty years later, that little patch still gives us plenty of asparagus—and what better way to use it up than in a light and colorful pasta dish? This recipe can be made any time of year with whichever vegetables are in season.
—Wendy Ball, Battle Creek, MI

Prep: 20 min. • **Cook:** 20 min.
Makes: 6 servings

9 oz. uncooked whole wheat linguine
1 lb. fresh asparagus, trimmed and cut into 2-in. pieces
2 medium carrots, thinly sliced
1 small red onion, chopped
2 medium zucchini or yellow summer squash, thinly sliced
½ lb. sliced fresh mushrooms
2 garlic cloves, minced
1 cup half-and-half cream
⅔ cup reduced-sodium chicken broth
1 cup frozen petite peas
2 cups cubed fully cooked ham
2 Tbsp. julienned fresh basil
¼ tsp. pepper

½ cup grated Parmesan cheese
Optional: Additional fresh basil and Parmesan cheese

1. In a 6-qt. stockpot, cook linguine according to package directions, adding asparagus and carrots during the last 3-5 minutes of cooking. Drain; return to pot.
2. Place a large skillet coated with cooking spray over medium heat. Add onion; cook and stir 3 minutes. Add squash, mushrooms, and garlic; cook and stir until crisp-tender, 4-5 minutes.
3. Add cream and broth; bring to a boil, stirring to loosen browned bits from pan. Reduce heat; simmer, uncovered, until sauce is thickened slightly, about 5 minutes. Stir in peas, ham, 2 Tbsp. basil and pepper; heat through.
4. Add to the linguine mixture; stir in ½ cup cheese. If desired, top with additional basil and cheese.

2 cups: 338 cal., 9g fat (4g sat. fat), 53mg chol., 817mg sod., 46g carb. (8g sugars, 8g fiber), 23g pro. **Diabetic exchanges:** 2½ starch, 2 lean meat, 1 vegetable, ½ fat.

DID YOU KNOW?

The peak months for buying asparagus are April and May. Look for firm, straight, uniform spears. The tips should be closed with crisp stalks. It's best to use asparagus within a few days of purchase. To clean, soak asparagus in cold water. Cut or snap off the tough white portion.

Soups, Stews & Chilis

favorites

Soups

SAUSAGE & SPINACH TORTELLINI SOUP

My husband's grandmother used to make this soup with her own homemade sausage and tortellini. We don't make those by hand anymore, but this version is almost as good as hers. It's also an excellent way to get the kids to eat their spinach!
—Joyce Lulewicz, Brunswick, OH

Prep: 10 min. • **Cook:** 30 min.
Makes: 2 servings

- ½ lb. bulk Italian sausage
- 1 small onion, thinly sliced
- 1 garlic clove, minced
- 1 can (14½ oz.) reduced-sodium chicken broth
- ½ cup water
- 1½ cups torn fresh spinach
- ¾ cup refrigerated cheese tortellini
- 2 Tbsp. shredded Parmesan cheese Crushed red pepper flakes, optional

1. In a small saucepan, cook sausage over medium heat until no longer pink; drain. Add onion; cook and stir until tender. Add garlic; cook 1 minute longer. Stir in broth and water; bring to a boil. Reduce heat; simmer, uncovered, for 10 minutes.
2. Return to a boil. Reduce heat, add the spinach and tortellini; cook until tortellini is tender, 7-9 minutes. Sprinkle with cheese. If desired, top with crushed red pepper flakes.
1¾ cups: 354 cal., 19g fat (8g sat. fat), 64mg chol., 1360mg sod., 23g carb. (4g sugars, 2g fiber), 23g pro.

CHICKEN CASSOULET SOUP

After my sister spent a year in France as an au pair, I created this lighter, easier version of a traditional French cassoulet for her. It uses chicken instead of the usual duck.
—Bridget Klusman, Otsego, MI

Prep: 35 min. • **Cook:** 6 hours
Makes: 7 servings (2¾ qt.)

- ½ lb. bulk pork sausage
- 5 cups water
- ½ lb. cubed cooked chicken
- 1 can (16 oz.) kidney beans, rinsed and drained
- 1 can (15 oz.) black beans, rinsed and drained
- 1 can (15 oz.) garbanzo beans or chickpeas, rinsed and drained
- 2 medium carrots, shredded
- 1 medium onion, chopped
- ¼ cup dry vermouth or chicken broth
- 5 tsp. chicken bouillon granules
- 4 garlic cloves, minced
- 1½ tsp. minced fresh thyme or ½ tsp. dried thyme
- ¼ tsp. fennel seed, crushed
- 1 tsp. dried lavender flowers, optional
- ½ lb. bacon strips, cooked and crumbled Additional fresh thyme, optional

1. In a large skillet, cook the sausage over medium heat until no longer pink; drain.
2. Transfer to a 4- or 5-qt. slow cooker. Add water, chicken, beans, carrots, onion, vermouth, bouillon, garlic, thyme, fennel and, if desired, lavender. Cover and cook on low for 6-8 hours or until heated through.
3. Divide among bowls; sprinkle with bacon. If desired, top with additional fresh thyme.
Note: Look for dried lavender flowers suitable for culinary use in spice shops. If using lavender from the garden, make sure the plant hasn't been treated with chemicals.
1½ cups: 494 cal., 23g fat (7g sat. fat), 77mg chol., 1821mg sod., 34g carb. (6g sugars, 9g fiber), 34g pro.

BEEFY MINESTRONE

I know lots of meatless minestrone recipes, but my husband believes a true meal must contain some sort of meat. By his standard, this is the perfect dish. The pretty soup is flavorful, hearty and soul-satisfying.
—Juli Snaer, Enid, OK

Prep: 20 min. • **Cook:** 6½ hours
Makes: 8 servings (3 qt.)

6	cups chicken broth
1	can (16 oz.) kidney beans, rinsed and drained
1	can (15 oz.) crushed tomatoes
1	can (14½ oz.) diced tomatoes with basil, oregano and garlic, undrained
1	beef top round steak (1 lb.), cut onto ½-in. cubes
15	fresh baby carrots, halved
2	celery ribs, chopped
1	small onion, chopped
½	cup dry red wine
4	garlic cloves, minced
1	tsp. dried oregano
1	tsp. dried basil
¼	tsp. pepper
1	cup uncooked ditalini or other small pasta
	Optional: Fresh oregano and shredded Parmesan cheese

1. Combine the first 13 ingredients in a 5- or 6-qt. slow cooker. Cover and cook on low for 6-7 hours or until the meat is tender.
2. Stir in pasta. Cover and cook on high for 30 minutes or until the pasta is tender. If desired, top with fresh oregano and shredded Parmesan cheese.

1½ cups: 255 cal., 3g fat (1g sat. fat), 35mg chol., 1124mg sod., 33g carb. (7g sugars, 6g fiber), 21g pro.

DEB'S MUSHROOM & BARLEY SOUP

Nothing is more comforting than coming home to a steaming bowl of this rich soup! I prep the ingredients the evening before, and I start the slow cooker in the morning on my way out the door.
—Debra Kamerman, New York, NY

- -

Prep: 25 min. • **Cook:** 6 hours
Makes: 10 servings (3½ qt.)

- 1   lb. sliced baby portobello mushrooms
- 3   medium carrots, finely chopped
- 3   celery ribs, finely chopped
- 1   medium onion, finely chopped
- 1   cup medium pearl barley
- 1   tsp. dried thyme
- 1   tsp. pepper
- 5   cups water
- 4   cups beef stock
- 3   tsp. salt, divided
- 1   large egg, lightly beaten
- 1   lb. ground turkey

1. Place first 9 ingredients and 2½ tsp. salt in a 6- or 7-qt. slow cooker.
2. In a large bowl, mix egg and remaining salt. Add turkey; mix lightly but thoroughly. Shape into 1¼-in. balls; drop gently into slow cooker. Cook, covered, on low until vegetables and barley are tender, 6-8 hours.
1⅓ cups: 180 cal., 4g fat (1g sat. fat), 49mg chol., 967mg sod., 22g carb. (4g sugars, 5g fiber), 15g pro.

MARYLAND-STYLE CRAB SOUP

Try this beautiful dish that incorporates the best of vegetable soup and flavorful crab. Whole crabs and claws can be broken into pieces and dropped into the soup, which is my personal preference. I serve the soup with saltine crackers and a cold beer.
—Freelove Knott, Palm Bay, FL

- -

Prep: 20 min. • **Cook:** 6¼ hours
Makes: 8 servings (3 qt.)

- 2   cans (14½ oz. each) diced tomatoes with green peppers and onions, undrained
- 2   cups water
- 1½ lbs. potatoes, cut into ½-in. cubes (about 5 cups)
- 2   cups cubed peeled rutabaga
- 2   cups chopped cabbage
- 1   medium onion, finely chopped
- 1   medium carrot, sliced
- ½   cup frozen corn, thawed
- ½   cup frozen lima beans, thawed
- ½   cup frozen peas, thawed
- ½   cup cut fresh green beans (1-in. pieces)
- 4   tsp. seafood seasoning
- 1   tsp. celery seed
- 1   vegetable bouillon cube
- ¼   tsp. salt
- ¼   tsp. pepper
- 1   lb. fresh or lump crabmeat, drained

1. In a 6-qt. slow cooker, combine the first 16 ingredients. Cook, covered, on low for 6-8 hours or until the vegetables are tender.
2. Stir in fresh or lump crabmeat. Cook, covered, on low 15 minutes longer or until heated through.
Note: This recipe was prepared with Knorr vegetable bouillon.
1½ cups: 202 cal., 1g fat (0 sat. fat), 55mg chol., 1111mg sod., 34g carb. (11g sugars, 7g fiber), 15g pro.

CHICKEN GNOCCHI PESTO SOUP

After tasting a similar soup at a restaurant, I created this quick and tasty version. The pesto adds an extra-nice Italian flavor that is often missing from other gnocchi soups.
—Deanna Smith, Des Moines, IA

Takes: 25 min. • **Makes:** 4 servings (1½ qt.)

- 1 jar (15 oz.) roasted garlic Alfredo sauce
- 2 cups water
- 2 cups rotisserie chicken, roughly chopped
- 1 tsp. Italian seasoning
- ¼ tsp. salt
- ¼ tsp. pepper
- 1 pkg. (16 oz.) potato gnocchi
- 3 cups coarsely chopped fresh spinach
- 4 tsp. prepared pesto

In a large saucepan, combine the first 6 ingredients; bring to a gentle boil, stirring occasionally. Stir in gnocchi and spinach; cook until the gnocchi float, 3-8 minutes. Top each serving with pesto.

1½ cups: 586 cal., 26g fat (11g sat. fat), 158mg chol., 1650mg sod., 56g carb. (3g sugars, 4g fiber), 31g pro.

CHIPOTLE CHICKEN SOUP WITH CORNMEAL DUMPLINGS

I combined two of my favorite soup recipes and the result was this filling bowl with a Tex-Mex flair. The cornmeal dumplings are the perfect finishing touch.
—Nancy Granaman, Burlington, IA

Prep: 20 min. • **Cook:** 30 min.
Makes: 6 servings

- 1 can (15 oz.) black beans, rinsed and drained
- 1 can (14½ oz.) no-salt-added stewed tomatoes, cut up
- 1 can (14½ oz.) reduced-sodium chicken broth
- 1¾ cups water
- 1 tsp. ground cumin
- 1 tsp. minced chipotle pepper in adobo sauce
- 2 cups cubed cooked chicken breast
- 1 large egg
- 1 large egg white
- 1 pkg. (8½ oz.) cornbread/ muffin mix
- ⅓ cup reduced-fat biscuit/ baking mix
- 1 Tbsp. fat-free milk
- ¼ cup minced fresh cilantro

1. In a small bowl, mash half the beans. Transfer mashed and remaining beans to a Dutch oven. Add the tomatoes, broth, water, cumin and chipotle pepper. Bring to a boil. Reduce heat; cover and simmer for 15 minutes. Add chicken.

2. In a small bowl, combine egg, egg white, muffin mix and baking mix; stir in milk. Drop batter by tablespoonfuls onto the simmering soup. Cover and simmer until a toothpick inserted in a dumpling comes out clean (do not lift the cover while simmering), 10-12 minutes. Ladle soup into bowls. Sprinkle each serving with cilantro if desired.

1⅓ cups: 356 cal., 7g fat (2g sat. fat), 80mg chol., 808mg sod., 48g carb. (13g sugars, 5g fiber), 24g pro.

1 lb. uncooked shrimp
   (31-40 per lb.), peeled
   and deveined
6 oz. uncooked thick rice noodles
1 cup bean sprouts
4 green onions, sliced
   Chopped peanuts, optional
   Lime wedges

1. In a 6-qt. stockpot, heat oil over medium heat. Add shallots and chili pepper; cook and stir 4-6 minutes or until tender. Stir in crushed tomatoes, peanut butter and soy sauce until blended; add broth. Bring to a boil; cook, uncovered, 15 minutes to allow the flavors to blend.

2. Add the shrimp and noodles; cook until shrimp turn pink and noodles are tender, 4-6 minutes longer. Top each serving with bean sprouts, green onions and, if desired, chopped peanuts and additional chopped chili pepper. Serve with lime wedges.

1⅓ cups: 252 cal., 7g fat (1g sat. fat), 69mg chol., 755mg sod., 31g carb. (5g sugars, 4g fiber), 17g pro. **Diabetic exchanges:** 2 lean meat, 1½ starch, 1 vegetable, 1 fat.

Looking to incorporate more whole grains into your meals? Whole grain brown rice noodles are available, but they can be hard to find. Whole wheat angel hair pasta is a healthy stand-in, and it adds 6g of fiber per serving.

SHRIMP PAD THAI SOUP

Pad Thai is one of my favorite foods, but it is usually loaded with calories. This soup is a healthier option that has all the flavors of traditional versions.
—Julie Merriman, Seattle, WA

- -

Prep: 15 min. • **Cook:** 30 min.
Makes: 8 servings (2¾ qt.)

1 Tbsp. sesame oil
2 shallots, thinly sliced
1 Thai chili pepper or serrano
   pepper, seeded and finely chopped
1 can (28 oz.) no-salt-added
   crushed tomatoes
¼ cup creamy peanut butter
2 Tbsp. reduced-sodium soy sauce
   or fish sauce
6 cups reduced-sodium
   chicken broth

CURRIED CHICKEN SOUP

My grandmother used to make this yummy soup, and I recently added some of my own touches to it, including chickpeas, coconut milk and fresh cilantro.

—Deanna Hindenach, Paw Paw, MI

- -

Prep: 25 min. • **Cook:** 45 min.
Makes: 8 servings (2½ qt.)

    4 tsp. curry powder
    ½ tsp. salt
    ½ tsp. pepper
    ½ tsp. cayenne pepper
    1 lb. boneless skinless chicken
       breasts, cut into 1-in. cubes
    3 medium carrots, chopped
    1 medium sweet red pepper,
       chopped
    1 small onion, chopped
    2 Tbsp. olive oil
    1 garlic clove, minced
    1 can (15 oz.) garbanzo beans or
       chickpeas, rinsed and drained
    1 can (14½ oz.) chicken broth
    1 can (14½ oz.) diced tomatoes,
       drained
    1 cup water
    1 can (13.66 oz.) coconut milk
    ¾ cup minced fresh cilantro

1. In a large shallow dish, combine curry, salt, pepper and cayenne. Add chicken, a few pieces at a time, and turn to coat.
2. In a large saucepan over medium heat, cook the chicken, carrots, red pepper and onion in oil for 4 minutes. Add garlic; cook 1-2 minutes longer or until the chicken is browned and vegetables are tender; drain.
3. Stir in garbanzo beans, broth, tomatoes and water. Bring to a boil. Reduce heat; cover and simmer for 30 minutes. Stir in coconut milk; heat through. Garnish each serving with cilantro.
1¼ cups: 270 cal., 16g fat (10g sat. fat), 32mg chol., 555mg sod., 17g carb. (5g sugars, 5g fiber), 16g pro.

CHICKPEA TORTILLA SOUP

This vegan tortilla soup recipe is so healthy, filling and family-friendly! Everyone raves about how hearty and flavorful it is, and we like to play around with different toppings each time it's served.

—Julie Peterson, Crofton, MD

- -

Takes: 30 min. • **Makes:** 8 servings (3 qt.)

    1 Tbsp. olive oil
    1 medium red onion, chopped
    4 garlic cloves, minced
    1 to 2 jalapeno peppers, seeded and
       chopped, optional
    ¼ tsp. pepper
    8 cups vegetable broth
    1 cup red quinoa, rinsed
    2 cans (15 oz. each) no-salt-added
       chickpeas or garbanzo beans,
       rinsed and drained
    1 can (15 oz.) no-salt-added black
       beans, rinsed and drained
    3 medium tomatoes, chopped
    1 cup frozen corn
    ⅓ cup minced fresh cilantro
       Optional: Crushed tortilla chips,
       cubed avocado, lime wedges
       and additional chopped cilantro

Heat oil in a Dutch oven over medium-high heat. Add the red onion, garlic, jalapeno, if desired, and pepper; cook and stir until tender, 3-5 minutes. Add vegetable broth and quinoa. Bring to a boil; reduce heat. Simmer, uncovered, until the quinoa is tender, about 10 minutes. Add black beans, tomatoes, corn and cilantro; heat through. If desired, serve with optional ingredients.
1½ cups: 289 cal., 5g fat (0 sat. fat), 0 chol., 702mg sod., 48g carb. (5g sugars, 9g fiber), 13g pro.

ONE-POT SPINACH BEEF SOUP

My idea of a winning weeknight meal is this beefy soup that simmers to perfection in one big pot. Grate some Parmesan cheese, and pass the crackers!
—Julie Davis, Jacksonville, FL

Takes: 30 min. • **Makes:** 8 servings (2½ qt.)

- 1 lb. ground beef
- 3 garlic cloves, minced
- 2 cartons (32 oz. each) reduced-sodium beef broth
- 2 cans (14½ oz. each) diced tomatoes with green pepper, celery and onion, undrained
- 1 tsp. dried basil
- ½ tsp. pepper
- ½ tsp. dried oregano
- ¼ tsp. salt
- 3 cups uncooked bow tie pasta
- 4 cups fresh spinach, coarsely chopped
  Grated Parmesan cheese

In a 6-qt. stockpot, cook beef and garlic over medium heat until beef is no longer pink, breaking up the beef into crumbles, 6-8 minutes; drain. Stir in broth, tomatoes and seasonings; bring to a boil. Stir in pasta; return to a boil. Cook, uncovered, until the pasta is tender, 7-9 minutes. Stir in spinach until wilted. Sprinkle servings with cheese.
1⅓ cups: 258 cal., 7g fat (3g sat. fat), 40mg chol., 909mg sod., 30g carb. (8g sugars, 3g fiber), 17g pro.

GRANDMA'S SEAFOOD CHOWDER

My grandmother serves this every year on Christmas morning—it's the only time we ever had it. But why wait, when you can enjoy this satisfying chowder anytime? It's also delicious topped with biscuits!
—Melissa Obernesser, Utica, NY

- -

Prep: 15 min. • **Cook:** 25 min.
Makes: 10 servings (3¼ qt.)

- 3 Tbsp. plus ¼ cup butter, divided
- 1 lb. sliced fresh mushrooms
- ⅓ cup all-purpose flour
- 1 tsp. salt
- ⅛ tsp. pepper
- 4 cups half-and-half cream
- 1½ cups 2% milk
- 1 lb. haddock fillets, skin removed, cut into 1-in. pieces
- 1 lb. uncooked medium shrimp, peeled and deveined
- 2 cups frozen peas (about 10 oz.)
- ¾ cup shredded cheddar cheese
- 1 cup lump crabmeat (about 5 oz.), drained
- 1 jar (4 oz.) diced pimientos, drained
- 1 tsp. paprika

1. In a 6-qt. stockpot, heat 3 Tbsp. butter over medium-high heat. Add mushrooms; cook and stir until tender, 8-10 minutes. Remove from pot.
2. In same pot, heat remaining butter over medium heat. Stir in flour, salt and pepper until smooth; gradually whisk in cream and milk. Bring to a boil, stirring constantly; cook and stir until thickened, 2-3 minutes.
3. Stir in haddock, shrimp, peas and sauteed mushrooms; cook until fish just begins to flake easily with a fork and shrimp turn pink, 5-7 minutes. Add the cheese, crab and pimientos; stir gently until cheese is melted. If desired, sprinkle servings with paprika.
1¼ cups: 390 cal., 23g fat (14g sat. fat), 176mg chol., 596mg sod., 14g carb. (8g sugars, 2g fiber), 28g pro.

HEARTY CHICKEN & WILD RICE SOUP

Garlic and herb cream cheese adds subtle notes of flavor to this creamy, tasty soup. On a chilly day, it feels exactly like eating a bowlful of comfort.
—Shelisa Terry, Henderson, NV

- -

Takes: 25 min. • **Makes:** 6 servings (2¼ qt.)

- 1 pkg. (6.2 oz.) fast-cooking long grain and wild rice mix
- 2 cans (10¾ oz. each) condensed cream of chicken and mushroom soup, undiluted
- 3 cups 2% milk
- 2 pkg. (6 oz. each) ready-to-use grilled chicken breast strips
- 2 cups frozen California-blend vegetables, thawed and coarsely chopped
- ¾ cup spreadable garlic and herb cream cheese

Prepare rice mix according to package directions using a Dutch oven. Stir in the remaining ingredients; heat through.
1½ cups: 425 cal., 17g fat (8g sat. fat), 85mg chol., 1832mg sod., 45g carb. (10g sugars, 7g fiber), 24g pro.

SKILLET SOUTHWESTERN CHICKEN SOUP

This hearty bowl is brimming with chicken, corn, black beans and diced tomatoes, all seasoned with zippy southwestern flavor. Serve alongside Mexican cornbread for a delicious accompaniment.
—Terri Stevens, Ardmore, OK

- -

Prep: 10 min. • **Cook:** 25 min.
Makes: 4 servings (1 qt.)

- 2 Tbsp. olive oil
- ½ lb. boneless skinless chicken breast, cut into ½-in. cubes
- ¼ cup finely chopped onion
- 2 garlic cloves, minced
- 1 can (15¼ oz.) whole-kernel corn, drained
- 1 can (15 oz.) black beans, rinsed and drained
- 1 can (14½ oz.) chicken broth
- 1 can (10 oz.) diced tomatoes and green chiles, undrained
- 1 tsp. ground cumin
- ½ tsp. salt
- ½ tsp. chili powder
- ⅛ tsp. cayenne pepper
  Optional: Plain yogurt and minced fresh cilantro

1. In a large skillet, heat oil over medium heat. Add chicken and onion; cook and stir 5-6 minutes or until chicken is no longer pink. Add garlic; cook 1 minute longer.
2. Stir in corn, beans, broth, tomatoes and seasonings. Bring to a boil. Reduce heat; simmer, covered, 10-15 minutes to allow flavors to blend. Top servings with yogurt and cilantro if desired.
1 cup: 302 cal., 9g fat (1g sat. fat), 31mg chol., 1106mg sod., 32g carb. (6g sugars, 7g fiber), 19g pro.

ROAST PORK SOUP

A rich and full-bodied broth is the secret to making this soup, full of tender chunks of pork, potatoes and navy beans, stand out. It's been a family-favorite comfort food for years, especially when served in the winter with warm cornbread.
—Sue Gulledge, Springville, AL

- -

Prep: 15 min. • **Cook:** 55 min.
Makes: 9 servings

- 3 cups cubed cooked pork roast
- 2 medium potatoes, peeled and chopped
- 1 large onion, chopped
- 1 can (15 oz.) navy beans, rinsed and drained
- 1 can (14½ oz.) Italian diced tomatoes, undrained
- 4 cups water
- ½ cup unsweetened apple juice
- ½ tsp. salt
- ½ tsp. pepper
  Minced fresh basil

In a soup kettle or Dutch oven, combine the first 9 ingredients. Bring to a boil. Reduce heat; cover and simmer until vegetables are crisp-tender, 45 minutes. Sprinkle with basil.
1 cup: 206 cal., 5g fat (2g sat. fat), 42mg chol., 435mg sod., 23g carb. (6g sugars, 4g fiber), 18g pro. **Diabetic exchanges:** 1 starch, 1 meat, 1 vegetable.

CHEESEBURGER SOUP

A local restaurant serves a cheeseburger soup I love, but wouldn't give out its recipe. Undeterred, I developed my own version by experimenting and modifying a recipe for potato soup. I was pleased with the way this all-American bowl turned out.
—Joanie Shawhan, Madison, WI

- -

Prep: 45 min. • **Cook:** 10 min.
Makes: 8 servings (2¼ qt.)

½ lb. ground beef
4 Tbsp. butter, divided
¾ cup chopped onion
¾ cup shredded carrots
¾ cup diced celery
1 tsp. dried basil
1 tsp. dried parsley flakes
1¾ lbs. (about 4 cups) cubed peeled potatoes
3 cups chicken broth
¼ cup all-purpose flour
2 to 4 cups shredded Velveeta
1½ cups whole milk
¾ tsp. salt
¼ to ½ tsp. pepper
¼ cup sour cream

1. In a large saucepan over medium heat, cook and crumble beef until no longer pink; drain and set aside. In same saucepan, melt 1 Tbsp. butter over medium heat. Saute onion, carrots, celery, basil and parsley until vegetables are tender, about 10 minutes. Add potatoes, ground beef and broth; bring to a boil. Reduce heat; simmer, covered, until potatoes are tender, 10-12 minutes.
2. Meanwhile, in a small skillet, melt the remaining butter. Add flour; cook and stir until bubbly, 3-5 minutes. Add to soup; bring to a boil. Cook and stir 2 minutes. Reduce heat to low. Stir in cheese, milk, salt and pepper; cook until cheese melts. Remove from heat; blend in sour cream.
1 cup: 450 cal., 27g fat (15g sat. fat), 100mg chol., 1421mg sod., 33g carb. (8g sugars, 3g fiber), 19g pro.

TEST KITCHEN TIP

To prevent your soup from curdling, remove it from the heat before adding the sour cream.

ASIAN VEGETABLE-BEEF SOUP

My husband is Korean American, so I enjoy working Asian flavors into our menu. This tasty soup was something I put together one night with what I found in our fridge. Everyone loved it!
—Mollie Lee, Rockwall, TX

Prep: 30 min. • **Cook:** 1¾ hours
Makes: 6 servings

- 1 lb. beef stew meat, cut into 1-in. cubes
- 1 Tbsp. canola oil
- 2 cups water
- 1 cup beef broth
- ¼ cup sherry or additional beef broth
- ¼ cup reduced-sodium soy sauce
- 6 green onions, chopped
- 3 Tbsp. brown sugar
- 2 garlic cloves, minced
- 1 Tbsp. minced fresh gingerroot
- 2 tsp. sesame oil
- ¼ tsp. cayenne pepper
- 1½ cups sliced fresh mushrooms
- 1½ cups julienned carrots
- 1 cup sliced bok choy
- 1½ cups uncooked long grain rice
  Chive blossoms, optional

1. In a large saucepan, brown meat in oil on all sides; drain. Add water, broth, sherry, soy sauce, onions, brown sugar, garlic, ginger, sesame oil and cayenne. Bring to a boil. Reduce heat; cover and simmer for 1 hour.
2. Stir in mushrooms, carrots and bok choy; cover and simmer 20-30 minutes longer or until the vegetables are tender. Meanwhile, cook rice according to package directions.
3. Divide rice among 6 soup bowls, ¾ cup in each; top each with 1 cup soup. Garnish with chive blossoms if desired.

1 cup soup with ¾ cup rice: 379 cal., 10g fat (2g sat. fat), 47mg chol., 621mg sod., 50g carb. (9g sugars, 2g fiber), 20g pro.

SEAFOOD CIOPPINO

If you're looking for a great seafood recipe for your slow cooker, this classic fish stew is just the ticket. It's full of juicy clams, crab, fish and shrimp, and fancy enough to make for an elegant meal.
—Lisa Moriarty, Wilton, NH

Prep: 20 min. • **Cook:** 4½ hours
Makes: 8 servings (2½ qt.)

- 1 can (28 oz.) diced tomatoes, undrained
- 2 medium onions, chopped
- 3 celery ribs, chopped
- 1 bottle (8 oz.) clam juice
- 1 can (6 oz.) tomato paste
- ½ cup white wine or ½ cup vegetable broth
- 5 garlic cloves, minced
- 1 Tbsp. red wine vinegar
- 1 Tbsp. olive oil
- 1 to 2 tsp. Italian seasoning
- 1 bay leaf
- ½ tsp. sugar
- 1 lb. haddock fillets, cut into 1-in. pieces
- 1 lb. uncooked shrimp (41-50 per lb.), peeled and deveined
- 1 can (6 oz.) chopped clams, undrained
- 1 can (6 oz.) lump crabmeat, drained
- 2 Tbsp. minced fresh parsley

1. In a 4- or 5-qt. slow cooker, combine the first 12 ingredients. Cook, covered, on low 4-5 hours.
2. Stir in seafood. Cook, covered, until fish just begins to flake easily with a fork and shrimp turn pink, 20-30 minutes longer Remove bay leaf. Stir in parsley.

1¼ cups: 205 cal., 3g fat (1g sat. fat), 125mg chol., 483mg sod., 15g carb. (8g sugars, 3g fiber), 29g pro. **Diabetic exchanges:** 3 lean meat, 2 vegetable.

SOUTHWEST BARLEY & LENTIL SOUP

My family has made lentil soup every New Year since I was little. We've tweaked the recipe over time, and now all our friends love it, too!

—Kristen Heigl, Staten Island, NY

Prep: 15 min. • **Cook:** 55 min.
Makes: 12 servings (4½ qt.)

- 1 Tbsp. olive oil
- 1 pkg. (14 oz.) smoked kielbasa or Polish sausage, halved lengthwise and sliced
- 4 medium carrots, chopped
- 1 medium onion, chopped
- 2 garlic cloves, minced
- ¾ tsp. ground cumin
- 1 can (28 oz.) crushed tomatoes
- 1 pkg. (16 oz.) dried brown lentils, rinsed
- 1 can (15 oz.) black beans, rinsed and drained
- ¾ cup medium pearl barley
- ½ cup frozen corn
- 10 cups reduced-sodium chicken broth

1. In a 6-qt. stockpot, heat oil over medium heat. Add smoked kielbasa; cook and stir 6-8 minutes or until browned. Remove from pan with a slotted spoon.

2. Add the carrots and onion to same pot; cook and stir 6-8 minutes or until tender. Add garlic and cumin; cook 1 minute longer. Stir in kielbasa and remaining ingredients; bring to a boil. Reduce heat and simmer, covered, 35-45 minutes or until lentils and barley are tender, stirring occasionally.

1½ cups: 366 cal., 11g fat (3g sat. fat), 22mg chol., 904mg sod., 48g carb. (7g sugars, 17g fiber), 21g pro.

THE ULTIMATE CHICKEN NOODLE SOUP

My first Wisconsin winter was so cold that all I wanted to eat was soup. Then I moved to Colorado, and found the winters almost as cold! I keep this warm bowl of goodness in heavy rotation from November to April.
—Gina Nistico, Denver, CO

- -

Prep: 15 min. • **Cook:** 45 min. + standing
Makes: 10 servings (about 3½ qt.)

2½ lbs. bone-in chicken thighs
1¼ tsp. pepper, divided
½ tsp. salt
1 Tbsp. canola oil
1 large onion, chopped
1 garlic clove, minced
10 cups chicken broth
4 celery ribs, chopped
4 medium carrots, chopped
2 bay leaves
1 tsp. minced fresh thyme
  or ¼ tsp. dried thyme
3 cups uncooked kluski or other
  egg noodles (about 8 oz.)
1 Tbsp. chopped fresh parsley
1 Tbsp. lemon juice

1. Pat chicken thighs dry with paper towels; sprinkle with ½ tsp. pepper and salt. In a 6-qt. stockpot, heat oil over medium-high heat. Add chicken in batches, skin side down, and cook until dark golden brown, 3-4 minutes. Remove chicken from pan; remove and discard skin. Discard drippings, reserving 2 Tbsp..

2. Add onion to drippings; cook and stir over medium-high heat until tender, 4-5 minutes. Add garlic; cook 1 minute longer. Add broth, stirring to loosen browned bits from pan. Bring to a boil. Return chicken to pan. Add celery, carrots, bay leaves and thyme. Reduce heat; simmer, covered, until chicken is tender, 25-30 minutes.

3. Transfer chicken to a plate. Remove soup from heat. Add noodles; let stand, covered, until noodles are tender, 20-22 minutes.

4. Meanwhile, when chicken is cool enough to handle, remove the meat from bones; discard bones. Shred meat into bite-sized pieces. Return meat to stockpot. Stir in parsley and lemon juice. Adjust seasoning with salt and the remaining ¾ tsp. pepper. Discard bay leaves.

1⅓ cups: 239 cal., 12g fat (3g sat. fat), 68mg chol., 1176mg sod., 14g carb. (3g sugars, 2g fiber), 18g pro.

TEST KITCHEN TIP

Save chicken bones and vegetable scraps to make your own broth for the next pot of soup.

SLOW-COOKER POTATO & HAM SOUP

In our house, this recipe is a win-win. It's so easy for me to whip up and even easier for my family to devour. Serving crusty bread for dipping is the perfect finishing touch.
—Linda Haglund, Buffalo, MN

Prep: 10 min. • **Cook:** 6¼ hours
Makes: 8 servings (2½ qt.)

- 1 carton (32 oz.) chicken broth
- 1 pkg. (30 oz.) frozen shredded hash brown potatoes, thawed
- 1 small onion, finely chopped
- ¼ tsp. pepper
- 4 oz. cream cheese, softened and cubed
- 1 cup cubed deli ham
- 1 can (5 oz.) evaporated milk
  Optional: Sour cream and chopped green onions

1. In a 4- or 5-qt. slow cooker, combine the broth, potatoes, onion and pepper. Cook, covered, on low until vegetables are tender, 6-8 hours.
2. Mash potatoes to desired consistency. Whisk in cream cheese until melted. Stir in ham and milk. Cook, covered, until heated through, 15-20 minutes longer. Serve with sour cream and green onions if desired.
1¼ cups: 257 cal., 10g fat (5g sat. fat), 45mg chol., 1053mg sod., 31g carb. (6g sugars, 2g fiber), 12g pro.

SIMPLE TACO SOUP

We first tried this thick-as-chili soup at a church dinner. It's a warm dish ideal for a cold day and easy to prepare with kitchen staples. So what are you waiting for? Dig in!
—Glenda Taylor, Sand Springs, OK

Takes: 25 min.
Makes: 8 servings (about 2 qt.)

- 2 lbs. ground beef
- 1 envelope taco seasoning
- 1½ cups water
- 1 can (16 oz.) mild chili beans, undrained
- 1 can (15¼ oz.) whole kernel corn, drained
- 1 can (15 oz.) pinto beans, rinsed and drained
- 1 can (14½ oz.) stewed tomatoes
- 1 can (10 oz.) diced tomato with green chiles
- 1 can (4 oz.) chopped green chiles, optional
- 1 envelope ranch salad dressing mix

In a Dutch oven, cook beef over medium heat until no longer pink; drain. Add taco seasoning and mix well. Stir in the remaining ingredients. Bring to a boil. Reduce heat; simmer, uncovered, for 15 minutes or until heated through, stirring occasionally.
1 cup: 370 cal., 14g fat (5g sat. fat), 70mg chol., 1369mg sod., 35g carb. (7g sugars, 7g fiber), 27g pro.

1 tsp. Sriracha chili sauce
1 can (13.66 oz.) light coconut milk
1 carton (32 oz.) chicken broth
2 cups thinly sliced Chinese or napa cabbage
1 cup thinly sliced fresh snow peas
  Thinly sliced green onions
  Lime wedges

1. Toss chicken with cornstarch. In a 6-qt. stockpot, heat 2 Tbsp. oil over medium-high heat; saute the chicken until lightly browned, 2-3 minutes. Remove from pot.

2. In same pan, saute onion, jalapeno and garlic in remaining oil over medium-high heat until onion is tender, 3-4 minutes. Stir in seasonings, chili sauce, coconut milk and broth; bring to a boil. Reduce heat; simmer, covered, 20 minutes.

3. Stir in cabbage, snow peas and chicken; cook, uncovered, just until the cabbage is crisp-tender and chicken is cooked through, 3-4 minutes. Serve with green onions and lime wedges.

1⅓ cups: 244 cal., 14g fat (5g sat. fat), 45mg chol., 1017mg sod., 11g carb. (4g sugars, 2g fiber), 17g pro.

TEST KITCHEN TIP

Adding lime juice too soon will turn the snow peas and cabbage an unattractive olive green color. Instead, serve with lime wedges so the acid doesn't have time to change the color of the vegetables.

SPICY THAI COCONUT CHICKEN SOUP

January is national soup month, and one year, I came up with a new recipe for every day of the month. This one, with its special Thai flavors, is my favorite! For an even richer flavor, try using whole coconut milk.
—Diane Nemitz, Ludington, MI

Prep: 20 min. • **Cook:** 40 min.
Makes: 6 servings (2 qt.)

1 lb. boneless skinless chicken breasts, cut into ¾-in. cubes
3 Tbsp. cornstarch
3 Tbsp. peanut or canola oil, divided
1 large onion, chopped
1 small jalapeno pepper, seeded and minced
2 garlic cloves, minced
2 tsp. red curry powder
1 tsp. ground ginger
¾ tsp. salt
½ tsp. ground turmeric

PRESSURE-COOKER ITALIAN SAUSAGE & KALE SOUP

The first time I made this colorful soup, our home smelled wonderful. We knew it was a keeper to see us through cold winter days.
—Sarah Stombaugh, Chicago, IL

- -

Prep: 20 min. • **Cook:** 15 min.
Makes: 8 servings (3½ qt.)

- 1   lb. bulk hot Italian sausage
- 6   cups chopped fresh kale
- 2   cans (15½ oz. each) great northern beans, rinsed and drained
- 1   can (28 oz.) crushed tomatoes
- 4   large carrots, finely chopped (about 3 cups)
- 1   medium onion, chopped
- 3   garlic cloves, minced
- 1   tsp. dried oregano
- ¼   tsp. salt
- ⅛   tsp. pepper
- 5   cups chicken stock
      Grated Parmesan cheese, optional

1. Select saute setting on a 6-qt. electric pressure cooker and adjust for medium heat. Add Italian sausage. Cook and stir, crumbling meat, until no longer pink. Press cancel. Remove sausage; drain, then return to pressure cooker.
2. Add the next 10 ingredients. Lock lid; close pressure-release valve. Adjust to pressure-cook on high for 10 minutes. Allow the pressure to naturally release for 5 minutes, then quick-release any remaining pressure. Top individual servings with cheese, if desired.
1¾ cups: 297 cal., 13g fat (4g sat. fat), 31mg chol., 1105mg sod., 31g carb. (7g sugars, 9g fiber), 16g pro.

ZIPPY CHICKEN & CORN CHOWDER

This gently spiced corn chowder is always a good option for kids, but adults can rev up their servings with hot pepper sauce. It's my go-to on busy nights.
—Andrea Early, Harrisonburg, VA

- -

Prep: 15 min. • **Cook:** 25 min.
Makes: 8 servings (3 qt.)

- ¼   cup butter
- 1   large onion, chopped
- 1   medium green pepper, chopped
- ¼   cup all-purpose flour
- 1   Tbsp. paprika
- 2   medium potatoes, peeled and chopped
- 1   carton (32 oz.) chicken broth
- 1   skinned rotisserie chicken, shredded
- 6   cups fresh or frozen corn
- 1   Tbsp. Worcestershire sauce
- ½   to 1 tsp. hot pepper sauce
- 1   tsp. salt
- 1   cup 2% milk

1. In a stockpot, heat the butter over medium-high heat. Add chopped onion and pepper; cook, stirring, until vegetables are crisp-tender, 3-4 minutes. Stir in flour and paprika until blended.
2. Add potatoes; stir in broth. Bring to a boil; reduce heat and simmer, covered, until tender, 12-15 minutes.
3. Stir in chicken, corn, sauces and salt; bring to a boil. Reduce heat and cook, uncovered, until corn is tender, 4-6 minutes. Add milk; heat through (do not boil).
1½ cups: 351 cal., 12g fat (5g sat. fat), 75mg chol., 920mg sod., 39g carb. (7g sugars, 4g fiber), 25g pro.

Stews

SQUASH & CHICKEN STEW

This satisfying stew is not only nutritious but family-friendly. Chicken thighs are slowly simmered with stewed tomatoes, butternut squash, green peppers and onion for meal-in-one convenience and flavor that can't be beat.
—*Taste of Home* Test Kitchen

Prep: 15 min. • **Cook:** 6 hours
Makes: 5 servings

- 2 lbs. boneless skinless chicken thighs, cut into ½-in. pieces
- 1 can (28 oz.) stewed tomatoes, cut up
- 3 cups cubed peeled butternut squash
- 2 medium green peppers, cut into ½-in. pieces
- 1 small onion, sliced and separated into rings
- 1 cup water
- 1 tsp. salt
- 1 tsp. ground cumin
- ½ tsp. ground coriander
- ½ tsp. pepper
- 2 Tbsp. minced fresh parsley
   Hot cooked couscous, optional

In a 5-qt. slow cooker, combine the first 10 ingredients. Cover; cook on low for 6-7 hours or until the chicken is no longer pink. Sprinkle with parsley. Serve with couscous if desired.
1½ cups: 384 cal., 14g fat (4g sat. fat), 121mg chol., 867mg sod., 31g carb. (13g sugars, 7g fiber), 37g pro.

FAVORITE HAMBURGER STEW

I got this recipe from a woman at church as a way to use our home-canned tomatoes. My husband loves it, and I like that it makes a carefree dinner in the winter months. No wonder it's our favorite meal now!
—Marcia Clay, Truman, MN

Prep: 20 min. • **Cook:** 65 min.
Makes: 16 servings (4 qt.)

- 2 lbs. ground beef
- 2 medium onions, chopped
- 4 cans (14½ oz. each) stewed tomatoes, undrained
- 8 medium carrots, thinly sliced
- 4 celery ribs, thinly sliced
- 2 medium potatoes, peeled and cubed
- 2 cups water
- ½ cup uncooked long grain rice
- 3 tsp. salt
- 1 tsp. pepper

1. In a Dutch oven, cook beef and onions over medium heat until the meat is no longer pink; drain. Add the tomatoes, carrots, celery, potatoes, water, rice, salt and pepper; bring to a boil. Reduce heat; cover and simmer 30 minutes or until the vegetables and rice are tender.
2. Uncover; simmer 20-30 minutes longer or until thickened to desired consistency.
Freeze option: Freeze cooled stew in freezer containers. To use, partially thaw in refrigerator overnight. Heat through in a saucepan, stirring occasionally and adding a little water if necessary.
1 cup: 191 cal., 7g fat (3g sat. fat), 35mg chol., 689mg sod., 21g carb. (8g sugars, 2g fiber), 12g pro.

SHRIMP & COD STEW IN TOMATO-SAFFRON BROTH

I love when I come inside on a chilly day and am greeted by the comforting aroma of my seafood stew simmering in the kitchen.
—Lydia Jensen, Kansas City, MO

- -

Prep: 20 min. • **Cook:** 25 min.
Makes: 8 servings (3 qt.)

2	Tbsp. olive oil
1	large onion, chopped
3	garlic cloves, minced
1	Tbsp. minced fresh or
	1 tsp. dried thyme
¼	tsp. saffron threads or
	1 tsp. ground turmeric
2	bay leaves
2	cans (14½ oz. each)
	no-salt-added diced tomatoes
1	lb. cod fillet, cut into 1-in. cubes
1	lb. uncooked large shrimp,
	peeled and deveined
2	cups water
1	can (14½ oz.) vegetable broth
1	cup whole kernel corn
¼	tsp. pepper
1	pkg. (6 oz.) fresh baby spinach
	Lemon wedges, optional

1. In a 6-qt. stockpot, heat oil over medium heat. Add onion; cook and stir until tender. Add garlic, thyme, saffron and bay leaves. Cook and stir 1 minute longer. Add the tomatoes, fish, shrimp, water, broth, corn and pepper.

2. Bring to a boil. Reduce heat; simmer, uncovered, 8-10 minutes or until shrimp turn pink and fish flakes easily with a fork, adding spinach during the last 2-3 minutes of cooking. Discard bay leaves. If desired, serve with lemon wedges.

1½ cups: 250 cal., 6g fat (1g sat. fat), 121mg chol., 1005mg sod., 18g carb. (7g sugars, 3g fiber), 27g pro.

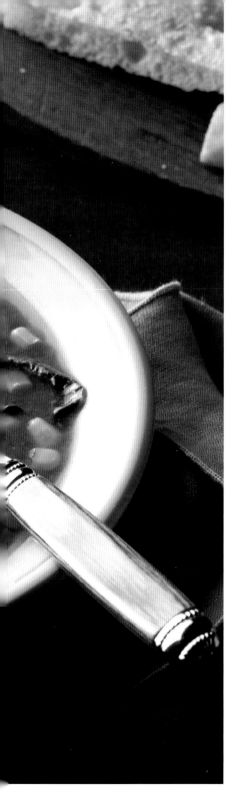

SLOW-COOKED VEGETABLE CURRY

I like the no-fuss nature of the slow cooker, but sometimes slow dishes sacrifice flavor for convenience. Luckily, this cozy spiced stew gives a home cook the best of both.
—Susan Smith, Mead, WA

Prep: 35 min. • **Cook:** 5 hours
Makes: 6 servings

- 1 **Tbsp. canola oil**
- 1 **medium onion, finely chopped**
- 4 **garlic cloves, minced**
- 3 **tsp. ground coriander**
- 1½ **tsp. ground cinnamon**
- 1 **tsp. ground ginger**
- 1 **tsp. ground turmeric**
- ½ **tsp. cayenne pepper**
- 2 **Tbsp. tomato paste**
- 2 **cans (15 oz. each) garbanzo beans or chickpeas, rinsed and drained**
- 3 **cups cubed peeled sweet potatoes (about 1 lb.)**
- 3 **cups fresh cauliflower florets (about 8 oz.)**
- 4 **medium carrots, cut into ¾-in. pieces (about 2 cups)**
- 2 **medium tomatoes, seeded and chopped**
- 2 **cups chicken broth**
- 1 **cup light coconut milk**
- ½ **tsp. pepper**
- ¼ **tsp. salt**
  Minced fresh cilantro
  Hot cooked brown rice
  Lime wedges
  Plain yogurt, optional

1. In a large skillet, heat oil over medium heat; saute the onion until soft and lightly browned, 5-7 minutes. Add the garlic and spices; cook and stir 1 minute. Stir in the tomato paste; cook 1 minute. Transfer to a 5- or 6-qt. slow cooker.

2. Mash 1 can of beans until smooth; add to slow cooker. Stir in the remaining can of beans, vegetables, broth, coconut milk, pepper and salt.

3. Cook, covered, on low until vegetables are tender, 5-6 hours. Sprinkle with minced cilantro. Serve with hot brown rice, lime wedges and, if desired, yogurt.

1⅔ cups curry: 304 cal., 8g fat (2g sat. fat), 2mg chol., 696mg sod., 49g carb. (12g sugars, 12g fiber), 9g pro.

DID YOU KNOW?

Where's the curry powder? What is commonly called curry is actually a blend of spices like those used in this dish. The curry powder you see in grocery stores is simply a premixed spice blend. Every curry blend is a little bit different.

HEARTY BAKED BEEF STEW

This is a super easy way to make a beautiful, yummy stew. You don't need to brown the meat first—just combine it with chunks of carrots, potatoes and celery, and then let it all cook together in a flavorful gravy. My daughter Karen came up with the recipe for her busy family.
—Doris Sleeth, Naples, FL

Prep: 15 min. • **Bake:** 1¾ hours
Makes: 8 servings

- 1 can (14½ oz.) diced tomatoes, undrained
- 1 cup water
- 3 Tbsp. quick-cooking tapioca
- 2 tsp. sugar
- 1½ tsp. salt
- ½ tsp. pepper
- 2 lbs. beef stew meat, cut into 1-in. cubes
- 4 medium carrots, cut into 1-in. chunks
- 3 medium potatoes, peeled and quartered
- 2 celery ribs, cut into ¾-in. chunks
- 1 medium onion, cut into chunks
- 1 slice bread, cubed

1. Preheat oven to 375°. In a large bowl, combine the diced tomatoes, water, tapioca, sugar, salt and pepper. Stir in the remaining ingredients.
2. Pour into a greased 13x9-in. or 3-qt. baking dish. Cover and bake 1¾-2 hours or until meat and vegetables are tender. Serve in bowls.
1 cup: 300 cal., 8g fat (3g sat. fat), 70mg chol., 628mg sod., 31g carb. (7g sugars, 4g fiber), 25g pro. **Diabetic exchanges:** 3 lean meat, 2 starch.

SATAY-STYLE PORK STEW

Thai cuisine features flavors that are sweet and sour, salty and spicy. This dish balances all of them using ginger, honey, red pepper, rice vinegar and garlic, with peanuts and creamy peanut butter.
—Nicole Werner, Ann Arbor, MI

Prep: 25 min. • **Cook:** 8 hours
Makes: 6 servings

- 1 boneless pork shoulder butt roast (3 to 4 lbs.), cut into 1½-in. cubes
- 2 medium parsnips, peeled and sliced
- 1 small sweet red pepper, thinly sliced
- 1 cup chicken broth
- ¼ cup reduced-sodium teriyaki sauce
- 2 Tbsp. rice vinegar
- 1 Tbsp. minced fresh gingerroot
- 1 Tbsp. honey
- 2 garlic cloves, minced
- ½ tsp. crushed red pepper flakes
- ¼ cup creamy peanut butter
  Hot cooked rice, optional
- 2 green onions, chopped
- 2 Tbsp. chopped dry roasted peanuts

In a 3-qt. slow cooker, combine the first 10 ingredients. Cover and cook on low until pork is tender, 8-10 hours. Skim fat; stir in peanut butter. Serve with rice if desired; top with onions and peanuts.
Freeze option: Before adding toppings, freeze cooled stew in freezer containers. To use, partially thaw in refrigerator overnight. Heat through in a saucepan, stirring occasionally and adding a little broth or water if necessary.
1 cup: 519 cal., 30g fat (10g sat. fat), 135mg chol., 597mg sod., 19g carb. (9g sugars, 3g fiber), 44g pro.

3 celery ribs, cut into ¾-in. pieces
2 medium onions, cut into wedges
¼ cup all-purpose flour
¼ cup water
  Fresh thyme sprigs, optional

1. In a Dutch oven, brown the beef on all sides in oil over medium-high heat; drain. Add the cider, broth, vinegar, salt, thyme and pepper; bring to a boil. Reduce heat; cover and simmer for 1¼ hours.

2. Add the potatoes, carrots, celery and onions; return to a boil. Reduce heat; cover and simmer for 30-35 minutes or until beef and vegetables are tender.

3. Combine flour and water until smooth; stir into stew. Bring to a boil; cook and stir for 2 minutes or until thickened. If desired, serve with fresh thyme.

1 cup: 330 cal., 12g fat (3g sat. fat), 72mg chol., 628mg sod., 31g carb. (14g sugars, 2g fiber), 24g pro. **Diabetic exchanges:** 3 lean meat, 1½ starch, 1 vegetable.

DID YOU KNOW?

About 2,500 different varieties of apples are grown in the U.S., but there are more than 7,500 apple varieties in the world, so if you had the recommended "apple a day," it would take 20 years to try them all.

HOMEMADE APPLE CIDER BEEF STEW

This meal is especially nice in fall, when the weather gets crisp and Nebraska's apple orchards start selling fresh cider. Its subtle sweetness is a welcome change from other savory stews. We enjoy it with biscuits and apple slices, or sometimes cheddar cheese.
—Joyce Glaesemann, Lincoln, NE

- -

Prep: 30 min. • **Cook:** 1¾ hours
Makes: 8 servings

2 lbs. beef stew meat, cut into 1-in. cubes
2 Tbsp. canola oil
3 cups apple cider or juice
1 can (14½ oz.) reduced-sodium beef broth
2 Tbsp. cider vinegar
1½ tsp. salt
¼ to ½ tsp. dried thyme
¼ tsp. pepper
3 medium potatoes, peeled and cubed
4 medium carrots, cut into ¾-in. pieces

2. Add bouillon, herbs, 2 cups water and wine to same pan; bring to a boil, stirring to loosen browned bits from pan. Add beef; return to a boil. Transfer to oven; bake, covered, 1 hour.

3. Stir in vegetables and, if desired, thin with additional water. Bake, covered, until beef and vegetables are tender, 45-60 minutes.

1½ cups: 419 cal., 15g fat (5g sat. fat), 106mg chol., 949mg sod., 33g carb. (5g sugars, 4g fiber), 37g pro.

ORZO SHRIMP STEW

My husband and I are big fans of seafood, so I don't skimp on the shrimp in this mildly seasoned stew. We also love getting our veggies in with the broccoli and tomatoes.
—Lisa Stinger, Hamilton, NJ

- -

Takes: 20 min. • **Makes:** 4 servings (1¾ qt.)

2½ cups reduced-sodium
    chicken broth
5 cups fresh broccoli florets
1 can (14½ oz.) diced tomatoes,
    undrained
1 cup uncooked orzo
1 lb. uncooked medium shrimp,
    peeled and deveined
¾ tsp. salt
¼ tsp. pepper
2 tsp. dried basil
2 Tbsp. butter

1. Bring broth to a boil in a Dutch oven. Add the broccoli, tomatoes and orzo. Reduce heat; simmer, uncovered, for 5 minutes, stirring occasionally.

2. Add the shrimp, salt and pepper. Cover and cook for 4-5 minutes or until the shrimp turn pink and the orzo is tender. Stir in the basil and butter.

1¾ cups: 401 cal., 10g fat (5g sat. fat), 190mg chol., 919mg sod., 45g carb. (0 sugars, 4g fiber), 35g pro. **Diabetic exchanges:** 3 lean meat, 2½ starch, 1 vegetable

SLOW-SIMMERED BURGUNDY BEEF STEW

My mother-in-law shared this recipe with me many years ago. Ever since then, it's been a go-to whenever I need good food without a lot of fussing.
—Mary Lou Timpson, Colorado City, AZ

- -

Prep: 30 min. • **Bake:** 1¾ hours
Makes: 4 servings

1½ lbs. beef stew meat,
    cut into 1¼-in. pieces
3 Tbsp. all-purpose flour
¾ tsp. salt
2 to 4 tsp. canola oil, divided
2 tsp. beef bouillon granules
2 tsp. dried parsley flakes
1½ tsp. Italian seasoning
2 cups water
1 cup Burgundy wine or
    beef stock
3 medium potatoes
    (about 1⅓ lbs.),
    peeled and quartered
1 cup fresh mushrooms, halved
1 medium onion, cut into 8 wedges
2 medium carrots, cut
    into 1-in. pieces
2 celery ribs, cut into ½-in. pieces
    Additional water, optional

1. Preheat oven to 350°. Toss beef with flour and salt to coat lightly; shake off excess. In an ovenproof Dutch oven, heat 2 tsp. oil over medium heat. Brown beef in batches, adding additional oil as needed. Remove from pan.

SEAFOOD GUMBO

Gumbo is one of Louisiana's most famous dishes, and even though we live across the state line in Texas, we just can't seem to get enough of this traditional Cajun meal. This recipe calls for seafood, but you could also use chicken, duck or sausage.

—Ruth Aubey, San Antonio, TX

Prep: 20 min. • **Cook:** 30 min.
Makes: 24 servings (6 qt.)

- 1 **cup all-purpose flour**
- 1 **cup canola oil**
- 4 **cups chopped onion**
- 2 **cups chopped celery**
- 2 **cups chopped green pepper**
- 1 **cup sliced green onion and tops**
- 4 **cups chicken broth**
- 8 **cups water**
- 4 **cups sliced okra**
- 2 **Tbsp. paprika**
- 2 **Tbsp. salt**
- 2 **tsp. oregano**
- 1 **tsp. ground black pepper**
- 6 **cups small shrimp, rinsed and drained, or seafood of your choice**
- 1 **cup minced fresh parsley**
- 2 **Tbsp. Cajun seasoning**

1. In a heavy Dutch oven, combine flour and oil until smooth. Cook over medium-high heat for 5 minutes, stirring constantly. Reduce heat to medium. Cook and stir about 10 minutes more, or until mixture is reddish brown.

2. Add onion, celery, green pepper and green onion; cook and stir 5 minutes. Add chicken broth, water, okra, paprika, salt, oregano and pepper. Bring to a boil; reduce heat and simmer, covered, 10 minutes.

3. Add the shrimp and parsley. Simmer, uncovered, about 5 minutes more or until the seafood is done. Remove from heat; stir in Cajun seasoning.

1 cup: 175 cal., 9g fat (1g sat. fat), 115mg chol., 1574mg sod., 10g carb. (3g sugars, 2g fiber), 12g pro.

PRESSURE-COOKER BEEF DAUBE PROVENCAL

This makes the perfect meal on cold winter days, especially after we have been outside cutting wood or hunting. If you're lucky enough to have venison, try it in this dish for melt-in-your-mouth goodness.
—Brenda Ryan, Marshall, MO

- -

Prep: 30 min. • **Cook:** 30 min. + releasing
Makes: 8 servings

- 1 boneless beef chuck roast or venison roast (about 2 lbs.), cut into 1-in. cubes
- 1½ tsp. salt, divided
- ½ tsp. coarsely ground pepper, divided
- 2 tsp. olive oil
- 2 cups chopped carrots
- 1½ cups chopped onion
- 12 garlic cloves, crushed
- 1 Tbsp. tomato paste
- 1 cup dry red wine
- 1 can (14½ oz.) diced tomatoes, undrained
- ½ cup beef broth
- 1 tsp. chopped fresh rosemary
- 1 tsp. chopped fresh thyme
- 1 bay leaf
  Dash ground cloves
  Hot cooked pasta or mashed potatoes

1. Sprinkle beef with ½ tsp. salt and ¼ tsp. pepper. Select saute or browning setting on a 6-qt. electric pressure cooker. Adjust for medium heat; add oil. When oil is hot, brown beef in batches.
2. Add the carrots, onions and garlic to pressure cooker; cook and stir until golden brown, 4-6 minutes. Add tomato paste; cook and stir until fragrant, about 1 minute. Add wine, stirring to loosen any browned bits. Return the beef to pressure cooker. Add the tomatoes, broth, rosemary, thyme, bay leaf, cloves and remaining 1 tsp. salt and ¼ tsp. pepper. Press cancel.
3. Lock lid; close pressure-release valve. Adjust to pressure-cook on high for 30 minutes. Let pressure release naturally for 10 minutes; quick-release any remaining pressure. A thermometer inserted in beef should read at least 160°. Discard the bay leaf. Serve with hot cooked pasta. If desired, sprinkle with additional thyme.
Freeze option: Place beef and vegetables in freezer containers; top with cooking juices. Cool and freeze. To use, partially thaw in refrigerator overnight. Heat through in a covered saucepan, stirring gently and adding a little broth if necessary.
1 cup beef mixture: 248 cal., 12g fat (4g sat. fat), 74mg chol., 652mg sod., 10g carb. (5g sugars, 2g fiber), 24g pro. **Diabetic exchanges:** 3 lean meat, 1 vegetable.

SOUTHWEST TURKEY STEW

I prefer mains that help me stay on my diet while still allowing me to eat what the rest of the family eats. This one is a hit with my husband and our young children.
—Stephanie Hutchinson, Helix, OR

- -

Prep: 15 min. • **Cook:** 5 hours
Makes: 6 servings

- 1½ lbs. turkey breast tenderloins, cubed
- 2 tsp. canola oil
- 1 can (15 oz.) turkey chili with beans, undrained
- 1 can (14½ oz.) diced tomatoes, undrained
- 1 medium sweet red pepper, chopped
- 1 medium green pepper, chopped
- ¾ cup chopped onion
- ¾ cup salsa
- 3 garlic cloves, minced
- 1½ tsp. chili powder
- ½ tsp. ground cumin
- ¼ tsp. salt
- 1 Tbsp. minced fresh cilantro, optional

1. In a nonstick skillet, brown turkey in oil; transfer to a 3-qt. slow cooker. Stir in chili, tomatoes, peppers, onion, salsa, garlic, chili powder, cumin and salt.
2. Cover and cook on low for 5-6 hours or until the turkey is no longer pink and the vegetables are tender. Garnish with cilantro if desired.
1¼ cups: 238 cal., 4g fat (1g sat. fat), 65mg chol., 837mg sod., 17g carb. (7g sugars, 5g fiber), 33g pro. **Diabetic exchanges:** 4 lean meat, 1 vegetable, ½ starch.

ZESTY BEEF STEW

Preparation of this hearty dish couldn't be simpler. I created it when I didn't have some of my usual ingredients for vegetable beef soup. My husband says it's the best thing I have ever made!
—Margaret Turza, South Bend, IN

- -

Prep: 10 min. • **Cook:** 3½ hours
Makes: 6 servings (1½ qt.)

- 1 lb. beef stew meat, cut into 1-in. cubes
- 1 pkg. (16 oz.) frozen mixed vegetables, thawed
- 1 can (15 oz.) pinto beans, rinsed and drained
- 1½ cups water
- 1 can (8 oz.) pizza sauce
- 2 Tbsp. medium pearl barley
- 1 Tbsp. dried minced onion
- 2 tsp. beef bouillon granules
- ¼ tsp. crushed red pepper flakes

In a 3-qt. slow cooker, combine all the ingredients. Cover and cook on low until the meat is tender, 3½-4½ hours.
1 cup: 251 cal., 6g fat (2g sat. fat), 47mg chol., 526mg sod., 28g carb. (5g sugars, 8g fiber), 21g pro. **Diabetic exchanges:** 3 lean meat, 2 starch.

3 garlic cloves, minced
1 cup dried brown lentils, rinsed
4 cups cubed peeled butternut squash (about 1 lb.)
2 cups chopped fresh spinach
¼ cup minced fresh cilantro
¼ cup lime juice

1. In a 5- or 6-qt. slow cooker, whisk first 7 ingredients. In a large skillet, heat 2 tsp. oil over medium heat; brown the lamb in batches. Add to slow cooker.
2. In the same skillet, saute the chopped onions in remaining oil over medium heat until tender, 4-5 minutes. Add the ginger and garlic; cook and stir 1 minute. Add to slow cooker. Stir in lentils and squash.
3. Cook, covered, on low until the meat and lentils are tender, 6-8 hours. Stir in spinach until wilted. Stir in cilantro and lime juice.
Freeze option: Freeze cooled stew in freezer containers. To use, partially thaw in refrigerator overnight. Heat through in a saucepan, stirring occasionally and adding broth if necessary.
1¼ cups: 411 cal., 21g fat (11g sat. fat), 38mg chol., 777mg sod., 34g carb. (7g sugars, 6g fiber), 23g pro.

TEST KITCHEN TIP

No peeking! Opening the slow cooker allows steam to escape, causing the temperature to drop. You may need to add 20-30 minutes to the cook time for each time the lid is lifted.

SQUASH & LENTIL LAMB STEW

My family lived in New Zealand when I was younger. Every Sunday, my mother made a lamb stew—it was Dad's favorite! I changed the recipe slightly to suit my family's more modern palates, but it's just as delicious.
—Nancy Heishman, Las Vegas, NV

Prep: 30 min. • **Cook:** 6 hours
Makes: 8 servings (2½ qt.)

1 can (13.66 oz.) coconut milk
½ cup creamy peanut butter
2 Tbsp. red curry paste
1 Tbsp. hoisin sauce
1 tsp. salt
½ tsp. pepper
1 can (14½ oz.) chicken broth
3 tsp. olive oil, divided
1 lb. lamb or beef stew meat, cut into 1½ in. pieces
2 small onions, chopped
1 Tbsp. minced fresh gingerroot

FROGMORE STEW

This picnic-style medley of shrimp, smoked kielbasa, corn and potatoes is a specialty of South Carolina cuisine. It's commonly been dubbed Frogmore Stew or Beaufort Stew after the two low country communities that lay claim to its origin. No matter what you call it, this one-pot wonder is sure to be a hit with everyone who tastes it!
—*Taste of Home* Test Kitchen

Prep: 10 min. • **Cook:** 35 min.
Makes: 8 servings

16 cups water
1 large sweet onion, quartered
3 Tbsp. seafood seasoning
2 medium lemons, halved, optional
1 lb. small red potatoes
1 lb. smoked kielbasa or
   fully cooked hot links,
   cut into 1-in. pieces
4 medium ears sweet corn,
   cut into thirds
2 lbs. uncooked medium shrimp,
   peeled and deveined
   Seafood cocktail sauce
   Melted butter
   Additional seafood seasoning

1. In a stockpot, combine water, onion, seafood seasoning and, if desired, lemons; bring to a boil. Add the potatoes; cook, uncovered, 10 minutes. Add kielbasa and corn; return to a boil. Reduce heat; simmer, uncovered, 10-12 minutes or until potatoes are tender. Add shrimp; cook 2-3 minutes longer or until the shrimp turn pink.
2. Drain; transfer to a bowl. Serve with cocktail sauce, butter and additional seafood seasoning.
1 serving: 369 cal., 18g fat (6g sat. fat), 175mg chol., 751mg sod., 24g carb. (7g sugars, 2g fiber), 28g pro.

ANCIENT GRAIN BEEF STEW

This version of beef stew is comfort food with a healthy twist. Rather than potatoes, I use lentils and red quinoa. If leftover stew seems too thick, just add more beef stock when reheating.
—Margaret Roscoe, Keystone Heights, FL

Prep: 25 min. • **Cook:** 6 hours
Makes: 10 servings

2 Tbsp. olive oil
1 lb. beef stew meat, cut into
   1-in. cubes
4 celery ribs with leaves, chopped
2 medium carrots, peeled, chopped
1 large onion, chopped
1½ cups dried lentils, rinsed
½ cup red quinoa, rinsed
5 large bay leaves
2 tsp. ground cumin
1½ tsp. salt
1 tsp. dried tarragon
½ tsp. pepper
2 cartons (32 oz. each) beef stock

Heat oil in a large skillet over medium heat. Add beef; brown on all sides. Transfer meat and drippings to a 5- or 6-qt. slow cooker. Stir in the remaining ingredients. Cook, covered, on low until stew meat is tender, 6-8 hours. Discard bay leaves.
1⅓ cups: 261 cal., 7g fat (2g sat. fat), 28mg chol., 797mg sod., 29g carb. (5g sugars, 5g fiber), 21g pro. **Diabetic exchanges:** 2 starch, 2 lean meat, ½ fat.

BRUNSWICK STEW

This thick stew is filled to the brim with a bounty of potatoes, lima beans, corn and tomatoes. Authentic versions call for rabbit or squirrel, but I think you'll love the tender chunks of chicken.

—Mildred Sherrer, Fort Worth, TX

Prep: 1 hour + cooling • **Cook:** 45 min.
Makes: 6 servings

- 1 broiler/fryer chicken (3½ to 4 lbs.), cut up
- 2 cups water
- 4 medium potatoes, peeled and cubed
- 2 medium onions, sliced
- 1 can (15¼ oz.) lima beans, rinsed and drained
- 1 tsp. salt
- ½ tsp. pepper
  Dash cayenne pepper
- 1 can (15¼ oz.) corn, drained
- 1 can (14½ oz.) diced tomatoes, undrained
- ¼ cup butter
- ½ cup dry bread crumbs

1. In a Dutch oven, slowly bring the chicken and water to a boil. Cover and simmer for 45-60 minutes or until the chicken is tender, skimming the surface as foam rises.

2. Remove chicken and set aside until cool enough to handle. Remove and discard skin and bones. Cube the chicken and return to broth.

3. Add the potatoes, onions, beans and seasonings. Bring to a boil. Reduce heat; simmer, uncovered, until potatoes are tender, 30 minutes. Stir in the remaining ingredients. Simmer, uncovered, about 10 minutes or until slightly thickened.

1 serving: 589 cal., 25g fat (9g sat. fat), 123mg chol., 1147mg sod., 47g carb. (9g sugars, 7g fiber), 40g pro.

TURKEY DUMPLING STEW

My mom made this when I was young, and it was always everyone's favorite. Since it's not too time-consuming, I often make it on weekends for our children, who love the tender dumplings.

—Becky Mohr, Appleton, WI

- -

Prep: 20 min. • **Cook:** 50 min.
Makes: 6 servings

- 4 bacon strips, finely chopped
- 1½ lbs. turkey breast tenderloins, cut into 1-in. pieces
- 4 medium carrots, sliced
- 2 small onions, quartered
- 2 celery ribs, sliced
- 1 bay leaf
- ¼ tsp. dried rosemary, crushed
- 2 cups water, divided
- 1 can (14½ oz.) reduced-sodium chicken broth
- 3 Tbsp. all-purpose flour
- ½ tsp. salt
- ⅛ to ¼ tsp. pepper
- 1 cup reduced-fat biscuit/baking mix
- ⅓ cup plus 1 Tbsp. fat-free milk
   Optional: Coarsely ground pepper and chopped fresh parsley

1. In a Dutch oven, cook the bacon over medium heat, stirring occasionally, until crisp. Remove with a slotted spoon; drain on paper towels. Reserve 2 tsp. drippings.
2. In the reserved drippings, saute turkey over medium-high heat until lightly browned. Add the vegetables, herbs, 1¾ cups water and the broth; bring to boil. Reduce heat; simmer, covered, until the vegetables are tender, 20-30 minutes.
3. Mix flour and the remaining water until smooth; stir into the turkey mixture. Bring to a boil; cook and stir until thickened, about 2 minutes. Discard bay leaf. Stir in salt, pepper and bacon.
4. In a small bowl, mix the biscuit mix and milk to form a soft dough; drop dough in 6 equal mounds on top of the simmering stew. Cover; simmer 15 minutes or until a toothpick inserted in dumplings comes out clean. If desired, sprinkle with pepper and parsley before serving.
1 serving: 284 cal., 6g fat (1g sat. fat), 52mg chol., 822mg sod., 24g carb. (6g sugars, 2g fiber), 34g pro. **Diabetic exchanges:** 4 lean meat, 1 starch, 1 vegetable, ½ fat.

If you want an even more veggie-laden stew, stir frozen peas and corn into the pot just before the vegetables are done. Then add the flour mixture and the dumplings as directed.

HEARTY HUNTER'S STEW

Tender meat and thick, rich gravy are the hallmarks of this delicious rustic stew. This is warm, homemade comfort at its finest.
—Joyce Worsech, Catawba, WI

- -

Prep: 25 min. • **Cook:** 2 hours 50 min.
Makes: 8 servings

- 2 lbs. boneless venison or beef chuck roast, cut in 1-in. cubes
- 2 Tbsp. canola oil
- 4¼ cups water, divided
- ½ cup tomato juice
- 2 medium onions, cut in wedges
- 2 celery ribs, sliced
- 1 tsp. Worcestershire sauce
- 2 bay leaves
- 2 to 3 tsp. salt
- ½ tsp. pepper
- 6 medium carrots, quartered
- 1 large rutabaga, peeled and cubed
- 6 medium potatoes, peeled and quartered
- 1 cup frozen peas
- 1 Tbsp. cornstarch

1. In a Dutch oven, brown meat in oil over medium heat. Add 4 cups water and scrape to loosen any browned drippings from the pan. Add the tomato juice, onions, celery, Worcestershire sauce, bay leaves, salt and pepper. Bring to a boil. Reduce heat; cover and cook for 2 hours, stirring occasionally.
2. Discard bay leaves; add the carrots, rutabaga and potatoes. Cover and cook for 40-60 minutes.
3. Stir in the peas; cook for 10 minutes. Combine cornstarch and remaining water until smooth; stir into stew. Bring to a boil. Cook and stir 2 minutes or until thickened.
1 cup: 351 cal., 7g fat (2g sat. fat), 96mg chol., 778mg sod., 42g carb. (14g sugars, 7g fiber), 31g pro.

TUSCAN PORTOBELLO STEW

This heart-healthy, one-skillet stew is quick and easy to prepare yet elegant enough for company. When I take this tasty vegetarian dish to my school's potlucks, it is devoured by teachers and students alike.
—Jane Siemon, Viroqua, WI

- -

Prep: 20 min. • **Cook:** 20 min.
Makes: 4 servings

- 2 large portobello mushrooms, coarsely chopped
- 1 medium onion, chopped
- 3 garlic cloves, minced
- 2 Tbsp. olive oil
- ½ cup white wine or vegetable broth
- 1 can (28 oz.) diced tomatoes, undrained
- 2 cups chopped fresh kale
- 1 bay leaf
- 1 tsp. dried thyme
- ½ tsp. dried basil
- ½ tsp. dried rosemary, crushed
- ¼ tsp. salt
- ¼ tsp. pepper
- 2 cans (15 oz. each) cannellini beans, rinsed and drained

1. In a large skillet, saute the mushrooms, onion and garlic in oil until tender. Add the wine. Bring to a boil; cook until liquid is reduced by half. Stir in the tomatoes, kale and seasonings. Bring to a boil. Reduce heat; cover and simmer for 8-10 minutes.
2. Add the beans; heat through. Discard the bay leaf.
1¼ cups: 309 cal., 8g fat (1g sat. fat), 0 chol., 672mg sod., 46g carb. (9g sugars, 13g fiber), 12g pro. **Diabetic exchanges:** 2 starch, 2 vegetable, 1½ fat, 1 lean meat.

2 garlic cloves, minced
1 can (14½ oz.) diced tomatoes, undrained
1 cup dry red wine or reduced-sodium beef broth
2 Tbsp. red currant jelly
2 bay leaves
2 fresh oregano sprigs
1 can (15 oz.) cannellini beans, rinsed and drained
  Minced fresh parsley, optional

1. Preheat oven to 350°. Toss beef with flour and steak seasoning.
2. In an ovenproof Dutch oven, heat 1 Tbsp. oil over medium heat. Brown beef in batches; remove with a slotted spoon.
3. In same pan, heat remaining oil over medium heat. Add onion, celery, parsnips and carrots; cook and stir until onion is tender. Add garlic; cook 1 minute longer. Stir in tomatoes, wine, jelly, bay leaves, oregano and beef; bring to a boil.
4. Bake, covered, 1½ hours. Stir in beans; bake, covered, 30-40 minutes longer or until beef and vegetables are tender. Remove bay leaves and oregano sprigs. If desired, sprinkle with parsley.

Freeze option: Freeze cooled stew in freezer containers. To use, partially thaw in refrigerator overnight. Heat through in a saucepan, stirring occasionally and adding a little broth or water if necessary.

1 cup: 310 cal., 9g fat (3g sat. fat), 64mg chol., 373mg sod., 26g carb. (8g sugars, 5g fiber), 25g pro. **Diabetic exchanges:** 3 lean meat, 1 starch, 1 vegetable, 1 fat.

WINTERTIME BRAISED BEEF STEW

This wonderful beef stew makes an easy Sunday meal. Because it's even better a day or two later, we usually make a double batch so we're sure to have leftovers.
—Michaela Rosenthal, Woodland Hills, CA

- -

Prep: 40 min. • **Bake:** 2 hours
Makes: 8 servings (2 qt.)

2 lbs. boneless beef sirloin steak or chuck roast, cut into 1-in. pieces
2 Tbsp. all-purpose flour
2 tsp. Montreal steak seasoning
2 Tbsp. olive oil, divided
1 large onion, chopped
2 celery ribs, chopped
2 medium parsnips, peeled and cut into 1½-in. pieces
2 medium carrots, peeled and cut into 1½-in. pieces

APPLE CHICKEN STEW

My husband and I enjoy exploring our local apple orchards in the fall. We always make sure to buy extra cider so we can cook up this sensational supper.

—Carol Mathias, Lincoln, NE

Prep: 35 min. • **Cook:** 3 hours
Makes: 8 servings (2 qt.)

- 1½ tsp. salt
- ¾ tsp. dried thyme
- ½ tsp. pepper
- ¼ to ½ tsp. caraway seeds
- 1½ lbs. potatoes (about 4 medium), cut into ¾-in. pieces
- 4 medium carrots, cut into ¼-in. slices
- 1 medium red onion, halved and sliced
- 1 celery rib, thinly sliced
- 2 lbs. boneless skinless chicken breasts, cut into 1-in. pieces
- 2 Tbsp. olive oil
- 1 bay leaf
- 1 large tart apple, peeled and cut into 1-in. cubes
- 1 Tbsp. cider vinegar
- 1¼ cups apple cider or juice
  Minced fresh parsley

1. Mix first 4 ingredients. In a 5-qt. slow cooker, layer vegetables; sprinkle with half the salt mixture.
2. Toss chicken with oil and the remaining salt mixture. In a large skillet over medium-high heat, brown chicken in batches. Add to slow cooker. Top with bay leaf and apple. Add vinegar and cider.
3. Cook, covered, on high until the chicken is no longer pink and the vegetables are tender, 3-3½ hours. Discard bay leaf. Stir before serving. Sprinkle with parsley.
1 cup: 284 cal., 6g fat (1g sat. fat), 63mg chol., 533mg sod., 31g carb. (9g sugars, 4g fiber), 26g pro. **Diabetic exchanges:** 3 lean meat, 2 starch, 1 fat.

CREAMY BRATWURST STEW

I adapted a baked stew recipe I found in the newspaper to make a slow-cooked version. Rich, hearty and creamy, it's perfect when you need something simple and savory.

—Susan Holmes, Germantown, WI

Prep: 20 min. • **Cook:** 6½ hours
Makes: 8 servings (2 qt.)

- 1¾ lbs. potatoes (about 4 medium), peeled and cubed
- 2 medium carrots, chopped
- 2 celery ribs, chopped
- 1 medium onion, chopped
- 1 medium green pepper, chopped
- 2 lbs. uncooked bratwurst links
- ½ cup chicken broth
- 1 tsp. salt
- 1 tsp. dried basil
- ½ tsp. pepper
- 2 cups half-and-half cream
- 1 Tbsp. cornstarch
- 3 Tbsp. cold water

1. Place first 5 ingredients in a 5-qt. slow cooker; toss to combine. Top with the bratwurst. Mix the broth and seasonings; pour over top.
2. Cook, covered, on low until the sausage is cooked through and the vegetables are tender, 6-7 hours. Remove sausages from slow cooker; cut into 1-in. slices. Return sausage to potato mixture; stir in cream.
3. Mix cornstarch and water until smooth; stir into stew. Cook, covered, on high until thickened, about 30 minutes.
1 cup: 544 cal., 39g fat (15g sat. fat), 114mg chol., 1367mg sod., 25g carb. (5g sugars, 2g fiber), 19g pro.

Chilis

FIREHOUSE CHILI

As one of the cooks at the firehouse, I used to prepare meals for 10 men. This chili was among their favorites.
—Richard Clements, San Dimas, CA

- -

Prep: 20 min. • **Cook:** 1½ hours
Makes: 16 servings (4 qt.)

- 2   Tbsp. canola oil
- 4   lbs. lean ground beef (90% lean)
- 2   medium onions, chopped
- 1   medium green pepper, chopped
- 4   cans (16 oz. each) kidney beans, rinsed and drained
- 3   cans (28 oz. each) stewed tomatoes, cut up
- 1   can (14½ oz.) beef broth
- 3   Tbsp. chili powder
- 2   Tbsp. ground coriander
- 2   Tbsp. ground cumin
- 4   garlic cloves, minced
- 1   tsp. dried oregano

In a Dutch oven, heat the canola oil over medium heat. Brown beef in batches, crumbling the meat, until no longer pink; drain and set aside. Add onions and green pepper; cook until tender. Return meat to Dutch oven. Stir in the remaining ingredients. Bring to a boil. Reduce heat; simmer, covered, until the flavors are blended, about 1½ hours.

1 cup: 354 cal., 12g fat (4g sat. fat), 71mg chol., 657mg sod., 32g carb. (10g sugars, 8g fiber), 31g pro. **Diabetic exchanges:** 3 lean meat, 2 starch.

Serving to kids who pick the kidney beans out of chili? To ensure they get their fill, puree half the beans and half a can of tomato sauce. Add this mixture to the chili along with the whole beans.

SPICY WHITE CHILI

The original version of this dish was great, but my son just can't get enough spice, so I added green chiles and other seasonings to create this final version of a quick and easy chili he's wild about.
—Carlene Bailey, Bradenton, FL

- -

Prep: 20 min. • **Cook:** 15 min.
Makes: 8 servings (2 qt.)

- 2   medium onions, chopped
- 1   Tbsp. canola oil
- 4   garlic cloves, minced
- 2   cans (4 oz. each) chopped green chiles
- 2   tsp. ground cumin
- 1   tsp. dried oregano
- ¼   tsp. cayenne pepper
- ¼   tsp. ground cloves
- 2   cans (14½ oz. each) chicken broth
- 4   cups cubed cooked chicken
- 3   cans (15½ oz. each) great northern beans, rinsed and drained
- 2   cups shredded Monterey Jack cheese
    Optional: Sour cream and sliced jalapeno peppers

1. In a Dutch oven or soup kettle, saute onions in oil until tender. Stir in garlic, chiles, cumin, oregano, cayenne and cloves; cook and stir 2-3 minutes more. Add the broth, chicken and beans; simmer, uncovered, for 15 minutes.

2. Remove from the heat. Stir in cheese until melted. Garnish with sour cream and jalapeno peppers if desired.

1 cup: 324 cal., 16g fat (7g sat. fat), 87mg chol., 609mg sod., 13g carb. (3g sugars, 4g fiber), 31g pro.

CHICKEN CHILI WITH BLACK BEANS

Because this dish looks different from traditional chili, my family was hesitant to try it at first. But thanks to its full, rich flavor, it's become a real favorite.
—Jeanette Urbom, Louisburg, KS

- -

Prep: 10 min. • **Cook:** 25 min.
Makes: 10 servings (3 qt.)

- 3 whole boneless skinless chicken breasts (1¾ lbs.), cubed
- 2 medium sweet red peppers, chopped
- 1 large onion, chopped
- 3 Tbsp. olive oil
- 1 can (4 oz.) chopped green chiles
- 4 garlic cloves, minced
- 2 Tbsp. chili powder
- 2 tsp. ground cumin
- 1 tsp. ground coriander
- 2 cans (15 oz. each) black beans, rinsed and drained
- 1 can (28 oz.) Italian stewed tomatoes, cut up
- 1 cup chicken broth or beer
- ½ to 1 cup water

In a Dutch oven, saute chicken, red peppers and onion in oil until the chicken is no longer pink, about 5 minutes. Add the green chiles, garlic, chili powder, cumin and coriander; cook 1 minute longer. Stir in the beans, tomatoes, broth and ½ cup water; bring to a boil. Reduce heat and simmer, uncovered, for 15 minutes, stirring often and adding water as necessary.

1¼ cups: 236 cal., 6g fat (1g sat. fat), 44mg chol., 561mg sod., 21g carb. (5g sugars, 6g fiber), 22g pro. **Diabetic exchanges:** 2 lean meat, 1½ starch, 1 fat.

CONTEST-WINNING PEPPERONI PIZZA CHILI

Pizza and chili together in one dish—what could be better? Dish up big bowlfuls to fill folks up at halftime or serve for a delicious weeknight meal.

—Jennifer Gelormino, Pittsburgh, PA

- -

Prep: 20 min. • **Cook:** 30 min.
Makes: 12 servings (3 qt.)

- 2 lbs. ground beef
- 1 lb. bulk hot Italian sausage
- 1 large onion, chopped
- 1 large green pepper, chopped
- 4 garlic cloves, minced
- 1 jar (16 oz.) salsa
- 1 can (16 oz.) hot chili beans, undrained
- 1 can (16 oz.) kidney beans, rinsed and drained
- 1 can (12 oz.) pizza sauce
- 1 pkg. (8 oz.) sliced pepperoni, halved
- 1 cup water
- 2 tsp. chili powder
- ½ tsp. salt
- ½ tsp. pepper
- 3 cups shredded part-skim mozzarella cheese

1. In Dutch oven, cook beef, sausage, onion, green pepper and garlic over medium heat until the meat is no longer pink; drain.
2. Stir in the salsa, beans, pizza sauce, pepperoni, water, chili powder, salt and pepper. Bring to a boil. Reduce heat; cover and simmer until heated through, about 20 minutes. Sprinkle servings with cheese.
Freeze option: Before adding cheese, cool chili. Freeze chili in freezer containers. To use, partially thaw in refrigerator overnight. Heat through in a saucepan; stir occasionally and add a little water if necessary. Sprinkle each serving with cheese.
1 cup chili with ¼ cup cheese: 464 cal., 28g fat (11g sat. fat), 94mg chol., 1240mg sod., 21g carb. (6g sugars, 5g fiber), 33g pro.

JUMPIN' ESPRESSO BEAN CHILI

Chili is my favorite dish to experiment with, and this meatless version I created is low in fat but high in flavor. Everyone always tries to guess the secret ingredient, but nobody ever thinks it's coffee!

—Jessie Apfe, Berkeley, CA

- -

Prep: 15 min. • **Cook:** 35 min.
Makes: 7 servings

- 3 medium onions, chopped
- 2 Tbsp. olive oil
- 2 Tbsp. brown sugar
- 2 Tbsp. chili powder
- 2 Tbsp. ground cumin
- 1 Tbsp. instant coffee granules
- 1 Tbsp. baking cocoa
- ¾ tsp. salt
- 2 cans (14½ oz. each) no-salt-added diced tomatoes
- 1 can (15 oz.) black beans, rinsed and drained
- 1 can (15 oz.) kidney beans, rinsed and drained
- 1 can (15 oz.) garbanzo beans or chickpeas, rinsed and drained
   Optional: Sour cream, sliced green onions, shredded cheddar cheese and pickled jalapeno slices

1. In a Dutch oven, saute onions in olive oil until tender. Add brown sugar, chili powder, cumin, coffee granules, cocoa and salt; cook and stir for 1 minute.
2. Stir in tomatoes and beans. Bring to a boil. Reduce heat; cover and simmer for 30 minutes to allow flavors to blend. Serve with sour cream, onions, cheddar cheese and jalapeno slices if desired.
1 cup: 272 cal., 6g fat (1g sat. fat), 0 chol., 620mg sod., 45g carb. (14g sugars, 12g fiber), 12g pro. **Diabetic exchanges:** 2½ starch, 2 vegetable, 1 lean meat.

BEER BRAT CHILI

My husband and I love this chili because it smells so good as it's simmering in the slow cooker all day. I can't think of a better way to use up leftover brats, and he can't think of a better way to eat them!
—Katrina Krumm, Apple Valley, MN

Prep: 10 min. • **Cook:** 5 hours
Makes: 8 servings (2½ qt.)

- 1   can (15 oz.) cannellini beans, rinsed and drained
- 1   can (15 oz.) pinto beans, rinsed and drained
- 1   can (15 oz.) southwestern black beans, undrained
- 1   can (14½ oz.) Italian diced tomatoes, undrained
- 1   can (10 oz.) diced tomatoes and green chiles, undrained
- 1   pkg. (14 oz.) fully cooked beer bratwurst links, sliced
- 1½ cups frozen corn
- 1   medium sweet red pepper, chopped
- 1   medium onion, finely chopped
- ¼   cup chili seasoning mix
- 1   garlic clove, minced

In a 5-qt. slow cooker, combine all the ingredients. Cook, covered, on low for 5-6 hours.
1¼ cups: 383 cal., 16g fat (5g sat. fat), 34mg chol., 1256mg sod., 42g carb. (7g sugars, 10g fiber), 17g pro.

THAI-STYLE CHICKEN CHILI

I love this Asian take on the classic one-pot meal. It's quick, easy, nutritious and, most importantly, delicious.
—Roxanne Chan, Albany, CA

Takes: 30 min. • **Makes:** 6 servings (2 qt.)

- 2   Tbsp. sesame oil
- 1   lb. boneless skinless chicken thighs, cut into 1-in. pieces
- 1   medium carrot, diced
- 1   celery rib, chopped
- 1   tsp. minced fresh gingerroot
- 1   large garlic clove, minced
- 1   can (28 oz.) diced tomatoes
- 1   can (13.66 oz.) light coconut milk
- 1   Tbsp. red curry paste
- ¾   tsp. salt
- ¼   tsp. pepper
- 1   cup frozen shelled edamame, thawed
- 2   cups fresh baby spinach
- 1   green onion, minced
- ½   tsp. grated lemon zest
     Fresh cilantro leaves
     Dry roasted peanuts

1. In a large saucepan, heat sesame oil over medium heat. Add the chicken, carrot and celery; cook and stir until the vegetables are slightly softened, 3-4 minutes. Add ginger and garlic; cook 1 minute more.
2. Stir in tomatoes, coconut milk, curry paste, salt and pepper. Bring to a boil. Reduce heat; simmer, covered, 10 minutes. Add edamame; cook 5 minutes more. Stir in spinach, green onion and lemon zest until spinach wilts. Remove from heat; top with cilantro and peanuts.
1⅓ cups: 270 cal., 16g fat (6g sat. fat), 50mg chol., 635mg sod., 12g carb. (7g sugars, 4g fiber), 18g pro.

- 2 cans (4 oz. each) chopped green chiles
- ½ cup creamy peanut butter
- 1 to 2 Tbsp. ground ancho chili pepper
- 1 tsp. kosher salt
- 1 tsp. smoked paprika
  Optional: Shredded smoked cheddar cheese and chopped peanuts

1. In a large skillet, heat oil over medium-high heat; add beef and cook in batches 7-10 minutes or until no longer pink, breaking into crumbles. Remove with slotted spoon; drain. Add green pepper, onion and carrot; cook and stir until slightly browned, about 2 minutes. Add garlic; cook 1 minute longer. Transfer meat, vegetables and drippings to a 5- or 6-qt. slow cooker.
2. Stir in the next 7 ingredients until combined. Cook, covered, on low until vegetables are tender, about 4 hours. If desired, sprinkle with shredded cheese and peanuts.
1 cup: 279 cal., 15g fat (4g sat. fat), 59mg chol., 878mg sod., 13g carb. (6g sugars, 4g fiber), 23g pro.

TEST KITCHEN TIP

Be sure to use smoked paprika! Regular paprika is made from peppers that have been dried and ground. For smoked paprika, peppers are smoked before grinding, creating big flavor.

SMOKY PEANUT BUTTER CHILI

Just for fun, I decided to take the beans out of my standard chili recipe and instead add peanut butter and peanuts—wow! I tried it on my family and they all loved it.
—Nancy Heishman, Las Vegas, NV

- -

Prep: 25 min. • **Cook:** 4 hours
Makes: 12 servings (3 qt.)

- 1 Tbsp. peanut oil or canola oil
- 2½ lbs. lean ground beef (90% lean)
- 1 large green pepper, chopped
- 1 large red onion, chopped
- 1 large carrot, peeled and chopped
- 2 garlic cloves, minced
- 2 cans (15 oz. each) tomato sauce
- 2 cans (14½ oz. each) diced tomatoes with basil, oregano and garlic, undrained

SPICY PEANUT CHICKEN CHILI

I discovered Mexican peanut chicken when I was in the Southwest, which inspired this chili. Chipotle peppers give the dish a nice spice that's extra warming on a cool day.
—Crystal Schlueter, Babbitt, MN

- -

Takes: 30 min. • **Makes:** 6 servings (2 qt.)

- 1 can (15 oz.) pinto beans, rinsed and drained
- 1 can (14½ oz.) Mexican diced tomatoes, undrained
- 1 can (14½ oz.) no-salt-added diced tomatoes, undrained
- 1 can (14½ oz.) reduced-sodium chicken broth
- 1 pkg. (12 oz.) frozen southwestern corn
- 3 Tbsp. creamy peanut butter
- 1 to 2 Tbsp. minced chipotle peppers in adobo sauce
- 2 tsp. chili powder
- ½ tsp. ground cinnamon
- 3 cups coarsely shredded rotisserie chicken
- 6 Tbsp. reduced-fat sour cream
  Minced fresh cilantro, optional

1. Place the first 9 ingredients in a 6-qt. stockpot; bring to a boil. Reduce heat; simmer, covered, until flavors are blended, about 15 minutes.
2. Stir in chicken; heat through. Serve with sour cream and, if desired, cilantro.
Freeze option: Freeze the cooled chili in freezer containers. To use, partially thaw in refrigerator overnight. Heat through in a saucepan, stirring occasionally; add a little broth if necessary.
1⅓ cups soup with 1 Tbsp. sour cream: 368 cal., 13g fat (3g sat. fat), 67mg chol., 797mg sod., 33g carb. (11g sugars, 6g fiber), 30g pro.

TURKEY CHILI

I've taken my mother's milder recipe for chili and made it thicker and more robust. It's a favorite, especially in fall and winter.
—Celesta Zanger, Bloomfield Hills, MI

- -

Prep: 20 min. • **Cook:** 6½ hours
Makes: 12 servings (3 qt.)

- 1 lb. lean ground turkey
- ¾ cup chopped celery
- ¾ cup chopped onion
- ¾ cup chopped green pepper
- 2 Tbsp. chili powder
- 1 tsp. ground cumin
- ¼ tsp. pepper
- ⅛ to ¼ tsp. cayenne pepper
- 2 cans (14½ oz. each) no-salt-added diced tomatoes, undrained
- 1 jar (24 oz.) meatless pasta sauce
- 1 can (16 oz.) hot chili beans, undrained
- 1½ cups water
- ½ cup frozen corn
- 1 can (16 oz.) kidney beans, rinsed and drained
- 1 can (15 oz.) pinto beans, rinsed and drained
  Optional: Sour cream, cubed avocado, diced jalapenos

1. In a large skillet, cook and crumble the turkey with celery, onion and pepper over medium-high heat until the turkey is no longer pink, 6-8 minutes. Transfer to a 5-qt. slow cooker. Stir in seasonings, tomatoes, pasta sauce, chili beans, water and corn.
2. Cook, covered, on high 1 hour. Reduce setting to low; cook, covered, until flavors are blended, 5-6 hours.
3. Stir in the kidney and pinto beans; cook, covered, on low 30 minutes longer. If desired, serve with sour cream, avocado and jalapeno.
1 cup: 200 cal., 4g fat (1g sat. fat), 26mg chol., 535mg sod., 29g carb. (8g sugars, 8 fiber), 15g pro. **Diabetic exchanges:** 2 lean meat, 2 vegetable, 1 starch.

TURKEY WHITE CHILI

Growing up in a Pennsylvania Dutch area, I was surrounded by excellent cooks and wonderful food. I enjoy experimenting with new recipes, like this change-of-pace chili.
—Kaye Whiteman, Charleston, WV

Prep: 15 min. • **Cook:** 70 min.
Makes: 6 servings (1½ qt.)

- 2 Tbsp. canola oil
- ½ cup chopped onion
- 3 garlic cloves, minced
- 2½ tsp. ground cumin
- 1 lb. boneless skinless turkey breast, cut into 1-in. cubes
- ½ lb. ground turkey
- 3 cups chicken broth
- 1 can (15 oz.) garbanzo beans or chickpeas, rinsed and drained
- 1 Tbsp. minced jalapeno pepper
- ½ tsp. dried marjoram
- ¼ tsp. dried savory
- 2 tsp. cornstarch
- 1 Tbsp. water
  Optional: Shredded Monterey Jack cheese, sliced red onion

1. In a large saucepan or Dutch oven, heat canola oil over medium heat. Add onion and saute until tender, about 5 minutes. Add garlic and cook 1 minute more. Stir in cumin; cook 5 minutes. Add turkey and cook until no longer pink. Add broth, beans, jalapeno, marjoram and savory. Bring to a boil. Reduce heat; simmer, covered, for 45 minutes, stirring occasionally.

2. Uncover; cook 15 minutes more. Dissolve cornstarch in water; stir into the chili. Bring to a boil. Cook and stir 2 minutes. If desired, top servings with shredded cheese and sliced red onion.

1 cup: 288 cal., 12g fat (2g sat. fat), 73mg chol., 635mg sod., 15g carb. (3g sugars, 3g fiber), 29g pro. **Diabetic exchanges:** 3 lean meat, 1 starch, 1 fat.

BLACK BEAN, CHORIZO & SWEET POTATO CHILI

Chili is an all-time favorite meal of mine, and this recipe takes the beloved dish to the next level by changing up the flavors and adding a surprise—sweet potatoes.
—Julie Merriman, Seattle, WA

Prep: 20 min. • **Cook:** 6 hours
Makes: 16 servings (4 qt.)

- 1   lb. uncooked chorizo, casings removed, or spicy bulk pork sausage
- 1   large onion, chopped
- 2   poblano peppers, finely chopped
- 2   jalapeno peppers, seeded and finely chopped
- 3   Tbsp. tomato paste
- 3   large sweet potatoes, peeled and cut into ½-in. cubes
- 4   cans (14½ oz. each) fire-roasted diced tomatoes, undrained
- 2   cans (15 oz. each) black beans, rinsed and drained
- 2   cups beef stock
- 2   Tbsp. chili powder
- 1   Tbsp. dried oregano
- 1   Tbsp. ground coriander
- 1   Tbsp. ground cumin
- 1   Tbsp. smoked paprika
- ¼   cup lime juice
  Optional: Chopped jalapenos, chopped red onion and crumbled queso fresco

1. In a large skillet, cook and stir chorizo, onion, poblanos and jalapenos over medium heat for 8-10 minutes or until the chorizo is cooked. Using a slotted spoon, transfer to a 6-qt. slow cooker.

2. Stir in tomato paste. Add the potatoes, tomatoes, beans, stock and spices; stir to combine. Cover and cook on low for 6-7 hours or until potatoes are tender. Stir in lime juice. If desired, top with chopped jalapenos, chopped red onion and crumbled queso fresco.

1 cup: 263 cal., 9g fat (3g sat. fat), 25mg chol., 823mg sod., 33g carb. (11g sugars, 6g fiber), 12g pro.

DID YOU KNOW?

What's the difference between sweet potatoes and yams? A true yam is an edible root with dry starchy flesh and dark barklike skin. Sweet potatoes are moist, generally with orange flesh and a smoother outer appearance, and are high in beta carotene and vitamins C and B-6.

CHUNKY CHIPOTLE PORK CHILI

Perfect for using leftover pork roast, this wonderful recipe can be made ahead and reheated. It's even better the second day!
—Peter Halferty, Corpus Christi, TX

- -

Prep: 15 min. • **Cook:** 20 min.
Makes: 4 servings (1 qt.)

- 1 medium green pepper, chopped
- 1 small onion, chopped
- 1 chipotle pepper in adobo sauce, finely chopped
- 1 Tbsp. canola oil
- 3 garlic cloves, minced
- 1 can (16 oz.) red beans, rinsed and drained
- 1 cup beef broth
- ½ cup salsa
- 2 tsp. ground cumin
- 2 tsp. chili powder
- 2 cups shredded cooked pork
- ¼ cup sour cream
   Sliced jalapeno pepper, optional

1. In a large saucepan, saute green pepper, onion and chipotle pepper in oil until tender. Add garlic; cook 1 minute longer.
2. Add the beans, broth, salsa, cumin and chili powder. Bring to a boil. Reduce heat; simmer, uncovered, for 10 minutes or until thickened. Add the pork; heat through. Serve with sour cream and, if desired, jalapeno slices.
Freeze option: Cool chili and transfer to freezer containers. Freeze up to 3 months. To use, thaw in the refrigerator. Transfer to a large saucepan; heat through, adding water to thin if desired. Serve with sour cream and jalapeno slices, if desired.
1 cup: 340 cal., 14g fat (4g sat. fat), 73mg chol., 834mg sod., 24g carb. (3g sugars, 7g fiber), 27g pro.

BARBECUED BEEF CHILI

Two friends inspired the recipe for this hearty, slow-cooked chili when we were talking about what to make for a potluck.
—Phyllis Shyan, Elgin, IL

- -

Prep: 10 min. • **Cook:** 6 hours
Makes: 12 servings (3 qt.)

- 7 tsp. chili powder
- 1 Tbsp. garlic powder
- 2 tsp. celery seed
- 1 tsp. coarsely ground pepper
- ¼ to ½ tsp. cayenne pepper
- 1 fresh beef brisket (3 to 4 lbs.)
- 1 medium green pepper, chopped
- 1 small onion, chopped
- 1 bottle (12 oz.) chili sauce
- 1 cup ketchup
- ½ cup barbecue sauce
- ⅓ cup packed brown sugar
- ¼ cup cider vinegar
- ¼ cup Worcestershire sauce
- 1 tsp. ground mustard
- 1 can (16 oz.) hot chili beans, undrained
- 1 can (15½ oz.) great northern beans, rinsed and drained
   Optional: Shredded cheddar cheese, chopped white onion and sliced jalapeno peppers

1. Combine first 5 ingredients; rub over brisket. Cut into 8 pieces; place in a 5-qt. slow cooker. Combine green pepper, onion, chili sauce, ketchup, barbecue sauce, brown sugar, vinegar, Worcestershire sauce and mustard; pour over meat. Cover and cook on high 5-6 hours or until meat is tender.
2. Remove meat; cool slightly. Meanwhile, skim fat from cooking juices. Shred meat with 2 forks; return to slow cooker. Reduce heat to low. Stir in the beans. Cover and cook for 1 hour or until heated through. If desired, top with shredded cheddar, chopped white onion and sliced jalapenos.
1 cup: 302 cal., 6g fat (2g sat. fat), 48mg chol., 1037mg sod., 36g carb. (20g sugars, 5g fiber), 28g pro.

1 pkg. (8 oz.) cream cheese, cubed
¼ cup water or chicken broth
2 Tbsp. ranch salad dressing mix
1 Tbsp. chili powder
1 tsp. onion powder
1 tsp. ground cumin
¼ tsp. crushed red pepper flakes
   Optional: Shredded cheddar
     cheese, sour cream and
     cooked crumbled bacon

1. Select saute setting on a 6-qt. electric pressure cooker and adjust for medium heat; add butter. When the butter is hot, cook and stir chicken, onion, jalapenos and garlic until the chicken is no longer pink and the vegetables are tender, 6-8 minutes, breaking up chicken into crumbles. Stir in corn, beans, diced tomatoes and chiles, cream cheese, water, dressing mix and seasonings. Press cancel.
2. Lock lid; close pressure-release valve. Adjust to pressure-cook on high for 8 minutes. Quick-release pressure. Stir before serving. Garnish with shredded cheddar cheese, sour cream, bacon and additional jalapenos as desired.
Freeze option: Before adding toppings, cool chili. Freeze chili in freezer containers. To use, partially thaw in refrigerator overnight. Heat through in a saucepan, stirring occasionally; add a little water if necessary. Sprinkle with toppings.
Note: Wear disposable gloves when cutting hot peppers; the oils can burn skin. Avoid touching your face.

1 cup: 344 cal., 20g fat (10g sat. fat), 84mg chol., 1141mg sod., 25g carb. (6g sugars, 5g fiber), 17g pro.

PRESSURE-COOKER JALAPENO POPPER CHICKEN CHILI
It doesn't get much better than this quick and comforting chili that tastes like liquid jalapeno poppers. You'll be back for more!
—Natasha Galbreath, Spanaway, WA

- -

Prep: 30 min. • **Cook:** 10 min.
Makes: 7 servings (1¾ qt.)

2 Tbsp. butter
1 lb. ground chicken
1 large onion, chopped
2 to 4 jalapeno peppers, seeded and finely chopped
4 garlic cloves, minced
1 can (15¼ oz.) whole kernel corn, undrained
1 can (15 oz.) black beans, rinsed and drained
1 can (10 oz.) diced tomatoes and green chiles, undrained

SLOW-COOKER SPICY PORK CHILI

Tender pork adds extra flavor and texture to this slow-cooked chili. Whether you use pork tenderloin, boneless pork roast or boneless pork chops, you can't go wrong when you cook up this delicious dish!
—*Taste of Home* Test Kitchen

Prep: 10 min. • **Cook:** 6 hours
Makes: 6 servings (about 2½ qt.)

- 2 lbs. boneless pork, cut into ½-in. cubes
- 1 Tbsp. canola oil
- 1 can (28 oz.) crushed tomatoes
- 2 cups frozen corn
- 1 can (15 oz.) black beans, rinsed and drained
- 1 cup chopped onion
- 2 cups beef broth
- 1 can (4 oz.) chopped green chiles
- 1 Tbsp. chili powder
- 1 tsp. minced garlic
- ½ tsp. salt
- ½ tsp. cayenne pepper
- ½ tsp. pepper
- ¼ cup minced fresh cilantro
  Shredded cheddar cheese, optional

1. In a large skillet, cook pork in oil over medium-high heat until browned, 5-6 minutes. Transfer the pork and drippings to a 5-qt. slow cooker. Stir in tomatoes, corn, beans, onion, broth, chiles, chili powder, garlic, salt, cayenne and pepper.
2. Cover and cook on low until the pork is tender, 6-7 hours. Stir in cilantro. Serve with cheese if desired.
1¾ cups: 395 cal., 12g fat (4g sat. fat), 89mg chol., 1055mg sod., 34g carb. (9g sugars, 8g fiber), 39g pro.

🍎 BUTTERNUT SQUASH CHILI

Adding nutrient-packed squash to these hearty bowls makes for a tasty and filling dish your whole family will love. Mine does!
—Jeanne Larson, Rancho Santa Margarita, CA

Prep: 20 min. • **Cook:** 30 min.
Makes: 8 servings (2 qt.)

- 1 lb. ground beef or turkey
- ¾ cup chopped red onion
- 5 garlic cloves, minced
- 3 Tbsp. tomato paste
- 1 Tbsp. chili powder
- 1 tsp. ground cumin
- ½ to 1 tsp. salt
- 1¾ to 2 cups water
- 1 can (15 oz.) black beans, rinsed and drained
- 1 can (15 oz.) pinto beans, rinsed and drained
- 1 can (14½ oz.) diced tomatoes
- 1 can (14½ to 15 oz.) tomato sauce
- 3 cups cubed peeled butternut squash, (½-in. cubes)
- 2 Tbsp. cider vinegar
  Optional: Chopped avocado, plain Greek yogurt and shredded mozzarella cheese

1. In a Dutch oven over medium heat, cook the beef and onion, crumbling meat, until beef is no longer pink and the onion is tender, 6-8 minutes.
2. Add the next 5 ingredients and cook 1 minute longer. Stir in water, both types of beans, diced tomatoes and the tomato sauce. Bring to a boil; reduce heat. Stir in squash; simmer, covered, until the squash is tender, 20-25 minutes. Stir in vinegar.
3. If desired, serve with chopped avocado, Greek yogurt and shredded mozzarella.
1 cup: 261 cal., 8g fat (3g sat. fat), 35mg chol., 704mg sod., 32g carb. (6g sugars, 8g fiber), 18g pro. **Diabetic exchanges:** 2 starch, 2 lean meat.

LAMB & WHITE BEAN CHILI

I created this fresh take on chili using lamb and Moroccan seasoning with a garnish of goat cheese and almonds. My husband and son asked me to make a second batch almost right away! If you like spicier chili, add harissa paste or use medium salsa instead of mild.

—Arlene Erlbach, Morton Grove, IL

- -

Prep: 25 min. • **Cook:** 6¼ hours
Makes: 4 servings (1 qt.)

1 lb. ground lamb
1 cup coarsely chopped red onion
1 can (15 oz.) cannellini beans, undrained
1 jar (16 oz.) mild chunky salsa
3 Tbsp. Moroccan seasoning (ras el hanout), divided
4½ tsp. finely chopped lemon zest, divided
3 Tbsp. orange marmalade
¼ cup minced fresh parsley
¼ cup crumbled goat cheese
2 Tbsp. sliced almonds
  Optional: Additional chopped red onion; toasted naan flatbread or pita bread

1. In a large nonstick skillet, cook lamb and onion over medium-high heat 6-8 minutes or until no longer pink, breaking into crumbles; drain. Transfer the lamb mixture to a 3- or 4-qt. slow cooker. Add beans.

2. In a small bowl, combine salsa, 1½ Tbsp. Moroccan seasoning and 1 Tbsp. lemon zest. Pour over the beans and lamb; stir until well combined. Cook, covered, on low until onions are tender, about 6 hours.

3. In a small bowl, combine marmalade with the remaining Moroccan seasoning and lemon zest; stir into the slow cooker. Cook, covered, 15 minutes longer. Sprinkle each serving with parsley, cheese and almonds. Serve with additional red onion and naan or pita bread if desired.

1 cup: 438 cal., 18g fat (8g sat. fat), 84mg chol., 840mg sod., 39g carb. (16g sugars, 7g fiber), 28g pro.

> **TEST KITCHEN TIP**
>
> If you're watching your budget, use ½ lb. of lamb and boost the amount of beans or chickpeas.

 VEGETARIAN CHILI OLE!

I combine the ingredients for this yummy chili the night before, start my trusty slow cooker in the morning, and come home to a rich, spicy meal at night!
—Marjorie Au, Honolulu, HI

- -

Prep: 35 min. • **Cook:** 6 hours
Makes: 7 servings (1¾ qt.)

- 1 can (16 oz.) kidney beans, rinsed and drained
- 1 can (15 oz.) black beans, rinsed and drained
- 1 can (14½ oz.) diced tomatoes, undrained
- 1½ cups frozen corn
- 1 large onion, chopped
- 1 medium zucchini, chopped
- 1 medium sweet red pepper, chopped
- 1 can (4 oz.) chopped green chiles
- 1 oz. Mexican chocolate, chopped
- 1 cup water
- 1 can (6 oz.) tomato paste
- 1 Tbsp. cornmeal
- 1 Tbsp. chili powder
- ½ tsp. salt
- ½ tsp. dried oregano
- ½ tsp. ground cumin
- ¼ tsp. hot pepper sauce, optional
  Optional: Diced tomatoes, chopped green onions and crumbled queso fresco

In a 4-qt. slow cooker, combine the first 9 ingredients. Combine water, tomato paste, cornmeal, chili powder, salt, oregano, cumin and, if desired, pepper sauce until smooth; stir into slow cooker. Cover and cook on low 6-8 hours or until vegetables are tender. Serve with the toppings of your choice.

1 cup: 216 cal., 1g fat (0 sat. fat), 0 chol., 559mg sod., 43g carb. (11g sugars, 10g fiber), 11g pro. **Diabetic exchanges:** 2½ starch, 1 lean meat.

LIME CHICKEN CHILI

Lime juice gives this chili a zesty twist, while canned tomatoes and beans make preparation a snap. Try serving bowls with toasted tortilla strips.
—Linda Randazzo, Egg Harbor County, NJ

Prep: 25 min. • **Cook:** 40 min.
Makes: 6 servings (2 qt.)

- 1   medium onion, chopped
- 1   each medium sweet yellow, red and green pepper, chopped
- 2   Tbsp. olive oil
- 3   garlic cloves, minced
- 1   lb. ground chicken
- 1   Tbsp. all-purpose flour
- 1   Tbsp. baking cocoa
- 1   Tbsp. ground cumin
- 1   Tbsp. chili powder
- 2   tsp. ground coriander
- ½   tsp. salt
- ½   tsp. garlic pepper blend
- ¼   tsp. pepper
- 2   cans (14½ oz. each) diced tomatoes, undrained
- ¼   cup lime juice
- 1   tsp. grated lime zest
- 1   can (15 oz.) cannellini beans, rinsed and drained
- 2   flour tortillas (8 in.), cut into ¼-in. strips
- 6   Tbsp. reduced-fat sour cream

1. In a large saucepan, saute onion and peppers in oil for 7-8 minutes or until crisp-tender. Add garlic; cook 1 minute longer. Add chicken; cook and stir over medium heat for 8-9 minutes or until no longer pink.
2. Stir in the flour, cocoa and seasonings. Add the tomatoes, lime juice and lime zest. Bring to a boil. Reduce heat; simmer, uncovered, for 20-25 minutes or until thickened, stirring frequently. Stir in beans; heat through.
3. Meanwhile, place tortilla strips on a baking sheet coated with cooking spray. Bake at 400° for 8-10 minutes or until crisp.

Serve individual servings of chili with tortilla strips and sour cream.
1¼ cups with 10 tortilla strips and 1 Tbsp. sour cream: 357 cal., 14g fat (4g sat. fat), 55mg chol., 643mg sod., 40g carb. (4g sugars, 8g fiber), 21g pro.

❄ CHEESY CHILI

My six grandchildren enjoy feasting on big bowls of this zesty chili. It's so creamy and tasty you can even serve it as a dip at parties.
—Codie Ray, Tallulah, LA

Takes: 25 min.
Makes: 12 servings (about 3 qt.)

- 2   lbs. ground beef
- 2   medium onions, chopped
- 2   garlic cloves, minced
- 3   cans (10 oz. each) diced tomatoes and green chiles, undrained
- 1   can (28 oz.) diced tomatoes, undrained
- 2   cans (4 oz. each) chopped green chiles
- ½   tsp. pepper
- 2   lbs. Velveeta, cubed
     Optional: Sour cream, sliced jalapeno pepper, chopped tomato, minced fresh cilantro

1. In a large saucepan, cook beef, onions and garlic until the meat is no longer pink; drain. Stir in tomatoes, chiles and pepper; bring to a boil.
2. Reduce heat; simmer, uncovered, for 10-15 minutes. Stir in cheese until melted. Serve immediately. If desired, top with sour cream, jalapenos, tomatoes and cilantro.
Freeze option: Cool chili and transfer to freezer containers. Freeze up to 3 months. To use, thaw in the refrigerator; heat in a saucepan or microwave.
1 cup: 396 cal., 25g fat (15g sat. fat), 85mg chol., 1166mg sod., 13g carb. (9g sugars, 2g fiber), 29g pro.

SLOW-COOKER QUINOA CHILI

This is the recipe that turned my husband into a quinoa lover. I made it the day he got good news on a new job, and we'll always remember how excited we were as we ate this beautiful meal.
—Claire Gallam, Alexandria, VA

- -

Prep: 25 min. • **Cook:** 4 hours
Makes: 10 servings (about 3½ qt.)

- 1   lb. lean ground beef (90% lean)
- 1   medium onion, chopped
- 2   garlic cloves, minced
- 1   can (28 oz.) diced tomatoes with mild green chiles, undrained
- 1   can (14 oz.) fire-roasted diced tomatoes, undrained
- 1   can (15 oz.) garbanzo beans or chickpeas, rinsed and drained
- 1   can (15 oz.) black beans, rinsed and drained
- 2   cups reduced-sodium beef broth
- 1   cup quinoa, rinsed
- 2   tsp. onion soup mix
- 1   to 2 tsp. crushed red pepper flakes
- 1   tsp. garlic powder
- ¼   to ½ tsp. cayenne pepper
- ¼   tsp. salt
  Optional: Shredded cheddar cheese, chopped avocado, chopped red onion, sliced jalapeno, sour cream and cilantro

1. In a large skillet, cook beef, onion and garlic over medium-high heat, breaking meat into crumbles, 6-8 minutes or until meat is no longer pink; drain.
2. Transfer mixture to a 5- or 6-qt. slow cooker. Add the next 11 ingredients; stir to combine. Cook, covered, on low 4-5 hours or until the quinoa is tender. Serve with optional toppings as desired.
1½ cups: 318 cal., 7g fat (2g sat. fat), 37mg chol., 805mg sod., 41g carb. (7g sugars, 8g fiber), 21g pro. **Diabetic exchanges:** 2½ starch, 2 lean meat.

GAME-STOPPER CHILI

A hearty chili with sausage, beef, beans and barley is perfect for the halftime food rush. At watch parties, people cheer when they see me come in with my slow cooker!
—Barbara Lento, Houston, PA

- -

Prep: 25 min. • **Cook:** 6 hours
Makes: 12 servings (4 qt.)

- 1   can (28 oz.) diced tomatoes, undrained
- 1   can (15 oz.) black beans, rinsed and drained
- 1   can (15 oz.) kidney beans, rinsed and drained
- 1   lb. boneless beef chuck steak, cut into 1-in. cubes
- 1   lb. bulk spicy pork sausage, cooked and drained
- 2   medium onions, chopped
- 1   medium sweet red pepper, chopped
- 1   medium green pepper, chopped
- 1   cup hot chunky salsa
- ⅓   cup medium pearl barley
- 2   Tbsp. chili powder
- 2   tsp. jarred roasted minced garlic
- 1   tsp. salt
- 1   tsp. ground cumin
- 4   cups beef stock
- 2   cups shredded Mexican cheese blend
  Corn chips

1. Place all ingredients except the cheese and chips in a 6-qt. slow cooker. Cook, covered, on low until the beef is tender, 6-8 hours.
2. Stir in the cheese until melted. Serve chili with chips.
Freeze option: Freeze cooled chili in freezer containers. To use, partially thaw in refrigerator overnight. Heat through in a saucepan, stirring occasionally.
1⅓ cups: 359 cal., 18g fat (7g sat. fat), 62mg chol., 1062mg sod., 26g carb. (6g sugars, 6g fiber), 23g pro.

Oven Baked
favorites

Beef

RAMONA'S CHILAQUILES

A dear neighbor shared this recipe, which she used to make from scratch. My version takes a few shortcuts.
—Marina Castle Kelley, Canyon Country, CA

- -

Takes: 30 min. • **Makes:** 4 servings

- ½ lb. lean ground beef (90% lean)
- ½ lb. fresh chorizo or bulk spicy pork sausage
- 1 medium onion, finely chopped
- 1 garlic clove, minced
- 1 can (14½ oz.) diced tomatoes with mild green chiles, undrained
- 1 can (10 oz.) diced tomatoes and green chiles, undrained
- 4 cups tortilla chips (about 6 oz.)
- 1 cup shredded Monterey Jack cheese
  Chopped fresh cilantro
  Optional: Sour cream, diced avocado, sliced red onion

1. Preheat oven to 350°. In a large skillet, cook and crumble beef and chorizo with onion and garlic over medium heat until beef is no longer pink, 5-7 minutes; drain. Stir in both tomatoes; bring to a boil. In a greased 1½-qt. or 8-in. square baking dish, layer 2 cups chips, half the meat mixture and ½ cup cheese; repeat layers.
2. Bake, uncovered, until the cheese is melted, 12-15 minutes. Sprinkle with cilantro. If desired, serve with toppings.
1 serving: 573 cal., 35g fat (14g sat. fat), 110mg chol., 1509mg sod., 28g carb. (5g sugars, 4g fiber), 33g pro.

TEST KITCHEN TIP

Chilaquiles are indulgent any way you fix them, but they can be lightened up. Use chorizo chicken sausage and baked chips to lop off 15 grams fat.

INSIDE-OUT STUFFED PEPPERS

My daughters don't care for the usual hollowed-out green peppers stuffed with a meat-and-rice mixture, so one of the girls dreamed up this alternative. The peppers are chopped and combined with the other ingredients in a casserole. Simply genius!
—Darlene Brenden, Salem, OR

- -

Prep: 15 min. • **Bake:** 65 min.
Makes: 6 servings

- 1 lb. ground beef
- ½ cup chopped onion
- 1 can (14½ oz.) stewed tomatoes, cut up
- 1 large green pepper, chopped
- ½ cup uncooked long grain rice
- ½ cup water
- 2 tsp. Worcestershire sauce
- ½ tsp. salt
- ¼ tsp. pepper
- 1 cup shredded cheddar cheese

1. Preheat oven to 350°. In a large skillet, cook ground beef over medium heat until no longer pink; drain. Transfer to a greased 2-qt. casserole. Add the next 8 ingredients.
2. Cover and bake until the rice is tender, about 1 hour. Uncover and sprinkle with cheese; cook until the cheese is melted, about 5 minutes longer.
1 serving: 276 cal., 12g fat (7g sat. fat), 57mg chol., 516mg sod., 22g carb. (5g sugars, 2g fiber), 19g pro.

BEEF & TATER BAKE

The entire family will enjoy this heartwarming, all-in-one dinner. Plus, it offers easy cleanup!
—Mike Tchou, Pepper Pike, OH

- -

Prep: 10 min. • **Bake:** 35 min.
Makes: 8 servings

- 4 **cups frozen Tater Tots**
- 1 **lb. ground beef**
- ¼ **tsp. garlic powder**
- ⅛ **tsp. pepper**
- 1 **can (10¾ oz.) condensed cream of broccoli soup, undiluted**
- ⅓ **cup 2% milk**
- 1 **pkg. (16 oz.) frozen chopped broccoli, thawed**
- 1 **can (2.8 oz.) french-fried onions, divided**
- 1 **cup shredded Colby-Monterey Jack cheese, divided**
- 1 **medium tomato, chopped**

1. Preheat oven to 400°. Spread Tater Tots evenly in an ungreased 13x9-in. baking dish. Bake, uncovered, 10 minutes.
2. Meanwhile, in a large skillet, cook and crumble beef over medium heat until no longer pink, 5-7 minutes; drain. Stir in seasonings, soup, milk, broccoli, ¾ cup onions, ½ cup cheese and tomato; heat through. Pour over potatoes.
3. Bake, covered, for 20 minutes. Sprinkle with remaining onions and cheese. Bake, uncovered, until the cheese is melted, 5-10 minutes.

1 piece: 400 cal., 24g fat (9g sat. fat), 50mg chol., 805mg sod., 29g carb. (3g sugars, 4g fiber), 17g pro.

Corn, Beef & Tater Bake: Substitute 1 package frozen corn for the broccoli and 1 can cream of celery soup for the cream of broccoli soup.

ITALIAN HOT DISH
My husband had a poor perception of healthy food until he tried this beefy casserole. The combination of pasta, oregano, mushrooms and green peppers makes it a favorite in our house.
—Theresa Smith, Sheboygan, WI

- -

Prep: 30 min. • **Bake:** 40 min.
Makes: 4 servings

- 1½ **cups uncooked multigrain bow tie pasta (about 4 oz.)**
- 1 **lb. lean ground beef (90% lean)**
- 1 **cup sliced fresh mushrooms, divided**
- ½ **cup chopped onion**
- ½ **cup chopped green pepper**
- 1 **tsp. dried oregano**
- ½ **tsp. garlic powder**
- ¼ **tsp. onion powder**
- ⅛ **tsp. pepper**
- 1 **can (15 oz.) tomato sauce**
- ½ **cup shredded part-skim mozzarella cheese, divided**
- 2 **Tbsp. grated Parmesan cheese, divided**

1. Preheat oven to 350°. Cook pasta according to the package directions for al dente; drain.
2. Meanwhile, in a large skillet coated with cooking spray, cook and crumble beef with ½ cup mushrooms, onion and green pepper over medium-high heat until meat is no longer pink, 5-7 minutes. Stir in seasonings and tomato sauce; bring to a boil. Reduce heat; simmer, covered, 15 minutes.
3. Place pasta in an 8-in. square baking dish coated with cooking spray. Top with meat sauce and the remaining mushrooms. Sprinkle with ¼ cup mozzarella cheese and 1 Tbsp. Parmesan cheese.
4. Bake, covered, for 35 minutes. Uncover; sprinkle with the remaining cheeses. Bake until heated through and the cheese is melted, 5-10 minutes.
1 serving: 394 cal., 15g fat (6g sat. fat), 82mg chol., 704mg sod., 32g carb. (5g sugars, 5g fiber), 34g pro. **Diabetic exchanges:** 2 starch, 3 lean meat, 2 vegetable, ½ fat.

To clean mushrooms, gently remove any surface dirt by rubbing with a soft mushroom brush or a damp paper towel. Do not peel mushrooms. Trim the stems.

MAINLY MUSHROOM BEEF CARBONNADE

This is the ultimate comfort food, an earth-and-turf combo that smells amazing while it's cooking and tastes even better. The mushrooms are so meaty, you can cut the amount of beef and add more portabellos if you like. Serve over mashed potatoes, egg noodles or rice—or on its own with bread to sop up the goodness!
—Susan Asanovic, Wilton, CT

- -

Prep: 45 min. • **Bake:** 2 hours
Makes: 6 servings

- 2 Tbsp. plus 1½ tsp. canola oil, divided
- 1½ lbs. beef stew meat, cut into 1-in. cubes
- ¾ tsp. salt
- ¼ tsp. plus ⅛ tsp. pepper
- 3 medium onions, chopped
- 1¼ lbs. portobello mushrooms, stems removed, cut into ¾-in. dice
- 4 garlic cloves, minced
- 2 Tbsp. tomato paste
- ½ lb. fresh baby carrots
- 1 thick slice day-old rye bread, crumbled (about 1½ cups)
- 3 bay leaves
- 1½ tsp. dried thyme
- 1 tsp. beef bouillon granules
- 1 bottle (12 oz.) light beer or beef broth
- 1 cup water
- 1 oz. bittersweet chocolate, grated

1. Preheat oven to 325°. In an ovenproof Dutch oven, heat 2 Tbsp. oil over medium-high heat. Sprinkle beef with salt and pepper; brown in batches. Remove with a slotted spoon.

2. Reduce heat to medium. Add onions to the pan drippings; cook, stirring frequently, until dark golden brown, about 8 minutes. Stir in the remaining oil; add mushrooms and garlic. Saute until the mushrooms begin to brown and release their liquid. Stir in tomato paste.

3. Add carrots, bread, bay leaves, thyme and bouillon. Add beer and water, stirring to loosen browned bits from pan. Bring to a boil; return beef to pan.

4. Bake, covered, until the meat is tender, 2-2¼ hours. Remove from oven; discard bay leaves. Stir in chocolate until melted.

1 cup: 333 cal., 16g fat (4g sat. fat), 71mg chol., 547mg sod., 18g carb. (7g sugars, 4g fiber), 26g pro.

TEST KITCHEN TIP

A light-bodied beer can be replaced with dark beer or red wine in most recipes.

SHEPHERD'S PIE

When you need a real meat-and-potatoes fix, try this satisfying layered casserole. It combines creamy from-scratch mashed potatoes with a savory meat filling. Your favorite barbecue sauce gives the dish an extra tang.

—Cindy Kliskey, Pepperell, MA

- -

Prep: 25 min. • **Bake:** 25 min.
Makes: 2 casseroles (8 servings each)

5   lbs. potatoes
     (about 10 medium),
     peeled and cubed
2   lbs. ground beef
2   large onions, chopped
2   garlic cloves, minced
2   cans (15½ oz. each) whole kernel
     corn, drained
1½   cups barbecue sauce
2   pkg. (8 oz. each) cream cheese,
     softened
¼   cup butter, cubed

1   tsp. salt
¼   tsp. pepper
2   cups shredded cheddar cheese

1. Preheat oven to 350°. Place potatoes in a stockpot and cover with water. Bring to a boil. Reduce heat; cover and cook until tender, 15 minutes.
2. Meanwhile, cook beef, onions and garlic in a Dutch oven until the meat is no longer pink; drain. Stir in corn and barbecue sauce.
3. Drain the potatoes; mash with cream cheese, butter, salt and pepper. Spoon the meat mixture into 2 greased 13x9-in. baking dishes. Spread mashed potatoes over top; sprinkle with cheese.
4. Bake shepherd's pie, uncovered, until bubbly, 25-30 minutes.

Freeze option: Cool unbaked casseroles; cover and freeze up to 3 months. To use, partially thaw in refrigerator overnight. Remove from refrigerator 30 minutes before baking. Cover and bake at 350° until bubbly, 1¼ hours. Uncover; bake until the cheese is melted and a thermometer inserted in center reads 165°, 5-10 minutes longer.

1¼ cups: 443 cal., 25g fat (13g sat. fat), 88mg chol., 820mg sod., 38g carb. (15g sugars, 3g fiber), 18g pro.

SWEET POTATO ENCHILADA STACK

Mexican flavors abound in this awesome enchilada stack jam-packed with black beans and sweet potato.
—*Taste of Home* Test Kitchen

Prep: 20 min. • **Bake:** 20 min.
Makes: 6 servings

- 1 large sweet potato, peeled and cut into ½-in. cubes
- 1 Tbsp. water
- 1 lb. ground beef
- 1 medium onion, chopped
- 1 can (15 oz.) black beans, rinsed and drained
- 1 can (10 oz.) enchilada sauce
- 2 tsp. chili powder
- ½ tsp. dried oregano
- ½ tsp. ground cumin
- 3 flour tortillas (8 in.)
- 2 cups shredded cheddar cheese

1. Preheat oven to 400°. In a large microwave-safe bowl, combine sweet potatoes and water. Cover and microwave on high for 4-5 minutes or until potatoes are almost tender.
2. Meanwhile, in a large skillet, cook beef and onion over medium heat until meat is no longer pink; drain. Stir in the beans, enchilada sauce, chili powder, oregano, cumin and sweet potato; heat through.
3. Place a flour tortilla in a greased 9-in. deep-dish pie plate; layer with a third of the beef mixture and a third of the cheese. Repeat layers twice. Bake 20-25 minutes or until bubbly.
1 piece: 457 cal., 22g fat (12g sat. fat), 87mg chol., 804mg sod., 39g carb. (6g sugars, 6g fiber), 29g pro.

SPINACH & FETA FLANK STEAK

While this dish may look difficult, it's actually very easy to do. Fancy spirals of flavor are perfect for holiday meals but easy enough for a weeknight dinner.
—Josh Carter, Birmingham, AL

Prep: 15 min. • **Bake:** 40 min.
Makes: 6 servings

- 1 beef flank steak (1½ to 2 lbs.)
- 1 pkg. (10 oz.) frozen chopped spinach, thawed and squeezed dry
- 1 pkg. (4 oz.) crumbled feta cheese
- ⅓ cup minced fresh parsley
- 3 Tbsp. snipped fresh dill
- 3 Tbsp. chopped green onions
- 1 tsp. salt
- ½ tsp. pepper
- 1 Tbsp. olive oil

1. Cut flank steak horizontally from a long side to within ½ in. of opposite side. Open steak so it lies flat; flatten to ¼-in. thickness.
2. Combine the spinach, cheese, parsley, dill and onions. Spread over steak to within 1 in. of edges. Roll up jelly-roll style, starting with a short side; tie with kitchen string. Sprinkle with salt and pepper.
3. In a large skillet, brown meat in oil on all sides; transfer to the greased rack of a shallow roasting pan. Bake at 400° until the meat reaches desired doneness (for medium-rare, a thermometer should read 135°; medium, 140°; medium-well, 145°), 40-45 minutes. Remove from oven and let stand 15 minutes. To serve, remove string; slice into 1-in.-thick slices.
2 slices: 242 cal., 14g fat (6g sat. fat), 58mg chol., 662mg sod., 3g carb. (0 sugars, 2g fiber), 24g pro.

GRANDMA'S RICE DISH

My grandmother often made this casserole when I was young. I forgot about it until I found myself adding the same ingredients to leftover rice one day. The memories came flooding back.
—Lorna Moore, Glendora, CA

Prep: 20 min. • **Bake:** 15 min.
Makes: 4 servings

- 1 lb. ground beef
- ⅓ cup chopped onion
- ½ cup chopped green pepper
- 2 cups cooked long grain rice
- 1 can (14½ oz.) diced tomatoes, undrained
- 1 can (11 oz.) whole kernel corn, drained
- 1 can (2¼ oz.) sliced ripe olives, drained
- 6 bacon strips, cooked and crumbled
- 2 tsp. chili powder
- 1 tsp. garlic powder
- ½ tsp. salt
- 1½ cups shredded cheddar cheese, divided
- ½ cup dry bread crumbs
- 1 Tbsp. butter, melted

1. Preheat oven to 350°. In a large skillet, cook beef, onion and green pepper over medium heat until the meat is no longer pink; drain.
2. Stir in rice, tomatoes, corn, olives, bacon and seasonings; heat through. Stir in 1 cup cheese until melted.
3. Transfer to a greased 11x7-in. baking dish. Sprinkle with the remaining cheese. Toss bread crumbs with butter; sprinkle over the top of the casserole.
4. Bake, uncovered, 15-20 minutes or until cheese is melted.
1½ cups: 719 cal., 37g fat (18g sat. fat), 136mg chol., 1397mg sod., 52g carb. (9g sugars, 5g fiber), 41g pro.

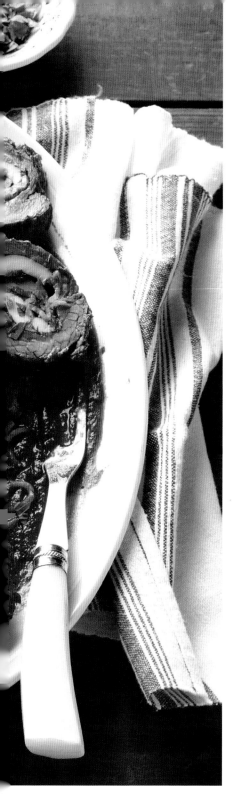

NANA'S ITALIAN ROULADE

My great-aunt from Sicily taught my mother how to stuff and bake a steak in a jelly-roll style. It's unique and really special in our family.

—Roseanne McDonald, Days Creek, OR

- -

Prep: 30 min. • **Cook:** 1½ hours
Makes: 8 servings

- 6 bacon strips
- 2 garlic cloves, minced
- ¾ tsp. Italian seasoning
- ½ tsp. salt
- ½ tsp. pepper
- 1 beef flank steak (1½ to 2 lbs.)
- ¼ cup grated Parmesan cheese
- 3 hard-boiled large eggs, sliced
- ¼ cup minced fresh parsley
- 2 Tbsp. olive oil
- 3 jars (24 oz. each)
  meatless pasta sauce
  Hot cooked spaghetti
  Additional minced fresh parsley

1. Preheat oven to 350°. Place bacon on a microwave-safe plate lined with paper towels. Cover with additional paper towels; microwave on high 3-5 minutes or until partially cooked but not crisp. In a small bowl, mix garlic, Italian seasoning, salt and pepper.

2. Starting with a long side, cut flank steak horizontally in half to within ½ in. of opposite side. Open steak flat; pound with a meat mallet to ¼-in. thickness.

3. Spread garlic mixture over steak; sprinkle with cheese. Layer with eggs and bacon to within 1 in. of edges; sprinkle with parsley. Starting with a long side of the steak, roll up jelly-roll style (along the grain); tie at 1½-in. intervals with kitchen string.

4. In a Dutch oven, heat oil over medium-high heat. Brown roulade on all sides. Pour pasta sauce over top. Bake, covered, for 1½-1¾ hours or until meat is tender.

5. Remove roulade from pot; remove string and cut into slices. Serve with sauce over spaghetti. Sprinkle with additional parsley.

1 slice with ¾ cup sauce: 331 cal., 15g fat (5g sat. fat), 119mg chol., 1491mg sod., 24g carb. (17g sugars, 4g fiber), 26g pro.

The French word *roulade* is the common term for steak rolled around a filling. In Italy, roulades are known as *involtini*. The name encompasses the style of dish, rather than the particular filling ingredients, leading to lots of interesting regional variations.

BEEF STEW SKILLET PIE

Puff pastry makes a pretty topping for this homey skillet potpie—and it's such an easy way to get a show-stopping result.
—Josh Rink, Milwaukee, WI

Prep: 1½ hours • **Bake:** 30 min. + standing
Makes: 6 servings

6	Tbsp. all-purpose flour, divided
1½	tsp. salt
½	tsp. pepper
1	lb. boneless beef round steak, cut into 1-in. pieces
2	Tbsp. canola oil
1	large onion, chopped
2	garlic cloves, minced
¼	cup dry red wine
2	cups beef broth, divided
1	Tbsp. tomato paste
½	tsp. Italian seasoning
½	tsp. dried basil
1	bay leaf
2	medium potatoes, cubed
3	large carrots, peeled and sliced
½	cup frozen peas
2	Tbsp. minced fresh parsley
1	sheet frozen puff pastry, thawed
1	large egg, beaten

1. In a large resealable container, combine 3 Tbsp. flour, salt and pepper. Add beef in batches; shake to coat. Invert a 10-in. ovenproof skillet onto parchment; trace circle around pan ¼ in. larger than rim. Cut out the parchment circle and set it aside. In same skillet, saute beef in oil until browned. Add onion and garlic; cook and stir until the onion is tender. Add wine, stirring to loosen browned bits.

2. Combine 1½ cups broth, tomato paste, Italian seasoning and basil; stir into skillet. Add bay leaf. Bring to a boil. Reduce heat; cover and simmer until the meat is tender, about 45 minutes. Add the potatoes and carrots; cook until vegetables are tender, 20-25 minutes longer.

3. Meanwhile, roll out puff pastry to fit the skillet using the parchment circle as a guide; cut venting slits in the pastry. Keep chilled until ready to use.

4. Combine the remaining flour and broth until smooth; gradually stir into the skillet. Bring to a boil; cook and stir for 2 minutes or until thickened and bubbly. Discard bay leaf. Stir in peas and parsley.

5. Brush beaten egg around edge of skillet to help the pastry adhere; carefully place pastry over filling. Using a fork, press pastry firmly onto rim of pan; brush with beaten egg. Bake pie at 425° until the pastry is dark golden brown, 30-35 minutes. Let stand for 10 minutes before serving.

1 slice: 473 cal., 19g fat (4g sat. fat), 73mg chol., 1088mg sod., 49g carb. (4g sugars, 6g fiber), 25g pro.

CABBAGE ROLL CASSEROLE

I layer cabbage with tomato sauce and beef to create a hearty casserole that tastes like cabbage rolls—but without all the work.
—Doreen Martin, Kitimat, BC

- -

Prep: 20 min. • **Bake:** 55 min.
Makes: 12 servings

- 2 lbs. ground beef
- 1 large onion, chopped
- 3 garlic cloves, minced
- 2 cans (15 oz. each) tomato sauce, divided
- 1 tsp. dried thyme
- ½ tsp. dill weed
- ½ tsp. rubbed sage
- ¼ tsp. salt
- ¼ tsp. pepper
- ¼ tsp. cayenne pepper
- 2 cups cooked rice
- 4 bacon strips, cooked and crumbled
- 1 medium head cabbage (2 lbs.), shredded
- 1 cup shredded part-skim mozzarella cheese
   Coarsely ground pepper, optional

1. Preheat oven to 375°. In a large skillet, cook beef and onion over medium heat, crumbling beef, until meat is no longer pink. Add garlic; cook 1 minute longer. Drain. Stir in 1 can tomato sauce and next 6 ingredients. Bring to a boil. Reduce heat; simmer, covered, 5 minutes. Stir in rice and bacon; remove from heat.

2. Layer a third of the cabbage in a greased 13x9-in. baking dish. Top with half the meat mixture. Repeat layers; top with remaining cabbage. Pour the remaining tomato sauce over top.

3. Cover and bake 45 minutes. Uncover; sprinkle with cheese. Bake until the cheese is melted, about 10 minutes. Let stand for 5 minutes before serving. If desired, sprinkle with coarsely ground pepper.

1 piece: 256 cal., 13g fat (5g sat. fat), 56mg chol., 544mg sod., 17g carb. (4g sugars, 3g fiber), 20g pro.

TEST KITCHEN TIP

Minimize mess by using 90% lean ground beef or ground sirloin (so you can skip the draining step) and use coleslaw mix (so you don't have to chop the cabbage).

CHILES RELLENOS CASSEROLE

I love green chiles and cook with them often when I entertain. This easy version of the classic Mexican dish gives you big chile pepper taste in every meaty bite.
—Nadine Estes, Alto, NM

- -

Prep: 15 min. • **Bake:** 45 min.
Makes: 6 servings

- 1   can (7 oz.) whole green chiles
- 1½ cups shredded Colby-Monterey Jack cheese
- ¾   lb. ground beef
- ¼   cup chopped onion
- 1   cup whole milk
- 4   large eggs
- ¼   cup all-purpose flour
- ¼   tsp. salt
- ⅛   tsp. pepper

1. Preheat oven to 350°. Split the chiles and remove seeds; dry on paper towels. Arrange chiles on the bottom of a greased 2-qt. baking dish. Top with cheese. In a skillet, cook beef and onion over medium heat until meat is no longer pink; drain. Spoon over the cheese.
2. In a bowl, beat the milk, eggs, flour, salt and pepper until smooth; pour over the beef mixture. Bake, uncovered, until a knife inserted in the center comes out clean, 45-50 minutes. Let stand 5 minutes before serving.
Note: Wear disposable gloves when cutting hot peppers; the oils can burn skin. Avoid touching your face.
1 piece: 321 cal., 20g fat (11g sat. fat), 212mg chol., 406mg sod., 9g carb. (3g sugars, 0 fiber), 24g pro.

TORTILLA PIE

My husband and I love this delicious dinner pie because it's lighter than traditional lasagnas made with pasta. Even our two young daughters get excited when I bring it to the table!
—Lisa King, Caledonia, MI

- -

Takes: 30 min. • **Makes:** 4 servings

- ½   lb. lean ground beef (90% lean)
- ½   cup chopped onion
- 2   garlic cloves, minced
- 1   tsp. chili powder
- ½   tsp. ground cumin
- 1   can (14½ oz.) Mexican diced tomatoes, drained
- ¾   cup reduced-fat ricotta cheese
- ¼   cup shredded part-skim mozzarella cheese
- 3   Tbsp. minced fresh cilantro, divided
- 4   whole wheat tortillas (8 in.)
- ½   cup shredded cheddar cheese

1. Preheat oven to 400°. In a large skillet, cook and crumble beef with onion and garlic over medium heat until no meat is longer pink, 4-6 minutes. Stir in spices and tomatoes. Bring to a boil; remove from heat. In a small bowl, mix ricotta cheese, mozzarella cheese and 2 Tbsp. cilantro.
2. Place a tortilla in a 9-in. round baking pan coated with cooking spray. Layer with half the meat sauce, a tortilla, ricotta mixture, another tortilla and remaining meat sauce. Top with remaining tortilla; sprinkle with cheddar cheese and the remaining cilantro.
3. Bake, covered, until heated through, 15-20 minutes.
1 serving: 356 cal., 14g fat (6g sat. fat), 65mg chol., 574mg sod., 32g carb. (7g sugars, 5g fiber), 25g pro. **Diabetic exchanges:** 3 medium-fat meat, 2 starch

BROCCOLI BEEF SUPPER

Broccoli is one of my favorite vegetables, so I'm constantly on the lookout for new ways of preparing it. This casserole is a great entree.
—Connie Bolton, San Antonio, TX

- -

Prep: 15 min. • **Bake:** 35 min.
Makes: 8 servings

- 4 cups frozen cottage fries
- 1 lb. ground beef
- 3 cups frozen chopped broccoli, thawed
- 1 can (2.8 oz.) french-fried onions, divided
- 1 medium tomato, chopped
- 1 can (10¾ oz.) condensed cream of celery soup, undiluted
- 1 cup shredded cheddar cheese, divided
- ½ cup 2% milk
- ¼ tsp. garlic powder
- ¼ tsp. pepper

1. Preheat oven to 400°. Line the bottom and sides of a greased 13x9-in. baking dish with cottage fries. Bake, uncovered, for 10 minutes.

2. Meanwhile, in a large skillet, cook beef over medium heat until no longer pink; drain. Layer the beef, broccoli, half the onions and the tomato over the fries. In a small bowl, combine the soup, ½ cup cheese, milk, garlic powder and pepper; pour over top.

3. Cover and bake for 20 minutes. Uncover; sprinkle with the remaining cheese and onions. Bake 2 minutes longer or until the cheese is melted.

1 cup: 420 cal., 22g fat (9g sat. fat), 46mg chol., 529mg sod., 40g carb. (3g sugars, 3g fiber), 18g pro.

SPAGHETTI SQUASH MEATBALL CASSEROLE

One of our favorite comfort food dinners is spaghetti and meatballs. We're crazy about this lightened-up, healthier version featuring so many veggies. The same beloved flavors with more nutritious ingredients!
—Courtney Stultz, Weir, KS

- -

Prep: 35 min. • **Bake:** 30 min.
Makes: 6 servings

- 1 **medium spaghetti squash (about 4 lbs.)**
- ½ **tsp. salt, divided**
- ½ **tsp. fennel seed**
- ¼ **tsp. ground coriander**
- ¼ **tsp. dried basil**
- ¼ **tsp. dried oregano**
- 1 **lb. lean ground beef (90% lean)**
- 2 **tsp. olive oil**
- 1 **medium onion, chopped**
- 1 **garlic clove, minced**
- 2 **cups chopped collard greens**
- 1 **cup chopped fresh spinach**
- 1 **cup reduced-fat ricotta cheese**
- 2 **plum tomatoes, chopped**
- 1 **cup pasta sauce**
- 1 **cup shredded part-skim mozzarella cheese**

1. Cut squash lengthwise in half; discard seeds. Place the halves on a microwave-safe plate, cut side down. Microwave, uncovered, on high until squash is tender, 15-20 minutes. Cool slightly.
2. Preheat oven to 350°. Mix ¼ tsp. salt with the remaining seasonings; add to the beef, mixing lightly but thoroughly. Shape into 1½-in. balls. In a large skillet, brown the meatballs over medium heat; remove from pan.
3. In same pan, heat oil over medium heat; saute onion until tender, 3-4 minutes. Add garlic; cook and stir 1 minute. Stir in collard greens, spinach, ricotta cheese and the remaining salt; remove from heat.
4. Using a fork, separate the strands of the spaghetti squash; stir into the greens mixture. Transfer to a greased 13x9-in. baking dish. Top with tomatoes, meatballs, sauce and cheese. Bake, uncovered, until the meatballs are cooked through, 30-35 minutes.

1 serving: 362 cal., 16g fat (6g sat. fat), 69mg chol., 618mg sod., 32g carb. (7g sugars, 7g fiber), 26g pro. **Diabetic exchanges:** 3 lean meat, 2 starch, 1 fat.

ULTIMATE POT ROAST

Pot roast recipes are the ultimate comfort food. When a juicy pot roast simmers in garlic, onions and veggies, everyone comes running to ask, "When can we eat?" The answer? "Just wait—it will be worth it!"
—Nick Iverson, Denver, CO

- -

Prep: 55 min. • **Bake:** 2 hours
Makes: 8 servings

- 1 boneless beef chuck-eye or other chuck roast (3 to 4 lbs.)
- 2 tsp. pepper
- 2 tsp. salt, divided
- 2 Tbsp. canola oil
- 2 medium onions, cut into 1-in. pieces
- 2 celery ribs, chopped
- 3 garlic cloves, minced
- 1 Tbsp. tomato paste
- 1 Tbsp. minced fresh thyme or 1 tsp. dried thyme
- 2 bay leaves
- 1 cup dry red wine or reduced-sodium beef broth
- 2 cups reduced-sodium beef broth
- 1 lb. small red potatoes, quartered
- 4 medium parsnips, peeled and cut into 2-in. pieces
- 6 medium carrots, cut into 2-in. pieces
- 1 Tbsp. red wine vinegar
- 2 Tbsp. minced fresh parsley
   Salt and pepper to taste

1. Preheat oven to 325°. Pat roast dry with a paper towel; tie at 2-in. intervals with kitchen string. Sprinkle with pepper and 1½ tsp. salt. In a Dutch oven, heat oil over medium-high heat. Brown roast on all sides. Remove from pot.
2. Add onions, celery and ½ tsp. salt to the same pot; cook and stir over medium heat 8-10 minutes or until onions are browned. Add garlic, tomato paste, thyme and bay leaves; cook and stir 1 minute longer.

3. Add wine, stirring to loosen browned bits from pot; stir in broth. Return roast to pot. Arrange potatoes, parsnips and carrots around roast; bring to a boil. Bake, covered, until meat is fork-tender, 2-2½ hours.
4. Remove roast and vegetables from pot; keep warm. Discard bay leaves; skim fat from cooking juices. On stovetop, bring juices to a boil; cook until liquid is reduced by half (about 1½ cups), 10-12 minutes. Stir in vinegar and parsley; season with salt and pepper to taste.
5. Remove string from roast. Serve with vegetables and sauce.
3 oz. cooked beef with 1 cup vegetables and 3 Tbsp. sauce: 459 cal., 20g fat (7g sat. fat), 112mg chol., 824mg sod., 32g carb. (8g sugars, 6g fiber), 37g pro.

TEST KITCHEN TIP

Chuck is the ideal cut for this type of low-and-slow braising because it has plenty of marbling and collagen. This translates to tenderness and flavor! Brisket is a good choice, too. Very lean cuts like rump and round roasts will work but will not be nearly as moist and fall-apart tender.

LAYERED BEEF CASSEROLE

With my busy days, I treasure meal-in-one recipes like this. Toss together a salad, and dinner is ready in no time at all.
—Dorothy Wiedeman, Eaton, CO

- -

Prep: 25 min. • **Bake:** 2 hours + standing
Makes: 8 servings

6   medium potatoes, peeled and thinly sliced
1   can (15¼ oz.) whole kernel corn, drained
½   cup chopped green pepper
1   cup chopped onion
2   cups sliced fresh carrots
1½ lbs. lean ground beef (90% lean)
1   can (8 oz.) tomato sauce
  Salt and pepper to taste
1   cup shredded process cheese (Velveeta)

1. Preheat oven to 350°. In a greased 13x9-in. baking dish, layer the potatoes, corn, green pepper, onion and carrots. Crumble beef over the vegetables. Pour tomato sauce over top. Sprinkle with salt and pepper.

2. Cover and bake for 2 hours or until the meat is no longer pink and a thermometer reads 160°. Sprinkle with cheese. Let stand for 10 minutes before serving.

Freeze option: Before baking, cover and freeze for up to 3 months. Thaw in the refrigerator overnight and bake as directed, increasing time as needed to reach 160°. Sprinkle with cheese before serving.

1 serving: 341 cal., 11g fat (5g sat. fat), 64mg chol., 526mg sod., 35g carb. (8g sugars, 4g fiber), 23g pro.

TEST KITCHEN TIP

Rather than baking in one pan to serve eight, this casserole can be divided between two 1½ qt. baking dishes. Bake one to enjoy now and freeze the other for another meal.

PINWHEEL STEAK POTPIE

On cool nights, nothing hits the spot like a steaming homemade potpie— especially one you can get on the table so quickly. The pinwheel crust on top has become my signature.
—Kristin Shaw, Castleton, NY

- -

Prep: 25 min. • **Bake:** 20 min.
Makes: 6 servings

- 2 Tbsp. butter
- 1¼ lbs. beef top sirloin steak, cut into ½-in. cubes
- ¼ tsp. pepper
- 1 pkg. (16 oz.) frozen vegetables for stew
- 2 Tbsp. water
- ½ tsp. dried thyme
- 1 jar (12 oz.) mushroom or beef gravy
- 1 tube (8 oz.) refrigerated crescent rolls

1. Preheat oven to 375°. In a 10-in. cast-iron or other ovenproof skillet, heat butter over medium-high heat. Brown beef in batches; remove from pan. Sprinkle with pepper; keep warm.
2. In the same skillet, combine vegetables, water and thyme; stir in gravy. Bring to a boil. Reduce heat; simmer, uncovered, until the vegetables are thawed. Stir in beef; remove from heat.
3. Unroll crescent dough and separate into 8 triangles. Starting from the wide end of each triangle, roll up a third of the length and place over the beef mixture with the pointed end toward the center.
4. Bake, uncovered, until golden brown, 16-18 minutes.
1 piece: 365 cal., 18g fat (6g sat. fat), 67mg chol., 716mg sod., 29g carb. (4g sugars, 1g fiber), 22g pro.

REUBEN BREAD PUDDING

Our Aunt Renee always brought this casserole to family picnics in Chicago. It became so popular that she started bringing two or three. I have also made it using dark rye bread or marbled rye, and ham instead of corned beef—all the variations are delicious!
—Johnna Johnson, Scottsdale, AZ

- -

Prep: 20 min. • **Bake:** 35 min.
Makes: 6 servings

- 4 cups cubed rye bread (about 6 slices)
- 2 Tbsp. butter, melted
- 2 cups cubed or shredded cooked corned beef (about ½ lb.)
- 1 can (14 oz.) sauerkraut, rinsed and well drained
- 1 cup shredded Swiss cheese, divided
- 3 large eggs
- 1 cup 2% milk
- ⅓ cup prepared Thousand Island salad dressing
- 1½ tsp. prepared mustard
- ¼ tsp. pepper

1. Preheat oven to 350°. In a large bowl, toss bread cubes with butter. Stir in corned beef, sauerkraut and ½ cup Swiss cheese; transfer to a greased 11x7-in. baking dish.
2. In the same bowl, whisk eggs, milk, salad dressing, mustard and pepper; pour over top. Bake, uncovered, 30 minutes. Sprinkle with remaining cheese. Bake until golden and a knife inserted in the center comes out clean, 5-7 minutes longer.
1 piece: 390 cal., 25g fat (10g sat. fat), 165mg chol., 1295mg sod., 21g carb. (7g sugars, 3g fiber), 19g pro.

Chicken & Turkey

ARTICHOKE RATATOUILLE CHICKEN

I loaded all the fresh produce I could find into this speedy chicken dinner. Serve it on its own or over pasta.
—Judy Armstrong, Prairieville, LA

Prep: 25 min. • **Bake:** 1 hour
Makes: 6 servings

- 3 Japanese eggplants (about 1 lb.)
- 4 plum tomatoes
- 1 medium sweet yellow pepper
- 1 medium sweet red pepper
- 1 medium onion
- 1 can (14 oz.) water-packed artichoke hearts, drained and quartered
- 2 Tbsp. minced fresh thyme
- 2 Tbsp. capers, drained
- 2 Tbsp. olive oil
- 2 garlic cloves, minced
- 1 tsp. Creole seasoning, divided
- 1½ lbs. boneless skinless chicken breasts, cubed
- 1 cup white wine or chicken broth
- ¼ cup grated Asiago cheese
  Hot cooked pasta, optional

1. Preheat oven to 350°. Cut eggplants, tomatoes, peppers and onion into ¾-in. pieces; transfer to a large bowl. Stir in artichoke hearts, thyme, capers, oil, garlic and ½ tsp. Creole seasoning.
2. Sprinkle chicken with the remaining Creole seasoning. Transfer chicken to a 13x9-in. baking dish coated with cooking spray; spoon the vegetable mixture over top. Drizzle wine over the vegetables.
3. Bake, covered, for 30 minutes. Uncover; bake until the chicken is no longer pink and the vegetables are tender, 30-45 minutes longer. Sprinkle with cheese. If desired, serve with pasta.

1⅔ cups: 252 cal., 9g fat (2g sat. fat), 67mg chol., 468mg sod., 15g carb. (4g sugars, 4g fiber), 28g pro. **Diabetic exchanges:** 3 lean meat, 1 starch, 1 fat.

SPINACH & CHICKEN PHYLLO PIE

For a showstopper, we make chicken pie with crispy layers of phyllo pastry and spinach. Even our kids go for it. It's so good served with a minty fruit salad.
—Katie Ferrier, Houston, TX

Prep: 35 min. • **Bake:** 35 min.
Makes: 8 servings

- 2 lbs. ground chicken
- 1 large onion, chopped
- 1 tsp. pepper
- 1 tsp. dried oregano
- ¾ tsp. salt
- ½ tsp. ground nutmeg
- ¼ tsp. crushed red pepper flakes
- 3 pkg. (10 oz. each) frozen chopped spinach, thawed and squeezed dry
- 4 large eggs, lightly beaten
- 3 cups crumbled feta cheese
- 20 sheets phyllo dough (14x9-in. size)
  Cooking spray

1. Preheat oven to 375°. In a large skillet, cook the ground chicken and onion over medium-high heat 7-9 minutes or until the chicken is no longer pink, breaking up meat into crumbles; drain. Stir in the seasonings. Add spinach; cook and stir until liquid is evaporated. Transfer to a large bowl; cool slightly. Stir in beaten eggs and cheese.
2. Layer 10 sheets phyllo dough in a greased 13x9-in. baking dish, spritzing each with cooking spray. (Keep remaining phyllo dough covered with a damp towel to prevent it from drying out.) Spread the spinach mixture over phyllo. Top with remaining sheets of phyllo, spritzing each with cooking spray. Cut into 8 rectangles.
3. Bake, uncovered, 35-40 minutes or until golden brown. If necessary, recut rectangles before serving.

1 piece: 442 cal., 23g fat (8g sat. fat), 191mg chol., 921mg sod., 25g carb. (3g sugars, 6g fiber), 35g pro.

CHICKEN CHILES RELLENOS STRATA

This versatile dish can be made as an entree, brunch or potluck dish. It's also one of the easiest meals to assemble on a busy weeknight.
—Kallee Krong-McCreery, Escondido, CA

Prep: 20 min. + chilling
Bake: 35 min. + standing
Makes: 10 servings

- 6 cups cubed French bread (about 6 oz.)
- 2 cans (4 oz. each) chopped green chiles
- 2 cups shredded Monterey Jack cheese
- 2 cups shredded cooked chicken
- 12 large eggs
- 1½ cups 2% milk
- 2 tsp. baking powder
- 1 tsp. garlic salt
- 1 cup shredded cheddar cheese
  Salsa

1. In a greased 13x9-in. baking dish, layer half of each of the following: bread cubes, chiles, Monterey Jack cheese and chicken. Repeat the layers.

2. In a large bowl, whisk eggs, milk, baking powder and garlic salt until blended. Pour over the layers. Sprinkle with cheddar cheese. Refrigerate, covered, overnight.

3. Preheat oven to 350°. Remove strata from refrigerator while oven heats. Bake, uncovered, 35-40 minutes or until puffed and golden at edges. Let stand 10 minutes before serving. Serve with salsa.

1 piece: 338 cal., 20g fat (9g sat. fat), 282mg chol., 820mg sod., 13g carb. (3g sugars, 1g fiber), 27g pro.

CHICKEN-STUFFED CUBANELLE PEPPERS

Here's a new take on traditional stuffed peppers. I substituted chicken for the beef and used Cubanelle peppers in place of the usual green peppers.
—Bev Burlingame, Canton, OH

- -

Prep: 20 min. • **Bake:** 1 hour
Makes: 6 servings

- 6 Cubanelle peppers or mild banana peppers
- 2 large eggs, lightly beaten
- 3 cups shredded cooked chicken breast
- 1 cup salsa
- ¾ cup soft bread crumbs
- ½ cup cooked long grain rice
- 2 cups meatless pasta sauce

1. Preheat oven to 350°. Cut and discard tops from peppers; remove seeds. In a large bowl, mix eggs, chicken, salsa, bread crumbs and rice. Spoon into the peppers.
2. Spread pasta sauce onto bottom of a 13x9-in. baking dish coated with cooking spray. Top with peppers. Bake, covered, 60-65 minutes or until the peppers are tender and a thermometer inserted in stuffing reads at least 165°.
Note: To make soft bread crumbs, tear bread into pieces and place in a food processor or blender. Cover and pulse until crumbs form. A slice of bread yields ½-¾ cup crumbs.
1 stuffed pepper: 230 cal., 4g fat (1g sat. fat), 125mg chol., 661mg sod., 20g carb. (7g sugars, 5g fiber), 26g pro. **Diabetic exchanges:** 3 lean meat, 2 vegetable, 1 starch.

CURRIED CHICKEN TURNOVERS

Whenever I have leftover chicken, these turnovers are on the menu. The tasty secret is in the curry.
—Laverne Kohut, Manning, AB

- -

Prep: 30 min. • **Bake:** 15 min.
Makes: 8 servings

- 1 cup finely chopped cooked chicken
- 1 medium apple, peeled and finely chopped
- ½ cup mayonnaise
- ¼ cup chopped cashews or peanuts
- 1 green onion, finely chopped
- 1 to 2 tsp. curry powder
- ¼ tsp. salt
- ¼ tsp. pepper
  Pastry for double-crust pie
- 1 large egg, lightly beaten

1. Preheat oven to 425°. In a small bowl, combine the first 8 ingredients.
2. Divide pastry dough into 8 portions. On a lightly floured surface, roll each portion into a 5-in. circle. Place about ¼ cup filling on 1 side of each circle. Moisten the edges of each with water. Fold the crust over the filling; press edges with a fork to seal.
3. Place turnovers on greased baking sheets. Brush with egg. Cut ½-in. slits in the top of each. Bake 15-20 minutes or until golden brown.
Pastry for double-crust pie (9 in.): Combine 2½ cups all-purpose flour and ½ tsp. salt; cut in 1 cup cold butter until crumbly. Gradually add ⅓-⅔ cup ice water, tossing with a fork until dough holds together when pressed. Wrap dough and refrigerate 1 hour.
1 turnover: 512 cal., 37g fat (17g sat. fat), 101mg chol., 526mg sod., 34g carb. (2g sugars, 2g fiber), 11g pro.

CRANBERRY CHICKEN & WILD RICE

This tender chicken in a sweet-tart cranberry sauce is delicious, and it's so easy to prepare. I love that I can do other things while it bakes.
—Evelyn Lewis, Independence, MO

Prep: 10 min. • **Bake:** 35 min.
Makes: 6 servings

- 6 boneless skinless chicken breast halves (4 oz. each)
- 1½ cups hot water
- 1 pkg. (6.2 oz.) fast-cooking long grain and wild rice mix
- 1 can (14 oz.) whole-berry cranberry sauce
- 1 Tbsp. lemon juice
- 1 Tbsp. reduced-sodium soy sauce
- 1 Tbsp. Worcestershire sauce

1. Preheat oven to 350°. Place chicken in a 13x9-in. baking dish coated with cooking spray. In a bowl, mix hot water, rice mix and contents of the seasoning packet; pour around chicken.
2. In a small bowl, mix the remaining ingredients; pour over chicken. Bake, covered, until a thermometer inserted in chicken reads 165°, 35-45 minutes.

1 chicken breast half with ½ cup rice mixture: 332 cal., 3g fat (1g sat. fat), 63mg chol., 592mg sod., 50g carb. (19g sugars, 2g fiber), 26g pro.

CHICKEN ZUCCHINI CASSEROLE

A co-worker shared this recipe—it was originally her grandmother's. When I make it, I use rotisserie chicken from the grocery store and fresh zucchini my neighbor gives me from his garden.
—Bev Dutro, Dayton, OH

Prep: 20 min. • **Bake:** 45 min.
Makes: 6 servings

- 1 pkg. (6 oz.) stuffing mix
- ¾ cup butter, melted
- 3 cups diced zucchini
- 2 cups cubed cooked chicken breast
- 1 can (10¾ oz.) condensed cream of chicken soup, undiluted
- 1 medium carrot, shredded
- ½ cup chopped onion
- ½ cup sour cream

1. Preheat oven to 350°. In a large bowl, combine the stuffing mix and butter. Set aside ½ cup stuffing mixture for the topping. Add zucchini, chicken, soup, carrot, onion and sour cream to the remaining stuffing mixture.
2. Transfer to a greased 11x7-in. baking dish. Sprinkle with the reserved stuffing mixture. Bake, uncovered, until golden brown and bubbly, 40-45 minutes.

1 cup: 481 cal., 31g fat (18g sat. fat), 115mg chol., 1174mg sod., 27g carb. (6g sugars, 2g fiber), 21g pro.

CITRUS-HERB ROAST CHICKEN

This dish is one of my all-time favorites...
flavorful, juicy chicken with the aromas
of spring: fresh herbs, lemon and spring
onions. It's the perfect one-pot meal.
I make the gravy right in the pan, too.
—Megan Fordyce, Fairchance, PA

- -

Prep: 25 min. • **Bake:** 2 hours + standing
Makes: 8 servings

6   garlic cloves
1   roasting chicken (6 to 7 lbs.)
3   lbs. baby red potatoes, halved
6   medium carrots, halved lengthwise
     and cut into 1-in. pieces
4   fresh thyme sprigs
4   fresh dill sprigs
2   fresh rosemary sprigs
1   medium lemon
1   small navel orange
1   tsp. salt
½   tsp. pepper
3   cups chicken broth, warmed
6   green onions, cut into 2-in. pieces

1. Preheat oven to 350°. Peel garlic and
cut into quarters. Place chicken on cutting
board. Tuck wings under chicken. With a
sharp paring knife, cut 24 small slits in the
breasts, drumsticks and thighs. Insert garlic
in the slits. Tie drumsticks together.
2. Place potatoes and carrots in a shallow
roasting pan; top with herbs. Place chicken,
breast side up, over the vegetables and
herbs. Cut the lemon and orange in half;
gently squeeze juices over the chicken and
vegetables. Place the squeezed fruits inside
the chicken cavity. Sprinkle chicken with
salt and pepper. Pour broth around chicken.
3. Roast until a thermometer inserted in
the thickest part of thigh reads 170°-175°,
about 2-2½ hours, sprinkling green onions
over vegetables during the last 20 minutes.
(Cover loosely with foil if chicken browns
too quickly.)
4. Remove chicken from oven; tent with
foil. Let stand 5 minutes before carving.
Discard herbs. If desired, skim the fat and
thicken pan drippings for gravy. Serve with
chicken and vegetables.
**7 oz. cooked chicken with 1¼ cups
vegetables:** 561 cal., 24g fat (7g sat. fat),
136mg chol., 826mg sod., 39g carb.
(5g sugars, 5g fiber), 47g pro.

BAKED CHICKEN FAJITAS

I can't remember when or where I found this recipe, but I've used it nearly every week since. We like it with hot sauce for added spice.

—Amy Trinkle, Milwaukee, WI

- -

Prep: 15 min. • **Bake:** 20 min.
Makes: 6 servings

- 1 lb. boneless skinless chicken breasts, cut into thin strips
- 1 can (14½ oz.) diced tomatoes and green chiles, drained
- 1 medium onion, cut into thin strips
- 1 medium green pepper, cut into thin strips
- 1 medium sweet red pepper, cut into thin strips
- 2 Tbsp. canola oil
- 2 tsp. chili powder
- 2 tsp. ground cumin
- ¼ tsp. salt
- 12 flour tortillas (6 in.), warmed
  Optional toppings: Sliced avocado, tomato wedges and lime wedges

1. Preheat oven to 400°. In a 13x9-in. baking dish coated with cooking spray, combine the chicken, tomatoes, onion and peppers. Combine oil, chili powder, cumin and salt. Drizzle over chicken mixture; toss to coat.
2. Bake, uncovered, for 20-25 minutes or until the chicken is no longer pink and the vegetables are tender. Spoon onto tortillas; fold or roll tortillas to serve. If desired, serve with optional toppings.
2 fajitas: 375 cal., 14g fat (3g sat. fat), 42mg chol., 838mg sod., 40g carb. (3g sugars, 5g fiber), 22g pro.

CHICKEN & RICE CASSEROLE

Everyone loves this casserole because it's a tasty combination of hearty and crunchy ingredients mixed in a creamy sauce. It's a time-tested classic.

—Myrtle Matthews, Marietta, GA

- -

Prep: 15 min. • **Bake:** 1 hour
Makes: 12 servings

- 4 cups cooked white rice or a combination of wild and white rice
- 4 cups diced cooked chicken
- ½ cup slivered almonds
- 1 small onion, chopped
- 1 can (8 oz.) sliced water chestnuts, drained
- 1 pkg. (10 oz.) frozen peas, thawed
- ¾ cup chopped celery
- 1 can (10¾ oz.) condensed cream of celery soup, undiluted
- 1 can (10¾ oz.) condensed cream of chicken soup, undiluted
- 1 cup mayonnaise
- 2 tsp. lemon juice
- 1 tsp. salt
- 2 cups crushed potato chips
  Paprika

1. Preheat oven to 350°. In a greased 13x9-in. baking dish, combine the first 7 ingredients. In a large bowl, combine soups, mayonnaise, lemon juice and salt. Pour over chicken mixture and toss to coat.
2. Sprinkle with potato chips and paprika. Bake until heated through, about 1 hour.
1 cup: 439 cal., 26g fat (5g sat. fat), 51mg chol., 804mg sod., 31g carb. (3g sugars, 3g fiber), 19g pro.

LEMONY CHICKEN & RICE

I couldn't say who loves this recipe best, because every time I serve it, it gets raves! Occasionally I even get a phone call or email from a friend requesting the recipe, and it's certainly a favorite for my grown children and 15 grandchildren.

—Maryalice Wood, Langley, BC

- -

Prep: 15 min. + marinating • **Bake:** 55 min.
Makes: 2 casseroles (4 servings each)

2	**cups water**
½	**cup reduced-sodium soy sauce**
¼	**cup lemon juice**
¼	**cup olive oil**
2	**garlic cloves, minced**
2	**tsp. ground ginger**
2	**tsp. pepper**
16	**bone-in chicken thighs, skin removed (about 6 lbs.)**
2	**cups uncooked long grain rice**
4	**Tbsp. grated lemon zest, divided**
2	**medium lemons, sliced**

1. In a large shallow dish, combine the first 7 ingredients. Add chicken thighs; turn to coat and cover. Refrigerate for 4 hours or overnight.

2. Preheat oven to 325°. Spread 1 cup rice into each of 2 greased 13x9-in. baking dishes. Top each with 1 Tbsp. lemon zest, 8 chicken thighs and half the marinade. Top with sliced lemons.

3. Bake, covered, for 40 minutes. Bake, uncovered, until a thermometer inserted in chicken reads 170°-175°, 15-20 minutes longer. Sprinkle with remaining lemon zest.

2 chicken thighs with ¾ cup rice mixture: 624 cal., 26g fat (6g sat. fat), 173mg chol., 754mg sod., 41g carb. (1g sugars, 1g fiber), 53g pro.

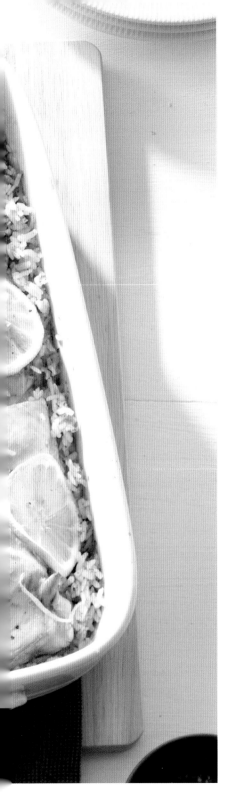

VEGETABLE CHICKEN

I adapted a recipe for one of my favorite all-vegetable dishes by adding chicken. Now it's a mouthwatering main meal.
—Dorothy McGrew Hood, Northbrook, IL

- -

Prep: 20 min. • **Bake:** 1½ hours
Makes: 4 servings

- 1 broiler/fryer chicken (3½ to 4 lbs.), cut up and skin removed
- 2 cups sliced celery
- 2 cups fresh or frozen cut green beans
- 1½ cups sliced carrots
- 1 large onion, sliced
- 1 small zucchini, diced
- 1 can (14½ oz.) diced tomatoes, undrained
- 3 Tbsp. quick-cooking tapioca
- 1 Tbsp. sugar
- 2 tsp. salt, optional
- ½ tsp. pepper

1. Preheat oven to 350°. Place the chicken, celery, green beans, carrots and onion in an ungreased 13-x-9-in. baking dish.
2. In a small bowl, combine the zucchini, tomatoes, tapioca, sugar, salt if desired and pepper. Pour over chicken and vegetables.
3. Cover tightly and bake until the chicken juices run clear and the vegetable mixture thickens, about 1½ hours. Stir vegetables occasionally during baking.

14 oz. cooked chicken and vegetables: 242 cal., 4g fat (0 sat. fat), 62mg chol., 298mg sod., 27g carb. (0 sugars, 0 fiber), 25g pro. **Diabetic exchanges:** 3 lean meat, 3 vegetable.

MEXICALI CASSEROLE

Kids gobble up this satisfying Mexican-style supper. It's mild enough for them and seasoned enough for anyone.
—Gertrudis Miller, Evansville, IN

- -

Prep: 15 min. • **Bake:** 55 min.
Makes: 6 servings

- 1 lb. lean ground turkey
- 2 medium onions, chopped
- 1 small green pepper, chopped
- 1 garlic clove, minced
- 1 can (16 oz.) kidney beans, rinsed and drained
- 1 can (14½ oz.) diced tomatoes, undrained
- 1 cup water
- ⅔ cup uncooked long grain rice
- ⅓ cup sliced ripe olives
- 1 tsp. chili powder
- ½ tsp. salt
- ½ cup shredded reduced-fat cheddar cheese

1. Preheat oven to 375°. In a large skillet coated with cooking spray, cook turkey, onions and pepper over medium heat until the meat is no longer pink and the vegetables are tender, breaking up turkey into crumbles, 6-8 minutes. Add garlic; cook 1 minute longer. Drain. Stir in beans, tomatoes, water, rice, sliced olives, chili powder and salt.
2. Transfer to an 11x7-in. baking dish coated with cooking spray. Bake, covered, until the rice is tender, 50-55 minutes. Sprinkle with cheese. Bake, uncovered, until the cheese is melted, about 5 minutes longer.

1 serving: 331 cal., 9g fat (3g sat. fat), 59mg chol., 604mg sod., 38g carb. (5g sugars, 6g fiber), 25g pro. **Diabetic exchanges:** 3 lean meat, 2 starch, 2 vegetable.

INDIAN BAKED CHICKEN

Cumin and turmeric give this hearty entree just the right amount of Indian flavor, but it still appeals to picky eaters in the bunch.
—Stephanie Kurin, Muncie, IN

Prep: 15 min. • **Bake:** 1 hour
Makes: 6 servings

- 1 lb. small red potatoes, quartered
- 4 medium carrots, cut into 1-in. pieces
- 1 large onion, cut into 1-in. pieces
- 6 boneless skinless chicken thighs (about 1½ lbs.)
- 1 can (14½ oz.) chicken broth
- 1 can (6 oz.) tomato paste
- 2 Tbsp. olive oil
- 1 Tbsp. ground turmeric
- 1 tsp. chili powder
- 1 tsp. ground cumin
- ½ tsp. salt
- ½ tsp. garlic powder
- ½ tsp. pepper

1. Preheat oven to 400°. Place potatoes, carrots and onion in a greased 13x9-in. baking dish; add chicken. In a small bowl, combine the remaining ingredients and pour over top.
2. Cover and bake for 1-1¼ hours or until a thermometer inserted into chicken reads 180° and the vegetables are tender.
1 serving: 323 cal., 13g fat (3g sat. fat), 77mg chol., 612mg sod., 25g carb. (7g sugars, 4g fiber), 25g pro. **Diabetic exchanges:** 3 lean meat, 2 vegetable, 1 starch, 1 fat.

CRESCENT TURKEY CASSEROLE

How do you make a dinner of turkey and vegetables appealing to kids? You turn it into a pie, of course! My version tastes classic, but won't take much time at all.
—Daniela Essman, Perham, MN

Takes: 30 min. • **Makes:** 4 servings

- ½ cup mayonnaise
- 2 Tbsp. all-purpose flour
- 1 tsp. chicken bouillon granules
- ⅛ tsp. pepper
- ¾ cup 2% milk
- 2 cups frozen mixed vegetables (about 10 oz.), thawed
- 1½ cups cubed cooked turkey breast
- 1 tube (4 oz.) refrigerated crescent rolls

1. Preheat oven to 375°. In a saucepan, mix first 4 ingredients until smooth; gradually stir in milk. Bring to a boil over medium heat; cook and stir until thickened, about 2 minutes. Add vegetables and turkey; cook and stir until heated through. Transfer to a greased 8-in. square baking pan.
2. Unroll the crescent dough and separate into 8 triangles; arrange over the turkey mixture. Bake until the casserole is heated through and the topping is golden brown, 15-20 minutes.
1 piece: 453 cal., 28g fat (6g sat. fat), 48mg chol., 671mg sod., 26g carb. (7g sugars, 3g fiber), 22g pro.
Turkey Biscuit Potpie: Thaw vegetables; combine in a bowl with turkey breast, one 10¾-oz. can condensed cream of chicken soup and ¼ tsp. dried thyme. Place in a deep-dish 9-in. pie plate. Mix 1 cup biscuit/baking mix, ½ cup milk and 1 egg; spoon over top. Bake at 400° for 25-30 minutes.
Turkey Asparagus Casserole: Thaw a 10-oz. package of frozen cut asparagus; combine in a bowl with turkey breast, one 10¾-oz. can condensed cream of chicken soup and ¼ cup water. Bake at 350° for 30 minutes, topping with a 2.8-oz. can french-fried onions during last 5 minutes.

LEMONY ROASTED CHICKEN & POTATOES

This one-dish meal tastes like it needs hours of hands-on time to put together, but it's just minutes to prep the simple ingredients. The meat juices cook the veggies to perfection.
—Sherri Melotik, Oak Creek, WI

- -

Prep: 20 min. • **Bake:** 40 min.
Makes: 4 servings

1½ lbs. red potatoes
    (about 5 medium),
    cut into ¾-in. cubes
1 large onion, coarsely chopped
1 medium lemon, halved and sliced
3 Tbsp. olive oil, divided
3 garlic cloves, minced
1¼ tsp. salt, divided
1 tsp. dried rosemary,
    crushed, divided
1 tsp. pepper, divided

4 bone-in chicken thighs
    (about 1½ lbs.)
4 chicken drumsticks (about 1 lb.)
1 tsp. paprika
6 cups fresh baby spinach
    (about 5 oz.)
Lemon wedges, optional

1. Preheat oven to 425°. Place potatoes, onion and sliced lemon in a large bowl; toss with 2 Tbsp. oil, garlic and ½ tsp. each salt, rosemary and pepper. Spread evenly in a greased roasting pan. Roast on an upper oven rack for 20 minutes.
2. Meanwhile, toss chicken with paprika and the remaining salt, rosemary and pepper. In a large skillet, heat the remaining oil over medium-high heat. Brown chicken in batches.
3. Place chicken over the potato mixture. Roast until a thermometer inserted in chicken reads 170° and the potatoes are tender, 15-20 minutes. Remove chicken from pan. Immediately add spinach to vegetables, stirring to wilt slightly. Serve with chicken and, if desired, lemon wedges.
1 serving: 589 cal., 31g fat (7g sat. fat), 128mg chol., 898mg sod., 35g carb. (4g sugars, 5g fiber), 42g pro.

The red potatoes add nice color to this dish, but you can use others. Try Yukon gold or fingerling potatoes—any low-starch, high-moisture potato will do!

THAI PEANUT CHICKEN CASSEROLE

I used traditional pizza sauce and toppings in this recipe for years. After becoming a fan of Thai peanut chicken pizza, I decided to use those flavors instead. Serve with stir-fried vegetables or a salad with sesame dressing for an easy, delicious meal.
—Katherine Wollgast, Troy, MO

- -

Prep: 30 min. • **Bake:** 30 min.
Makes: 10 servings

- 2 tubes (12 oz. each) refrigerated buttermilk biscuits
- 3 cups shredded cooked chicken
- 1 cup sliced fresh mushrooms
- 1 bottle (11½ oz.) Thai peanut sauce, divided
- 2 cups shredded mozzarella cheese, divided
- ½ cup chopped sweet red pepper
- ½ cup shredded carrot
- 4 green onions, sliced
- ¼ cup honey-roasted peanuts, coarsely chopped

1. Preheat oven to 350°. Cut each biscuit into 4 pieces. Place in a greased 13x9-in. baking pan.
2. In a large bowl, combine the chicken, mushrooms and 1 cup peanut sauce; spread over the biscuits. Top with 1 cup cheese, red pepper, carrot and green onions. Sprinkle with the remaining cheese.
3. Bake until the topping is set, cheese is melted and the biscuits have cooked all the way through, about 40 minutes. Sprinkle with peanuts and serve with the remaining peanut sauce.
1 serving: 490 cal., 25g fat (8g sat. fat), 55mg chol., 1013mg sod., 43g carb. (13g sugars, 1g fiber), 26g pro.

MAPLE-ROASTED CHICKEN & ACORN SQUASH

When I became a new mother, my mom helped me find comforting recipes to have on hand. This one was a happy discovery!
—Sara Eilers, Surprise, AZ

- -

Prep: 15 min. • **Bake:** 35 min.
Makes: 6 servings

- 1 medium acorn squash
- 4 medium carrots, chopped (about 2 cups)
- 1 medium onion, cut into 1-in. pieces
- 6 bone-in chicken thighs (about 2¼ lbs.)
- ½ cup maple syrup
- 1 tsp. salt
- ½ tsp. coarsely ground pepper

1. Preheat oven to 450°. Cut squash lengthwise in half; remove and discard seeds. Cut each half crosswise into ½-in. slices; discard ends. Place squash, carrots and onion in a greased 13x9-in. baking pan; top with chicken, skin side down. Roast 10 minutes.
2. Turn chicken over; drizzle with maple syrup and sprinkle with salt and pepper. Roast 25-30 minutes longer or until a thermometer inserted in chicken reads 170°-175° and the vegetables are tender.
1 serving: 363 cal., 14g fat (4g sat. fat), 81mg chol., 497mg sod., 36g carb. (23g sugars, 3g fiber), 24g pro. **Diabetic exchanges:** 3 lean meat, 2 starch, 1 vegetable.

FAVORITE COMPANY CASSEROLE

Even my friends who don't eat a lot of broccoli or mushrooms admit that this casserole is a winner. It's so easy to throw together, and the leftovers are fabulous.
—Suzann Verdun, Lisle, IL

- -

Prep: 15 min. • **Bake:** 45 min.
Makes: 8 servings

- 1 pkg. (6 oz.) wild rice, cooked
- 3 cups frozen chopped broccoli, thawed
- 1½ cups cubed cooked chicken
- 1 cup cubed cooked ham
- 1 cup shredded cheddar cheese
- 1 jar (4½ oz.) sliced mushrooms, drained
- 1 cup mayonnaise
- 1 tsp. prepared mustard
- ½ to 1 tsp. curry powder
- 1 can (10¾ oz.) condensed cream of mushroom soup, undiluted
- ¼ cup grated Parmesan cheese

1. Preheat oven to 350°. In a greased 2-qt. baking dish, layer the first 6 ingredients in order listed. Combine mayonnaise, mustard, curry and soup. Spread over top. Sprinkle with Parmesan cheese.
2. Bake, uncovered, 45-60 minutes or until top is light golden brown.

1 cup: 405 cal., 32g fat (8g sat. fat), 61mg chol., 872mg sod., 11g carb. (1g sugars, 2g fiber), 18g pro.

ROASTED CHICKEN THIGHS WITH PEPPERS & POTATOES

My family loves this fragrant dish! Fresh peppers and herbs from the garden make the chicken and potatoes special.
—Patricia Prescott, Manchester, NH

Prep: 20 min. • **Bake:** 35 min.
Makes: 8 servings

2	lbs. red potatoes (about 6 medium)
2	large sweet red peppers
2	large green peppers
2	medium onions
2	Tbsp. olive oil, divided
4	tsp. minced fresh thyme or 1½ tsp. dried thyme, divided
3	tsp. minced fresh rosemary or 1 tsp. dried rosemary, crushed, divided
8	boneless skinless chicken thighs (about 2 lbs.)
½	tsp. salt
¼	tsp. pepper

1. Preheat oven to 450°. Cut the potatoes, peppers and onions into 1-in. pieces. Place vegetables in a roasting pan. Drizzle with 1 Tbsp. oil; sprinkle with 2 tsp. each thyme and rosemary and toss to coat. Place the chicken over vegetables. Brush chicken with remaining oil; sprinkle with remaining thyme and rosemary. Sprinkle the vegetables and chicken with salt and pepper.

2. Roast until a thermometer inserted in chicken reads 170° and vegetables are tender, 35-40 minutes.

1 chicken thigh with 1 cup vegetables:
308 cal., 12g fat (3g sat. fat), 76mg chol., 221mg sod., 25g carb. (5g sugars, 4g fiber), 24g pro. **Diabetic exchanges:** 3 lean meat, 1 starch, 1 vegetable, ½ fat.

TEST KITCHEN TIP

Common olive oil works better for roasting at high heat than extra-virgin olive oil. If you don't want the flavor of olive oil, try a mild, neutral cooking oil, like vegetable, canola or grapeseed. Avoid coconut oil; its smoke point is much lower than this high roasting temperature, so it might add a burnt or bitter taste to food.

CHEDDAR CHICKEN POTPIE

Cheese soup is one of my favorites, but it's a bit too rich for my husband's taste. Now I make a variation of potpie we both enjoy. If I'm in a hurry, I'll skip the crust, add extra milk and serve it as a chowder.
—Sandra Cothran, Ridgeland, SC

- -

Prep: 30 min. • **Bake:** 40 min.
Makes: 6 servings

CRUST
- 1 cup all-purpose flour
- ½ tsp. salt
- 5 Tbsp. cold butter, cubed
- 3 Tbsp. cold water

FILLING
- 1½ cups chicken broth
- 2 cups peeled cubed potatoes
- 1 cup sliced carrots
- ½ cup sliced celery
- ½ cup chopped onion
- ¼ cup all-purpose flour
- 1½ cups whole milk
- 2 cups shredded sharp cheddar cheese
- 4 cups cubed cooked chicken
- ¼ tsp. poultry seasoning
  Salt and pepper to taste

1. To make the crust, in a small bowl, combine flour and salt. Cut in butter until the mixture resembles coarse crumbs. Gradually add water, mixing gently with a fork. Gather into a ball. Cover and chill at least 30 minutes.
2. Preheat oven to 425°. To make the filling, pour chicken broth in a Dutch oven; bring to a boil over high heat. Add vegetables. Reduce heat; simmer until the vegetables are tender, 10-15 minutes.
3. In a small bowl, combine the flour and milk; stir into the vegetable mixture. Cook and stir over medium heat until slightly thickened and bubbly. Stir in cheese, chicken, poultry seasoning, salt and pepper. Heat until the cheese melts. Spoon into a 10-in. cast-iron or other ovenproof skillet. Set aside.

4. On a lightly floured surface, roll dough for crust to fit the top of the casserole; trim edges as necessary. Place on casserole over filling; seal edges. Make several slits in center of crust for steam to escape.
5. Bake until golden brown, about 40 minutes.

1 piece: 603 cal., 31g fat (18g sat. fat), 161mg chol., 902mg sod., 38g carb. (6g sugars, 3g fiber), 42g pro.

SALSA VERDE CHICKEN CASSEROLE

This is a rich and surprisingly tasty rendition of all the Tex-Mex dishes molded into one packed, beautiful casserole. Best of all, it's ready in only half an hour.
—Janet McCormick, Proctorville, OH

Takes: 30 min. • **Makes:** 6 servings

- 2 cups shredded rotisserie chicken
- 1 cup sour cream
- 1½ cups salsa verde, divided
- 8 corn tortillas (6 in.)
- 2 cups chopped tomatoes
- ¼ cup minced fresh cilantro
- 2 cups shredded Monterey Jack cheese

Optional: Avocado slices, thinly sliced green onions or fresh cilantro leaves

1. Preheat oven to 400°. In a small bowl, combine chicken, sour cream and ¾ cup salsa. Spread ¼ cup salsa on the bottom of a greased 8-in. square baking dish.
2. Layer with half the tortillas and half the chicken mixture; sprinkle with half the tomatoes, the cilantro and half the cheese. Repeat layers with the remaining tortillas, chicken mixture, tomatoes and cheese.
3. Bake, uncovered, until bubbly, 20-25 minutes. Serve with the remaining salsa and, if desired, optional toppings.
1 serving: 400 cal., 23g fat (13g sat. fat), 102mg chol., 637mg sod., 22g carb. (5g sugars, 3g fiber), 26g pro.

CAPRESE CHICKEN

I love a Caprese salad of tomatoes, basil and cheese, so why not use the same ingredients with chicken? You can grill this dish, but my family agrees it's juicier straight from the oven.
—Dana Johnson, Scottsdale, AZ

Prep: 10 min. + marinating • **Bake:** 20 min.
Makes: 4 servings

- ⅔ cup Italian salad dressing
- 2 tsp. chicken seasoning
- 2 tsp. Italian seasoning
- 4 boneless skinless chicken breast halves (6 oz. each)
- 2 Tbsp. canola oil
- ½ lb. fresh mozzarella cheese, cut into 4 slices
- 2 medium tomatoes, sliced
- 1 Tbsp. balsamic vinegar or balsamic glaze
  Torn fresh basil leaves

1. In a large shallow dish, combine salad dressing, chicken seasoning and Italian seasoning. Add chicken and turn to coat. Refrigerate 4-6 hours. Drain chicken and discard marinade.
2. Preheat oven to 450°. In an ovenproof skillet, heat oil over medium-high heat. Brown chicken on both sides. Transfer skillet to oven; bake 15-18 minutes or until a thermometer reads 165°.
3. Top chicken with mozzarella cheese and tomato. Bake 3-5 minutes longer or until the cheese is melted. Drizzle with vinegar; top with basil.
1 serving: 525 cal., 34g fat (11g sat. fat), 139mg chol., 761mg sod., 5g carb. (4g sugars, 1g fiber), 45g pro.

FIESTA CHICKEN

Chili powder and picante sauce add just the right dash of zip to this hearty main dish. It's a snap to assemble since it uses convenience foods.
—Teresa Peterson, Kasson, MN

Prep: 15 min. • **Bake:** 40 min.
Makes: 8 servings

- 1 can (10¾ oz.) condensed cream of chicken soup, undiluted
- 1 can (10¾ oz.) condensed cream of mushroom soup, undiluted
- 2 small tomatoes, chopped
- ⅓ cup picante sauce
- 1 medium green pepper, chopped
- 1 small onion, chopped
- 2 to 3 tsp. chili powder
- 12 corn tortillas (6 in.), cut into 1-in. strips
- 3 cups cubed cooked chicken
- 1 cup shredded Colby cheese

1. Preheat oven to 350°. In a large bowl, combine the soups, tomatoes, picante sauce, green pepper, onion and chili powder. In a greased 13x9-in. baking dish, layer half the tortilla strips, chicken, soup mixture and cheese. Repeat layers.
2. Cover and bake for 40-50 minutes or until bubbly.

Freeze option: Cover unbaked casserole and freeze. To use, partially thaw in the refrigerator overnight. Remove from refrigerator 30 minutes before baking. Preheat oven to 350°. Bake casserole as directed, increasing time as necessary to heat through and for a thermometer inserted in center to read 165°.

1 serving: 324 cal., 14g fat (5g sat. fat), 65mg chol., 802mg sod., 28g carb. (3g sugars, 4g fiber), 23g pro.

THAI CHICKEN & SLAW

This chicken recipe's combination of flavors—including a little sweetness from the honey—is popular with my friends and family. I make it whenever I have visitors.
—Karen Norris, Philadelphia, PA

Prep: 25 min. + marinating • **Cook:** 30 min.
Makes: 8 servings

- ½ cup canola oil
- ½ cup white wine vinegar
- ½ cup honey
- 2 Tbsp. minced fresh gingerroot
- 2 Tbsp. reduced-sodium soy sauce
- 2 garlic cloves, minced
- 1 tsp. sesame oil
- 8 boneless skinless chicken thighs (about 2 lbs.)

SLAW
- 6 cups coleslaw mix
- 1 cup frozen shelled edamame, thawed
- 1 medium sweet pepper, chopped
- 1 Tbsp. creamy peanut butter
- ½ tsp. salt
- 4 green onions, sliced

1. In a small bowl, whisk first 7 ingredients until blended. Pour 1 cup marinade into a bowl or shallow dish. Add chicken and turn to coat. Refrigerate overnight. Cover and refrigerate the remaining marinade.
2. Preheat oven to 350°. Drain chicken, discarding marinade from the bowl. Place chicken in a 13x9-in. baking dish coated with cooking spray. Bake, uncovered, until a thermometer reads 170°, 30-40 minutes.
3. Meanwhile, place coleslaw mix, edamame and pepper in a large bowl. Add peanut butter and salt to reserved marinade; whisk until blended. Pour over coleslaw mixture; toss to coat. Refrigerate until serving.
4. Serve chicken with slaw. Sprinkle with green onions.

3 oz. cooked chicken with ⅔ cup slaw: 326 cal., 18g fat (3g sat. fat), 76mg chol., 171mg sod., 16g carb. (12g sugars, 2g fiber), 24g pro. **Diabetic exchanges:** 3 lean meat, 2 fat, 1 vegetable, ½ starch.

MEXICAN TURKEY ROLL-UPS

I whip up this recipe when my family is craving Mexican food and when I have turkey I need to use up. These roll-ups are so fun and tasty, even picky kids like them.
—Marlene Muckenhirn, Delano, MN

- -

Prep: 10 min. • **Bake:** 30 min.
Makes: 5 servings

2½ cups cubed cooked turkey
1½ cups sour cream, divided
3 tsp. taco seasoning, divided
1 can (10¾ oz.) condensed cream of mushroom soup, undiluted, divided
1½ cups shredded cheddar cheese, divided
1 small onion, chopped
½ cup salsa
¼ cup sliced ripe olives
10 flour tortillas (6 in.)
Shredded lettuce
Chopped tomatoes
Optional: Additional salsa and sliced ripe olives

1. Preheat oven to 350°. In a bowl, combine turkey, ½ cup sour cream, 1½ tsp. taco seasoning, half the soup, 1 cup cheese, the onion, salsa and olives. Place ⅓ cup filling on each tortilla. Roll up and place, seam side down, in a greased 13x9-in. baking dish.

2. Combine the remaining sour cream, taco seasoning and soup; pour over the tortillas. Cover and bake for 30 minutes or until heated through.

3. Sprinkle with the remaining cheese. Serve with shredded lettuce and chopped tomatoes. Top with additional salsa and sliced ripe olives if desired.

2 roll-ups: 639 cal., 35g fat (18g sat. fat), 140mg chol., 1501mg sod., 38g carb. (5g sugars, 2g fiber), 37g pro.

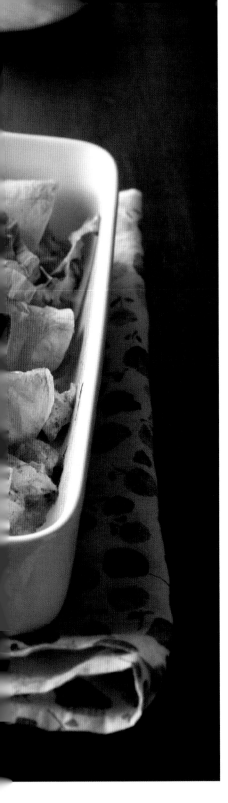

TURKEY & SPINACH STUFFING CASSEROLE

I know dried cranberries may seem to be an odd ingredient for this dish, but they add just a hint of sweetness that makes this simple casserole special.
—Gilda Lester, Millsboro, DE

Takes: 25 min. • **Makes:** 4 servings

- 1 can (14½ oz.) reduced-sodium chicken broth
- 3 Tbsp. butter
- 3 cups stuffing mix
- 3 cups cubed cooked turkey
- 2 cups fresh baby spinach
- ½ cup dried cranberries
- ¾ cup shredded cheddar cheese

1. Preheat the oven to 350°. In a large saucepan, bring broth and butter to a boil. Remove from heat. Add the stuffing mix; stir until moistened. Stir in turkey, spinach and cranberries.
2. Transfer to a greased 11x7-in. baking dish. Sprinkle with cheese. Bake, uncovered, for 10-15 minutes or until the cheese is melted.
1¼ cups: 565 cal., 24g fat (12g sat. fat), 125mg chol., 1259mg sod., 43g carb. (15g sugars, 2g fiber), 42g pro.

ROASTED CHICKEN & RED POTATOES

Pop this homey dinner in the oven for about an hour, then enjoy! It has so much flavor—the meat juices help cook the veggies just perfectly.
—Sherri Melotik, Oak Creek, WI

Prep: 15 min. • **Bake:** 55 min.
Makes: 6 servings

- 2 lbs. red potatoes, cut into 1-in. pieces
- 1 pkg. (9 oz.) fresh spinach
- 1 large onion, cut into 1-in. pieces
- 2 Tbsp. olive oil
- 4 garlic cloves, minced
- 1 tsp. salt, divided
- 1 tsp. dried thyme
- ¾ tsp. pepper, divided
- 6 chicken leg quarters
- ¾ tsp. paprika

1. Preheat oven to 375°. Place potatoes, spinach and onion in a greased shallow roasting pan. Add oil, garlic, ¾ tsp. salt, thyme and ½ tsp. pepper; toss to combine.
2. Arrange chicken over the vegetables; sprinkle with paprika and the remaining salt and pepper. Roast on an upper oven rack for 55-60 minutes or until a thermometer inserted in chicken reads 180° and the potatoes are tender.
1 chicken leg quarter with 1 cup vegetable mixture: 449 cal., 21g fat (5g sat. fat), 105mg chol., 529mg sod., 29g carb. (3g sugars, 4g fiber), 35g pro.

CHICKEN VEGGIE PACKETS

People think I went to a lot of trouble when I serve these packets. Individual pouches hold the juices in during baking to keep the herbed chicken moist and tender. It saves time and makes cleanup a breeze.
—Edna Shaffer, Beulah, MI

- -

Takes: 30 min. • **Makes:** 4 servings

4	boneless skinless chicken breast halves (4 oz. each)
½	lb. sliced fresh mushrooms
1½	cups fresh baby carrots
1	cup pearl onions
½	cup julienned sweet red pepper
¼	tsp. pepper
3	tsp. minced fresh thyme
½	tsp. salt, optional
	Lemon wedges, optional

1. Preheat oven to 375°. Flatten chicken breasts to ½-in. thickness; place each on a piece of heavy-duty foil (about 12-in. square). Layer mushrooms, carrots, onions and red pepper over the chicken; sprinkle with pepper, thyme and salt if desired.
2. Fold foil around chicken and vegetables and seal tightly. Place on a baking sheet. Bake for 30 minutes or until the chicken juices run clear. If desired, serve with lemon wedges.
1 serving: 175 cal., 3g fat (1g sat. fat), 63mg chol., 100mg sod., 11g carb. (6g sugars, 2g fiber), 25g pro. **Diabetic exchanges:** 3 lean meat, 2 vegetable.

CHICKEN STIR-FRY BAKE

One night I decided to try using frozen vegetables in my stir-fry. Not wanting to stand watch over the stovetop, I baked the entree in the oven. People say this tastes like it's hot from the skillet. What's more, it's ready in little more than half an hour.
—Carly Carter, Nashville, TN

- -

Prep: 10 min. • **Bake:** 25 min.
Makes: 4 servings

2	cups uncooked instant rice
1	can (8 oz.) sliced water chestnuts, drained
2	cups cubed cooked chicken
1	pkg. (16 oz.) frozen stir-fry vegetables, thawed
1	can (14½ oz.) chicken broth
¼	cup soy sauce
1	garlic clove, minced
½	to ¾ tsp. ground ginger

Preheat the oven to 375°. Place rice in a greased 11x7-in. baking dish. Layer with water chestnuts, chicken and vegetables. Combine the remaining ingredients; pour over top. Cover and bake for 25 minutes or until the rice is tender.

1 cup: 427 cal., 6g fat (1g sat. fat), 62mg chol., 1442mg sod., 62g carb. (3g sugars, 6g fiber), 30g pro.

ARTICHOKE CHICKEN

Rosemary, mushrooms and artichokes combine to give chicken a wonderful, savory flavor. I've served this dish for a large group by doubling the recipe. It's always a big hit with everyone—especially my family!
—Ruth Stenson, Santa Ana, CA

- -

Prep: 15 min. • **Bake:** 50 min.
Makes: 8 servings

8   boneless skinless chicken breast halves (4 oz. each)
2   Tbsp. butter
2   jars (6 oz. each) marinated quartered artichoke hearts, drained
1   jar (4½ oz.) whole mushrooms, drained
½   cup chopped onion
⅓   cup all-purpose flour
1½ tsp. dried rosemary, crushed
¾   tsp. salt

¼   tsp. pepper
2   cups chicken broth or 1 cup broth and 1 cup dry white wine
    Hot cooked noodles
    Minced fresh parsley

1. Preheat oven to 350°. In a large skillet, brown chicken in butter. Remove chicken to an ungreased 13x9-in. baking dish. Arrange the artichokes and mushrooms on top of chicken; set aside.
2. Saute chopped onion in pan juices until crisp-tender. Combine the flour, rosemary, salt and pepper. Stir into pan until blended. Add chicken broth. Bring to a boil; cook and stir until thickened and bubbly, about 2 minutes. Spoon over chicken.
3. Bake, uncovered, until a thermometer inserted in the chicken reads 165°, about 40 minutes. Serve with noodles and sprinkle with parsley.

Freeze option: Cool, cover and freeze unbaked casserole. To use, partially thaw in refrigerator overnight; remove 30 minutes before baking. Bake as directed, increasing time as necessary to heat through and for a thermometer inserted in the chicken to read 165°.

1 serving: 232 cal., 9g fat (3g sat. fat), 81mg chol., 752mg sod., 7g carb. (1g sugars, 1g fiber), 28g pro. **Diabetic exchanges:** 4 lean meat, 1½ fat, ½ starch.

DID YOU KNOW?

If you prefer, you can use fresh mushrooms instead of jarred. Get button mushrooms or baby portobellos; if they're large, you can halve them. Fresh mushrooms give up some liquid as they cook, so you can skimp a little on the added broth if you like.

Pork

HAM & SWISS STROMBOLI

This is an ideal meal to take to someone for dinner. It's also easy to change up the recipe with your favorite meats or cheeses.
—Tricia Bibb, Hartselle, AL

Takes: 30 min. • **Makes:** 6 servings

- 1 tube (11 oz.) refrigerated crusty French loaf
- 6 oz. sliced deli ham
- ¼ cup finely chopped onion
- 8 bacon strips, cooked and crumbled
- 6 oz. sliced Swiss cheese
  Honey mustard, optional

1. Preheat oven to 375°. Unroll dough on a baking sheet. Place ham down the center third of the dough to within 1 in. of ends; top with onion, bacon and cheese. Fold the long sides of the dough over the filling, pinching seam and ends to seal; tuck ends under. Cut several slits in top.
2. Bake until golden brown, 20-25 minutes. Cut into serving slices. If desired, serve with honey mustard.
Freeze option: Securely wrap and freeze cooled unsliced stromboli in heavy-duty foil. To use, reheat stromboli on an ungreased baking sheet in a preheated 375° oven until heated through and a thermometer inserted in center reads 165°.
1 slice: 272 cal., 11g fat (5g sat. fat), 40mg chol., 795mg sod., 26g carb. (3g sugars, 1g fiber), 18g pro.

STUFFED IOWA CHOPS

Here's a hearty dish for big appetites. The corn and apples make a tasty stuffing for the chops.
—Judith Smith, Des Moines, IA

Prep: 20 min. • **Bake:** 50 min.
Makes: 4 servings

- 4 bone-in pork loin chops (1½ in. thick and 8 oz. each)
- 1 Tbsp. canola oil

- 1 Tbsp. finely chopped onion
- 1 Tbsp. minced fresh parsley
- 1 Tbsp. 2% milk
- ¼ tsp. salt
- ¼ tsp. rubbed sage
- ¼ tsp. pepper
- 1 cup chopped peeled apple
- 1 cup whole kernel corn
- 1 cup dry bread crumbs

SAUCE
- ⅓ cup honey
- 3 to 4 Tbsp. Dijon mustard
- ¾ tsp. minced fresh rosemary or ⅛ tsp. dried rosemary, crushed

1. Preheat oven to 350°. Cut a pocket in each pork chop by slicing almost to the bone. In a large skillet, heat oil over medium heat. Brown the chops on each side; cool slightly.

2. In a bowl, mix onion, parsley, milk and seasonings. Add apple, corn and bread crumbs; toss to combine. Spoon mixture into the pork chops; place in a greased 13x9-in. baking dish.
3. In a small bowl, mix sauce ingredients; reserve half the sauce for brushing. Pour the remaining sauce over pork chops. Bake, uncovered, for 50-60 minutes or until a thermometer inserted in the stuffing reads 165°, brushing occasionally with reserved sauce during the last 20 minutes.
1 stuffed pork chop: 601 cal., 24g fat (8g sat. fat), 112mg chol., 875mg sod., 54g carb. (31g sugars, 3g fiber), 41g pro.

CREOLE PORK TENDERLOIN WITH VEGETABLES

Fresh summer vegetables are paired with lean pork and tasty Greek olives for a healthy and quick dinner that's great for family or friends.
—Judy Armstrong, Prairieville, LA

- -

Prep: 30 min. • **Bake:** 20 min.
Makes: 8 servings

3½ tsp. reduced-sodium Creole seasoning, divided
2 pork tenderloins (1 lb. each)
2 Tbsp. canola oil
2 medium fennel bulbs, trimmed and cut into 1-in. wedges
1 medium eggplant, cut into 1-in. cubes
2 medium yellow summer squash, halved and cut into ½-in. slices
1 large sweet red pepper, cut into 1-in. pieces
2 shallots, thinly sliced
½ cup pitted Greek olives, coarsely chopped
3 garlic cloves, minced
½ cup vegetable broth
4 tsp. minced fresh thyme or 1¼ tsp. dried thyme

1. Preheat oven to 350°. Sprinkle 3 tsp. Creole seasoning over tenderloins. In a 6-qt. stockpot, heat oil over medium-high heat. Brown the meat on all sides. Transfer to a roasting pan.

2. Add fennel, eggplant, squash, pepper and shallots to the pot; cook and stir over medium heat 3-4 minutes or until lightly browned. Add olives and garlic; cook and stir 1 minute longer. Stir in broth, thyme and the remaining Creole seasoning; bring to a boil. Reduce heat; simmer, covered, 6-8 minutes or until fennel is crisp-tender. Spoon vegetables and liquid around pork.

3. Bake, uncovered, 20-25 minutes or until vegetables are tender and a thermometer inserted in pork reads 145°. Let stand for 5 minutes before serving. Cut pork into slices; serve with vegetables.

3 oz. cooked pork with 1 cup vegetables: 247 cal., 10g fat (2g sat. fat), 64mg chol., 575mg sod., 15g carb. (7g sugars, 5g fiber), 25g pro. **Diabetic exchanges:** 3 lean meat, 2 vegetable, 1 fat.

TEST KITCHEN TIP

Select eggplant with smooth skin; avoid those with soft or brown spots. Young and tender eggplants do not need to be peeled before using, but larger eggplants may be bitter and will taste better when peeled.

HAM & LEEK PIES

I've been making these pies for years, so many of my friends and family now have the recipe. If you can't find leeks, a sweet or mild onion works just as well.
—Bonny Tillman, Acworth, GA

Prep: 40 min. • **Bake:** 20 min.
Makes: 4 servings

- ¼ cup butter, cubed
- 4 cups sliced leeks (white portion only)
- ½ lb. sliced fresh mushrooms
- 3 medium carrots, sliced
- ½ cup all-purpose flour
- 1¼ cups 2% milk
- 1¼ cups vegetable broth
- 1¾ cups cubed fully cooked ham
- 2 Tbsp. minced fresh parsley
- ¼ to ½ tsp. ground nutmeg
  Dash pepper
- 1 sheet frozen puff pastry, thawed
- 1 large egg, lightly beaten

1. Preheat oven to 425°. In a large saucepan, heat butter over medium-high heat. Add leeks, mushrooms and carrots; cook and stir until tender.

2. Stir in flour until blended. Gradually stir in the milk and broth. Bring to a boil over medium heat, stirring constantly; cook and stir until thickened, about 2 minutes. Remove from heat; stir in ham, parsley, nutmeg and pepper.

3. On a lightly floured surface, unfold puff pastry; roll to ¼ in. thickness. Using a 10-oz. ramekin as a template, cut out 4 tops for the pies. Fill 4 greased 10-oz. ramekins with the leek mixture; top with pastry. Cut slits in pastry. Brush tops with egg.

4. Bake 18-22 minutes or until the crust is golden brown. Let stand for 5 minutes before serving.

1 pie equals: 713 cal., 37g fat (15g sat. fat), 123mg chol., 1,461mg sod., 72g carb., 9g fiber, 25g pro.

SAUSAGE HASH BROWN BAKE

For this all-in-one breakfast casserole, I like to sandwich pork sausage between layers of hash browns with creamy soup and French onion dip. Cheddar cheese tops it all off.
—Esther Wrinkles, Vanzant, MO

- -

Prep: 15 min. • **Bake:** 55 min.
Makes: 12 servings

- 2   lbs. bulk pork sausage
- 2   cups shredded cheddar cheese, divided
- 1   can (10¾ oz.) condensed cream of chicken soup, undiluted
- 1   cup sour cream
- 1   carton (8 oz.) French onion dip
- 1   cup chopped onion
- ¼   cup chopped green pepper
- ¼   cup chopped sweet red pepper
- ⅛   tsp. pepper
- 1   pkg. (30 oz.) frozen shredded hash brown potatoes, thawed

1. Preheat oven to 350°. In a large skillet, cook the sausage over medium heat until no longer pink; drain on paper towels. In a large bowl, combine 1¾ cups cheese and the next 7 ingredients; fold in potatoes.
2. Spread half the mixture into a greased shallow 3-qt. baking dish. Top with sausage and the remaining potato mixture. Sprinkle with the remaining cheese. Cover and bake for 45 minutes. Uncover; bake 10 minutes longer or until heated through.

1 serving: 382 cal., 27g fat (14g sat. fat), 63mg chol., 776mg sod., 20g carb. (4g sugars, 2g fiber), 13g pro.

SPINACH & GOUDA-STUFFED PORK CUTLETS

This started as a restaurant copycat dish at home. Cheese just oozes out of the center, and mustard lends a lot of flavor.
—Joan Oakland, Troy, MT

- -

Takes: 30 min. • **Makes:** 2 servings

- 3   Tbsp. dry bread crumbs
- 2   Tbsp. grated Parmesan cheese
- 2   pork sirloin cutlets (3 oz. each)
- ¼   tsp. salt
- ⅛   tsp. pepper
- 2   slices smoked Gouda cheese (about 2 oz.)
- 2   cups fresh baby spinach
- 2   Tbsp. horseradish mustard

1. Preheat oven to 400°. In a shallow bowl, mix bread crumbs and Parmesan cheese.
2. Sprinkle the tops of cutlets with salt and pepper. Layer half of each with the Gouda cheese and spinach. Fold cutlets in half, enclosing the filling; secure with toothpicks. Brush mustard over outsides of pork; dip in the bread crumb mixture, patting to help the coating adhere.
3. Place on a greased foil-lined baking sheet. Bake until coating is golden brown and pork is tender, 12-15 minutes. Discard toothpicks before serving.

1 stuffed cutlet: 299 cal., 16g fat (7g sat. fat), 91mg chol., 898mg sod., 10g carb. (2g sugars, 2g fiber), 30g pro.

3. In a greased 13x9-in. baking dish, layer potatoes and onion. Pour the broth mixture over the layers. Place pork chops on top.
4. Cover and bake for 1 hour; uncover and bake 30 minutes longer or until the meat and potatoes are tender. If desired, sprinkle with paprika and parsley.

1 serving: 574 cal., 29g fat (11g sat. fat), 128mg chol., 1015mg sod., 36g carb. (3g sugars, 3g fiber), 40g pro.

BAKED CHOPS & COTTAGE FRIES

Convenience items such as frozen vegetables and a jar of cheese sauce make it a snap to assemble this delectable pork chop supper. It's a simple one-dish meal.
—Gregg Voss, Emerson, NE

Prep: 20 min. • **Bake:** 55 min.
Makes: 6 servings

- 6   bone-in pork loin chops (1 in. thick and 7 oz. each)
- 1   Tbsp. olive oil
- ½   tsp. seasoned salt
- 1   cup cheese dip
- ½   cup 2% milk
- 4   cups frozen cottage (waffle) fries
- 1   can (2.8 oz.) french-fried onions, divided
- 4   cups frozen broccoli florets

1. Preheat oven to 350°. In a large skillet, brown the pork chops in oil; sprinkle with seasoned salt. In a small bowl, combine cheese sauce and milk until blended.
2. Spread into a greased 13x9-in. baking dish. Top with cottage fries and half the onions. Layer with broccoli and pork chops.
3. Cover and bake for 45 minutes. Sprinkle with the remaining onions. Bake until a thermometer inserted in pork reads 160°, 10 minutes longer.

1 serving: 533 cal., 28g fat (11g sat. fat), 116mg chol., 1208mg sod., 28g carb. (6g sugars, 3g fiber), 38g pro.

PORK CHOPS WITH SCALLOPED POTATOES

Mom always managed to put a delicious hearty meal on the table for us and for our farmhands. This comforting dish reminds me of home.
—Bernice Morris, Marshfield, MO

Prep: 25 min. • **Bake:** 1½ hours
Makes: 6 servings

- 3   Tbsp. butter
- 3   Tbsp. all-purpose flour
- 1½   tsp. salt
- ¼   tsp. pepper
- 1   can (14½ oz.) chicken broth
- 6   pork rib or loin chops (¾ in. thick)
- 2   Tbsp. canola oil
    Additional salt and pepper, optional
- 6   cups thinly sliced peeled potatoes
- 1   medium onion, sliced
    Optional: Paprika and minced fresh parsley

1. Preheat oven to 350°. Melt butter In a small saucepan; stir in the flour, salt and pepper until smooth. Add broth. Bring to a boil; cook and stir for 1 minute or until thickened. Remove from heat and set aside.
2. In a large skillet, brown the pork chops on both sides in oil; sprinkle with additional salt and pepper if desired.

SUNDAY CHOPS & STUFFING

My family likes to make these savory chops for Sunday dinner. The recipe lets us spend more time having fun together and less time cooking.
—Georgiann Franklin, Canfield, OH

- -

Prep: 30 min. • **Bake:** 25 min.
Makes: 6 servings

- 2 cups water
- 2 celery ribs, chopped (about 1 cup)
- 7 Tbsp. butter, divided
- ¼ cup dried minced onion
- 6 cups seasoned stuffing cubes
- 1 Tbsp. canola oil
- 6 bone-in pork loin chops (7 oz. each)
- ¼ tsp. salt
- ¼ tsp. pepper
- 2 medium tart apples, sliced
- ¼ cup packed brown sugar
- ⅛ tsp. pumpkin pie spice

1. Preheat oven to 350°. In a saucepan, combine water, celery, 6 Tbsp. butter and dried minced onion. Bring to a boil. Remove from heat; stir in stuffing cubes. Spoon into a greased 13x9-in. baking dish.
2. In a large skillet, heat oil over medium heat. Brown pork chops on both sides. Arrange over stuffing. Sprinkle with salt and pepper.
3. In a small bowl, toss apples with brown sugar and pie spice; place over pork chops. Dot with remaining butter.
4. Bake, uncovered, 25-30 minutes or until a thermometer inserted in pork reads 145°. Let stand 5 minutes before serving.
1 serving: 600 cal., 26g fat (12g sat. fat), 122mg chol., 1018mg sod., 56g carb. (19g sugars, 4g fiber), 36g pro.

PORK SPANISH RICE

My family wasn't fond of pork roast until I used it in this yummy casserole.
—Betty Unrau, MacGregor, MB

- -

Prep: 20 min. • **Bake:** 20 min.
Makes: 4 servings

- 1 medium green pepper, chopped
- 1 small onion, chopped
- 2 Tbsp. butter
- 1 can (14½ oz.) diced tomatoes, drained
- 1 cup chicken broth
- ½ tsp. salt
- ¼ tsp. pepper
- 1¾ cups cubed cooked pork
- 1 cup uncooked instant rice
  Optional: Lime wedges and minced cilantro

1. Preheat oven to 350°. In a large skillet, saute green pepper and onion in butter until tender. Stir in the tomatoes, broth, salt and pepper. Bring to a boil; stir in pork and rice.
2. Transfer to a greased 2-qt. baking dish. Cover and bake until the rice is tender and the liquid is absorbed, 20-25 minutes. Stir before serving. If desired, serve with lime wedges and top with minced cilantro.
1 cup: 304 cal., 12g fat (6g sat. fat), 71mg chol., 756mg sod., 29g carb. (5g sugars, 3g fiber), 21g pro. **Diabetic exchanges:** 3 lean meat, 2 starch, 1½ fat.

Chopped green peppers can be frozen in airtight freezer containers up to 6 months. A medium green pepper, chopped, will yield about 1 cup. A large green pepper, chopped, will yield 1⅓-1½ cups.

FARMHOUSE PORK & APPLE PIE

I've always loved pork and apples together, and this recipe combines them nicely to create a comforting dish. It takes a bit of preparation, but my family and I agree the wonderful flavor is well worth the effort.
—Suzanne Strocsher, Bothell, WA

Prep: 70 min. • **Bake:** 2 hours
Makes: 10 servings

- 1 lb. sliced bacon, cut into 2-in. pieces
- 3 medium onions, chopped
- 3 lbs. boneless pork, cut into 1-in. cubes
- ¾ cup all-purpose flour
  Canola oil, optional
- 3 medium tart apples, peeled and chopped
- 1 tsp. rubbed sage
- 1 tsp. salt
- ½ tsp. ground nutmeg
- ¼ tsp. pepper
- 1 cup apple cider
- ½ cup water
- 4 medium potatoes, peeled and cubed
- 5 Tbsp. butter, divided
- ½ cup 2% milk
  Additional salt and pepper to taste
  Minced fresh parsley, optional

1. Preheat oven to 350°. In a large cast-iron or ovenproof skillet, cook the bacon over medium heat, stirring occasionally, until crisp. Remove with a slotted spoon; drain on paper towels. Discard all but 2 Tbsp. drippings. Increase heat to medium-high. Add onions to drippings; cook until tender, 5-7 minutes. Remove with a slotted spoon; drain. Reduce heat to medium.

2. Toss pork with flour. Working in batches, brown the pork in the drippings, adding oil if needed. Remove with a slotted spoon; drain. Remove skillet from heat; discard drippings. Return pork to the skillet. Add bacon, onions, apples, sage, salt, nutmeg, and pepper. Stir in cider and water.

3. Bake, covered, until the pork is tender, about 2 hours. Meanwhile, place potatoes in a large saucepan; add water to cover. Bring to a boil. Reduce heat and cook, uncovered, until the potatoes are tender, 10-15 minutes.

4. Preheat broiler. Drain potatoes. Mash, gradually adding 3 Tbsp. butter, enough milk to reach desired consistency and salt and pepper. Spread the potatoes over the pork mixture. Melt the remaining butter; brush over potatoes. Broil 6 in. from heat until topping is browned, about 5 minutes. If desired, sprinkle with parsley.

1 serving: 467 cal., 22g fat (9g sat. fat), 110mg chol., 603mg sod., 32g carb. (11g sugars, 3g fiber), 36g pro.

PORK CHOPS OLE

This recipe is a fun and simple way to give pork chops south-of-the-border flair. The flavorful seasoning, rice and melted cheddar cheese make the dish a certain crowd-pleaser.

—Laura Turner, Channelview, TX

Prep: 15 min. • **Bake:** 1 hour
Makes: 6 servings

6	pork loin chops (½ in. thick)
2	Tbsp. canola oil
	Seasoned salt and pepper to taste
1½	cups water
1	can (8 oz.) tomato sauce
¾	cup uncooked long grain rice
2	Tbsp. taco seasoning
1	medium green pepper, chopped
½	cup shredded cheddar cheese

1. Preheat oven to 350°. In a large skillet, brown pork chops in oil; sprinkle with seasoned salt and pepper.

2. Meanwhile, in a greased 13x9-in. baking dish, combine the water, tomato sauce, rice and taco seasoning.

3. Arrange chops over rice; top with green pepper. Cover and bake for 1 hour or until the rice and meat are tender. Uncover and sprinkle with cheese.

Freeze option: Omit water and substitute 1 package (8.8 oz.) ready-to-serve long grain rice for the uncooked rice. Assemble the casserole as directed. Cool unbaked casserole; cover and freeze. To use, partially thaw in refrigerator overnight. Remove from the refrigerator 30 minutes before baking. Bake casserole as directed, increasing time as necessary.

1 serving: 515 cal., 27g fat (9g sat. fat), 121mg chol., 587mg sod., 25g carb. (1g sugars, 1g fiber), 41g pro.

EASY CHEESY LOADED GRITS

A tasty bowl of grits inspired me to develop my own with sausage, green chiles and cheeses. It just might be better than the original!
—Joan Hallford, North Richland Hills, TX

Prep: 35 min. • **Bake:** 50 min. + standing
Makes: 8 servings

- 1 lb. mild or spicy bulk pork sausage
- 1 small onion, chopped
- 4 cups water
- ½ tsp. salt
- 1 cup quick-cooking grits
- 3 cans (4 oz. each) chopped green chiles
- 1½ cups shredded sharp cheddar cheese, divided
- 1½ cups shredded Monterey Jack cheese, divided
- 2 Tbsp. butter
- ¼ tsp. hot pepper sauce
- 2 large eggs, lightly beaten
- ¼ tsp. paprika
  Chopped fresh cilantro

1. Preheat oven to 325°. In a large skillet, cook the sausage and onion over medium heat 6-8 minutes or until sausage is no longer pink, breaking up the sausage into crumbles; drain.

2. In a large saucepan, bring water and salt to a boil. Slowly stir in grits. Reduce the heat to medium-low; cook, covered, about 5 minutes or until thickened, stirring occasionally. Remove from heat.

3. Add green chiles, ¾ cup cheddar cheese, ¾ cup Monterey Jack cheese, butter and pepper sauce; stir until cheese is melted. Stir in eggs, then the sausage mixture.

4. Transfer to a greased 13x9-in. baking dish. Top with the remaining cheeses and sprinkle with paprika. Bake, uncovered, until golden brown and set, 50-60 minutes. Let stand 10 minutes before serving. Sprinkle with cilantro.

1 cup: 399 cal., 28g fat (15g sat. fat), 116mg chol., 839mg sod., 19g carb. (2g sugars, 2g fiber), 18g pro.

1 tsp. ground cumin
½ cup shredded cheddar cheese
Sliced jalapeno pepper, optional

1. Preheat oven to 350°. In a large skillet, brown pork in oil; drain. Stir in the beans, soup, tomatoes, chiles, rice, water, salsa and cumin.

2. Pour into an ungreased 2-qt. baking dish. Bake, uncovered, until bubbly, about 30 minutes. Sprinkle with cheese; let stand 5 minutes before serving. If desired, serve with jalapeno slices.

Freeze option: Sprinkle cheese over cooled unbaked casserole. Cover and freeze. To use, partially thaw in refrigerator overnight. Remove from refrigerator 30 minutes before baking. Preheat oven to 350°. Bake casserole as directed, increasing time as necessary to heat through and for a thermometer inserted in center to read 165°. If desired, serve with jalapeno slices.

1 serving: 390 cal., 15g fat (6g sat. fat), 81mg chol., 814mg sod., 29g carb. (3g sugars, 6g fiber), 32g pro.

DID YOU KNOW?

Many recipes (such as this one) call for rinsing and draining canned beans, but then add water. The rinsing and draining removes extra salt used in the canning process. If you like, you can use the bean liquid, but be sure to reduce both the amount of salt and water in the recipe.

PORK & GREEN CHILE CASSEROLE

I work at a local hospital and also part time for some area doctors, so I'm always on the lookout for good, quick recipes to fix for my family. Some of my co-workers and I often exchange recipes. This zippy casserole is one that was brought to a picnic at my house. People raved about it.
—Dianne Esposite, New Middletown, OH

- -

Prep: 20 min. • **Bake:** 30 min.
Makes: 6 servings

1½ lbs. boneless pork, cut into ½-in. cubes
1 Tbsp. canola oil
1 can (15 oz.) black beans, rinsed and drained
1 can (10¾ oz.) condensed cream of chicken soup, undiluted
1 can (14½ oz.) diced tomatoes, undrained
2 cans (4 oz. each) chopped green chiles
1 cup quick-cooking brown rice
¼ cup water
2 to 3 Tbsp. salsa

PORK SHEPHERD'S PIE

Of all the shepherd's pie recipes I've tried through the years, this one is definitely the best. I enjoy cooking for my family, who all agree this meat pie is a keeper.
—Mary Arthurs, Etobicoke, ON

- -

Prep: 30 min. • **Bake:** 45 min.
Makes: 6 servings

PORK LAYER
- 1   lb. ground pork
- 1   small onion, chopped
- 2   garlic cloves, minced
- 1   cup cooked rice
- ½   cup pork gravy or
- ¼   cup chicken broth
- ½   tsp. salt
- ½   tsp. dried thyme

CABBAGE LAYER
- 1   medium carrot, diced
- 1   small onion, chopped
- 2   Tbsp. butter or margarine
- 6   cups chopped cabbage
- 1   cup chicken broth
- ½   tsp. salt
- ¼   tsp. pepper

POTATO LAYER
- 2   cups mashed potatoes
- ¼   cup shredded cheddar cheese

1. Preheat oven to 350°. In a skillet over medium heat, brown pork until no longer pink. Add onion and garlic. Cook until vegetables are tender; drain. Stir in rice, gravy, salt and thyme. Spoon into a greased 11x7-in. baking dish.

2. In the same skillet, saute carrot and onion in butter over medium heat for 5 minutes. Stir in cabbage; cook for 1 minute. Add broth, salt and pepper; cover and cook for 10 minutes.

3. Spoon over pork layer. Spoon or pipe mashed potatoes on top; sprinkle with cheese. Bake, uncovered, for 45 minutes or until browned.

1 cup: 365 cal., 19g fat (8g sat. fat), 66mg chol., 1045mg sod., 28g carb. (5g sugars, 4g fiber), 19g pro.

HAM & VEGGIE CASSEROLE

I've paired ham with broccoli and cauliflower for years. To complete this delicious casserole dinner, I pass around dinner rolls.
—Sherri Melotik, Oak Creek, WI

- -

Takes: 30 min. • **Makes:** 4 servings

- 1   pkg. (16 oz.) frozen broccoli florets
- 1   pkg. (16 oz.) frozen cauliflower
- 2   tsp. plus 2 Tbsp. butter, divided
- ¼   cup seasoned bread crumbs
- 2   Tbsp. all-purpose flour
- 1½   cups 2% milk
- ¾   cup shredded sharp cheddar cheese
- ½   cup grated Parmesan cheese
- 1½   cups cubed fully cooked ham (about 8 oz.)
- ¼   tsp. pepper

1. Preheat oven to 425°. Cook broccoli and cauliflower according to the package directions; drain.

2. Meanwhile, in a small skillet, melt 2 tsp. butter. Add bread crumbs; cook and stir over medium heat for 2-3 minutes or until lightly toasted. Remove from heat.

3. In a large saucepan, melt the remaining butter over medium heat. Stir in flour until smooth; gradually whisk in milk. Bring to a boil, stirring constantly; cook and stir for 1-2 minutes or until thickened. Remove from heat; stir in cheeses until blended. Stir in ham, pepper and vegetables.

4. Transfer mixture to a greased 8-in. square baking dish. Sprinkle with toasted crumbs. Bake, uncovered, until heated through, 10-15 minutes.

1½ cups: 420 cal., 23g fat (13g sat. fat), 89mg chol., 1233mg sod., 25g carb. (10g sugars, 6g fiber), 28g pro.

ROASTED PORK TENDERLOIN & VEGETABLES

There are no complicated steps to follow when preparing this medley of tender pork and veggies. Just season with herbs, then pop it in the oven.
—Diane Martin, Brown Deer, WI

- -

Prep: 20 min. • **Bake:** 25 min.
Makes: 6 servings

- 2 pork tenderloins (¾ lb. each)
- 2 lbs. red potatoes, quartered
- 1 lb. carrots, halved and cut into 2-in. pieces
- 1 medium onion, cut into wedges
- 1 Tbsp. olive oil
- 2 tsp. dried rosemary, crushed
- 1 tsp. rubbed sage
- ½ tsp. salt
- ¼ tsp. pepper

1. Preheat oven to 450°. Place the pork in a shallow roasting pan coated with cooking spray; arrange the potatoes, carrots and onion around pork. Drizzle with olive oil. Combine the seasonings; sprinkle over the meat and vegetables.
2. Bake, uncovered, 25-35 minutes or until the meat reaches desired doneness (for medium-rare, a thermometer should read 145°; medium, 160°) and vegetables are tender, stirring vegetables occasionally. Remove pork from oven; tent with foil. Let stand 5 minutes before slicing.
Note: If the pork is done before vegetables are tender, remove from the oven and keep warm. Continue cooking until the roasted vegetables are tender.
1 serving: 301 cal., 7g fat (2g sat. fat), 64mg chol., 304mg sod., 33g carb. (6g sugars, 5g fiber), 26g pro. **Diabetic exchanges:** 3 lean meat, 2 starch, 1 vegetable.

CORDON BLEU CASSEROLE

We love everything about traditional cordon bleu, and this variation is so easy to make. It's a delicious way to eat Thanksgiving leftovers.
—Kristine Blauert, Wabasha, MN

- -

Prep: 20 min. • **Bake:** 25 min.
Makes: 8 servings

- 2 cups uncooked elbow macaroni
- 2 cans (10¾ oz. each) condensed cream of chicken soup, undiluted
- ¾ cup 2% milk
- ¼ cup grated Parmesan cheese
- 1 tsp. prepared mustard
- 1 tsp. paprika
- ½ tsp. dried rosemary, crushed
- ¼ tsp. garlic powder
- ⅛ tsp. rubbed sage
- 2 cups cubed cooked turkey
- 2 cups cubed fully cooked ham
- 2 cups shredded part-skim mozzarella cheese
- ¼ cup crushed Ritz crackers

1. Preheat oven to 350°. Cook macaroni according to package directions.
2. Meanwhile, whisk together soup, milk, Parmesan cheese, mustard and seasonings. Stir in turkey, ham and mozzarella cheese.
3. Drain macaroni; add to soup mixture and toss to combine. Transfer to greased 13x9-in. baking dish or 8 greased 8-oz. ramekins. Sprinkle with the crushed Ritz crackers. Bake, uncovered, until bubbly, 25-30 minutes.
Freeze option: Cover and freeze unbaked dish or ramekins. To use, partially thaw in refrigerator overnight. Remove from refrigerator 30 minutes before baking. Preheat oven to 350°. Bake as directed, increasing time as needed to heat through and for a thermometer inserted in center to read 165°.
1 cup: 327 cal., 14g fat (6g sat. fat), 64mg chol., 1090mg sod., 23g carb. (3g sugars, 1g fiber), 27g pro.

BEST EVER BEANS & SAUSAGE

My wife cooked up this dish, which is very popular with our friends and family. When she asks what she should bring, the reply is always: "Your beans and sausage—and a couple copies of the recipe!"
—Robert Saulnier, Clarksburg, MA

- -

Prep: 15 min. • **Bake:** 1 hour 20 min.
Makes: 16 servings

  1½ lbs. bulk spicy pork sausage
  1   medium green pepper, chopped
  1   medium onion, chopped
  1   can (31 oz.) pork and beans
  1   can (16 oz.) kidney beans,
      rinsed and drained
  1   can (15½ oz.) great northern
      beans, rinsed and drained
  1   can (15½ oz.) black-eyed
      peas, rinsed and drained
  1   can (15 oz.) pinto beans,
      rinsed and drained
  1   can (15 oz.) chickpeas,
      rinsed and drained
  1½ cups ketchup
  ¾   cup packed brown sugar
  2   tsp. ground mustard

1. Preheat oven to 325°. In a large skillet, cook sausage over medium heat until no longer pink; drain. Add green pepper and onion; saute until tender. Drain. Add the remaining ingredients.
2. Pour into a greased 13x9-in. baking dish. Cover and bake for 1 hour. Uncover. bake 20-30 minutes longer or until bubbly.
¾ cup: 316 cal., 9g fat (3g sat. fat), 15mg chol., 857mg sod., 48g carb. (19g sugars, 9g fiber), 13g pro.

TOMATO, SAUSAGE & CHEDDAR BREAD PUDDING

This savory dish is the perfect excuse to have bread pudding as the entire meal, not just as dessert.
—Holly Jones, Kennesaw, GA

Prep: 30 min. • **Bake:** 45 min.
Makes: 12 servings

- 3 cups shredded sharp cheddar cheese
- 1 can (28 oz.) diced tomatoes, drained
- 1 lb. bulk Italian sausage, cooked and crumbled
- 4 green onions, thinly sliced
- ¼ cup minced fresh basil or 1 Tbsp. dried basil
- ¼ cup packed brown sugar
- 1 tsp. dried oregano
- 1 tsp. garlic powder
- 3 cups cubed French bread
- 6 large eggs
- 1½ cups heavy whipping cream
- ½ tsp. salt
- ½ tsp. pepper
- ½ cup grated Parmesan cheese

1. Preheat oven to 350°. In a large bowl, combine the first 8 ingredients. Stir in bread. Transfer to a greased 13x9-in. baking dish.
2. In the same bowl, whisk eggs, cream, salt and pepper; pour over the bread mixture. Sprinkle with Parmesan cheese. Bake for 45-50 minutes or until a knife inserted in the center comes out clean.
1 piece: 430 cal., 32g fat (18g sat. fat), 206mg chol., 822mg sod., 16g carb. (8g sugars, 2g fiber), 19g pro.

HAM & SWISS CASSEROLE

When I prepare this noodle casserole for church gatherings, it's always a hit. It can easily be doubled or tripled for a crowd.
—Doris Barb, El Dorado, KS

Prep: 15 min. • **Bake:** 40 min.
Makes: 8 servings

- 1 pkg. (8 oz.) egg noodles, cooked and drained
- 2 cups cubed fully cooked ham
- 2 cups shredded Swiss cheese
- 1 can (10¾ oz.) condensed cream of celery soup, undiluted
- 1 cup sour cream
- ½ cup chopped green pepper
- ½ cup chopped onion

1. Preheat oven to 350°. In a greased 13x9-in. baking dish, layer half the egg noodles, ham and cheese.
2. In a large bowl, combine the soup, sour cream, green pepper and onion; spread half over the top. Repeat layers. Bake, uncovered, for 40-45 minutes or until heated through.
1 serving: 360 cal., 18g fat (10g sat. fat), 92mg chol., 815mg sod., 27g carb. (4g sugars, 1g fiber), 20g pro.

¾ cup finely chopped celery
¾ cup minced fresh parsley
½ tsp. rubbed sage
½ tsp. dried thyme
½ cup chicken broth
10 bacon strips
   Apricot preserves, optional

1. Preheat oven to 350°. To butterfly pork roast, cut a lengthwise slit down the center of the pork loin to within ½ in. of bottom. Open loin so it lies flat. Make another slit lengthwise down the center of each half to within ½ in. of bottom. Pound with a mallet to flatten to ¼-in. thickness. Sprinkle with salt, garlic powder and pepper.
2. In a large bowl, combine rice, apricots, onion, celery, parsley, sage, thyme and broth. Spread stuffing evenly over pork, ¼-½ in. thick (you will have stuffing left over). Roll up jelly-roll style, starting with a long side. Tie roast at 1½-2-in. intervals with kitchen string. Place the remaining stuffing in a greased shallow 2-qt. baking dish; set aside.
3. Bake the roast, uncovered, for 1 hour. Remove roast from oven; carefully remove string. Place bacon strips over top of roast, overlapping slightly. Bake until the bacon is browned and crisp, and a thermometer reads 160° 30-45 minutes longer. If needed, broil 4 in. from heat until bacon reaches desired crispness. Meanwhile, cover and bake the remaining stuffing until heated through, about 30 minutes.
4. Let roast stand for 10 minutes before slicing. If desired, brush with apricot preserves before slicing.
1 serving: 436 cal., 20g fat (7g sat. fat), 109mg chol., 547mg sod., 23g carb. (10g sugars, 3g fiber), 41g pro.

WILD RICE-STUFFED PORK LOIN

The earthy, slightly sweet stuffing tucked inside a tender pork roast means you get your main dish and side in every slice.
—Kim Rubner, Worthington, IA

- -

Prep: 20 min. • **Bake:** 1½ hours + standing
Makes: 10 servings

1   whole boneless pork loin
    roast (4 lbs.), trimmed
1   tsp. salt
½   tsp. garlic powder
¼   tsp. pepper
2   cups wild rice, cooked and drained
1½ cups coarsely chopped
    dried apricots
1   cup chopped onion

Freeze option: Cover and freeze unbaked casserole up to 3 months. Thaw in the refrigerator overnight. Remove from the refrigerator 30 minutes before baking. Preheat oven to 350°. Bake, uncovered, until golden brown and bubbly, 50-55 minutes.
1 cup: 428 cal., 26g fat (11g sat. fat), 69mg chol., 1193mg sod., 28g carb. (4g sugars, 3g fiber), 19g pro.

GLAZED SMOKED CHOPS WITH PEARS

My husband would eat pork chops every day if he could. Luckily, they're good all sorts of ways, so I can keep things interesting. This recipe, where they're cooked with pears, is one of my favorites.
—Lynn Moretti, Oconomowoc, WI

Takes: 30 min. • **Makes:** 4 servings

- 4 smoked boneless pork chops
- 1 Tbsp. olive oil
- 1 large sweet onion, cut into thin wedges
- ½ cup dry red wine or reduced-sodium chicken broth
- 2 Tbsp. balsamic vinegar
- 2 Tbsp. honey
- 2 large ripe pears, cut into 1-in. wedges

1. Preheat oven to 350°. In an ovenproof skillet over medium-high heat, brown pork chops on both sides; remove from pan.
2. In the same pan, heat oil over medium heat; saute onion until tender, 3-5 minutes. Add wine, vinegar and honey; bring to a boil, stirring to loosen any browned bits from the pan. Reduce heat; simmer, uncovered, until slightly thickened, about 5 minutes, stirring occasionally.
3. Return chops to pan; top with pears. Transfer to oven; bake until the pears are tender, 10-15 minutes.
1 serving: 313 cal., 4g fat (6g sat. fat), 41mg chol., 1056mg sod., 34g carb. (26g sugars, 4g fiber), 22g pro.

POLISH CASSEROLE

When I first made this dish, my 2-year-old liked it so much that he wanted it for every meal! You can use most any pasta that will hold the sauce.
—Crystal Jo Bruns, Iliff, CO

Prep: 25 min. • **Bake:** 45 min.
Makes: 2 casseroles (6 servings each)

- 4 cups uncooked penne pasta
- 1½ lbs. smoked Polish sausage or kielbasa, cut into ½-in. slices
- 2 cans (10¾ oz. each) condensed cream of mushroom soup, undiluted
- 1 jar (16 oz.) sauerkraut, rinsed and well drained
- 3 cups shredded Swiss cheese, divided
- 1⅓ cups 2% milk
- 4 green onions, chopped
- 2 Tbsp. Dijon mustard
- 4 garlic cloves, minced

1. Preheat oven to 350°. Cook the pasta according to package directions; drain and transfer to a large bowl. Stir in the sausage, soup, sauerkraut, 2 cups cheese, milk, onions, mustard and garlic.
2. Spoon into 2 greased 8-in. square baking dishes; sprinkle with remaining cheese. Bake, uncovered, until golden brown and bubbly, 45-50 minutes.

Seafood & Meatless

THAI SALMON BROWN RICE BOWLS

Turn to this salmon recipe for a quick and nourishing meal. Store-bought sesame ginger dressing saves time and adds extra flavor to this healthy dish.
—Naylet LaRochelle, Miami, FL

- -

Takes: 15 min. • **Makes:** 4 servings

- 4 **salmon fillets (4 oz. each)**
- ½ cup sesame ginger salad dressing, divided
- 3 cups hot cooked brown rice
- ½ cup chopped fresh cilantro
- ¼ tsp. salt
- 1 **cup julienned carrot**
   Thinly sliced red cabbage, optional

1. Preheat oven to 400°. Place salmon in a foil-lined 15x10x1-in. pan; brush with ¼ cup dressing. Bake until fish just begins to flake easily with a fork, 8-10 minutes. Meanwhile, toss rice with cilantro and salt.
2. To serve, divide the rice mixture among 4 bowls. Top with salmon, carrots and, if desired, sliced red cabbage. Drizzle with the remaining dressing.

1 serving: 486 cal., 21g fat (4g sat. fat), 57mg chol., 532mg sod., 49g carb. (8g sugars, 3g fiber), 24g pro.

ANGEL HAIR SHRIMP BAKE

Shrimp and pasta blend beautifully with herbs, salsa and three kinds of cheese in this hearty layered casserole. Whatever the occasion, bake up a dish of luscious shrimp goodness to share.
—Susan Davidson, Elm Grove, WI

- -

Prep: 25 min. • **Bake:** 25 min.
Makes: 8 servings

- 1 **pkg. (9 oz.) refrigerated angel hair pasta**
- 1½ **lbs. uncooked medium shrimp, peeled and deveined**
- ¾ **cup crumbled feta cheese**
- ½ **cup shredded Swiss cheese**
- 1 **jar (16 oz.) chunky salsa**
- ½ **cup shredded Monterey Jack cheese**
- ¾ **cup minced fresh parsley**
- 1 **tsp. dried basil**
- 1 **tsp. dried oregano**
- 2 **large eggs**
- 1 **cup half-and-half cream**
- 1 **cup plain yogurt**
   Chopped fresh parsley, optional

1. Preheat oven to 350°. In a greased 13x9-in. baking dish, layer half the pasta, shrimp, feta cheese, Swiss cheese and salsa. Repeat layers. Sprinkle with the Monterey Jack cheese, parsley, basil and oregano.
2. In a small bowl, whisk the eggs, cream and yogurt; pour over casserole. Bake, uncovered, until a thermometer reads 160°, 25-30 minutes. Let stand 5 minutes before serving. If desired, top with fresh chopped parsley.

1¼ cups: 340 cal., 13g fat (7g sat. fat), 203mg chol., 593mg sod., 25g carb. (5g sugars, 1g fiber), 27g pro.

OVEN-BAKED SHRIMP & GRITS

On chilly days, I doctor up grits and top them with shrimp for a comfy meal. If you're not a seafood lover, you can use chicken, ham or both.
—Jerri Gradert, Lincoln, NE

Prep: 20 min. • **Bake:** 45 min.
Makes: 6 servings

- 1 carton (32 oz.) chicken broth
- 1 cup quick-cooking grits
- 1 can (10 oz.) diced tomatoes and green chiles, drained
- 1 cup shredded Monterey Jack cheese
- 1 cup shredded cheddar cheese, divided
  Freshly ground pepper
- 2 Tbsp. butter
- 1 medium green pepper, chopped
- 1 medium onion, chopped
- 1 lb. uncooked shrimp (31-40 per lb.), peeled and deveined
- 2 garlic cloves, minced

1. Preheat the oven to 350°. In a 13x9-in. or 2½-qt. baking dish, combine the broth and grits. Bake, uncovered, until liquid is absorbed and the grits are tender, 30-35 minutes.
2. Stir in the tomatoes, Monterey Jack cheese and ½ cup cheddar cheese. Bake, uncovered, until heated through, about 10 minutes. Sprinkle with pepper and the remaining cheese; let stand 5 minutes.
3. In a large skillet, heat butter over medium-high heat; saute green pepper and onion until tender, 6-8 minutes. Add shrimp and garlic; cook and stir until the shrimp turn pink, 2-3 minutes. Spoon over the grits.

1⅔ cups: 360 cal., 18g fat (10g sat. fat), 141mg chol., 1199mg sod., 26g carb. (2g sugars, 2g fiber), 25g pro.

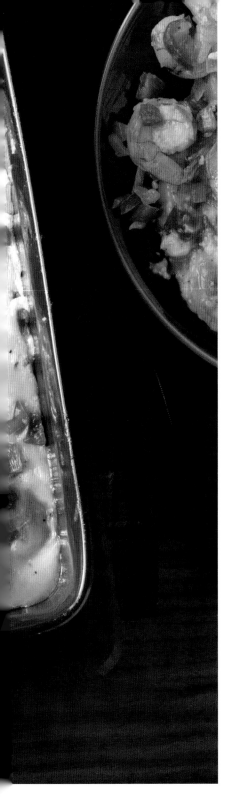

SEAFOOD CASSEROLE

A family favorite, this rice casserole is filled with plenty of seafood and veggies. It's hearty, homey and so easy to make!
—Nancy Billups, Princeton, Iowa

Prep: 20 min. • **Bake:** 40 min.
Makes: 6 servings

- 1 pkg. (6 oz.) long grain and wild rice
- 1 lb. frozen crabmeat, thawed, or 2½ cups lump crabmeat, drained
- 1 lb. cooked shrimp, peeled, deveined and cut into ½-in. pieces
- 2 celery ribs, chopped
- 1 medium onion, finely chopped
- ½ cup finely chopped green pepper
- 1 can (4 oz.) mushroom stems and pieces, drained
- 1 jar (2 oz.) diced pimientos, drained
- 1 cup mayonnaise
- 1 cup 2% milk
- ½ tsp. pepper
  Dash Worcestershire sauce
- ¼ cup dry bread crumbs

1. Cook rice according to package directions. Preheat oven to 375°.
2. In a large bowl, combine crab, shrimp, celery, onion, green pepper, mushrooms and pimientos. In a small bowl, whisk together the mayonnaise, milk, pepper and Worcestershire sauce; stir into the seafood mixture. Stir in the rice.
3. Transfer to a greased 13x9-in. baking dish. Sprinkle with bread crumbs. Bake, uncovered, until bubbly, 40-50 minutes.
1½ cups: 585 cal., 34g fat (5g sat. fat), 209mg chol., 1045mg sod., 31g carb. (5g sugars, 2g fiber), 37g pro.

TORTELLINI SPINACH CASSEROLE

Spinach gives this popular dish a fresh taste that delights even those who say they don't like spinach. People are often surprised at just how good it is! Whenever I bring it to a gathering, it never sits around long.
—Barbara Kellen, Antioch, IL

Prep: 20 min. • **Bake:** 20 min.
Makes: 12 servings

- 1 pkg. (19 oz.) frozen cheese tortellini
- 1 lb. sliced fresh mushrooms
- 1 tsp. garlic powder
- ¼ tsp. onion powder
- ¼ tsp. pepper
- ½ cup butter, divided
- 1 can (12 oz.) evaporated milk
- ½ lb. brick or Muenster cheese, cubed
- 3 pkg. (10 oz. each) frozen chopped spinach, thawed and squeezed dry
- 2 cups shredded part-skim mozzarella cheese

1. Preheat oven to 350°. Cook tortellini according to package directions.
2. Meanwhile, in a large skillet, saute sliced mushrooms, garlic powder, onion powder and pepper in ¼ cup butter until the mushrooms are tender. Remove and keep warm.
3. In same skillet, combine the milk and remaining butter. Bring to a gentle boil; stir in brick cheese until smooth. Drain tortellini; place in a large bowl. Stir in the mushroom mixture and spinach. Add cheese sauce and toss to coat.
4. Transfer to a greased 13x9-in. baking dish; sprinkle with mozzarella cheese. Cover and bake 15 minutes. Uncover; bake 5-10 minutes longer or until heated through and the cheese is melted.
1 cup: 281 cal., 19g fat (12g sat. fat), 64mg chol., 378mg sod., 13g carb. (4g sugars, 1g fiber), 15g pro.

SPINACH SALMON BUNDLES

Rich salmon encased in a flaky golden brown pastry will delight family and guests—and no one has to know how easy it is!

—Larissa Gedney, Myrtle Beach, SC

Takes: 30 min. • **Makes:** 4 servings

- 2 tubes (8 oz. each) refrigerated crescent rolls
- 4 salmon fillets (6 oz. each)
- ¼ tsp. salt
- ¼ tsp. pepper
- ⅓ cup garlic-herb spreadable cheese
- 1 pkg. (10 oz.) frozen chopped spinach, thawed and squeezed dry

1. Preheat oven to 400°. Unroll crescent dough and separate into 4 rectangles; seal perforations. Place a salmon fillet in the center of each rectangle; sprinkle with salt and pepper. Spoon spreadable cheese over each; top with spinach. Fold dough over the filling and pinch edges to seal.

2. Place on an ungreased baking sheet. Bake for 20-25 minutes or until golden brown.

Note: This recipe was tested with Alouette spreadable cheese.

1 bundle: 854 cal., 52g fat (16g sat. fat), 124mg chol., 1311mg sod., 48g carb. (8g sugars, 2g fiber), 45g pro.

FARMERS MARKET ENCHILADAS

These vegetarian enchiladas use lots of garden favorites for a quick weeknight meal. Do substitute whatever vegetables are ready in your garden—yellow summer squash, eggplant and corn all taste great here, too.

—Elisabeth Larsen, Pleasant Grove, UT

Prep: 20 min. • **Bake:** 45 min.
Makes: 7 servings

- 3 medium zucchini, quartered lengthwise and cut into ¼-in. pieces
- 1 poblano pepper, seeded and chopped
- 8 oz. sliced fresh mushrooms
- 8 oz. cherry tomatoes
- 1 Tbsp. olive oil
- 1 tsp. ground cumin
- ½ tsp. salt
- ¼ tsp. cayenne pepper
- 2 cups shredded Monterey Jack cheese
- 1 cup queso fresco or crumbled feta cheese, divided
- ½ cup minced fresh cilantro, divided
- 2 Tbsp. lime juice
- 14 corn tortillas (6 in.) warmed
- 1 can (15 oz.) enchilada sauce

1. Preheat oven to 400°. In a large bowl, combine zucchini, poblano, mushrooms and tomatoes; drizzle with oil and sprinkle with cumin, salt and cayenne. Toss to coat. Divide vegetable mixture between 2 lightly greased 15x10x1-in. baking pans. Roast for 15 minutes; rotate pans top to bottom. Roast an additional 10 minutes or until the vegetables are tender. Return to bowl and cool slightly.

2. Stir in the Monterey Jack cheese, ½ cup queso fresco, ¼ cup cilantro and lime juice. Place a scant ½ cup vegetable mixture off center on each tortilla. Roll up and place in a greased 13x9-in. baking dish, seam side down. Top with enchilada sauce; sprinkle with remaining queso fresco.

3. Bake, uncovered, until heated through and the cheese is melted, about 20 minutes. Top with the remaining cilantro.

2 enchiladas: 346 cal., 17g fat (9g sat. fat), 40mg chol., 780mg sod., 33g carb. (5g sugars, 5g fiber), 18g pro.

1. Preheat oven to 400°. In a bowl, combine beans, tomatoes, zucchini, onion, garlic, wine, ½ tsp. salt and ⅛ tsp. pepper.

2. Rinse fish and pat dry. Place each fillet on an 18x12-in. piece of heavy-duty foil; season with the remaining salt and pepper. Spoon bean mixture over the fish; top with lemon slices. Fold foil around fish and crimp edges to seal. Transfer packets to a baking sheet.

3. Bake until fish just begins to flake easily with a fork and the vegetables are tender, 15-20 minutes. Be careful of escaping steam when opening packet.

1 serving: 270 cal., 2g fat (1g sat. fat), 83mg chol., 658mg sod., 23g carb. (4g sugars, 7g fiber), 38g pro. **Diabetic exchanges:** 5 lean meat, 1 starch, 1 vegetable.

TEST KITCHEN TIP

If you hate to open a bottle of wine just for ¼ cup, look for wine in single-portion bottles. The small bottles are convenient for using in recipes. But remember—don't use wine for cooking that you wouldn't want to sip!

TUSCAN FISH PACKETS

My husband does a lot of fishing and I'm always looking for different ways to serve his catch. A professional chef was kind enough to share this recipe with me, and I played around with different veggie combinations until I found the one my family liked best.
—Kathy Morrow, Hubbard, OH

- -

Takes: 30 min. • **Makes:** 4 servings

1 can (15 oz.) great northern beans, rinsed and drained
4 plum tomatoes, chopped
1 small zucchini, chopped
1 medium onion, chopped
1 garlic clove, minced
¼ cup white wine
¾ tsp. salt, divided
¼ tsp. pepper, divided
4 tilapia fillets (6 oz. each)
1 medium lemon, cut into 8 thin slices

OVER-THE-BORDER SHRIMP ENCHILADAS

These enchiladas have a bit of a kick, thanks to chili powder and green chiles, but the deliciously creamy sauce balances it all.
—Beverly O'Ferrall, Linkwood, MD

Prep: 20 min. • **Bake:** 20 min.
Makes: 8 servings

- 1   medium onion, chopped
- 2   Tbsp. olive oil
- ¾   lb. uncooked medium shrimp, peeled and deveined
- 1   can (4 oz.) chopped green chiles
- ½   tsp. chili powder
- ¼   tsp. salt
- ¼   tsp. ground cumin
- ¼   tsp. pepper
- 1   pkg. (8 oz.) cream cheese, cubed
- 8   flour tortillas (8 in.), warmed
- 1½ cups chunky salsa
- 1½ cups shredded Monterey Jack cheese

1. Preheat oven to 350°. In a large skillet, saute onion in oil until tender. Add shrimp, green chiles, chili powder, salt, cumin and pepper. Cook 2-3 minutes or until shrimp turn pink. Stir in cream cheese until melted.

2. Place ⅓ cup shrimp mixture down the center of each tortilla. Roll up and place seam side down in a greased 13x9-in. baking dish. Pour salsa over the top; sprinkle with Monterey Jack cheese. Bake, uncovered, for 20-25 minutes or until heated through.
1 enchilada: 417 cal., 23g fat (11g sat. fat), 102mg chol., 809mg sod., 32g carb. (3g sugars, 1g fiber), 19g pro.

GREEK TILAPIA

While on a trip through the Greek islands, my husband and I had a dish that we loved. I tried to duplicate it by combining several different recipes and came up with this version. It's as close as we can get to being back in Greece!
—Sally Burrell, Idaho Falls, ID

Prep: 30 min. • **Bake:** 10 min.
Makes: 4 servings

- 4   tilapia fillets (4 oz. each)
- 4   tsp. butter
- 1   large egg
- ¾   cup crumbled tomato and basil feta cheese
- ¼   cup fat-free milk
- ¼   tsp. cayenne pepper
- 1   large tomato, seeded and chopped
- ¼   cup chopped ripe olives
- ¼   cup pine nuts, toasted
- 1   Tbsp. minced fresh parsley
- 1   Tbsp. lemon juice
- ⅛   tsp. pepper

1. Preheat oven to 425°. In a large cast-iron or other ovenproof skillet, brown fish fillets in butter.
2. In a small bowl, combine egg, cheese, milk and cayenne; spoon over fish. Sprinkle with tomato, olives and pine nuts. Bake, uncovered, until fish just begins to flake easily with a fork, 10-15 minutes.
3. In a small bowl, combine the parsley, lemon juice and pepper; drizzle over fish.
1 fillet: 279 cal., 16g fat (6g sat. fat), 123mg chol., 362mg sod., 5g carb. (2g sugars, 2g fiber), 29g pro.

TUNA NOODLE CASSEROLE

Families are sure to love the creamy texture and comforting taste of this traditional tuna casserole that goes together in a jiffy. I serve it with a green salad and warm rolls for a nutritious supper.
—Ruby Wells, Cynthiana, KY

Prep: 10 min. • **Bake:** 30 min.
Makes: 4 servings

- 1 can (10¾ oz.) reduced-fat reduced-sodium condensed cream of celery soup, undiluted
- ½ cup fat-free milk
- 2 cups cooked yolk-free wide noodles
- 1 cup frozen peas, thawed
- 1 can (6 oz.) light water-packed tuna, drained and flaked
- 1 jar (2 oz.) diced pimientos, drained
- 2 Tbsp. dry bread crumbs
- 1 Tbsp. butter, melted

1. Preheat oven to 400°. In a large bowl, combine soup and milk until smooth. Add noodles, peas, tuna and pimientos; mix well.
2. Pour into a 1½-qt. baking dish coated with cooking spray. Bake, uncovered, for 25 minutes. Toss bread crumbs and butter; sprinkle over the top. Bake 5 minutes longer or until golden brown.

1 cup: 238 cal., 5g fat (2g sat. fat), 27mg chol., 475mg sod., 32g carb. (6g sugars, 4g fiber), 15g pro. **Diabetic exchanges:** 2 starch, 2 lean meat, ½ fat.

BOMBAY RICE WITH SHRIMP

This recipe was given to me by a co-worker whose family is from India. I have served it many times at family get-togethers, brunches and even at an engagement shower for a friend. Along with her gift, I enclosed this recipe.
—Sherry Flaquel, Cutler Bay, FL

- -

Prep: 25 min. • **Bake:** 20 min.
Makes: 6 servings

1½ cups uncooked instant rice
1 can (10¾ oz.) condensed cream of celery soup, undiluted
½ cup water
2 tsp. curry powder
1 tsp. salt
1 lb. peeled and deveined cooked medium shrimp
1 medium onion, chopped
½ cup chopped walnuts
½ cup sweetened shredded coconut
½ cup golden raisins
1 small tart apple, chopped

1. Cook rice according to the package directions. Preheat oven to 350°.
2. Meanwhile, combine the soup, water, curry and salt in a large bowl. Stir in the shrimp, onion, walnuts, coconut, raisins, apple and rice. Transfer to a greased 11x7-in. baking dish.
3. Bake, uncovered, for 20-25 minutes or until heated through.

1⅓ cups: 367 cal., 13g fat (4g sat. fat), 117mg chol., 802mg sod., 43g carb. (14g sugars, 4g fiber), 20g pro.

NEW ENGLAND FISH BAKE

I've lived in Rhode Island for many years and love the fresh seafood dishes served here. This recipe from my mother-in-law is a favorite of mine.
—Norma DesRoches, Warwick, RI

- -

Prep: 25 min. • **Bake:** 20 min.
Makes: 4 servings

4 medium potatoes, peeled
1 tsp. all-purpose flour
1 small onion, sliced into rings
½ tsp. salt
¼ tsp. pepper
¾ cup 2% milk, divided
1½ lbs. cod fillets or freshwater fish (trout, catfish or pike)
3 Tbsp. grated Parmesan cheese, optional
2 Tbsp. minced fresh parsley or 2 tsp. dried parsley flakes
¼ tsp. paprika

1. Preheat oven to 375°. Place potatoes in a saucepan and cover with water. Bring to a boil. Reduce heat; cover and simmer until tender, 15-20 minutes. Drain; cool slightly.
2. Slice potatoes ⅛ in. thick; place in a greased shallow 2-qt. baking dish. Sprinkle with flour. Top with onion rings; sprinkle with salt and pepper. Pour half the milk over potatoes. Place fish on top; pour the remaining milk over the fish. Sprinkle with Parmesan cheese if desired.
3. Cover and bake until fish flakes easily with a fork, 20-30 minutes. Sprinkle with parsley and paprika.

1 serving: 281 cal., 2g fat (1g sat. fat), 68mg chol., 414mg sod., 34g carb. (5g sugars, 2g fiber), 31g pro. **Diabetic exchanges:** 4 lean meat, 2 starch.

SKINNY CRAB QUICHE

Crabmeat, zucchini, cheddar cheese and green onions flavor this savory crustless quiche. I take this to potlucks and cut it into appetizer-size slices. As a diabetic, I know there will be at least one dish there I can eat guilt-free.
—Nancy Romero, Clarkston, WA

- -

Prep: 15 min. • **Bake:** 25 min. + standing
Makes: 6 servings

1 **can (6 oz.) crab**
1½ **cups shredded reduced-fat cheddar cheese**
½ **cup shredded zucchini**
⅓ **cup chopped green onions**
1½ **cups egg substitute**
1 **can (12 oz.) fat-free evaporated milk**
¾ **tsp. ground mustard**
½ **tsp. salt**
¼ **tsp. salt-free lemon-pepper seasoning**
Dash paprika

1. Preheat oven to 400°. In a bowl, combine crab, cheese, zucchini and onions. Press onto the bottom and up the sides of a 9-in. deep-dish pie plate coated with cooking spray. In another bowl, combine the egg substitute, milk, ground mustard, salt and lemon-pepper; mix well. Pour into crust. Sprinkle with paprika.
2. Bake, uncovered, until a knife inserted in the center of quiche comes out clean, 25-30 minutes. Let stand for 10 minutes before cutting.
1 slice: 223 cal., 9g fat (5g sat. fat), 50mg chol., 736mg sod., 10g carb. (0 sugars, 1g fiber), 26g pro. **Diabetic exchanges:** 3 lean meat, ½ fat-free milk.

ARTICHOKE COD WITH SUN-DRIED TOMATOES

This cod is a great break from rich dishes around the holidays. I like to serve it over a bed of greens, pasta or quinoa. A squeeze of lemon gives it another layer of freshness.
—Hiroko Miles, El Dorado Hills, CA

- -

Takes: 30 min. • **Makes:** 6 servings

1 **can (14 oz.) quartered water-packed artichoke hearts, drained**
½ **cup julienned soft sun-dried tomatoes (not packed in oil)**
2 **green onions, chopped**
3 **Tbsp. olive oil**
1 **garlic clove, minced**
6 **cod fillets (6 oz. each)**
1 **tsp. salt**
½ **tsp. pepper**
Optional: Salad greens and lemon wedges

1. Preheat oven to 400°. In a small bowl, toss the first 5 ingredients.
2. Sprinkle both sides of the cod with salt and pepper; place in a 13x9-in. baking dish coated with cooking spray. Top with the artichoke mixture.
3. Bake, uncovered, for 15-20 minutes or until the fish just begins to flake easily with a fork. If desired, serve over greens with lemon wedges.
Note: This recipe was tested with sun-dried tomatoes that can be used without soaking. When using other sun-dried tomatoes that are not oil-packed, cover with boiling water and let stand until soft. Drain before using.
1 fillet with ⅓ cup artichoke mixture: 231 cal., 8g fat (1g sat. fat), 65mg chol., 665mg sod., 9g carb. (3g sugars, 2g fiber), 29g pro. **Diabetic exchanges:** 4 lean meat, 1½ fat, 1 vegetable.

TOPPING
- ½ cup grated Parmesan cheese
- ½ cup panko (Japanese) bread crumbs
- 3 garlic cloves, minced
- 2 Tbsp. olive oil
  Minced fresh parsley or basil, optional

1. Preheat oven to 350°. Cook ziti pasta according to the package directions for al dente; drain.
2. Meanwhile, in a large saucepan, combine the marinara sauce, Alfredo sauce, 1 cup mozzarella, ricotta, provolone and Romano cheeses. Heat over medium heat until sauce begins to simmer and cheeses are melted. Stir in cooked pasta; pour mixture into a greased 13x9-in. baking dish. Top with the remaining 1 cup mozzarella cheese.
3. In a small bowl, stir together Parmesan cheese, bread crumbs, garlic and olive oil; sprinkle over the pasta.
4. Bake, uncovered, until the mixture is bubbly and the topping is golden brown, 30-40 minutes. Let stand for 10 minutes before serving. Garnish with fresh parsley or basil if desired.

Freeze option: Cool unbaked casserole; cover and freeze. To use, partially thaw in refrigerator overnight. Remove from refrigerator 30 minutes before baking. Preheat oven to 350°. Cover casserole with foil; bake 50 minutes. Uncover; bake until heated through and a thermometer inserted in center reads 165°, 15-20 minutes longer.
1 cup: 449 cal., 15g fat (8g sat. fat), 32mg chol., 960mg sod., 59g carb. (11g sugars, 4g fiber), 21g pro.

FIVE-CHEESE ZITI AL FORNO
After having the five-cheese ziti at Olive Garden, I tried to make my own homemade version—and I think I got pretty close. I always double this and freeze the second one for another meal.
—Keri Whitney, Castro Valley, CA

- -

Prep: 20 min. • **Bake:** 30 min. + standing
Makes: 12 servings

- 1½ lbs. (about 7½ cups) ziti or small tube pasta
- 2 jars (24 oz. each) marinara sauce
- 1 jar (15 oz.) Alfredo sauce
- 2 cups shredded part-skim mozzarella cheese, divided
- ½ cup reduced-fat ricotta cheese
- ½ cup shredded provolone cheese
- ½ cup grated Romano cheese

CITRUS SALMON EN PAPILLOTE

This salmon dish is simple and easy to make yet so delicious, elegant and impressive.
—Dahlia Abrams, Detroit, MI

Prep: 20 min. • **Bake:** 15 min.
Makes: 6 servings

- 6 orange slices
- 6 lime slices
- 6 salmon fillets (4 oz. each)
- 1 lb. fresh asparagus, trimmed and halved
  Olive oil-flavored cooking spray
- ½ tsp. salt
- ¼ tsp. pepper
- 2 Tbsp. minced fresh parsley
- 3 Tbsp. lemon juice

1. Preheat oven to 425°. Cut parchment or heavy-duty foil into six 15x10-in. pieces; fold in half. Arrange citrus slices on 1 side of each piece of parchment. Top with fish and asparagus. Spritz with cooking spray. Sprinkle with salt, pepper and parsley. Drizzle with lemon juice.
2. Fold the parchment over fish; draw edges together and crimp with fingers to form tightly sealed packets. Place in baking pans.
3. Bake until the fish flakes easily with a fork, 12-15 minutes. Open packets carefully to allow steam to escape.

1 packet: 224 cal., 13g fat (2g sat. fat), 57mg chol., 261mg sod., 6g carb. (3g sugars, 1g fiber), 20g pro. **Diabetic exchanges:** 3 lean meat, 1 vegetable.

GREEK FISH BAKE

As a military spouse living overseas, I had the chance to try many styles of cooking. Here's a Mediterranean-inspired recipe that we still love today.
—Stacey Boyd, Springfield, VA

Takes: 30 min. • **Makes:** 4 servings

- 4 cod fillets (6 oz. each)
- 2 Tbsp. olive oil
- ¼ tsp. salt
- ⅛ tsp. pepper
- 1 small green pepper, cut into thin strips
- ½ small red onion, thinly sliced
- ¼ cup pitted Greek olives, sliced
- 1 can (8 oz.) tomato sauce
- ¼ cup crumbled feta cheese

1. Preheat oven to 400°. Place cod in a greased 13x9-in. baking dish. Brush with oil; sprinkle with salt and pepper. Top with green pepper, onion and olives.
2. Pour tomato sauce over top; sprinkle with cheese. Bake until fish just begins to flake easily with a fork, 15-20 minutes.
1 fillet with toppings: 246 cal., 12g fat (2g sat. fat), 68mg chol., 706mg sod., 6g carb. (2g sugars, 2g fiber), 29g pro. **Diabetic exchanges:** 4 lean meat, 1½ fat, 1 vegetable.

FOIL-PACKET SHRIMP & SAUSAGE JAMBALAYA

This hearty, satisfying dinner has all the flavors of an authentic jambalaya with little effort. The foil packets can be prepared a day ahead and cooked right before serving. These are also good on the grill!
—Allison Stroud, Oklahoma City, OK

Prep: 20 min. • **Bake:** 20 min.
Makes: 6 servings

- 12 oz. fully cooked andouille sausage links, cut into ½-in. slices
- 12 oz. uncooked shrimp (31-40 per lb.), peeled and deveined
- 1 medium green pepper, chopped
- 1 medium onion, chopped
- 2 celery ribs, chopped
- 3 garlic cloves, minced
- 2 tsp. Creole seasoning
- 1 can (14½ oz.) fire-roasted diced tomatoes, drained
- 1 cup uncooked instant rice
- 1 can (8 oz.) tomato sauce
- ½ cup chicken broth

Preheat oven to 425°. In a large bowl, combine all ingredients. Divide mixture among 6 greased 18x12-in. pieces of heavy-duty foil. Fold foil around mixture and crimp edges to seal, forming packets; place on a baking sheet. Bake until the shrimp turn pink and the rice is tender, 20-25 minutes.

1 packet: 287 cal., 12g fat (4g sat. fat), 143mg chol., 1068mg sod., 23g carb. (3g sugars, 2g fiber), 23g pro.

PORTOBELLO POLENTA BAKE

Any recipe with melted cheese in it is a favorite of mine. That's just one reason I love this polenta bake. It has a lot of protein for a meatless meal!
—Margee Berry, White Salmon, WA

- -

Prep: 25 min. • **Bake:** 25 min. + standing
Makes: 6 servings

1	can (14½ oz.) reduced-sodium chicken broth
1¼	cups water
1	cup cornmeal
2	tsp. olive oil
1	large onion, chopped
½	lb. sliced baby portobello mushrooms
¼	cup julienned soft sun-dried tomatoes (not packed in oil)
2	garlic cloves, minced
2	large eggs, lightly beaten
1	cup shredded Gruyere or fontina cheese
½	tsp. salt
1	cup part-skim ricotta cheese Minced fresh parsley

1. Preheat oven to 350°. In a large heavy saucepan, bring broth and water to a boil. Reduce heat to a gentle boil; slowly whisk in cornmeal. Cook and stir until thickened and cornmeal is tender, 8-10 minutes.

2. Meanwhile, in a large nonstick skillet, heat oil over medium-high heat; saute onion and mushrooms until tender, 4-5 minutes. Stir in tomatoes and garlic; cook 1 minute.

3. Mix eggs, Gruyere cheese and salt; stir into the polenta. Spread half the mixture into a greased 11x7-in. baking dish. Top with the vegetable mixture. Drop ricotta cheese by tablespoonfuls over top. Spread with the remaining polenta.

4. Bake, uncovered, until the edges are lightly browned, 25-30 minutes. Let stand 10 minutes before serving. Sprinkle with minced parsley.

Note: This recipe was tested with sun-dried tomatoes that can be used without soaking. When using other sun-dried tomatoes that are not oil-packed, cover with boiling water and let stand until soft. Drain before using.

1 serving: 304 cal., 13g fat (6g sat. fat), 96mg chol., 605mg sod., 29g carb. (4g sugars, 3g fiber), 17g pro. **Diabetic exchanges:** 2 starch, 2 medium-fat meat, ½ fat.

Baby portobello mushrooms are also known as cremini mushrooms. They can be used instead of white mushrooms for a flavor boost.

GREEK SPINACH BAKE

Spanakopita is the Greek name for this traditional dish featuring spinach and feta cheese. You can serve it as a side dish or meatless main dish.
—Sharon Olney, Galt, CA

- -

Prep: 10 min. • **Bake:** 1 hour
Makes: 6 servings

- 2 cups 4% cottage cheese
- 1 pkg. (10 oz.) frozen chopped spinach, thawed and squeezed dry
- 8 oz. crumbled feta cheese
- 6 Tbsp. all-purpose flour
- ½ tsp. pepper
- ¼ tsp. salt
- 4 large eggs, lightly beaten

1. Preheat oven to 350°. In a large bowl, combine the cottage cheese, spinach and feta cheese. Stir in the flour, pepper and salt. Add eggs and mix well.
2. Spoon into a greased 9-in. square baking dish. Bake, uncovered, until a thermometer reads 160°, about 1 hour.
1 serving: 262 cal., 13g fat (7g sat. fat), 178mg chol., 838mg sod., 14g carb. (4g sugars, 3g fiber), 21g pro.

SPINACH & BROCCOLI ENCHILADAS

I like to top this wonderful meatless meal with lettuce and serve it with extra picante sauce. It's quick, easy, filled with fresh flavor and definitely satisfying!
—Lesley Tragesser, Charleston, MO

- -

Prep: 25 min. • **Bake:** 25 min.
Makes: 8 servings

- 1 medium onion, chopped
- 2 tsp. olive oil
- 1 pkg. (10 oz.) frozen chopped spinach, thawed and squeezed dry
- 1 cup finely chopped fresh broccoli
- 1 cup picante sauce, divided
- ½ tsp. garlic powder
- ½ tsp. ground cumin
- 1 cup 1% cottage cheese
- 1 cup shredded reduced-fat cheddar cheese, divided
- 8 flour tortillas (8 in.), warmed

1. Preheat oven to 350°. In a large nonstick skillet over medium heat, cook and stir the chopped onion in oil until tender. Add the spinach, broccoli, ⅓ cup picante sauce, garlic powder and cumin; heat through.
2. Remove from heat; stir in cottage cheese and ½ cup cheddar cheese. Spoon about ⅓ cup spinach mixture down the center of each tortilla. Roll up and place seam side down in a 13x9-in. baking dish coated with cooking spray. Spoon the remaining picante sauce over top.
3. Cover and bake 20-25 minutes or until heated through. Uncover; sprinkle with the remaining cheese. Bake 5 minutes longer or until cheese is melted.
1 serving: 246 cal., 8g fat (3g sat. fat), 11mg chol., 614mg sod., 32g carb. (4g sugars, 2g fiber), 13g pro. **Diabetic exchanges:** 1½ starch, 1 lean meat, 1 vegetable, ½ fat.

¼ tsp. pepper
½ cup chopped red onion
1 can (2¼ oz.) sliced ripe olives, drained
1 cup shredded reduced-fat Mexican cheese blend

1. In a small saucepan, bring rice and water to a boil. Reduce heat; simmer, covered, until the rice is tender, 35-40 minutes.
2. Preheat oven to 350°. Place the beans, corn, tomatoes, cheddar cheese and rice in a large bowl; stir in salsa, sour cream and pepper. Transfer to a shallow 2½-qt. baking dish coated with cooking spray. Sprinkle with onion and olives.
3. Bake, uncovered, 30 minutes. Sprinkle with Mexican cheese; bake, uncovered, until heated through and cheese is melted, 5-10 minutes. Let stand another 10 minutes before serving.

1 cup: 285 cal., 10g fat (5g sat. fat), 21mg chol., 759mg sod., 36g carb. (6g sugars, 4g fiber), 15g pro. **Diabetic exchanges:** 2 starch, 2 vegetable, 1 lean meat, 1 fat.

TEST KITCHEN TIP

This casserole is incredibly versatile. Once you've learned the recipe, start experimenting. If you like things a little spicier, use medium or hot salsa instead of mild, or add a bit of taco seasoning. Sprinkle chopped avocados on top, or use it as a filling in a tortilla!

SOUTHWEST VEGETARIAN BAKE

This veggie-packed casserole hits the spot on chilly nights. But it's equally good any time I have a taste for Mexican food with all the fixings, too.
—Patricia Gale, Monticello, IL

- -

Prep: 40 min. • **Bake:** 35 min. + standing
Makes: 8 servings

¾ cup uncooked brown rice
1½ cups water
1 can (15 oz.) black beans, rinsed and drained
1 can (11 oz.) Mexicorn, drained
1 can (10 oz.) diced tomatoes and green chiles
1 cup shredded reduced-fat cheddar cheese
1 cup salsa
1 cup reduced-fat sour cream

3. Stir in garbanzo beans, cranberries, green onion, sage, lemon zest, lemon juice and the remaining oil and salt; spoon into squash. Sprinkle with cheese and pumpkin seeds.
1 stuffed squash half: 275 cal., 8g fat (2g sat. fat), 9mg chol., 591mg sod., 46g carb. (9g sugars, 10g fiber), 9g pro. **Diabetic exchanges:** 3 starch, 1 lean meat, ½ fat.

PEPPER & SALSA COD

After sampling a similar dish at the grocery store, my husband figured out how to make this awesome cod topped with salsa and peppers.
—Robyn Gallagher, Yorktown, VA

Takes: 30 min. • **Makes:** 2 servings

- 2 cod or haddock fillets (6 oz. each)
- 1 tsp. olive oil
- ¼ tsp. salt
  Dash pepper
- ⅓ cup orange juice
- ¼ cup salsa
- ⅓ cup julienned green pepper
- ⅓ cup julienned sweet red pepper
  Hot cooked rice

1. Preheat oven to 350°. Brush both sides of fillets with oil; place in a greased 11x7-in. baking dish. Sprinkle with salt and pepper. Pour orange juice over fish; top with salsa and peppers.
2. Bake, covered, until the fish just begins to flake easily with a fork, 17-20 minutes. Serve with rice.
1 serving: 183 cal., 3g fat (1g sat. fat), 65mg chol., 512mg sod., 9g carb. (6g sugars, 1g fiber), 27g pro. **Diabetic exchanges:** 4 lean meat, 1 vegetable, ½ fat.

QUINOA-STUFFED SQUASH BOATS

My colorful boats with quinoa, chickpeas and pumpkin seeds use delicata squash, a winter squash that's cream-colored with green stripes. If your market doesn't stock it, acorn squash will do nicely.
—Lauren Knoelke, Des Moines, IA

Takes: 30 min. • **Makes:** 8 servings

- 4 delicata squash (about 12 oz. each)
- 3 tsp. olive oil, divided
- ⅛ tsp. pepper
- 1 tsp. salt, divided
- 1½ cups vegetable broth
- 1 cup quinoa, rinsed
- 1 can (15 oz.) garbanzo beans or chickpeas, rinsed and drained
- ¼ cup dried cranberries
- 1 green onion, thinly sliced
- 1 tsp. minced fresh sage
- ½ tsp. grated lemon zest
- 1 tsp. lemon juice
- ½ cup crumbled goat cheese
- ¼ cup salted pumpkin seeds or pepitas, toasted

1. Preheat oven to 450°. Cut each squash lengthwise in half; remove and discard the seeds. Lightly brush cut sides with 1 tsp. oil; sprinkle with pepper and ½ tsp. salt. Place on a baking sheet, cut side down. Bake until tender, 15-20 minutes.
2. Meanwhile, in a large saucepan, combine broth and quinoa; bring to a boil. Reduce heat; simmer, covered, until the liquid is absorbed, 12-15 minutes.

Recipe Index

Index